AF262991

Named in remembrance of

the onetime *Antioch Review* editor

and longtime Bay Area resident,

the Lawrence Grauman, Jr. Fund

supports books that address

a wide range of human rights,

free speech, and social justice issues.

American Peril

The publisher and the University of California Press Foundation gratefully acknowledge the generous support of the Lawrence Grauman, Jr. Fund.

American Peril

THE VIOLENT HISTORY OF ANTI-ASIAN RACISM

Scott Kurashige

UNIVERSITY OF CALIFORNIA PRESS

University of California Press
Oakland, California

© 2026 by Scott Kurashige

All rights reserved.

Library of Congress Cataloging-in-Publication Data

Names: Kurashige, Scott author
Title: American peril : the violent history of anti-Asian racism / Scott
    Kurashige.
Description: Oakland, California : University of California Press, [2026] |
    Includes bibliographical references and index.
Identifiers: LCCN 2025045054 (print) | LCCN 2025045055 (ebook) |
    ISBN 9780520424777 cloth | ISBN 9780520424784 ebook
Subjects: LCSH: Racism against Asians—United States—History | Hate
    crimes—United States | Asian Americans—Political activity | White
    supremacy movements—United States | United States—Race relations—
    History
Classification: LCC E184.A75 K876 2026 (print) | LCC E184.A75 (ebook) |
    DDC 305.895/073—dc23/eng/20251113
LC record available at https://lccn.loc.gov/2025045054
LC ebook record available at https://lccn.loc.gov/2025045055

Manufactured in the United States of America

GPSR Authorized Representative: Easy Access System Europe, Mustamäe tee
50, 10621 Tallinn, Estonia, gpsr.requests@easproject.com

35   34   33   32   31   30   29   28   27   26
10   9   8   7   6   5   4   3   2   1

CONTENTS

AUTHOR'S NOTE

To accurately recount the history of anti-Asian racism and white supremacy, this book contains numerous references to offensive language, racist stereotypes, and graphic accounts of violence. Resurfacing painful and traumatic histories and understanding how and why they were erased and suppressed constitute crucial steps in the journey toward consciousness raising, collective empowerment, and social justice.

Unless quoting others, I avoid using *AAPI* as a blanket category, since it is too often used more or less as a synonym for *Asian American* or without the consent and participation of Pacific Islanders. Its use should be limited to specific instances when Asian Americans and Pacific Islanders voluntarily decide to build organizations or coalitions together (this tends to be indicated by the use of a slash, e.g., "AA/PI" or "A/PIA").

According to historical context, some persons in the book are listed with family name first, as is customary in some Asian cultures. When discussing minors, I have used pseudonyms except in some instances where the names of minors were reported by the media or appear in public sources.

Introduction

"NOT RACIALLY MOTIVATED"

These three words echoed across the nation in the aftermath of the mass shootings that struck Atlanta-area spas on March 16, 2021. I saw them flash on a breaking-news ticker as I followed coverage of the horrifying events.

Three facts immediately stood out:

1. The gunman was a twenty-one-year-old white male.
2. He shot and killed eight people: Daoyou Feng, Delaina Yaun Gonzalez, Hyun Jung Grant, Suncha Kim, Paul Andre Michels, Soon Chung Park, Xiaojie Tan, and Yong Ae Yue.
3. Asian women comprised six of the eight victims.[1]

The murders magnified the terror and sorrow emanating from thousands of anti-Asian attacks arising in the months preceding. Following the outbreak of COVID-19, bias incidents and assaults against Asian Americans soared to alarming heights as demagogues on the streets and in high office inflamed xenophobic fear and animosity. In the aftermath of the shootings, at least 70 percent of Asian Americans felt that violence and discrimination had become greater threats to the community during the pandemic.[2]

Against this backdrop, authorities carelessly repeated the claim of suspect Robert Aaron Long that the violence "was not racially motivated." In the words of the Cherokee County Sheriff's spokesman, Captain Jay Baker, he just had "a really bad day." Because Long was afflicted by a "sex addiction," Baker next conveyed, he viewed the massage parlors as "a temptation for him that he wanted to eliminate." But as Jina Moore of *Business Insider* countered, sex addiction is not a medical condition based on diagnostic criteria. It is, quite to the contrary, "a piece of evangelical theology." The shooter's projection of evil onto the spa workers betrayed his immersion within "purity culture." According to scholars Andrew L. Whitehead and Samuel L. Perry, the Christian nationalist mission to purify America of its would-be sins is rooted in "assumptions of nativism, white supremacy, patriarchy, and heteronormativity, along with divine sanction for authoritarian control and militarism."[3]

An informed response to Long's statement should, therefore, have probed how his ideas about sex and gender were interconnected with his thinking about race, religion, and colonialism. It was not necessary to prove that Long hated *all* Asians. The most pertinent question to ask was this: What led Long to target Asian women in the businesses he patronized yet derisively saw as ungodly? We do not need to read the killer's mind to know how the dehumanization of Asian women as sexualized labor, whose value lies only in its service to American men, pervades our culture. It is steeped in the history of exclusion, when Chinese women were stigmatized as prostitutes and a menace to public health. Since the mid-twentieth century, it has proliferated through the decades-long practice of "camptowns" set up to serve the recreational desires of U.S. soldiers stationed in Asia and "mail-order bride" catalogues promising to bring submissive women to American patrons. Directly or indirectly, these histories—including their dramatization on film and television—shape the image of "Oriental" massage parlors before one ever sets foot in them.

Soon enough, there was even more reason for outrage. Internet sleuths revealed that Baker had liked and shared a racist "CHY-NA virus" meme on social media. Placed under the national spotlight, Asian Americans were reminded how common it is for their fates to be determined by powerful figures committed to misrepresenting them. When called upon to validate the oppression of Black, Brown, and Indigenous peoples, Asian Americans are stereotyped as the high-achieving but docile "model minority." But the attacks of the pandemic accentuated the stereotype of Asians as the "perpetual foreigner" who must be contained or excised to make America great again.[4]

Tens of thousands of Asians and non-Asian allies responded with an unprecedented wave of protests and demonstrations spanning at least fifty cities. Hollywood celebrities joined grassroots community organizers. In 2021, over 8.4 million Twitter posts used the hashtag #StopAsianHate. Millions in donations and pledges were devoted to programs, events, advocacy groups, and awareness campaigns. In a sign of broader shifts among policymakers, Congress passed the COVID-19 Hate Crimes Act with rare and overwhelming bipartisan support to address anti-Asian attacks in May 2021. "Too often," President Joe Biden lamented as he signed it into law, anti-Asian hate "is met with silence—silence by the media, silence by our politics and silence by our history."[5]

As we will see in case studies from the past 175 years, that silence has been the product of a wide range of actors, including leaders on both sides of the aisle. Time and again, horrendous physical assaults and rampant discrimination have officially been deemed "not racially motivated." Although we can identify signs of overt bias in many instances, this is often just the tip of the iceberg. The reproduction of systemic racism occurs not simply through white denial but also through the promotion of cultural incompetency. "Racism is one of those crimes of which we in America seem content to allow the perpetrators to decide whether they are guilty," journalist Frank Shyong commented following the Atlanta shootings. "Like a conceited person staring into a mirror, America's white-dominated institutions investigate themselves for flaws and find none."[6]

Although confronting the scourge of anti-Asian violence has long been a priority for Asian American scholars and activists, their insights have too often been ignored or minimized by policymakers, educators, and journalists. The guardians of knowledge have customarily deemed the history and experience of Asian Americans to be inessential or peripheral to all levels of American education. Someone with a PhD will not necessarily possess more accurate information about Asian Americans than a high school graduate.

Anti-Asian violence thus presents a twofold problem. Physical acts of racist terror have been coupled with the violent erasure of history. This disturbing pattern has allowed anti-Asian violence and racism to escape both notice and censure. It stretches back to the nineteenth century, when white mobs and assailants subjected Asian immigrants to lynchings and pogroms with impunity. It also stretches overseas to encompass nearly every major U.S. war since Reconstruction. American soldiers wantonly committed scores of war crimes that the U.S. military routinely covered up. Such events are mostly or entirely missing from school textbooks. Thus, students learn a one-sided account of wars with Japan and Vietnam, and next to nothing about places like the Philippines, Okinawa, Korea, Cambodia, Indonesia, Laos, Bangladesh, and Afghanistan that have had their entire histories devastatingly remade by U.S. foreign policy.

While individuals may harbor unconscious bias, this calculated form of erasure stems from the *willful amnesia* at the core of the U.S. empire. The ideology of American exceptionalism set in place the myth that the United States was born free and uniquely destined to spread liberty and democracy, acting solely out of virtue. Under Donald Trump, the U.S. government is brutishly acting to rewrite history to promote white nationalism. Overcoming this willful amnesia is a crucial first step in addressing the problem. We cannot expect better policies or leadership to stop anti-Asian violence until we develop a better understanding of its historical and contemporary causes and manifestations. But power emanates from historical consciousness. It can reshape collective identity and foster the shared awareness necessary to build multiracial coalitions linking our struggles to transformative movements for social justice.

Given the long list of tragedies in American history, we should not have needed one more to function as a proverbial "teachable moment." Yet the Atlanta shootings served as a national wake-up call that has proven harder to ignore. Asian Americans have demonstrated overwhelming support for more educational measures to confront anti-Asian bias. Twelve states have now passed legislation requiring Asian American history to be taught in K–12 schools. Such an education is needed as much for Asians as for non-Asians. Only 24 percent of Asian Americans report being highly informed about the history of Asians in the United States. That equals the percentage saying they know little or nothing.[7]

What are we trying to remember? How should we go about recovering history? And most crucially, what must we do with this vital knowledge?

Much of this book is dedicated to dissecting episodes of anti-Asian violence that have been distorted or scrubbed from the official record. Beyond assigning individual blame or responsibility, I seek to place racist violence within the historical and political context necessary to understand root causes. My broader goal is to connect the dots—to reveal the patterns of racism and discrimination inherent within laws, ideologies, and institutions that render Asians vulnerable to pernicious forces. Finally, I highlight models of community organizing that seek not only to assist victims, but also to address the source of the problem and implement systemic change.

One point must be clear from the outset: Making sense of anti-Asian violence—or any form of oppression—necessitates grappling with the inequity and dehumanization that occur under capitalism. To be certain, some Asians have undoubtedly benefited from aligning with the privileged and powerful. But the racist assumption that Asian lives are "cheap" has underlain both the violence of imperialist wars in Asia and the rank exploitation of Asian workers in the United States. Moreover, capitalism maintains hegemony through deliberate divide-and-conquer strategies that pit subgroups of workers against each other. As a result, Asian Americans have repeatedly served as convenient scapegoats for the nation's woes. Anti-Asian violence erupted in response to the nation's first "Great Depression" that took off in the 1870s and the collapse of the "American Dream" of middle-class prosperity that began in the 1970s.

The title *American Peril* thus conveys a double meaning. From the nineteenth century through the COVID-19 pandemic, Asians have been cast as a "yellow peril," a "brown horde," and other forms of alien threat. At the same time, being cast as "dangerous" has greatly imperiled Asians and Asian Americans, making them the target of vigilante violence as well as state violence.

Part 1 recovers the expansive history of anti-Asian violence between the mid-nineteenth-century arrival of Chinese immigrants and the mass slaughters in Vietnam and other conflagrations of the Cold War era. In the making of the United States, white supremacy played a central role in the genocide of Indigenous peoples, the enslavement of Africans, and the conquest of Mexican land. The hatred this system produced served a material purpose: It motivated white hostility toward others, justified wealth accumulation through theft and exploitation, and rationalized elite rule. It went together with a patriarchal ideology that elevated men to leadership through a model of martial and economic dominance. This was the stage the nation set for Asian immigrants. They came to America—or, in the case of Hawaiian annexation and Philippine colonization, America came to them—as "colonized labor" in the age of Manifest Destiny and imperial expansion. Most were drawn to the U.S. West, where industrialists relied on their work to extract resources from newly captured territories and build the infrastructure necessary to incorporate the region into capitalist markets.

They came with dreams and fought to attain them. In some quarters, they were heartily welcomed. Frederick Douglass delivered a speech in 1869 that envisioned the United States as a "composite nation" of peoples from diverse backgrounds guided by the core principle of "human rights." Chinese immigrants, the great abolitionist declared, should be "invested with all the rights of American citizenship"—including the rights to vote and to hold elected office.[8]

But history took a different turn. Ling Sing, a Chinese immigrant who ventured to California to find gold, was killed by a white man attempting to rob a group of Chinese miners in 1853. Though this was one of countless brutal and senseless murders in this era, it claimed an infamous place in history when California's Supreme Court ruled that the murderer, George Hall, be set free because Chinese witnesses were not permitted to testify against whites. To be clear, Asian immigrants did not simply accept this type of oppression. They put up resistance by filing lawsuits, signing petitions, and waging strikes. To most white Americans, however, Asian labor was a disposable resource. Some workers literally died while performing treacherous jobs or fell victim to lynch mobs. The rest were discarded in the name of political expediency, setting in place patterns that similarly constrained the life chances of Japanese, Korean, Indian, and Filipino immigrants. Exclusionary laws both precluded new migration from Asia and barred those already here from naturalized citizenship and civil rights.

Violence was omnipresent. Though they often resented the monopolists who climbed atop the social order, white settlers used their power of numbers and citizenship to claim the spoils of empire, shutting out nonwhites they cast as rivals. Though they did not hesitate to act outside the law, they found that their actions were routinely validated by racist authorities and institutions. Thus, a deformed version of class struggle emerged. As white labor organizations rejected true proletarian solidarity, they leveraged their militancy for Asian exclusion. They attacked Chinese workers, physically and politically, as "coolies." In response, Chinese immigrants established enclaves for physical safety, cultural persistence, and mutual aid. But the exclusionists twisted these resilient acts of survival into proof of more depravity. They cast Chinatowns as dangerous sites of filth and vice, marking the inhabitants as inferior, degenerate, and unassimilable. On dozens of occasions, they moved to destroy and uproot entire Chinese communities. Going far beyond intimidation, they inflicted outright beatings and murders. While their heinous aim was nothing less than ethnic cleansing, the violence served a political purpose. By the late nineteenth century, the exclusionists pressured Congress and state legislatures to grant their major demands.

In the aftermath of Chinese exclusion, new sources of violence emanated from America's quest for global power in the age of multinational corporations. Its drive to colonize the Philippines touched off a deadly war near the turn of the twentieth century, creating an imperial footprint that engulfed the United States—directly or by proxy—in a series of conflicts that killed millions across Asia and the Pacific. Slaughtering civilians indiscriminately became a near ritual of combat. Maintaining the empire, as historian Moon-Ho Jung has argued, further entailed combating "anticolonial rage"— the dialectical other of colonial violence. From the deportation of Indian independence fighters to the mass incarceration of Japanese Americans, the U.S. government produced new rationales to repress Asians in the name of national security.[9]

Emerging from World War II as a victorious superpower, the United States established global standards for the new political and financial order and was the controlling influence over multilateral institutions like the United Nations, NATO, and the World Bank. While these bodies established a relative degree of postwar stability, the Cold War was anything but peaceful for much of the world's peoples. Beyond the cultural intrusion of American consumerism, the U.S. government violently disfigured foreign nations through self-serving diplomatic agendas and covert CIA operations purporting to contain communism. In conjunction with "containment," the American empire promoted the global integration of Asian peoples and nations into the "free world" centered on U.S. economic and geopolitical interests. In so doing, however, it subjected them to a pernicious form of inclusion. The U.S. military killed and sacrificed scores of "allies" it was purporting to save from the tyranny of communism, then foisted misogyny and violence on the Asian women and communities serving its permanent overseas bases. In 1955, an American sergeant raped and murdered five-year-old Yumiko Nagayama in Okinawa, part of a horrific pattern that would come to emblematize U.S. imperialism for far too many peoples in Asia and the Pacific.

The divisive, futile American war in Vietnam ultimately comprised the nation's involuntary turning point. In his 1968 speech "A Time to Break Silence," Dr. Martin Luther King Jr. condemned not only the U.S. invasion but also a system driven by racism, militarism, and materialism. Dr. King's call for a "revolution of values" coincided with the rise of a new wave of activism tied to a pan-Asian identity of resistance. Mike Nakayama was part of a generation of U.S. veterans politicized by the Vietnam War—but in a distinctly Asian manner. Chinese, Filipino, Korean, and Japanese Americans protested the racist drive to kill the "gooks," which went far beyond calls to defeat an enemy. They came together in the initial formation of "Asian American" identity, the birth of Asian American studies, and the forging of the Asian American movement during the late 1960s and early 1970s.

As the late philosopher-activist Grace Lee Boggs stated, "History is not the past. It is the stories we tell about the past. How we tell these stories— triumphantly or self-critically, metaphysically or dialectically—has a lot to do with whether we cut short or advance our evolution as human beings." By unearthing what the groundbreaking historian Yuji Ichioka called the "buried past," the first half of *American Peril* establishes the foundations for our endeavor to revisit and reimagine history. My goal is to provide a sense of history as trajectory—one whose past patterns we must understand to exercise our power in the present and chart a course toward a better future.[10]

I shift gears in part 2, examining cases and campaigns from the past five decades. Disturbingly, there is no shortage of tragedies to recollect from this period. I explain how the murder of Vincent Chin—the most well-known case of anti-Asian violence prior to the Atlanta shootings—remade Asian American identity and politics. If the concept of a distinctly "Asian American" social movement was born amid the hope and possibility of the radical 1960s, the term *anti-Asian violence* came into parlance through the Justice for Vincent Chin campaign amid the Reagan era's rightward shift.

In June 1982, Vincent Chin was celebrating his upcoming nuptials with friends at a club, when a squabble turned into a deadly encounter. A Chinese American raised in metro Detroit, Chin was beaten to death by two white men—one of whom scapegoated him for the loss of jobs in the U.S. auto industry to Japanese competition. A white judge compounded the tragedy by granting lenient sentences to the killers, who paid a small fine but avoided prison. Outrage over Chin's murder helped spawn a second wave of pan-Asian student and community activism during the 1980s and 1990s.

While continuing to delve into the public record to recover and reinterpret past events, my analysis in these chapters draws from my direct involvement in this work and from personal relationships with activists and organizations. When the original Vincent Chin movement sprouted up, I was too young to participate. But after moving to Detroit at the turn of the twenty-first century, I was fortunate to meet many of the family and community members who helped propel the movement and keep its memory alive. Along the way, I got to know others who expanded on this movement, including dedicated family members of Joseph Ileto, a Filipino American postal carrier killed in 1999 by a neo-Nazi who also shot up a Jewish community center in the San Fernando Valley section of Los Angeles.

On the one hand, it is impossible to overstate what a powerful catalyst Chin's legacy has been for Asian American consciousness raising and advocacy. The fear that anti-Asian violence can randomly strike anyone caught in the wrong place at the wrong time has been a vital unifying force—one that scholar Yen Le Espiritu has characterized as "reactive solidarity." Peoples of Asian ancestry in the United States are not necessarily bound together by a common language, culture, or lineage. As such, the perverse logic that "Asians all look alike" to racists provides a harrowing source of mutual identification. Antiracist organizing has served to bridge the ethnic, educational, and generational differences spanning the U.S.-born East Asian American activists and the Asian immigrants and refugees who arrived after Congress lifted discriminatory restrictions in 1965. It has also bridged class divides. The notorious "Dotbusters" attacks of the late 1980s, for instance, brought Indian American workers and professionals together in protest.[11]

The Chin story foregrounds the problem of *invisibility*, when Asian Americans are denied legal, political, and cultural representation, and *hypervisibility*, when the public transfixes on stereotypes that trigger moral panic. It draws attention to the institutionalization of racial bias within the judicial system, media, and broader society. And it celebrates the power and ability of activists to coalesce diverse Asian ethnicities within a multiracial coalition for civil rights and social justice.[12]

On the other hand, the pervasiveness of the Chin narrative exposes the limitations of panethnic identity and mobilization. It is too often told in a manner privileging a racial perspective that overshadows gender, sexuality, and class. We must also do more to ground our analysis of Chin's murder within the trials and tribulations of Detroit as a majority Black city. My reinterpretation of the Chin case seeks to illuminate wider pathways to coalition building and multiracial solidarity.

There is a danger of falling into a knee-jerk response to anti-Asian violence: First, look for signs of racial motivation, then demand that authorities arrest, prosecute, and imprison. In the difficult quest for resolution, the emotional weight that victims and their families place on such convictions is completely understandable. Frustrated by the repeated failure to bring perpetrators to justice, victims' advocates pushed to criminalize hate. Seeking to hold assailants *and* police accountable, new legislation expanded anti-hate prosecutions, enlarged protected categories, and enhanced sentencing. But this *hate crimes framework* also reinforced the power of policing, which functions to perpetuate social hierarchy. Viewing better policing as an antidote can further cause us to overlook victims of state violence, like Chonburi Xiong, a Hmong American teenager killed just outside of Detroit twenty-four years after Chin's demise. Though Xiong's family raised alarm after the police burst into their home to shoot him twenty-seven times, his story has not traveled nearly as far as Chin's.

As we turn from horror stories to the search for new solutions, it will become clear why hate crimes legislation and harsher punishment have not ended entrenched patterns of racist violence. As written and implemented, these laws place undue burden on proving individual culpability based on smoking-gun evidence of hate. Thus, they platform police officials like Jay Baker to make determinations of racial motivation. Prosecutions tend to be rare, and it is difficult to discern the degree to which such laws deter acts of hate. In a July 2021 study developed in partnership with civil rights advocates, the Movement Advancement Project cautioned that "hate crime laws are varied, often flawed, and can even harm the very communities they are meant to serve." The original premise was that enhanced law enforcement and stricter sentencing would protect minoritized communities. What we have witnessed since is movement in opposing directions: more policing and incarceration, but a retreat from civil rights enforcement. In Michigan, victim's rights and retributive justice measures carried out in the name of Vincent Chin have contributed to the mass incarceration crisis that is devastating Black communities.[13]

Transcending the legal definition of hate crimes, I adopt a wide-angle perspective to study anti-Asian violence. A minority of cases involve a random attack by a perpetrator who is overtly bigoted. But the effects of anti-Asian racism surface far more broadly. Violence and intimidation have been used to terrorize Asian communities and to achieve political objectives. Less directly, societal prejudice can inspire crimes of opportunity, when Asians are stereotyped as easy targets or perceived to hold wads of cash or bricks of gold. But the most sensational acts of violence against Asian Americans seem to be motivated by nothing more than anger. In January 2022, Michello Go was pushed in front of an oncoming New York subway in a murder that shocked and alarmed the public. Her tragic death turned out to be part of a string of violent incidents involving neglected persons who have experienced recurrent mental health crises, as well as bouts with the criminal justice system. To be clear, mental illness does not cause racism. People who are paranoid or distressed, however, can pick up racist cues from politicians and the media. Thus, a structural analysis and response is mandatory.

Our objective should be stopping anti-Asian violence before it happens. Getting to root causes means grappling with the dynamics of American capitalism in an era of right-wing counterrevolution, which began in reaction to the social progress of the 1960s and came to full power with the Trump presidencies. Until Trump's abrupt U-turn, global capital interests pushed trade liberalization, transnational migration, and intercultural exchange. The resulting increase in Asian American political, economic, and cultural influence created more visible targets of violence. In 2020, the Asian American population, including mixed-race persons, surpassed twenty-four million—a surge of more than 350 percent above the U.S. population of Asians in 1990. In many places, the effects were more pronounced. The Atlanta massacre occurred in a state where the Asian population has expanded more than sevenfold—double the national rate. Growing from 73,764 persons in 1990 to 565,644 by 2020, the Asian presence in Georgia rose from 1.1 percent to 5.3 percent of the population. Moreover, between 2016 and 2020, Asian American voter turnout rose by 84 percent in Georgia, adding sixty-one thousand votes, or five times Joe Biden's narrow victory margin. Comprising the fastest-growing racial group, percentagewise, in the United States, Asians are part of the emerging nonwhite majority that has prompted a xenophobic panic and a renewed exclusion movement.[14]

Whereas earlier periods marked the ascendance and zenith of American power, anti-Asian violence since the 1970s has resulted, in particular, from a bunker mentality tied to the perception of the United States as a declining empire. White nationalists equated the Vietnam War with liberal weakness and betrayal. But this was just a specific manifestation of the nationwide shock emanating from the defeat of the world's greatest superpower by a much smaller, impoverished country. Displaced by wars that the United States initiated and inflamed, Southeast Asian refugees faced the twisted notion that America has helped them too much already. Thus, antipathy toward "gooks" has lingered for decades.

Following 9/11, the stigmatization of Muslim and brown-skinned Asians as "terrorists" was a chest-thumping response to yet another exposed vulnerability. Balbir Singh Sodhi, a turban-wearing Sikh immigrant killed at the gas station where he worked in Mesa, Arizona, was among the first of dozens of Arab, Muslim, and South Asian Americans assaulted in the aftermath of the attacks on the Twin Towers and the Pentagon. Trade wars, first with Japan and then with China, invoke still more fragility. As the imperial mindset breeds hypocrisy, America has complained of being cheated in a contest for which it designed the global playing field and authored the rules.

Just as America's Cold War allies in Asia were expected to remain junior partners, the provisional acceptance of Asian Americans as a "model minority" was contingent on a submissive form of assimilation. As historian Robert G. Lee noted, the diligent, studious "model minority" adored by soft racists can morph back into the "gook" or "yellow peril" of hard racism when their success is perceived as a threat or provokes resentment. Contrary to the lopsided outcome of exclusion, however, Asian Americans have wound up on both the winning and losing sides of the intensified political and economic polarization that defines the era. This reflects the impact of a right-wing shift in ideology and public policy since the 1970s that scholars and activists have characterized by the term *neoliberalism*. This dramatic trend augmented corporate power while eviscerating the New Deal safety net, thus concentrating wealth at the top and poverty at the bottom, while hollowing out the middle. But the bifurcated experience of Asian Americans also reflects the specific effects of immigration laws and economic patterns since 1965 that have coveted the recruitment and advancement of highly educated professionals, while simultaneously increasing the nation's reliance on working-class migrants, including refugees and undocumented immigrants.[15]

Mirroring broader patterns in U.S. society, the polarization within Asian American communities profoundly reshaped the impact of anti-Asian racism and violence. Asian American professionals continued to endure multiple forms of mistreatment, including job discrimination, bullying, microaggressions, and media stereotyping. At the height of the COVID-19 pandemic, Natty Jumreornvong, a medical student in New York City, was kicked and dragged by a man who yelled racial slurs. She was part of a group of Asian medical clinicians who risked their own well-being to stop the virus, only to be harassed, threatened, and assaulted by racists blaming them for the spread of the "Chinese virus" and "kung flu." Surveys indicate that upper-income, highly educated Asian Americans have expressed the most elevated concern about hate incidents.[16]

But we need to be wary of promoting a form of "model minority" victimhood. The most clearly patterned forms of racist violence have tended to hit working-class Asian Americans, particularly Southeast Asian refugees and other residents of distressed urban neighborhoods, the hardest. The refugees had not only survived many years of gruesome wars; many were also combat veterans who had fought in intense battles. Some were, therefore, not inclined to turn the other cheek. When they chose to fight back, this prompted still more vigilante and state violence in response. Such conflicts reflect how the widening divide under neoliberalism concentrated problems socially and geographically in low-income communities of color, including police brutality, mass incarceration, redlining, predatory lending, unemployment, poverty, inadequate health care, public education crises, and toxic pollution.

While racist ideas and discrimination pervade the upper strata of American society, violent crime is overrepresented in places where people are most vulnerable and lacking social support—where frustrations boil as residents feel pitted against each other in the struggle to survive. We will travel back to the early 1990s to take a closer look at this phenomenon in Philadelphia, where the authorities were nonresponsive for weeks following the beating death of Heng Lim, a refugee from Cambodia, but immediately moved to arrest Asians accused of killing a white youth in what the media called a racial clash. Whereas the anti-Asian trade-war rhetoric of political elites troubles Wall Street financiers, the notion of Asian immigrants and refugees as unwelcome and unfair competitors has been a source of intense resentment in urban neighborhoods—often tied to unfounded rumors that they receive special handouts denied U.S. citizens. Thus, as white working-class attacks on Asians have carried over from the exclusion era, we have also seen more instances of interethnic conflict and violence amid the ravages of neoliberal retrenchment.

Since the 1990s, leading activists in organizations like Philadelphia's Asian Americans United and New York City's CAAAV: Organizing Asian Communities have reframed the way we define and address the problem of anti-Asian violence. Spotlighting their work helps us dispel the myth that Asians in the United States do not have an extensive history of social-justice activism or antiracist resistance. We will learn from organizers like Wei Chen, whose activism began when he was bullied as a high school student recently arrived from China, and Helen Gym, who became an influential figure on the Philadelphia City Council. Crucially, these movement builders in majority nonwhite cities fully comprehend that achieving social justice for Asian Americans cannot happen in isolation from organizing that seeks justice for the multiracial populations in which they reside. That is why their analysis and strategy cut across race, class, gender, sexuality, disability, citizenship status, and religion. Going beyond reactive protest, they are doing the difficult work of grassroots organizing to build community in the face of incessant attacks. They link the struggle against anti-Asian violence to a model of safety driven by restorative justice and a vision of collective care to promote sustainable housing, health, work, education, and youth leadership development.

With the United States standing at a historic crossroads, there are signs of possible futures in all the stories that follow. They point one way, toward more solidarity within a democratic, egalitarian system; or the other way, toward more conflict and violence within a plutocratic, authoritarian system. We should thus be prepared for these countervailing trends—rising anti-Asian hostility and Asian American political empowerment—to continue. They situate Asian Americans at the center of the decisive struggles and debates that will define the future.

PART ONE

How America Erased the Violent History of Anti-Asian Racism (1850s–1970s)

———

ONE

The Violence of Exclusion

In August 1885, a group of white workers demanded the removal of all Chinese immigrants who were mining with them in Rock Springs, a town of one thousand residents in Wyoming Territory. Around six hundred Chinese worked the mines—a large concentration for a site roughly a thousand-mile trek from San Francisco. More than three decades earlier, the discovery of gold in California had drawn the first major wave of migrants to the United States from China. While many hoped to discover riches in the land they called "Gold Mountain," the majority were relegated to arduous jobs at low wages and without the rights or protections of citizenship. The Chinese in Rock Springs were neither gold miners nor independent prospectors. They were hired by the Union Pacific railroad company to mine coal to fuel steam-powered locomotives.[1]

If an American student learns only a handful of things about Asian American history, one of the most common tidbits is that "the Chinese built the railroads." We need to look beyond the technological milestone, however, to consider the perspective of labor history. More than ten thousand Chinese worked for the Central Pacific Railroad, which the government had commissioned to build the transcontinental railroad starting in Sacramento and going east. In 1869, they famously met up with the mostly Irish workers hired by the Union Pacific, in Promontory Point, Utah, where the two lines were joined. But there was little to celebrate for the Chinese workers, many of whom had perished from the harsh weather and hazards of construction. Nearly all who survived became abruptly unemployed. They were not even afforded a free ride back to California on the tracks they had laid. But this corresponded with the promoters' xenophobic rationale for the transcontinental railroad's construction: It was urgently needed to boost *settlement* of whites in the U.S. West and restore order in the face of an overseas *invasion* of Celestials.[2]

As with their hiring of railroad construction crews, the Union Pacific had initially employed white workers, primarily immigrants, to mine bituminous coal at Rock Springs starting in 1868, on land expropriated from the Shoshone. This was an era of intense class conflict that was intertwined with unbridled anti-Asian racism. As decreasing yields cut into corporate profits, the company hired the first group of Chinese in 1875, when they were brought in to break a strike by white workers. Still, a relatively peaceful coexistence emerged over the next eight years, largely because the Chinese workers agreed to stay out of the higher-yield coal pits reserved for whites. Tension resurfaced in 1883. As greater and greater amounts of labor were needed to extract diminishing yields of coal, continued white migration to the West put further downward pressure on wages. In response, the Knights of Labor moved to organize the coal miners—but accepted only white workers as members. Nonetheless, the union demanded that the Chinese support their actions. Lines of segregation hardened in Rock Springs—a company town split into two distinct residential quarters: "Whitemen's Town" and "Chinatown." By the summer of 1885, there were nearly twice as many Chinese workers as whites, who complained that the company's practices were creating an entire workforce of so-called coolies. A management representative insisted that Chinese would need to be hired until the strikes ceased and the white workers respected the company's authority.[3]

Variations of this scenario occurred throughout the American West in towns where Asian immigrants were employed between the 1850s and the 1930s. Asians simultaneously became a useful tool for capitalism, a cheap source of ultimately disposable labor, and "the indispensable enemy" (to quote historian Alexander Saxton) of white agitators and demagogic politicians. Hostilities erupted in 1885, exploding the trope of the West as a "safety valve" for the social conflicts of the nation's densely settled areas east of the Mississippi. In Wyoming, white labor organizers developed a plan to drive out the Chinese miners, starting with the town of Carbon. But the Rock Springs workers jumped the gun. On the morning of September 2, 1885, Leo Qarqwang was working Coal Pit Number Six with a small group of Chinese miners. Claiming he had violated a whites-only space, a dozen or more whites moved to halt operations, forcing him and others out. They beat Leo over the head with a shovel and wounded another Chinese miner so badly that he later died. That pit was relatively far from town, but the fury reached Chinatown by afternoon. Armed to the teeth with guns and knives, a much larger group of seventy-five to one hundred whites gathered. They issued a stern warning: You have one hour to get out. But some began assaulting the Chinese residents within thirty minutes of the order to vacate.[4]

The primary account of the massacre that transpired comes from a statement signed by 559 Chinese workers at Rock Springs. Lor Sun Kit survived two shots in the arm and back. The first reported dead was Leo Dye Bah, a fifty-six-year-old immigrant with a wife and two children in China. He was shot through the chest, breaking his sternum. The mob killed Yip Ah Marn, who was thirty-eight and also had a wife and two children in China. Unarmed and defenseless, the Chinese community was caught "like a herd of frightened deer that let the huntsmen surround and kill them." Many tried to flee. Some were beaten. Others were robbed. At least fifteen were shot. White women joined the mob and engaged in shooting alongside the men. Amid vows from whites to kill all the Chinese, Chinatown was burned nearly to the ground. Some who hid inside for safety or were too infirm to flee were burned alive. The mob may also have thrown dead or wounded victims into the fire. Some who escaped to the hills died for lack of food or water. One man reportedly committed suicide after losing his wife and baby.[5]

By September 8, when President Grover Cleveland ordered troops into Rock Springs, many of the survivors had fled a hundred miles away to another company town, Evanston, with nothing but the clothes on their backs. The racist lynch mob killed twenty-eight Chinese and wounded fifteen—some of whom later died. Although sixteen whites were arrested, none were indicted by the grand jury. One influential white witness scurrilously blamed the Chinese for starting the deadly fires. Indeed, with the massacre covered by newspapers nationwide, many white Americans sided with the lynch mob. Incredibly, the head of the Knights of Labor determined that his union was totally blameless. "The recent assault upon the Chinese at Rock Springs," he declared, "is but the outcome of the feeling caused by the indifference of our lawmakers to the just demands of the people for relief." The company, nevertheless, remained determined to break the white workers' union. With federal troops becoming a long-standing presence, the Union Pacific fired the mob and strike leaders and insisted on bringing back the Chinese workers. In a sign of both resilience and desperation, 250 Chinese returned to the mines at Rock Springs within three weeks of the massacre. When whites refused to work with them, the bosses recruited more Chinese laborers. By the end of 1885, mining operations were back to full capacity, but Chinese now outnumbered whites by more than five to one.[6]

The Rock Springs massacre remains one of the worst mass murders of Asians in the continental United States by a racist mob. In terms of the number killed, it is rivaled only by the Hells Canyon massacre on May 25, 1887. A group of white men, led by a West Virginian transplant named Bruce "Blue" Evans, plotted a robbery of Chinese prospectors as they were mining for gold along the Snake River. It was a treacherous stretch, in Oregon near the Idaho border, where others dared not go. But the hoodlums chose not to rob and dash, even though they were in a remote area and would have been difficult to trace. The gang of eight whites, including a boy of only fifteen, slaughtered as many as thirty-four Chinese. Consequently, author R. Gregory Nokes concluded that racism must have influenced their actions. Meanwhile, the public knew nothing of the massacre until a body mysteriously appeared downstream several weeks later. More surfaced in the days that followed. All the suspects either were found innocent or fled to Canada. This outcome was not surprising, Nokes concluded, given that nothing more than a "half-hearted" investigation took place. For over a hundred years, the authorities buried the evidence until a county clerk found a handful of the surviving documents. We still do not even know most of the victims' names.[7]

Given how much has been lost to history, the statement by the survivors at Rock Springs serves as a broader comment on the horrors of the exclusion era:

> We never thought that the subjects of a nation entitled by treaty to the rights and privileges of the most favored nation could, in a country so highly civilized like this, so unexpectedly suffer the cruelty and wrong of being unjustly put to death, or of being wounded and left without the means of cure, or being abandoned to poverty, hunger, and cold, and without the means to betake themselves elsewhere.[8]

In this chapter, we will examine Chinese exclusion not simply as an event or a law but as a transnational process that played out over decades and shaped the life chances and experiences of Asian Americans broadly speaking. From the mid-nineteenth to the early twentieth century, anti-Asian racism intensified in concert with the rise of American capitalism and imperialism. Most immediately, exclusion entailed banning Asian migrants from entering the United States and barred those here from becoming naturalized citizens. But the effects of exclusion were sweeping in scope, limiting the prospects of Asian immigrants and their American-born descendants from full access to jobs, housing, political representation, and other civil rights.

Violence and exclusion went hand in hand. Denying fundamental rights to Asian Americans, such as the right to testify in court or equal protection from the police, rendered them vulnerable to racist assaults while granting white perpetrators effective immunity. At the same time, anti-Asian agitators deployed violence to drum up support for their causes. White labor organizers and mob leaders used peer pressure to gain adherents, while making an example of those who did not come along. Anti-Asian riots and massacres further served to define Asians as a social problem for white employers and policymakers to address. And through 1942, these violent, racist tactics repeatedly proved effective. Both major political parties closed ranks to support Chinese and Asian exclusion, Japanese American incarceration, and other measures intended to win over white voters and buy social peace.

CAPITALISM, IMPERIALISM, AND EXCLUSION

In what may come as a surprise for some readers, Americans did not start out hating the Chinese. Though they did harbor Orientalist stereotypes, the Founding Fathers and elites through the early 1800s developed a relatively favorable view of China. As historian John Kuo Wei Tchen has written, there emerged an "underlying consensus that the trade of goods and ideas with the empire of China would be beneficial to the building of distinction, independence, development, and wealth, and to the governing of the new nation." George Washington, who prized his collection of Chinese porcelain (what Americans simply call "china"), thought that Chinese people were white. But Washington's cultural fascination was eclipsed by the commercial interests of Alexander Hamilton. The ambitious first treasurer saw China as a key to the nation's growth and development—a concern that would develop over the course of the nineteenth century into a transcontinental and transnational imperial desire. In this growing lust for wealth and power, China and Chinese people were no longer abstractions.[9]

Anti-Asian racism was at least a partial byproduct of Manifest Destiny, the white supremacist ideology behind the Mexican-American War (1846–48) and the many wars tied to Indian removal. White Americans believed that they were chosen by God to expand the nation from sea to shining sea; hence, as they settled the West, they saw Indigenous and nonwhite peoples either as tools to exploit for the pursuit of wealth or as obstacles to progress that had to be eradicated. By the 1850s, the Chinese had morphed, in the

American mind, from curiosity to social problem. While Chinese laborers proved essential to the creation of infrastructure for capitalist development, they were precluded from citizenship in the nation that emerged. As historian Robert G. Lee has noted, the dominant image of Chinese and Asians shifted from merely foreign to alien—to that of a "pollutant" spoiling the white settlers' Edenic fantasy of the American West, a malady that must be expelled from the body politic, a race of people deemed not just inferior but ultimately disposable.[10]

While all aspects of Asian American history could benefit from additional research, we are fortunate to have an extensive body of works addressing the racist violence that accompanied the Chinese exclusion movement. Jean Pfaelzer, author of *Driven Out: The Forgotten War Against Chinese Americans*, has chronicled dozens of cases not only of Chinese being attacked and killed, but also of entire Chinese communities being forced en masse to leave towns under threats of violence. "The purges of the Chinese in the American West," Pfaelzer has written, "bring to my mind Kristallnacht, the night in 1938 when Nazi Germany violently exposed its intention to remove the Jews." She has further insisted that these accounts were not simply forgotten; they were erased. "Historians, librarians, archivists, filmmakers, and fiction writers have repressed a story whose evidence is in fact not hard to find." As a result, we have long underestimated the extent of anti-Chinese violence. Recovering many of these suppressed accounts, historian Beth Lew-Williams has documented at least 186 cases of Chinese residents being expelled from towns in the American West. In *The Chinese Must Go*, Lew-Williams describes the terrifying scale of these assaults: "The vigilantes targeted all Chinese people—young and old, male and female, rich and poor—planting bombs beneath businesses, shooting blindly through cloth tents, and setting homes ablaze."[11]

In one sense, this violence seems to speak for itself. Only a complete dehumanization of Chinese immigrants and a disregard for the sanctity of life—on the part not only of the assailants, but also of the authorities and bystanders who let matters get out of hand—could lead to massacres like the one at Rock Springs. Nevertheless, to understand the patterns and root causes of such violence, we need to ask critical questions: How and why did Chinese and Asian Americans, whose protest and resistance to discrimination and racist attacks are also well recorded, end up in this vulnerable position? What competing interests and power imbalances led some whites to embrace violence and intimidation more than others? What was distinct about the historical period in which exclusion predominated? And how were transnational connections central to the growth and expansion of American capitalism and global power between the mid-nineteenth and early twentieth centuries?

The era of Chinese exclusion in the United States began amid the reign of British imperialism over much of the globe. Through its defeat of China in the Opium Wars from 1839 to 1860, the British asserted a new level of military and economic power in East Asia. The conflict began as the British became voracious consumers of Chinese tea. While high tea was a custom of the elite, capitalists found that tea was also a useful stimulant to keep factory workers productive during the Industrial Revolution. With Chinese consumers uninterested in goods from England, the British pushed opium produced in colonial India. The illicit trade addicted Chinese users to such a degree that it not only erased the trade imbalance between the nations, but also created a large deficit for China. In response, China's embattled Qing emperor moved to halt the opium trade. This prompted the British to answer with superior and deadly military technology, subduing China and bringing the First Opium War to an end with the Treaty of Nanjing in 1842. Besides extracting a $21 million payment, the British forced open four new ports— on top of the sole existing port for international trade at Canton—and took possession of Hong Kong. Notably, the treaty further ensured that British subjects in China would only be "governed by such Laws and Regulations as Her Majesty the Queen of Great Britain, etc., shall see fit to direct." Unsatisfied with these gains, the British, with French assistance, launched a new round of attacks in 1856 to open more ports and gain more latitude for their merchants and commerce.[12]

The Opium Wars became a defining moment for Western imperialism, setting off what would become known as China's century of humiliation and establishing the rally cry for modern Chinese nationalism. Upwards of fifty thousand Chinese were killed or wounded, far outnumbering British and European casualties. The wars also set off a pattern of "unequal treaties" that emblematized the disparities of power between Asia and the West. Following China's defeat by Britain, the United States gained similar free trade rights just seventeen months later through the Treaty of Wanghia. Caleb Cushing, the U.S. diplomat who secured the treaty, explicitly advocated its imperialist aims. "I do not admit as my equals," Cushing stated, "either the red man of America, or the yellow man of Asia, or the black man of Africa." Secretary of State John Hay would argue near the turn of the twentieth century that

America's "open door" policy, which asserted the right of all foreign powers to trade equally in China, did "the Chinks a great service" by staving off formal colonization. Hay's "open door" rhetoric, however, contradicted the Monroe Doctrine's rationale for U.S. supremacy over the Western Hemisphere and masked America's increasingly aggressive posture toward Asia. In an act of gunboat diplomacy led by Commodore Matthew Perry, the United States sent a fleet of ships to Tokyo in 1853 and became the first to "open up" Japan to Western trade through the imposition of an unequal treaty in 1854. In response, after the relatively closed Tokugawa era, Japan began prioritizing modernization, militarization, and ultimately territorial expansion in the Meiji era. Before formally annexing Korea, Japan imposed a form of unequal relations similar to what the West had imposed on Japan and China. Thus, Chinese, Japanese, Koreans, and Indians—four of the main groups of immigrants from Asia prior to 1965—all came to the U.S. under conditions of severe inequity. Filipinos, as discussed in the next chapter, had their homeland formally colonized by the United States.[13]

The Opium Wars and unequal treaties set the stage for what was derisively called the "coolie trade." As British, Spanish, and American interests sought alternatives to enslaved Africans for work on colonial plantations, they turned to China and India as sources of indentured labor. Brokers arranged for the migration of Chinese workers, often with deceit or coercion, through the newly opened port of Xiamen, then known as Amoy. Some of the dirtiest forms of profit making came through this trade in human cargo. Conditions on ships were often so deplorable that migrants died en route to their destination. As a result, mutinies erupted frequently. In March 1852, captain Leslie Bryson of New Haven, Connecticut, arranged for the shipment of several hundred or more Chinese migrants on the *Robert Boyne*. As researched by historian Alexis Dudden, they may have been led to believe they were going to California, but found they were instead headed for the Chincha Islands of Peru, a place known for the profitable but dangerous harvest of guano fertilizer. Workers there routinely died from inhaling ammonia emitted by the massive deposits of bird excrement. To discipline the "coolies," Bryson reportedly ordered that their queues be cut off—an intolerable offense. The migrants rebelled and seized control of the ship. They subdued or killed the entire crew, chopping Bryson up into pieces. Unable to make it back to China, the mutineers were grounded on Ishigaki Island in the Ryukyu Kingdom. But word of the *Robert Boyne* mutiny made its way to Amoy, where residents were fed up with the kidnapping of men as captive labor. In

November 1852, hundreds revolted against the British colonists and their Chinese compradors. To put down the rebellion, British marines indiscriminately fired on the crowd, killing seven or eight Chinese, including a baby hit by a stray bullet. The tragedy helped bring an end to the formal "coolie" trade, though the term would persist as a racist stereotype of migrant wage laborers.[14]

Perhaps the most distinctive legal symbol of this hierarchy was the principle of extraterritoriality. What did it mean for British citizens in China to be governed only by laws as their queen saw fit? Historian Pär Cassel has stated that extraterritoriality (also referred to as consular jurisdiction) "developed into a practice that granted most foreigners nearly complete immunity from both local laws and jurisdiction." Not only did this apply to just about every conceivable encounter, but such privileges afforded under extraterritoriality "often went beyond the legal immunities that diplomatic personnel typically enjoy under international law." While Japan was able to end its unequal treaties by the 1890s, China remained under their stigma until World War II—a symbol of its derided status as "the sick man of Asia." In the United States, the denial of fundamental rights and protections to Asian immigrants comprised the perverse mirror image of Western immunity in Asia. White Westerners rationalized these twin inequities through the discourse of civilization. They should not themselves be subjected to barbaric laws in Asia allowing torture or corporal punishment, but Oriental savages could not be granted American constitutional rights without undermining the republic. The racist practice of legal immunity helped pave the way for white Americans to feel as if they had a license to kill and torture Asians on both sides of the Pacific with relative impunity.[15]

Beyond overseas warfare, racist violence was intertwined with the advance of American capitalism in two distinct ways. Capitalists can extract wealth through expropriation and exploitation. The process of exploitation is relatively well understood and straightforward. Capitalists by definition are those who own the means of production; they can produce goods for sale on the market. Workers, by contrast, have only their labor to sell and must therefore seek employment with a capitalist enterprise to survive. Assuming that the capitalists choose among their range of investment opportunities wisely, they will hire workers only when they can secure their labor power at wages that allow for sufficient realization of profits. Hence, workers cannot receive the full value of their labor. Once they are paid, the surplus value goes to the capitalists, who can magnify the class disparity by reinvesting their profits.

Moreover, capitalists can further benefit from the political oppression of minoritized workers whose opportunities for employment and political freedom are constrained, thus rendering them susceptible to greater levels of exploitation and what some have called super-exploitation.

Capitalists contend that when competition becomes cutthroat, expanding the pool of exploitable labor and driving down wages is not a luxury but an imperative. The scale and pace of war and development devastated Indigenous populations. Curtailment and eventual abolition of African slavery restricted its spread to the West. Industrialists in the U.S. West sought Asian labor as the quest for profit coincided with a race to secure federal contracts and market dominance in the expanding nation. In a landmark anthology, *Labor Immigration Under Capitalism: Asian Workers in the United States Before World War II*, Edna Bonacich and Lucie Cheng characterize Asian immigrant workers in this era as "colonized labor" to highlight the state of precarity they carried with them from their homelands. Here, we see the multiple effects of imperialism, marked by the interplay of exploitation and expropriation. Euro-American powers not only captured markets and seized resources overseas; they also created a cheaper source of labor to exploit both at home and abroad.[16]

Unfortunately, the role of expropriation under capitalism has been a source of some confusion. This stems largely from the awkward translation of a phrase in Marx's writings on the subject as "primitive accumulation," suggesting that this is only a prefatory stage to the maturation of capitalism as a system of exploitation. It is more clarifying to think of expropriation as constituting the original or primary form of accumulation—one that is never over and done, but recurring. For exploitation (i.e., capitalist profit) to occur, society must first be divided into classes, such that most of the populace becomes solely dependent on working for others to subsist. Thus, the westward expansion of U.S. capitalism necessitated dispossessing Native American and Mexican peoples of their land and the means of production. Aspects of life and nature that were sustainable, communal, and spiritual became privatized and commoditized. As historian Peter Linebaugh has pointed out, primary accumulation is an inherently violent process. Wars and militia actions enabled the outright theft of land and territory in what became the U.S. West, directly and indirectly creating a class of small entrepreneurs and big-time capitalists among the settlers. The colonizers garnered immediate wealth by extracting commodities like gold and silver. Industrialists, under contract from the federal government, then profited from the construction of the transcontinental railroad, which integrated the U.S. West into the national economy. As scholar Manu Karuka has written, the prospective seizure of Indigenous lands served as a "proprietary anchor" for railroad investors, who turned much of their profits from land grants. Finally, settlers accumulated wealth by developing the land they usurped—or selling it to others for development—first for agricultural production and later for urban uses.[17]

While it has become increasingly common to recognize the "contributions" that Asian Americans made to mining, railroads, and agriculture, it is more crucial to analyze the social relations that shaped these processes of capitalist development. Violence and expropriation created the class structure of the U.S. West. But that social hierarchy, in turn, rendered Asian immigrants susceptible to further violence. Chinese mining and railroad workers were called to perform grueling, dangerous labor with a high mortality rate, while compensated at one-quarter to one-third what whites were paid. They were, in effect, sacrificed to spare white workers from an equivalent level of risk and peril. For example, forced to work in the bitter cold on Christmas Day in 1866, at least four or five Chinese railroad workers were killed by an avalanche. Historian Gordon H. Chang estimates that hundreds of Chinese laborers—possibly more than one thousand—died building the transcontinental railroad. Toiling under hazardous conditions for paltry wages, they stopped working on June 24, 1867. The eight-day strike spread across thirty miles of track, shutting down operations and demanding equal wages and conditions with whites. It was possibly the largest in U.S. history by privately employed workers. Though the Chinese workers won a partial victory, their militancy, alas, did not foster multiracial labor solidarity.[18]

Rather than unite all workers to confront the capitalists, white workers opted, with few exceptions, for the more expedient battle to preserve their status over Chinese and, later, other Asian immigrant workers. As wage labor expanded, predominantly white working-class organizations repeatedly clashed with industrialists. Founded in 1869, the Knights of Labor pushed beyond narrow craft unionism that privileged skilled white male workers to expand its reach to farmers, unskilled labor, women, and African Americans. But full interracial solidarity among workers was scarcely a dream, let alone a reality. In the U.S. West, employers countered the success of labor organizing and the increased bargaining power of white workers by hiring Chinese workers to do "white" jobs. While the Knights welcomed European immigrants, even when they initially were hired at lower wages, it set the tone for organized labor's xenophobic, nationalist stance toward Asians. This was, to be clear, not an organization that merely *happened* to use racist agitation to advocate for the interests of labor. The union's anti-Chinese stance constituted the *core* identity of labor for these white workers. The Knights' influence soared as its geographic reach expanded west of the Mississippi and its membership peaked near 750,000 in 1885.[19]

Organized violence and the threat of violence became one of the principal tools of the trade to keep Asians in their place, rob them of the fruits of their labor, and, ultimately, exclude them entirely. Expropriation does not end when the exploitation of wage labor begins. It is a continuous force, as Linebaugh argues, that "intensifies exploitation."[20]

THE *HALL* OF INJUSTICE

Ling Sing was one of thousands of Chinese migrants who saw California as the Gold Mountain. George W. Hall was one of thousands of white men who felt he was more entitled to the gold rush than they were. On August 9, 1853, Hall confronted a group of Chinese immigrant miners camped near the Bear River in Nevada County (Nevada is the name of this county located in Northern California). Most Chinese who lived and worked in the continental United States at the time were in mining areas like this one; they comprised 13 percent of Nevada County in the 1860 census and 23 percent of nearby El Dorado County. They were initially tolerated within mining camps, so long as they agreed to perform essential but menial labor for the other miners and to restrict their prospecting to lower-yield sites or those that had already been picked over. But the Chinese were vastly outnumbered by white Americans from other states seeking a fortune. Leaving behind a wife in the Midwest, the blue-eyed, thirty-year-old Hall had arrived in gold country earlier that summer. Alongside his brother and another accomplice, he attempted to rob the Chinese group. According to witnesses, when Ling Sing came to assist a fellow miner, Hall shot and killed him "without the slightest provocation." The victim was found with fifteen wounds in his back.[21]

By this time, the nascent Chinese exclusion movement was already in motion. Most notably, California had passed two versions of the xenophobic Foreign Miners' Tax Law. The first incarnation in 1850 was intended to push out Mexican and Chilean miners. When the law was reinstituted in 1852, its primary targets were Chinese. With more than twenty thousand arriving from China that year, they had become the state's largest foreign migrant group. Unscrupulous actors exploited the discriminatory foreign miners' law even further, forcing many Chinese prospectors to pay for the mining license three or four times over as the tax became a pivotal and coveted source of revenue. Chinese immigration was further inhibited by a new surcharge the state required shipowners to pay per passenger. The effects were immediate. In 1853, the number of Chinese migrants coming to California fell to 4,270—fewer than the number that returned.[22]

Against those trends, justice was relatively swift for the murder of Ling Sing. The authorities arrested and tried George Hall for the crime in September 1853, and although his codefendants were acquitted, Hall was found guilty beyond a reasonable doubt. With the case arousing considerable public interest, Judge William T. Barbour sentenced him to death by hanging on the penultimate day of the year.[23]

But the convicted man continued to dispute the verdict. He was simply "unlucky," he said, "to be there when that Chinaman was killed." Offering to produce new witnesses, he begged the judge to reconsider. Barbour was unmoved. The unimpeachable evidence, he retorted, "would not have permitted the most incredulous to form any other conclusion." The judge then seized the moment to opine on the broader significance of the case:

> In the intendment and contemplation of law the lives of all men are held strictly sacred, without distinction; be he in high or low position, rich or poor, good or bad, his life belongs to his country and his God, and no self constituted authority can with impunity deprive him of the right. You most unfortunately, have participated in a delusion, which has prevailed to an alarming extent in California. Many persons here, have supposed that it is less heinous to kill a Negro, an Indian or a Chinaman, than a white person. This is a gross error. The law of our country throws the aegis of its protection upon all within its jurisdiction, it knows no race, color, or distinction.[24]

Barbour's statement would have been compelling in 1953, let alone 1853. Contra his timely eloquence and firm moral compass, however, the dominant social trend in 1850s California *did* value white lives above all others. Correspondingly, the law *did* flagrantly discriminate—in California and throughout America—on the basis of race, color, and nationality. In this historical context, Hall's plea for acquittal was sadly *not* delusional. When his appeal reached the state's supreme court, it was not elevated because of exculpatory evidence from his "other witnesses." Whiteness formed the sole basis for Hall's legal success.

The trial judge had flagged the decisive factors in the trial. There was, he affirmed, "clear and positive proof of the Chinese witnesses, corroborated by American testimony." Several Chinese immigrants had testified with the aid of Reverend William Speer, a translator recruited by the district attorney. The Presbyterian missionary had just returned from China the year before to establish a new mission in San Francisco. Speaking fluent Cantonese and well versed in Chinese history for a man of his time, Speer developed close ties to Chinatown community leaders and later started a groundbreaking bilingual newspaper called *Oriental*. Though otherwise culturally and politically conservative, Speer fervently opposed anti-Chinese racism in its many and varied forms and measures.[25]

While Speer's presence and support undoubtedly aided the successful prosecution of Hall, his advocacy ultimately hit a brick wall of blatant discrimination. A state act of 1850 read: "No Black or Mulatto person, or Indian, shall be allowed to give evidence in favor of, or against a white man." Hall's attorney, John McConnell (later elected California's attorney general), argued on appeal that the law prohibited the Chinese witnesses from testifying. In October 1854, this became the dispositive factor for a majority of the California Supreme Court, which vacated Hall's conviction. Only three judges decided the case. Chief Justice Hugh Campbell Murray, a twenty-eight-year-old veteran of the Mexican-American War, had arrived from Saint Louis amid the rush of 1849. He delivered the court's decision and was joined by Solomon Heydenfeldt, a Jewish southerner who had arrived just four years earlier. Alexander Wells, a northerner, dissented without comment, then died suddenly that same month.[26]

A proponent of the anti-immigrant Know Nothing Party, Hugh Murray wrote a specious opinion that bore the mark of both his political ideology and his reputation as a belligerent alcoholic. Not only did the law he referenced fail to mention Chinese or Asian persons, but Hall's counsel never objected to any of the Chinese witnesses testifying during the trial. The court itself had created the grounds for appeal. Failing to cite a single legal precedent to back his argument, Murray—largely echoing the appellant's argument—relied on a mix of contorted wordplay, racist ethnology, and practical discrimination.[27]

First, there was the need to define the legal meaning of *Indian*. Christopher Columbus, the chief justice argued, was searching for "a western passage to the Indies." Thus, when he named those he encountered "Indians," that name applied to "aboriginals of the New World, as well as of Asia." Consequently,

Murray reasoned, "the American Indians and the Mongoloid, or Asiatic" are "regarded as the same type of human species."

Next, Murray explained, "black" does not refer to the American "negro"; it must be more broadly construed as "the opposite of 'white.'" As such, the intent of the law was "to protect the white person" from testimony by "every one who is not of white blood." Even if one were to admit that "the Indian of this continent is not of the Mongolian type," Asians would still be barred from testimony simply because they could not claim whiteness.

Finally, the young chief justice said the quiet part out loud. Above and beyond the aforementioned definitions, Murray argued, Chinese immigrants must be excluded from testifying "on grounds of public policy." Allowing court testimony was a slippery slope that could lead to full citizenship rights and the pernicious sight of Chinese Americans "at the polls, in the jury box, upon the bench, and in our legislative halls." Any movement in this direction must be halted because the Chinese were "a race of people whom nature has marked as inferior, and who are incapable of progress or intellectual development beyond a certain point, as their history has shown."[28]

Aside from the outlandish rhetoric, the material effects of this decision were devastating. Statehood was already proving to have deadly consequences for California's Indigenous peoples, who were hit with a new wave of dispossession as rapacious forty-niners coveted their lands and as militias with a genocidal mentality hunted them down. Prior to Spanish colonization, there were more than three hundred thousand Native Californians. By 1846, the population had declined by half. Then, as historian Benjamin Madley has documented, it fell "at an even more astonishing rate" during the U.S. era. Though siding with the Union, California was anything but a free state for Indigenous peoples, thousands of whom were taken captive, held in debt bondage, and effectively enslaved. The 1880 U.S. Census counted only 16,277 California Indians. While many had died of disease and malnutrition, what American settlers recorded as "wars" were often one-sided massacres whose scores of victims routinely included women and children. Complementing bans on Indian voting and jury service, the ban on testimony against whites symbolized the impunity with which settlers could wantonly maim and kill those who got in the way of their plunder.[29]

Because the gold rush had prompted California's hasty admission as a state, federal legislation to address gold claims and mining was sorely lacking. Instead, might-makes-right frequently prevailed. Over four thousand murders occurred in just the half decade after gold was first struck. While the newly emerging Chinese population could not be decimated to the extent that Native Americans had been, their trek up Gold Mountain came at risk of life and limb. An 1862 investigation by the state legislature recorded the murders of eighty-eight Chinese miners. The actual number, according to Jean Pfaelzer, was likely in the hundreds. White mobs, who came west to strike gold one way or another, attacked and uprooted entire camps of Chinese miners. Routinely abusing their newfound authority, the official tax collectors—and fraudsters posing as such—extorted the miners, routinely deploying violence to achieve their purposes. One in eight of the reported Chinese victims were killed by tax collectors. Records compiled by Kenneth Gonzales-Day show that 352 people were lynched in California between 1850 and 1933, most of them during the nineteenth century, especially the 1850s. Mexicans comprised the largest ethnic group, with 126 victims. The twenty-nine documented lynchings of Chinese Americans place them between African Americans, with eight, and American Indians, with forty-one. When possible, however, Chinese immigrants armed themselves and fought back. In December 1866, a group of six Chinese gold miners outside of Sacramento killed two of the four white men who attacked them.[30]

Following the defeat of the Confederacy, the Radical Republicans in Congress established new bases for equal protection under the law through passage of the Fourteenth Amendment and a series of civil rights acts during the Reconstruction era. As California judges and politicians strained to evade the full implications of these laws, the state supreme court twice upheld the *Hall* decision. In 1868, it granted Black defendants the "equal" right as whites to exclude Chinese testimony. Again, in 1871, it granted that same perversion of rights to "the Chinaman." With Chinese activists repeatedly challenging the testimony ban, the state legislature finally relented, rescinding the ban when it updated penal and civil codes in 1872. By then, however, nearly two decades of unmitigated violence had occurred and anti-Chinese racism had been deeply woven into the fabric of society.[31]

The worst recorded anti-Asian massacre in California began in Los Angeles on the evening of October 24, 1871. There are competing accounts, but the most thorough documentation can be found in Scott Zesch's 2012 book *The Chinatown War*. The City of Angels was still a small town then— far from being the major metropolis that arose in the twentieth century. The hundred or so Chinese residents were generally confined to a street that was called Calle de los Negros but known colloquially in English by a moniker with an anti-Black epithet. The Chinese community's economic activities, including the illicit trafficking of women, mainly fell under the control of a few rival associations, or *tongs*. Reportedly, the riot began when a competition between the *tongs* over custody of a woman escalated into a gunfight that killed a local Anglo business owner and wounded a police officer. In response, a group of five hundred, mostly whites, developed a lynch-mob fervor. Its most zealous leaders sought to kill or drive out all the Chinese residents of the city. Gene Tong, a Chinese doctor who spoke English and Spanish, offered to give his $3,000 life savings to the rioters if they let him go. As he begged for his life, Tong was shot in the mouth, then hanged. Several others, who had nothing to do with the initial gunfight, innocently entered the fracas while walking home from work. They were also hanged, including Ah Loo, a fifteen-year-old boy who had just come from China. Whether through cruelty or amateurishness, the mob did not fashion a "legal hanging" that kills instantly by snapping the neck. Thus, some of the victims who were hanged suffered what one newspaper described as "a most barbarous process of slow and unreasoned strangulation." After a man named Tong Won managed to grab the rope to hold himself up, he was beaten until both his hands were broken, then stabbed and shot in the head. When the dust settled, the mob had killed no fewer than fifteen Chinese by hanging and three by gunfire. The police did little or nothing to intervene. Although the grand jury indicted twenty-five men for murder, only eight were found guilty of manslaughter, and even those convictions were effectively overturned.[32]

ANTI-ASIAN RACISM AS POLITICAL VIOLENCE

The end of *Hall* augured a new era for the rule of law. But instead of being diminished, anti-Asian violence increased during the 1870s and 1880s in concert with racist agitators escalating pressure on policymakers for Chinese exclusion. Anti-Chinese scapegoating further intensified with the Panic of 1873, which was called the "Great Depression" prior to the 1930s. Chinese labor had enriched railroad magnates and helped augur a massive boost in corporate investment during an era marked by Republican control of the federal government. But the frenzy of profiteering created a crisis of overproduction and a speculative bubble, most notably within the burgeoning railroad industry. The reckoning included a series of bank runs, skyrocketing unemployment, and heightened labor militancy. Moreover, the six-year depression of the 1870s bled into the "Long Depression" that extended into the 1890s. In contrast with Republican hegemony at the height of Reconstruction, staunch political competition characterized the subsequent Gilded Age. Prioritizing economic matters, northern Republicans yielded on the issue of racial equality, as Democrats began reclaiming the South and reinstituting white supremacist rule. While Republicans and Democrats split sharply over tariffs and the money supply, they both embraced immigration restrictions to compete for the votes of white male citizens.[33]

Distributed at Wells Fargo banks throughout the U.S. West starting in 1875, *An English-Chinese Phrase Book* offers a vivid snapshot of the violence that defined that historic moment. The collective authors, listed as "Wong Sam and Assistants," helped Chinese immigrants learn how to ask practical questions like "What goods have you for sale?" and understand household chores like "Empty the sugar into the milk-pan." But it was just as necessary for them to know statements like "The confession was extorted from him by force" and "He was choked to death with a lasso, by a robber." Author Shawn Wong has called this phrase book "the very first history of Chinese life in America from the Chinese point of view." Indeed, many of the would-be translations serve as narratives. One reads, "You have made an agreement to hire me, but if you find that I am not suitable you can discharge me, only you must not strike me."[34]

While this rising wave of violence was not controlled by a unitary leader or party, it was generally coordinated with political objectives. It thus behooves us to view such actions as an effective form of political violence. On a national level, the Republican Party was more friendly to Chinese immigrants before the Civil War and for the decade following the war. Its support for Black civil rights carried over significantly to Asians, at least to those born in the United States who were granted birthright citizenship through the Fourteenth Amendment. The party's business elites also supported immigration to boost the supply of labor needed for economic growth and to limit the power of white labor unions. California politics, however, did not fully align with these national trends. Although it was admitted to the union as a "free" state, many whites in California who opposed slavery also did not want Black people in their state. And the Golden State was unquestionably in the vanguard of anti-Asian racism. In February 1867, a large anti-Chinese riot engulfed San Francisco, setting an ominous political tone for the year. The Democrats surged with the support of white workers, reminiscent of Andrew Jackson's fusion of white supremacy with an embrace of the so-called common man. Democratic allies at the *San Francisco Examiner* called it "the party of the people" because it stood "for a white man's government, constitutionally administered, against a great Mongrel military despotism." And while the Republican Party's leaders included industrialists who owed their wealth to Chinese immigrant labor, it moved to keep pace by labeling Chinese immigration "an evil that should be restricted by legislation."[35]

A big win by the Democrats in 1867 demonstrated the power of anti-Chinese scapegoating, marking a vicious turning point in the drive toward exclusion. In his inaugural address, California governor Henry Haight railed against what he termed the "inferior races" and swore they would "never, with the consent of the people of this State, either vote or hold office." Reflecting the contortions of white supremacist political discourse, Haight insisted that "the opposition to giving the Negro and the Asiatic the ballot is not based upon prejudice or ill will against those races, but upon a conviction of the evils which would result to the whole country from corrupting the source of political power with elements so impure." We are to believe that the governor was not racist, but only meant to stop his white political opponents from using Black and Asian votes for ignoble purposes. Within a decade, both major parties were competing nationally to win the anti-Chinese vote. Congress passed the Page Act in 1875, barring "undesirable migrants" in a manner that targeted women brought from China as prostitutes. The racist violence spread nationally, too. In 1880, for instance, a mob killed a Chinese immigrant as it set out to destroy Denver's Chinatown.[36]

But California, where one out of every four workers was Chinese, remained ahead of the pack. In rural towns north of Sacramento, Chinese workers recruited for agricultural labor came under attack. The newly formed Supreme Order of Caucasians, a western version of the Ku Klux Klan, threatened Chinese workers and their white employers in Oroville, where Chinese immigrants had struck gold and established a substantial Chinatown with nearly one thousand residents. In 1876, assailants burned half of it down. The following year, the Laborers' Union demanded that the German owner of the Lemm Ranch in Chico stop employing Chinese. When he declined, a white mob aroused national infamy by murdering four Chinese workers execution style. Later that year, after Chinese men were accused of killing a white couple in Rocklin, hundreds of Chinese were expelled from the town. Four years into the depression, economic turbulence reached its peak, and white hatred was boiling. In July 1877, six thousand San Franciscans renewed anti-Chinese rioting in the state's largest city. The surging movement fed the rise of the Workingmen's Party, which became a third-party force in state politics and popularized the phrase "The Chinese Must Go!" It claimed one in three seats for California's 1878 constitutional convention, which augmented anti-Chinese measures, including the prohibition on voting in state elections that Haight had promised. When a single Chinese man voted in Monterey in July 1885, a white mob retaliated by lynching him. Ultimately, California's agitators succeeded in making Chinese exclusion a national issue, leading to the lopsided passage of the 1882 act officially known by the pedestrian title "An Act to execute certain treaty stipulations relating to Chinese."[37]

Today we call this law the Chinese Exclusion Act. It is rightfully known for the notorious precedent it set, singling out one ethnic group or nationality for a ban on entry to the United States. But Lew-Williams reminds us that the law was viewed in its time as a term-limited measure whose new restrictions did nothing to settle the "Chinese problem." The Knights of Labor complained it was both insufficient as written and inadequately enforced. Central to its vision of "class" consciousness was the conviction that Chinese immigrant workers were tools of monopoly capitalists, especially the railroad industry, whose only purpose in their eyes was the degradation of white labor.[38]

The Knights' argument for exclusion was circular. Chinese workers were inherently unassimilable—"the natural product of a pagan climate and a despotic soil," beneath humanity, acting more like a "swarm" of rats or "Asiatic locusts" than like male providers and citizen-subjects upholding the nation. One leader of the Knights ranked the Chinese below animals, deeming them "more slavish and brutish than the beasts that roam the fields." The union's leaders thus convinced themselves that Chinese workers were not only incapable of being organized; their very presence within American society undermined "civilization" and "Christianity." They thus blamed Chinese workers for conditions of life that were caused by systemic racism. Enforced segregation was read as "clannishness." Rampant labor exploitation and poverty led the Chinese to be cast as living cheaply and having low moral standards. Banned from union membership, the Chinese were perpetual competitors and strikebreakers. Prevented from forming families, they were "sojourners" with no concern for America's future. Excluded from jobs reserved for white men, they were both derided as "feminine" for doing domestic work and chastised as a threat to white womanhood.[39]

With the roads to solidarity so thoroughly barricaded, there was little opportunity for Chinese workers to challenge the stereotypes or prove that they belonged. Dehumanization of this degree provides a slippery slope toward physical harm, analogous to the defense of the home from vermin and infestation. Emboldened but far from satiated by their partial victory in 1882, the anti-Chinese forces escalated their violent attacks still further in the years that followed. On California's northern coast, Eureka first drew gold miners but subsequently thrived on lumbering. Around 1860, settler colonial militias carried out a series of massacres against hundreds of members of the Wiyot tribe, as well as Mattole, Eel River, and Mad River Indians. Industrialists then recruited Chinese immigrant workers, who formed a Chinatown covering one block. While large employers generally produced commodities for big cities and distant markets, the exclusionists organized and pressured whites who were dependent on the votes and patronage of local white workers. Through a mix of rioting and political agitation, white lumbermen drew support from municipal leaders and local businessmen as they launched a campaign to drive out Eureka's Chinese community. The hostility reached a boiling point in February 1885, after a white member of the city council was shot and killed when he was caught in the middle of a feud between two Chinese. A mob of six hundred looted stores and threatened to burn down Chinatown. Corralling every Chinese person they could find, the mob strung up a Chinese man in effigy and posted an ominous warning: "ANY CHINESE SEEN ON THIS STREET AFTER THREE O'CLOCK TODAY WILL BE HUNG TO THIS GALLOWS." Over the next two days, the entire Chinese community vacated the town, prompting the media to hail Eureka for its "peaceful" method of ethnic cleansing.[40]

In Juneau, Alaska, amid deferred hopes of striking gold through placer mining, dozens of Chinese were commissioned to work an industrialized lode mine for a white company in 1885. When the Chinese laborers were paid one-third less than the going rate for white and Alaskan Native miners, white mobs stormed and bombed their residences in June 1885 and January 1886. Eighty-six Chinese agreed to leave. Only one, known to whites as "China Joe," was allowed to stay. He became an early "model minority" example in Alaska. "Though his skin is yellow," went the legend, his "heart [is] all white." Indigenous to the land, the Tlingit could and would not "go back" to where they had come from. According to race and Indigenous studies scholar Juliana Hu Pegues, three Tlingit men were lynched in an episode characteristic of this period. The combination of Chinese removal and Native lynching did not, Pegues argues, represent the "lawlessness" of the "frontier." It was the deliberate implementation of a white supremacist system.[41]

Meanwhile, in the Pacific Northwest, though the Chinese population did not rival that of California, an outsized number of anti-Chinese pogroms took place during the 1880s. With the 1882 Chinese "restriction" enacted for ten years, the agitators moved to action as the clock ticked down. Furthermore, Canada's accelerated pace of exclusion increased the number of Chinese entering Washington from the northern border. U.S. officials moved to deport them, then held more than one hundred of them in what Lew-Williams has called the first case of "indefinite immigrant detention." Still, this did not satisfy the settler vigilantes. In September 1885, as news of the Rock Springs massacre spread nationwide, thirty-seven Chinese came to pick hops in Squak Valley (now the city of Issaquah) outside of Seattle. A violent mob burned their camp down, turned away others, and shot dead Fung Wai, Mong Goat, and Yung Son. They thereby set in motion a revolting pattern that would escalate that fall.[42]

Washington Territory's newly formed Knights of Labor, loosely tied to the national organization, galvanized white workers into the region's first significant labor organization. Workers had been drawn to the Pacific Northwest by the boom that resulted from railway construction connecting the region to the national economy. But the renewal of the economic depression in 1884 spurred interest in militant action among the Knights. In Tacoma, the Knights' Jacob Weisback, a German immigrant, won election to mayor with a call for the expulsion of all Chinese, who comprised nearly one in ten residents of the burgeoning city. Although Weisback swore that no violence would be deployed, the Knights disregarded the mayor when issuing their own vow in October 1885. Get out by the first of November, the mob demanded of the Chinese, or they would slit their throats. Two hundred immediately complied, but that did nothing to quell the mob. Several hundred armed men broke into buildings to pull the remaining Chinese out of their homes. Within a week, the rioters emptied the city of its Chinese community and burned Chinatown to the ground. During the forced eight-mile march through the cold and rain to an out-of-town train station, two Chinese immigrants died from exposure to the elements. Meanwhile, Washington gained infamy for the "Tacoma method" of ethnic cleansing. Chinatown never returned, but the Tacoma Chinese Reconciliation Park opened on the shores of Puget Sound in 2010 to commemorate the people and places that were lost.[43]

Nearby, in Seattle, similar agitation was fueled by so-called pro-labor organs like the *Seattle Daily Call*, which lambasted the "yellow heathen" Chinese workers and demanded action to curtail these "treacherous, almond-eyed sons of Confucius." Around 150 Chinese fled the city while their brethren were being forced out of Tacoma. But here, the intervention of federal troops on November 8, 1885, temporarily halted the exodus. It failed, however, to hold anyone accountable—all the rioters put on trial were quickly found not guilty—or put a stop to the violence. Indeed, some of the soldiers physically attacked and extorted cash from those they were ostensibly protecting. After several anti-Chinese bills fell just short of passage in the territorial legislature, the mob violence, prompted by the Knights of Labor, resumed on February 7, 1886. This time they wanted all the Chinese out by 1:00 p.m. They broke into the home of Chin Gee Hee, one of the community's most prosperous merchants and one of its few married men. As documented by Lew-Williams, a rioter pulled Chin's pregnant wife, Madam Wong, by her hair down the stairs. Three days later, the traumatized woman gave birth prematurely, but the baby did not survive. In response to such wanton acts of violence, Wan Lee, another merchant, hired a lawyer who convinced the court to halt the expulsion and review the matter. But fearing for their lives, around five hundred residents, half of Seattle's Chinese population, ultimately chose to leave. Nearly four hundred were marched onto a single ship to San Francisco. One of them, Chin Cheung, recounted many years later: "Many white people; same number Chinamen, lots of fight; not many Chinamen, no can fight."[44]

The Seattle and Tacoma riots made a political statement, too. The governor of Washington Territory, Watson C. Squire, was part of a white Republican elite that did business with Chinese merchants and saw the utility of immigrant labor. Amid the threats and assaults of fall 1885, however, Squire relented. The governor now embraced Chinese exclusion to ensure "domestic tranquility." Many, though not all, Republicans nationwide acceded to the exclusionists as well. With the passage of the Scott Act of 1888 and the Geary Act of 1892, the anti-Chinese movement made qualitative leaps toward comprehensive, permanent exclusion. Congress had foisted a new type of precarity onto Chinese Americans. As legal scholar Charles J. McClain noted, the Geary Act "created a legal presumption that every Chinese person was here unlawfully and threw on him or her the burden of proving the contrary."[45]

Exclusion would define the struggles of Chinese and all Asian immigrants and their descendants deep into the twentieth century, and the Progressive Era brought a new phase of anti-Asian violence. The lynchings and pogroms that marked the drive for Chinese exclusion would not end anytime soon, though they would occur with less frequency within the United States as the anti-Asian racism of the Wild West adapted to the regulatory state. This shift was embodied in the career of Terence Powderly, the former national head of the Knights of Labor. A sort of changing of the guard took place within organized labor as the Knights were eclipsed as the nation's largest union by the even more restrictive American Federation of Labor. In 1897, Powderly moved into President William McKinley's administration to serve as general commissioner of the U.S. Bureau of Immigration. Holding that authority for five years, he was afforded wide latitude to enforce the laws he had long championed. While students and merchants were exempt from exclusion, Powderly severely narrowed the eligibility of Chinese to enter the country through such categories. Claiming that most Chinese migrants were engaged in fraud, he turned entry and reentry into an even more Kafkaesque maze of inspections, interrogations, detentions, and delays. It proved to be nothing more than a slower form of killing for Ho Mun, who became gravely ill in a San Francisco jail and died in November 1899. When Chinese consular officials and local community leaders charged the government with neglect, Powderly brushed them off with the arrogance of power. He would neither spare the time nor shed a tear for those he presumed to be in the country illegally. Powderly not only urged his subordinates to escalate deportations *under* provisions of the law; he also rewarded them for deporting Chinese immigrants *outside* the rule of law.[46]

Tragically, the frontier justice of the nineteenth century was anything but extinct. But the thirst for conquest at the heart of Manifest Destiny ultimately led America overseas. Its pursuit of a global empire would bring violence and mass murder to a whole new level.

The Violence of Empire

"Mr. President, the times call for candor. The Philippines are ours forever, 'territory belonging to the United States,' as the Constitution calls them."[1] These were the words of the junior senator from Indiana, Albert Beveridge, on January 9, 1900. The Senate galleries filled ninety minutes before his speech. Lines ran out the doors with the overflow crowd. In the aftermath of the Spanish-American War, Beveridge called for indefinite American ownership and control of the Philippines. Filipino leaders had joined forces with the United States to end over three centuries of Spanish colonial rule. But their dreams of independence during the twilight of the Spanish empire bumped directly against the growing American desire for an empire of its own.[2]

The central thrust of Beveridge's speech was unmistakable. He was convinced the United States should control the entirety of North America from Canada to Mexico, as well as the Caribbean. Now it had not only an inalienable right, but a providential duty to seize the Philippine archipelago as its colonial possession. "We will not abandon our opportunity in the Orient," Beveridge proclaimed. "This island empire"—as he characterized the Philippine archipelago—constituted "the last land left in all the oceans." Through extensive travels, he had found these lands to be "a revelation of vegetable and mineral riches."[3]

With no regard for its Indigenous inhabitants, he urged Americans to commandeer the Philippines' gold, copper, coal, and wood—enough to "supply the furniture of the world for a century to come." Therein lay the requisite fuel to propel American ambition on the global stage. The Panic of 1893, an extended depression during the mid-1890s, had halted the nation's economic growth, putting a damper on the public's confidence and sweeping the Democrats out of power. Beveridge stood at the forefront of Republicans who saw imperialism as a solution to the crisis of overproduction. He foresaw the archipelago serving as a base for conquering "China's illimitable markets." The ultimate goal was "to establish the supremacy of the American republic over the Pacific and throughout the East till the end of time."[4]

Not surprisingly, Beveridge's thirst for plunder was intertwined with an unabashed white supremacism. His Senate floor speech—along with dozens of other writings and orations echoing its themes as he barnstormed the country—helped to popularize the racist logic used to justify imperialism and mass murder. Filipinos were a "barbarous race," a "dull and stupid" people stained by "hundreds of years of savagery." Because he saw them as wholly incapable of self-government, taking them under America's tutelage was an act of benevolence. Ultimately, colonizing the Philippines transcended politics. "It is elemental," Beveridge asserted. "It is racial."[5]

Advancing arguments that fused Christian nationalism with the scientific racism prevalent in his time, Beveridge proclaimed that God had made Anglo-Saxons "the master organizers of the world to establish system where chaos reigns." Now the moment had arrived for the United States to become the first among equals. "And of all our race," Beveridge rallied his countrymen, "He has marked the American people as His chosen nation to finally lead in the regeneration of the world."[6]

But any claims of benevolence and preordination rang hollow with the Filipinos, among whom a nationalist fervor arose with the prospect of liberation from Spanish rule. When Filipinos took up arms to liberate their homeland from their new occupiers, the Americans cast this act as an "insurrection." In fact, what broke out was a vicious war, one that consumed the U.S. nation and sparked intense political debates. Nonetheless, I do not recall hearing a single mention of the Philippine-American War during my entire K–12 education, and I have taught hundreds of students who recounted similar experiences.

Though erased from history, the war's effects were tragically all too memorable. Although Filipinos fought with dogged persistence, the combat proved incredibly one-sided, resulting directly or indirectly in the loss of at least a quarter of a million, and perhaps more than a million, Filipino lives. Beveridge helped make the case not only for a dramatic expansion of American military troops and investments, but also for the offensive use of force to achieve strategic objectives.[7]

"A lasting peace," he stated, "can be secured only by overwhelming forces in ceaseless action until universal and absolutely final defeat is inflicted on the enemy." He conveniently overlooked the fact that Filipinos had no interest in becoming the enemy of Americans—it was American imperialism and self-justification that had turned them into the "enemy." Beveridge closed with a call for his colleagues to close ranks and send a unified message to "these deluded children of our islands." Continued resistance was futile. Submit now and "this bloodshed will cease."[8]

Dozens of reporters were on hand. They plastered coverage of the speech on the front pages of newspapers across the nation, hailing the young senator as a "genius" and ruminating on "the magic of his eloquence."[9]

This chapter focuses on the Philippine-American War as a defining moment in U.S. history and in the specific history of anti-Asian racism and violence. During the first century of nationhood, Manifest Destiny was driven by wars of conquest over Mexico and Native American nations. Over the course of the twentieth century, American militarism increasingly pivoted toward Asia and the Pacific as the United States first established itself as *a* world power, then became *the* world's superpower.

The Philippine-American War marked the first test of whether Americans would assume responsibility for what Rudyard Kipling called the "white man's burden"—the willingness to do whatever was needed to conquer those deemed savages in the name of spreading so-called civilization. It popularized what historian Richard Welch characterized as a sense of "national superiority" and set a heinous standard for U.S. wars in Asia. This includes the "good war," when imperial Japan's move to seize lands the West had previously colonized or controlled clashed with U.S. objectives for power and hegemony in Asia and the Pacific.[10]

First, anti-Asian racism played a formative role in motivating both the American public to support the aims of war and soldiers to fight these wars.

Second, regardless of whether one considers American war aims generally justifiable, the racist dehumanization of Asian enemy combatants and civilians repeatedly facilitated the spread of torture, war crimes, and mass slaughter of civilians.

Third, whenever possible, the United States sought to cover up such atrocities, minimize their extent, or place blame for them on their foes.

Finally, wartime anti-Asian racism has never been confined to overseas zones of combat. A vicious cycle begins with domestic racism influencing decisions by American leaders to go to war and enabling the atrocities committed by commanders and soldiers during war. As was most notable in the case of Japanese Americans during World War II, these wartime events inflame discrimination and violence against Asians on the home front. And yet, despite the wars coming to an end, the racism they generate persists long after through stereotypes, epithets, discrimination, sexism, and violent assaults—all of which feed into the next inevitable war.

THE RACIST DRIVE FOR COLONIZATION

> We come, not as invaders or conquerors, but as friends, to protect the natives in their homes, in their employments, and in their personal and religious rights.
>
> *Executive order by President*
> **WILLIAM MCKINLEY**, December 21, 1898

McKinley's executive order proclaimed that American rule over the Philippines was a mission of "benevolent assimilation." To provide "the greatest good of the governed," he explained, "there must be sedulously maintained the strong arm of authority to repress disturbance and to overcome all obstacles to the bestowal of the blessings of good and stable government upon the people of the Philippine Islands under the free flag of the United States." In practice, this meant waging war against the very people America was claiming to liberate.[11]

With most leading Republicans attempting to refute arguments that U.S. objectives in the Philippines amounted to imperialism, the president proved more judicious with language than Senator Beveridge. Yet, as the Senate had yet to ratify the Treaty of Paris resolving the Spanish-American War, his proclamation was an aggressive assertion of dubious legal standing. It thus worked in coordination with Beveridge's aims. If McKinley's words sound like those of Dick Cheney and George W. Bush upon launching their disastrous preemptive war on Iraq, this reflected the running theme for the hundred years between these wars. Ever since the Founding Fathers declared independence from England, the leaders of the United States have viewed the nation as a beacon of liberty and justice for all. To maintain this self-image of American exceptionalism, they have strained to portray foreign intrusions and acts of conquest as consistent with a grand vision of spreading freedom and democracy. The contradictions reached new heights when the United States announced its arrival as a global power. With its smashing victory over Spain in 1898, it claimed Puerto Rico, Guam, and the Philippines as spoils of a colonial war.[12]

The Philippine-American War followed an even more forgotten war in Korea three decades earlier. As recounted by historian Gordon H. Chang, the United States sent a fleet of ships to open the "hermit kingdom" to commerce, just as Commodore Perry had done in Japan. The so-called Korean Expedition of 1871 was headed by Frederick C. Low, minister to China. While exhibiting a demonstration of force, the Americans portrayed their naval operation as a "peaceful mission in the interest of humanity." Low paternalistically believed that he was helping introduce "Christian civilization" to a savage people. Repulsed by this "utter contempt" for his country's sovereignty, King Kojong of Korea feared a full invasion by Western "barbarians." In what they deemed an act of self-defense, Korean troops fired their outmoded artillery on the trespassing U.S. ships in June 1871, failing to make contact. The Americans shot back, killing an estimated thirty Koreans. They returned with much greater forces to wipe out the Korean fortifications. At Kwangsong, the slaughter was so one-sided that U.S. soldiers found piles of Koreans burning and dismembered. While they officially counted 250 Korean dead, more were lost in fire, water, or ravines. By comparison, only three U.S. soldiers were killed and nine wounded.[13]

Though relatively brief, the Korean War of 1871 established precedents that would guide far more expansive U.S. military operations to come. Because the Americans left without any trade agreement—one would be achieved more diplomatically in 1882—Koreans hailed their fallen soldiers as national heroes and martyrs. But the intense fighting only confirmed the racist prejudices of the Americans. In the eyes of one U.S. soldier, the Koreans fought "more like demons than men." Describing his reaction to the gruesome scene, naval officer McLane Tilton wrote to his wife, "It didn't affect me more than looking at so many dead hogs." Frederick Low described Koreans as "mere automatons" educated "to meet death with the same indifference as the Indians of North America." In what would become a recurring trope of American imperialism, he concluded, "Human life is considered of little value." As corollary to his imperial expedition, Low, the former governor of California, returned to advocate Chinese exclusion.[14]

The same mentality would prevail among the next generation of U.S. leaders in the Philippines. Initially, Filipino leaders, eager to be rid of over three centuries of Spanish colonization, allied with the Americans and fought determinedly to defeat Spain. But the Americans outflanked them, staging a mock battle to allow Spain, a fallen power, to save face by surrendering to a Western nation. Next, they shut Filipinos out of the Treaty of Paris negotiations, through which the United States illegitimately purchased the Philippines from Spain at the bargain price of $20 million. Yet Filipinos made it clear that they had not sacrificed their dead merely to trade one set of rulers for another. When they refused to back down from their own declaration of independence, the Philippine-American War broke out. Fighting an asymmetric war against a much more heavily armed foe, Filipinos turned to guerrilla warfare. While most written records mark the war's duration as extending from 1899 to 1902, skirmishes continued over the next decade. Those the Americans had previously uplifted as heroes in the war against Spain were now depicted as criminals and bandits waging an insurrection against the prevailing authority.[15]

Concordant with growing American ambition, the war in the Philippines prompted a sharp and ultimately permanent rise in military spending, as well as an expansion of troops and a permanent U.S. presence in Asia and the Pacific. Still, any idea that the war would be a cakewalk was pure folly. "The armies of America can march unresisted from end to end of our country," declared the Comité Central Filipino in October 1901, "but wherever they are not present our people unite, drawn together by a common desire." Furthermore, the U.S. public became deeply divided over the war. Prominent citizens like Ida B. Wells, Jane Addams, Andrew Carnegie, and Grover Cleveland united within the Anti-Imperialist League, which declared "full sympathy with the heroic struggles for liberty of the people in the Spanish Islands." Mark Twain remarked that he was once a "red-hot imperialist" who wanted "the American eagle to go screaming into the Pacific." Yet, he concluded, "I have seen that we do not intend to free, but to subjugate the people of the Philippines. We have gone there to conquer, not to redeem." White labor leaders like Samuel Gompers of the American Federation of Labor initially condemned the war but later emphasized restrictions on Filipino immigration and trade.[16]

For many Americans, white supremacist ideology proved to be a driving motivation for the war. Proponents of U.S. empire drew on social Darwinist "theories of development" that portrayed white civilization as rising above savagery. These racist accounts of history and ethnology started from the assumption that white men were destined to be on top of the world—often adding that this was God's intention. Then they worked backward to find examples of white intelligence, bravery, and fortitude demonstrating how and why white world supremacy was attained. Nonwhite "races" were deemed to be either less evolved or wholly incapable of evolving. Eugenics and racist pseudoscience, such as the warped creation and interpretation of IQ tests, further rationalized white domination as the natural and desired societal order.[17]

Imperialism fused white and male supremacist ideologies. Before universal suffrage, political leadership was synonymous with manhood. But dramatic economic and social changes led to a redefinition of gender roles during the nineteenth century—even as a patriarchal order persisted. The rise of big cities and large corporations boosted white-collar employment as a primary site of men's work. Fretting that the new urban culture was making American men too effete, proponents of imperialism called for a restoration of the "savage virtues" necessary to win in a Darwinian struggle for survival. Mass participation in foreign wars, not unlike the spectacle of lynching at home, became a rite of passage for white men. Military service in the Philippines, historian Kristan Hoganson argued, became "a long-term remedy for the apparent problem of degeneracy in American men."[18]

Portraying the American nation as a vigorous young man coming of age, imperialists proffered Philippine annexation as a natural stage of maturation, reinforcing the depiction of Filipinos as children in need of tutelage. This stereotype became ubiquitous because it served dual purposes. Most immediately, the American colonial regime asserted that Filipinos were too immature to rule themselves. As usual, Beveridge was blunt and bigoted: "As a race, their general ability is not excellent." He found the natives of Paluan to be "primitive." The Moros were "vigorous and warlike, but have not the most elementary notions of civilization." Despite various assessments of ethnic groups, Beveridge drew a common conclusion. "We must never forget that in dealing with the Filipinos we deal with children," he declared. "And so our government must be simple and strong. Simple and strong!"[19]

At the same time, in the discourse of American exceptionalism, the language of tutelage served to distinguish the United States from other colonial powers. Central to the U.S. decision to hold the Philippines was a fear that a rival European power or Japan would seize control of the archipelago were it to relinquish said hold. Colonial tutelage thus comprised the "benevolent" paternalism of the Americans, who contended that the older imperialist powers never intended anything other than permanent exploitation and degradation of the natives. Still, the practical effect was minimal. Appointed commissioner of the Philippines in 1900, future president William Howard Taft declared that 90 percent of Filipinos were "in a hopeless condition of ignorance, and utterly unable intelligently to wield political control."

Referring to Filipinos by the patronizing but popular moniker of the time, Taft discerned that "our little brown brothers" would need fifty to one hundred years of tutelage under American rule "to develop anything resembling Anglo-Saxon political principles and skills."[20]

While we are wont to view racism as a reactionary yearning for an older hierarchy, Beveridge was known in his time as a "progressive" who uplifted the nation's spirits with visions of increased vigor. Raised in poverty with a father who was alternately absent and abusive, he eschewed support for the Ku Klux Klan and was arguably the most effective legislator at passing signature reforms of the Progressive Era, including food inspection, business regulation, and child labor protection. Born during the Civil War, Beveridge had nothing but scorn for the "fanatical reformers" who pushed the abolition of slavery. If they had only "let matters alone," the nation's sectional conflict could have been "straightened out without the white race killing itself off." Imperialism, he argued, provided the ideal vehicle for national reconciliation, uniting the North and South on the basis of a shared commitment to white supremacy after the fall of Reconstruction.[21]

But the war's racist undertones provoked widespread opposition from African Americans. To be certain, some prominent race men, including loyal Republicans, saw imperial expansion as an opportunity for Black economic and political advancement in an era of severely restricted opportunity. For those seeing the war as the triumph of civilization, the imperial battlefield became a place where Black men could vindicate their race by demonstrating their "manhood," too. Black newspapers, however, reported that most members of their communities opposed the war and imperialism. Editorials from a cross section of the Black press condemned the war as "highway robbery" and "unquestionably one of the foulest crimes ever attempted by a republic." Many drew comparisons between the struggles of Filipinos and Black Americans. "Every soldier in the Philippines who uses the term 'nigger' does so with hell-born contempt for the negro of the United States," stated Omaha's *Progress*, "and it is our one desire that he be cured of his fiendish malady by a Filipino bullet buried in the heart of such a wretch." Some embraced the Filipino liberation struggle and rejected calls for Black soldiers to enlist in what they perceived as a thankless mission "pitting negro against negro," particularly when troops and resources were better devoted to uplifting African Americans in the South. David Fagen, as Michael Morey has written, became "a mythic figure" as the head of a small group of African American Buffalo Soldiers whom Filipinos welcomed and encouraged to join the ranks of the guerrillas. Fed up with reporting to racist American officers, Fagen switched sides, launching repeated attacks on American troops and sprouting fears that Black soldiers would revolt en masse.[22]

Perhaps the best example of how freely and vociferously African Americans—in an era of notable precarity and disenfranchisement—spoke out against the colonization of the Philippines can be found in a statement by Frederick Douglass's son, Lewis, that circulated broadly in late 1899: "It is a sorry, though true, fact that wherever this government controls, injustice to dark races prevails," Douglass stated. "The people of Cuba, Puerto Rico, Hawaii, and Manila know it as well as do the wronged Indian and outraged black man in the United States." He proceeded to skewer McKinley's disingenuous assertion that America's motives were benevolent. "No sane, honest man in this country," Douglass remarked, "believes that equal and exact justice and that education without social distinctions will be had where the race hate indulged in by the men who denounce Filipinos as 'niggers' and only fit to be subjected to the white race has full sway." Instead, overseas expansion meant nothing more than the "extension of race hate and cruelty, barbarous lynchings and gross injustice to dark people."[23]

For Senator Beveridge, alongside Teddy Roosevelt and many American leaders, flagrant racism became the basis for a double standard denying Filipinos—made of "savage blood, oriental blood, Malay blood"—the "sacred" right of self-government. Filipino invocations of the Declaration of Independence were meaningless because that document "applies only to people capable of self-government"—just as the Constitution must be properly understood, he asserted, as a document written *by* white men *for* white men. Equating Filipinos and American Indians as similarly unfit for self-government, Beveridge scorned those who argued otherwise: "How dare any man prostitute this expression of the very elect of self-governing peoples to a race of Malay children of barbarism."[24]

WAR CRIMES IN THE PHILIPPINES

On the battlefield, such variations in racist discourse paled in comparison to the overt forms of dehumanization that reigned supreme. American soldiers commonly called Filipinos "niggers," "barbarians," "savages," and "goo-goos." According to historian David Roediger, *gook* may also have been used during the war. Possibly derived from *goo-goo,* its use as an anti-Filipino slur was documented at least as early as the 1930s, specifically to stigmatize Filipino natives lacking any European "blood." One veteran of the war characterized the American approach as follows: "The only good Filipino is a dead one. Take no prisoners; lead is cheaper than rice."[25]

This consistent, penetrating form of denigration underlay repeated massacres of outgunned Filipino guerrillas, as well as noncombatants. Scholar Luzviminda Francisco resurfaced much of this history in an essay published during the Vietnam War. After dominating an early battle in a lopsided manner, U.S. troops joked it was like a "quail shoot." They stacked the dead bodies so high that they used them as a fortification. The War Department customarily denied the occurrence of such atrocities, except when presented with incontrovertible evidence. In those instances, the military argued that it had used a proportionate level of force in the face of "savage" and "barbarous" attacks. But some early assessments by senior American military leaders foreshadowed casualties of immense proportions. "It may be necessary to kill half the Filipinos," declared General Rufus William Shafter, "in order that the remaining half of the population may be advanced to a higher plane of life than their present semi-barbarous state affords."[26]

There are clear parallels between the wars in Vietnam and in the Philippines. In both cases, U.S. soldiers, ill prepared to engage in a guerrilla war on unfamiliar territory, resorted to indiscriminate methods of collective punishment. This was the response to the Filipino tactic of resistance that Americans pejoratively characterized as "amigo warfare." As described by historian Reynaldo C. Ileto, "The Filipinos were friends during the day or when confronted, but at night or when no one was looking, they were guerrillas." Military leaders quickly dismissed McKinley's rhetoric of "benevolent assimilation," which Major General Lloyd Wheaton stated in 1901 was incompatible with ruling "semi-civilized natives belonging to a race whose every impulse is to treachery and perfidy." Since they could not trust their knowledge of who was friend or foe, civilian or soldier, American troops routinely burned down entire villages, willfully destroying all crops, storehouses, and livestock. Tens of thousands died through the direct and indirect effects of these scorched-earth policies. More than defeat in combat, these horrid conditions, compounded by a growing cholera epidemic that made basic survival untenable, laid the foundation for Filipino surrender.[27]

In the southern Luzon province of Batangas, General J. Franklin Bell launched a brutal crackdown on one of the areas that had offered the most dogged resistance. While the army would eventually capture guerrilla leader

Miguel Malvar in April 1902, Bell's counterinsurgency methods established a model for crimes against humanity. To separate the masses from the resistance, U.S. forces crammed the desolated population into concentration camps, euphemistically called "protected zones," where thousands died from disease and malnutrition. They deliberately destroyed food sources to starve the rest into submission. One American congressman, remaining anonymous to speak candidly, described the effects of similar campaigns in the north of Luzon, where the disturbances came to an end "because there isn't anybody there to rebel." The level of devastation was beyond his imagination. "The good Lord in heaven only knows the number of Filipinos that were put under ground," he stated. "Our soldiers took no prisoners, they kept no records; they simply swept the country and wherever and whenever they could get hold of a Filipino they killed him."[28]

It was the type of unrestrained action Senator Beveridge had foreseen in his unabashed defense of imperialism. "Our mistake has not been cruelty; it has been kindness," he said. "The friendly methods of peace have been thoroughly tried only to make peace more difficult. The Oriental does not understand our attempt to conciliate."[29]

Amid persistent fears of ambush by Filipino guerrillas wielding bolo knives—perhaps by the very servants or translators the Americans had come to embrace as "little brown brothers"—the U.S. military adopted a strategy of "pacification." There was no room for neutrality. Every Filipino who was not actively aiding the U.S. military was treated as the enemy. American soldiers routinely employed torture to coerce confessions, force villagers to inform on guerrillas, and sway those sitting on the fence. One common and notorious method was the "water cure." The harrowing practice—tacitly accepted by U.S. military leaders without their formal approval—was described in an April 1902 edition of *New York World*: "Water with handfuls of salt thrown in to make it more efficacious, is forced down the throats of the patients until their bodies become distended to the point of bursting." Soldiers would then "jump on the distended bodies" to dispel the water and "begin all over again." Some soldiers raped Filipina women and used sexual violence as a form of domination. In less common but repeated instances, American commanders ordered public executions of Filipinos by lynching or firing squad, leaving their bodies on display as a terrifying warning to others.[30]

While many victims' stories may never be recovered, one of the most well-documented massacres of the Philippine-American War occurred on the island of Samar. In September 1901, residents of the town of Balangiga were under siege by an American pacification campaign. The counterattack by Filipino guerrillas signaled their own ruthlessness in war. They ambushed the American troops while they were eating breakfast, killing fifty-four U.S. soldiers. Some were gruesomely beheaded. Only eighteen Americans managed to survive—most of them severely wounded. As stories of the "Balangiga massacre" sent shockwaves through the American public, U.S. commanders plotted revenge. They put in charge Brigadier General Jacob Smith, a veteran of the massacre at Wounded Knee, who gave orders to "kill and burn" the entire island. There was, he said, "no time to take prisoners." After he was court martialed, the press found accounts of Smith ordering the murder of Filipinos attempting to surrender, posing for photos in front of overstuffed makeshift jails he called "cattle pens," and bragging about soaring kill rates under his command. Testifying under oath, his subordinate officer spoke of the time he asked Smith to clarify the age range of Filipinos he wanted killed. "Everything over ten," replied the general.[31]

That Smith's actions were exposed and subjected him to prosecution should not imply that anything remotely resembling accountability occurred for the war crimes committed in the Philippines. While the U.S. colonial regime prided itself on bringing modern forms of sanitation to the archipelago, it simultaneously went to work sanitizing war narratives for domestic consumption. From January to June 1902, a truncated review of evidence of misconduct by the Senate's Lodge Committee proved to be little more than a whitewash operation, with Beveridge serving as the army's most adamant apologist. The highly partisan media was just as likely (or more likely) to defend or excuse as it was to chasten military officials for their actions. General Smith's champions portrayed him as a patriotic American hero being unfairly scapegoated. Members of the clergy came to his defense. A white protestant missionary, who witnessed Filipinos being administered the "water cure," found it to be a necessary and humane tactic. Boasting he had personally lynched thirty-five Filipinos, General "Fighting Fred" Funston went on a national speaking tour to rally support for Smith. Accusations of war crimes were nothing but "lies," he asserted. The military leaders spreading them should be "hung for treason." His rhetoric was so extreme that President Roosevelt felt it necessary to reprimand him. In response, Funston chastised the commander-in-chief as a weak leader who held back the military from using necessary force. As historian Stuart Creighton Miller pointed out, Funston's only mistake was saying the quiet part out loud. Roosevelt privately assured others that he considered the "water cure" to be a "mild" form of torture. "Nobody was seriously damaged," he believed, "whereas the Filipinos had inflicted incredible tortures on our people." Declaring the end of hostilities on July 4, 1902, the president admitted to no more than "a few acts of cruelty" by U.S. troops. These paled in comparison to "infinitely worse" acts by the Filipinos. Louis McComas, Roosevelt's ally in the Senate, concluded, "No war in history has been conducted with as much humanity."[32]

Despite the president's proclamation, U.S. colonial rule proved far less than peaceful, and the casualties continued to mount. In one of the most notorious instances, American troops led by General Leonard Wood massacred one thousand Moro people on Jolo Island in the Sulu region. In March 1906, the United States proudly recorded a victory in what it called the "Battle of Mount Dajo." Wood described the severely outgunned or unarmed men, women, and children as "religious fanatics" who used children as human shields. "They apparently desired that none be saved," stated the general. In fact, the army rained fire on the victims when they were trapped on the mountain summit. While many attempted to surrender, U.S. soldiers followed take-no-prisoner orders and gunned them down. As historian Kim Wagner has documented, the American newspapers discussed the massacre prominently for a couple weeks, then never mentioned it again.[33]

THE "FILIPINO PROBLEM" COMES TO AMERICA

Whether inspired by Americanized education in the Philippines or seeking work to support impoverished families, the first significant wave of Filipino migrants came to Hawai'i and the continental United States during the colonial period. Although they did not possess U.S. citizenship rights, their liminal status as U.S. "nationals" permitted them to migrate, even as other Asians were banned from doing so by the Chinese Exclusion Act and the Immigration Acts of 1917 and 1924. By 1930, over thirty thousand Filipino immigrants were working in the United States, primarily in California. In contrast to the idealistic images they had been fed in textbooks, of America as a land of democracy and opportunity, most wound up doing back-breaking labor in low-wage jobs. As late as the 1970s, historian Dawn Mabalon noted, many farmworkers lived "without electricity, running water, or flush toilets" in crowded, substandard, and makeshift dwellings.[34]

Wooed by democratic ideals, Filipino migrants entered a nation where large sectors of the American public remained under the sway of the racist language and imagery used to promote the war. Even some of the anti-imperialists drew on racist arguments, spreading fears that the Philippine colonization would lead to brown-skinned hordes polluting the American body politic. Though its sponsors intended to showcase America's benevolent process of assimilation, the vast and popular "Philippine reservation" at the 1904 St. Louis World's Fair left visitors with impressions of Filipinos as savages outside the bounds of civilization. The fair's live human displays centered well-groomed, Christian elites as models of evolution. But visitors were primarily drawn to the spectacle of Igorots and other Indigenous tribes performing rituals in g-strings and eating dogs in their "native" habitat. What was meant to extol the virtues of colonial tutelage only reinforced racist lines of difference and exclusion. Indeed, after some of the assimilated Filipino men were seen fraternizing with white women, they were attacked by a mob of white U.S. marines that grew as large as two hundred strong.[35]

Although Filipinos enjoyed migration rights denied other Asian immigrants, they were targeted by many of the same forces that pushed for exclusion: political demagogues, white labor organizations, and nativist groups. And despite their efforts to organize and strike for better working conditions, they were similarly accused of taking away jobs from whites or depressing wages. The anti-Filipino forces often controlled local newspapers that spread sensational and salacious stories about the "Filipino problem." According to historian Fred Cordova, no less than thirty Filipino communities were targeted by racist violence, riots, and intimidation in this era. On November 17, 1927, a white mob in the small town of Toppenish in central Washington moved to drive out all the Filipino immigrants who came to work in agriculture. Two years later, a mob of several hundred whites launched a similar attack in Exeter, California. The conflagration reportedly began after a Filipino laborer who had endured bullying and harassment stabbed a white man. With the general support of the local police chief, the mob burned down a labor camp housing Filipino farmworkers. Filipino social halls were bombed in San Francisco and Stockton, and Filipino lynching victims were found in the rural California towns of Lodi and Susanville. Law enforcement often did more harm than good, recalled Ray Corpuz, who grew up in Tacoma, Washington: "You fight with Caucasians. No questions asked; you go to jail." When attacked by someone much bigger than him, Corpuz acknowledged using a small knife to defend himself. "I spent several months in jail just for that," he stated. "There was no trial. You get kicked and put in jail." In the privacy of their homes, Filipino workers in Stockton practiced *escrima*, substituting asparagus-picking knives for bolos. They preserved the sacred martial art while preparing themselves for violent assaults.[36]

Xenophobia was particularly fueled by antipathy toward Filipino men dating white women—or the mere thought of them having relations—especially through the Filipino "taxi dance" halls. Catering to immigrant laborers, who were primarily single men, these clubs employed working-class white women, often from out of town, and routinely charged patrons ten cents per dance. Operating on the margins of society, they provided a small bit of respite and a larger dose of desire for workers, who otherwise toiled long hours performing arduous "stoop labor" in the sun-drenched fields. But in the minds of the exclusionists, the taxi dance hall was a menace to society rife with vice and crime, a glaring symbol of the danger posed by immigration. In March 1930, the *Stockton Daily Evening Record* warned the "little brown brothers" to stay in their subordinate place.[37]

Tensions intensified as the Great Depression set in. Anti-Filipino sentiments had built as the ranks of Filipino farm laborers grew during the mid- to late 1920s, especially in California. The most notorious recorded instance of white mob violence took place in the agricultural town of Watsonville, in California's Central Coast region. The largely one-sided white riot served to foreground the notion of the Filipino problem in the state. But underlying the disturbance were changes in the structure of the agricultural industry. Formerly home to smaller, locally owned apple orchards, the region had become one of the nation's primary suppliers of lettuce. Scapegoated by whites, low-wage Filipino labor facilitated mass corporate production for out-of-state markets. In December 1929, white residents complained about a taxi dance hall opening in nearby Palm Beach. Mobs of young white men roamed the streets, as organized groups railed against the Filipino presence. In January 1930, the conflict erupted into an all-out riot, with two hundred to seven hundred persons attacking the dance hall and sites of Filipino employment. Some of the rioters were armed; they set out to attack Filipinos at the John Murphy ranch. One assailant fired a machine gun into a bunkhouse, striking and killing Fermin Tobera, a twenty-two-year-old lettuce picker. For five days, Filipinos were beaten and robbed until the violence subsided. When police intervened, white xenophobes denounced them as "goo-goo lovers." In the meantime, the local newspaper blithely characterized the rioters as acting in "good humor."[38]

Although the police identified and arrested eight white men, they ended their half-hearted investigation into Tobera's murder, claiming they lacked sufficient evidence to charge anyone. While *People v. Hall* was a legal relic, prosecutors generally disregarded testimony by Filipino witnesses in practice. In the most blatant sign of bias, the case was assigned to Judge D. W. Rohrback, a leader of the Northern Monterey County Chamber of Commerce—one of the most prominent groups at the heart of the anti-Filipino agitation. Rohrback labeled Filipino immigrants "disease carriers" with a violent psyche. They were just "ten years removed from the bolo and breechcloth." He punctuated his screed with a warning that unless immigration was halted, interracial relations would produce "40,000 half-breeds" within a decade. No one from the D.A.'s office, however, called for Rohrback's recusal. Though the defendants pled guilty to rioting, the judge was on record advising the court to be "very lenient." They were sentenced in superior court to thirty days in jail and two years of probation.[39]

The Watsonville riot raised the level of alarm within the Filipino community to an unprecedented degree. On February 2, 1930, mobilized by labor activist Pablo Manlapit, one thousand Filipinos and their allies marched in Los Angeles to protest the riot and memorialize Tobera. Voices of outrage were raised across the Pacific, as well. In Manila, over ten thousand demonstrators marked a "National Day of Humiliation." But some Filipino American community leaders cautioned the workers to exercise restraint by refraining from actions that might arouse scorn from whites.[40]

The clamor of the exclusionists drowned them all out within the seats of political power, a disturbing sign of the broader effects of racist terror. In 1933, the California courts in *Roldan v. Los Angeles County* ruled that Filipinos could marry whites: The state's antimiscegenation law only barred yellow "Mongolians" and did not apply to brown "Malays." Immediately after, the state legislature amended the law to ensure that it banned Filipinos. Social segregation advanced, too. Businesses in cities like Stockton put up conspicuous signs reading "No Filipinos Allowed." In 1934, the U.S. Congress took its most definitive steps to resolve the so-called Filipino problem, when it passed the Tydings-McDuffie Act to end the formal colonization of the Philippines. But this was a less-than-benevolent gesture. In a sign of its true intent, the new law reclassified Filipinos from U.S. nationals to "aliens," closing the loophole that had allowed them free migration to the United States. While Congress deferred Philippine independence for at least a decade, it called for the immigration restriction to take effect as soon as possible. The new quota permitted only fifty Filipinos per year to enter the United States, including those attempting to come from the Territory of

Hawai'i. Through the Filipino Repatriation Act of 1935, Congress sought to reduce the existing Filipino population by providing one-way passage home. What the Immigration and Naturalization Service called a "Big Brotherly act" was but a thinly disguised vehicle for self-deportation. With many resolved to struggling for a better life in America, only 1 percent took the nation up on that offer.[41]

"THE GOVERNMENT WILL ALWAYS LIE ABOUT EMBARRASSING MATTERS"

Although the community persisted in the face of exclusion, countering the erasure of America's imperialist past has been a central concern of Filipino American historians and writers. "Amnesia over the horrors of the war of conquest in the Philippines set in early, during the summer of 1902," wrote Stuart Creighton Miller. The whitewashing that ensued over the following decades represented "the triumph of American innocence." By the time of the Cold War and the imposition of a repressive anticommunist environment, the Philippine-American War had been almost entirely forgotten. Even (or especially) in the Philippines, many came to see the Americans as the lesser evil that implemented a more democratic system than the Spanish and liberated the archipelago from the brutal rule of imperial Japan.[42]

The coeditors of the anthology *Vestiges of War* (2002) provide a sense of how pervasive this process of forgetting has been. Angel Velasco Shaw grew up hearing family members tell "stories about the joyous day the American tanks rolled into Manila" to end the Japanese occupation during World War II. Yet Shaw never knew of the Philippine-American War before turning eighteen. As the regular instructor of an Asian American literature course, Luis H. Francia found that only a few students each year, typically Filipino Americans, had any knowledge whatsoever of a war between the Philippines and the United States. "This simple fact," Francia wrote, "attests to the near-absence of the war in U.S. official narratives and forms the mantle of invisibility that shrouds Filipinos and Filipino Americans—an invisibility that unmoors and renders them contextless."[43]

Filipino American activists have also challenged the facile notion that the United States relinquished its colonial aims. Indeed, it continued to exert undue influence and commit human rights violations by proxy. Following its independence in 1946, the Philippines remained a special American ally hosting military bases and aiding U.S. operations in Korea and Vietnam. Consequently, the U.S. government backed Ferdinand Marcos, the anticommunist president, after he declared martial law on September 21, 1972. By 1977, the Marcos dictatorship had jailed seventy thousand political opponents and tortured thirty-four thousand Filipinos. Another 3,240 people disappeared. Given the authoritarian climate in the Philippines, Filipinos in the United States, both American-born and recent exiles, played an integral part in organizing against the Marcos regime and its U.S. sponsors. In some cases, the violence and repression followed them to America. Silme Domingo and Gene Viernes were labor organizers in Seattle and radical activists tied to the Katipunan ng mga Demokratikong Pilipino (KDP), or Union of Democratic Filipinos. On June 1, 1981, they were killed by hit men hired by Tony Baruso, a corrupt union president tied to Marcos. In response, Silme's sister Cindy and other KDP leaders and allies organized the Committee for Justice for Domingo and Viernes. Toiling for eight and a half years, they won a civil judgment in federal court holding Ferdinand and Imelda Marcos liable for their role in the conspiracy to murder the activists. Though the U.S. government was dismissed as a defendant, the committee also found evidence that U.S. agents were involved or complicit in the crime.[44]

For all the nuances of statecraft and policymaking, the devaluing of Asian lives has been a recurring theme in U.S. militarism. These Filipino Americans, who linked the history of imperialism to ongoing atrocities, were part of a broader wave of scholars and activists prompted by the Vietnam War to reexamine U.S. foreign policy. In the Philippine-American War, they found early examples of both American war crimes and antiwar protest. Many were moved by the exposure of the My Lai massacre to dig through the nation's ugly past. On the one hand, the American public finally learned that its soldiers were capable of systematically slaughtering civilians. On the other hand, the next worst thing to a complete cover-up was the conclusion that what happened at My Lai was an exceptional tragedy. "In the search for precedents," the *Washington Post* reported, "nothing can be found from World War I or World War II or the Korea conflict." In fact, the erasure from the official record of numerous massacres of Filipinos by U.S. forces established a pattern for the wars that followed. When news of the My Lai massacre made headlines, the U.S. military was covering up a horrific massacre of similar proportions that occurred during the early stages of the Korean War.[45]

While it had long been discussed among survivors in South Korea, the indiscriminate killing of as many as four hundred Korean civilians was withheld from the American public for nearly five decades, until a team of Associated Press (AP) reporters broke the story in 1999. After winning the Pulitzer Prize for Investigative Reporting, Sang-Hun Choe, Charles J. Hanley, and Martha Mendoza expanded their string of articles into a book-length exposé, *The Bridge at No Gun Ri: A Hidden Nightmare from the Korean War*. In the first major conflagration of the Cold War, President Harry Truman rushed in troops to stop North Korea from seizing control of the U.S.-backed South in 1950. The all-white Seventh Cavalry Regiment was one of the ill-prepared units called into action. They knew next to nothing about the land to which they were sent. During the first two weeks of U.S. action, nearly four hundred thousand refugees had fled the North and crossed into territory controlled by U.S. and South Korean forces. This raised a troubling problem for the Americans: Who was friend and who was foe? To the typical U.S. soldier, they all looked like "gooks." Chinese American veteran Suey Lee Wong recalled jumping out of the way just in time to avoid a jeep. He heard the white soldier driving the jeep yell, "Let's run down that damned gook kid." With American military leaders worried that North Korean combatants were hiding among the refugees, orders came down to halt the refugees. If they did not abide by these orders—many of which they may never have heard or understood—the Americans were to open fire. Veteran James McClure recalled seeing a scared young Korean girl, crying as she tried to flee rounds of machine-gun fire. "Mortars got her," he recounted.[46]

Before the refugees ultimately took cover under the bridge at No Gun Ri in late July, dozens were scrambling for cover. "The ground was shaking," Chun Choon-ja remembered. "It looked like heaven crashed on us." Only ten years old at the time, Choon-ja saw "fireballs" exploding all around as the Americans hit the unarmed refugees with a barrage of ammunition: strafing and bombing from fighter planes above; mortar fire from artillery in the distance; and seemingly endless rounds of bullets from soldiers armed with machine guns on the front line. Choon-ja ran to her mother. She found her moaning and gasping for air. "Part of her head was gone," she recounted. While others continued running, with no sanctuary in sight, Chung Koo-shik dropped to the ground for cover. The teenaged boy was then struck in the back by a flying object: It was the head of a baby. Elsewhere, one of the fireballs hit thirteen-year-old Hae-sook in the face. Screaming and crying in pain, she was blinded. Her right eye was sealed shut with blood clots. Her left eyeball was "the size of a fist dangling from her face." Hae-sook ripped her own eyeball off her face and kept fleeing.[47]

When the civilians took cover in a tunnel under the bridge, it proved scarcely a temporary refuge. Perhaps one hundred were already dead, with three hundred more to come. The Americans, who had followed them, kept firing, strafing, and bombing. Some U.S. soldiers reported that they saw return fire, but this was probably just their own bullets ricocheting back on them. As the number of dead steadily rose, the refugees took desperate measures to survive during three harrowing days in the tunnel. Park Hee-sook, a sixteen-year-old girl, had already watched her older sister, Hee-soon, die while bleeding, convulsing, and begging for water. She grew parched with thirst as well. "I drank like a mad person," Hee-sook recalled. "I couldn't really tell whether I drank blood or water." In the end, only two dozen Koreans were alive amid hundreds of dead under the bridge. While some who tried to flee were cut down, as many as two hundred may have escaped. One was Cho Nam-il, whose wife delivered a baby on the ground of the tunnel. After assisting with the birth, Cho's mother was killed by a round of fire that also wounded his father. Carrying his father on his back, Cho and his wife were able to flee but left the newborn to die. Han Soon-suk entered the tunnel pregnant, too. After she gave birth, U.S. soldiers gunned down mother, father, and baby. Nine other children aged one or younger were murdered.[48]

Chun Choon-ja survived the horrors of No Gun Ri with her father, who lost his wife, father, brother, and newlywed sister-in-law. But decades later, she was haunted by a revelation shared by a fellow survivor. Inside the tunnel, a baby boy understandably became distressed, crying intermittently despite repeated attempts by his father to calm him down. Every time the baby cried, the Americans intensified their gunfire. Amid pleading from the refugees to stop the noise, Choon-ja's anguished father pushed her brother's head under water until he stopped crying for good. All those years, she believed he had starved to death. "The baby comes back to me at night," Choon-ja told the AP reporters. "The souls of the dead won't rest until the full truth is known."[49]

The army went to great lengths to cover up the massacre, which was not mentioned in the Seventh Cavalry's official log, some of which mysteriously disappeared. When the AP's exposé compelled the Pentagon to issue a formal response, its January 2001 report was significantly a whitewash operation— the type of nonapology that says "we're sorry this happened" without admitting culpability. The death of civilians—finally acknowledged after years of denial—was a "regrettable" incident, an "unfortunate tragedy inherent to war." The Pentagon's claim that no orders were given to fire on the refugees, however, was disputed by U.S. veterans interviewed for a BBC documentary,

Kill 'em All: The American Military in Korea. "There was a lieutenant screaming like a madman," Seventh Cavalry veteran Joe Jackman admitted, "fire on everything, kill 'em all." Moreover, the No Gun Ri incident was part of a broader pattern of potential war crimes. "We burned down every town in North Korea," General Curtis E. LeMay concluded at the end of the war, "and South Korea, too." South Koreans have filed complaints charging the U.S. military with killing civilians on at least sixty-one occasions. On a scale comparable to No Gun Ri and My Lai, four hundred civilians, according to the testimony of survivors, died near Pohang at the hands of the U.S. Navy in September 1950. Former congressman Pete McCloskey, a Korean War veteran who advised the Pentagon on the investigation, acknowledged the lack of accountability. "I think it's almost a rule of political science," he told the BBC. "The government will always lie about embarrassing matters."[50]

This was the dirty underside of the American Century that Albert Beveridge envisioned on January 9, 1900. It was elemental. It was racial.

THREE

From Mass Incarceration to Mass Murder

On February 19, 1942, following a series of stunning advances by Japan's forces through large swaths of Asia and the Pacific, President Franklin D. Roosevelt issued Executive Order 9066. Purportedly designed to protect against espionage and prevent sabotage of sensitive national defense sites and materials, it authorized the U.S. military to designate areas "from which any or all persons may be excluded." As historians and activists have obliged the nation to remember, this order laid the groundwork for the mass incarceration of Japanese Americans from the West Coast. The order itself, however, was deliberately vague. It never mentioned Japan or Japanese Americans.[1]

For the time being, therefore, members of the press and public debated the implications of EO 9066:

- Would all "enemy aliens," including Germans and Italians, be excluded, or only Japanese immigrants?
- Where would the excluded be taken? And for how long?
- Would American-born citizens be excluded? If so, how would the military determine which citizens were a threat to commit sabotage?

California's attorney general, Earl Warren, weighed in quickly and forcefully, testifying in San Francisco on February 21, 1942, before the hearings of the House Select Committee Investigating National Defense Migration. The future, and famously liberal, chief justice of the Supreme Court of the United States thus established himself as arguably the most notorious anti-Japanese agitator in a prominent elected position during the war. Both Japanese American leaders and white progressives had hoped that the hearings would inject a heavy dose of reason into the jaundiced discourse and tamp down the most racist and maximalist calls. Warren shattered those hopes almost instantly. Emergency actions, he declared, must be "done immediately" to prevent "a Pearl Harbor incident" in California. But the next sneak attack would not come from overseas. The "greatest danger," he argued, emanated domestically from "well organized sabotage and fifth-column activity."[2]

To persuade the policymakers and the press, Warren propped up maps he prepared as visual aids to show that farms and residences of Japanese Americans were near national security sites that EO 9066 professed to protect. In his eyes, these exhibits demonstrated that "the Japanese had infiltrated themselves into every strategic spot in our coastal and valley counties." In fact, these "strategic" spots included ubiquitous sites—such as coastlines, airports, government buildings, train stations, highways, bridges, and defense factories—that would have coincided with the settlement patterns of all or most other racial and ethnic groups. In the case of power lines and radio towers, some Japanese immigrants, who were barred by state law from owning land, lived and operated small farms near these "strategic" spots because they were undesirable for whites. Many were part of rights-of-way that utility companies rented out for additional revenue. But Warren insisted that these patterns could not be accounted for "by coincidence alone." He thus raised alarm about the "grave and immediate danger" resulting from Japanese Americans being "ideally situated" to execute "a tremendous program of sabotage on a mass scale."[3]

Would all "enemy aliens," including Germans and Italians, be excluded, or only Japanese immigrants?

Warren's assertions were overtly racist and appealed to rank prejudice. "When we are dealing with the Caucasian race," he testified, "we have methods that will test the loyalty of them." There was no need to round up the Germans and the Italians en masse. "But when we deal with the Japanese," Warren objected, "we are in an entirely different field and we cannot form any opinion that we believe to be sound."[4]

Where would the excluded be taken? And for how long?

While Warren applauded EO 9066, he maintained that it addressed "only one-half of the problem." Exclusion from the West Coast was necessary but inadequate. Allowing Japanese Americans to move freely to other states would, he projected, cause "race riots and prejudice and hysteria and excesses of all kind." In other words, racist hostility justified detaining Japanese Americans behind barbed wire. Warren went so far as to rationalize attacks on Japanese Americans. Racists felt compelled to commit acts of vigilantism until the "Government through its agencies" demonstrated that it was "taking care of their most serious problem."[5]

Would American-born citizens be excluded? If so, how would the military determine which citizens were a threat to commit sabotage?

Because Warren harbored rampant stereotypes about the Oriental mind as devious and inscrutable, his alarm carried over to the flag-waving, American-born Nisei. Indeed, he barefacedly insisted that birthright citizens posed the gravest threat to home-front security. "There is more potential danger among the group of Japanese who are born in this country," Warren insisted, "than from the alien Japanese who were born in Japan."[6]

Then came the kicker. "We have had no sabotage and no fifth column activities in this State since the beginning of the war," Warren stipulated. "But I take the view that that is *the most ominous sign* in our whole situation. It convinces me more than perhaps any other factor that the sabotage that we are to get, the fifth column activities that we are to get, are timed just like Pearl Harbor was timed."

"They would be fools to tip their hands now, wouldn't they?" the chairman asked.

"Exactly," answered Warren.[7]

That Earl Warren is one of the most learned, judicious Americans in history is an incontrovertible statement. That he could so easily devolve into such Orwellian doublespeak and commence a frontal assault on constitutional rights showcases the pernicious power derived from decades of anti-Asian racism. The esteemed, liberal justice official was convinced that an unimpeachable record of law-abiding behavior by Japanese Americans served as proof that they would launch a deadly, Pearl Harbor–level attack on their fellow Americans.

When at war, governments and leaders need and summon national unity as at no other time. World War II set a new and grisly standard for "total war," involving the mobilization of the entirety of national resources. "In total war," as historian John Dower noted, "all aspects of the enemy community—including noncombatant men, women, and children—become legitimate targets." For the United States, anti-Japanese racism provided the linchpin for the call to service, offering a new level of inclusion for most while hardening lines with those cast as the enemy. Echoed by other politicians, Warren's line of argumentation influenced General John L. DeWitt, head of the Western Defense Command, who began carrying out the exclusion order against Japanese Americans the month after his testimony. No one was above suspicion. Widows, orphans, elders, the disabled, and the infirm were among the more than one hundred thousand Japanese Americans deemed a collective threat to national security. A majority of the Supreme Court would validate these actions when it delivered its notorious *Korematsu* decision.[8]

Let's be clear: FDR was not Hitler, and Manzanar was not Auschwitz.

But we will be sorely remiss if we conclude that the lessons of history end there. Any unchecked instance of this brand of extreme dehumanization is a slippery slope toward genocide. This chapter details how the exclusion movement spread beyond its anti-Chinese origins and paved the way for the mass incarceration of Japanese Americans. It further demonstrates how anti-Asian racism and violence operated in a transnational manner for Korean and South Asian Americans, as well as for Japanese Americans. World War II brought the fervor to the next level. The American fear and loathing of "Japs" that led to concentration camps at home produced a drive for extermination overseas. Evidence of real atrocities by Japan was combined with a projection in the minds of Americans that the Japanese race was unmatched in its savagery and uniquely prone to war crimes. This underlay the conviction— popular among U.S. military leaders and citizenry—that the mass slaughter of Japanese civilians was not merely justifiable, but a defensive act to save lives and preserve civilization.

PAN-ASIAN PATTERNS OF EXCLUSION

On May 7, 1891, a twenty-five-year-old Japanese woman named Nishimura Ekiu was detained by immigration officials upon arrival in San Francisco. Her appeal ultimately reached the U.S. Supreme Court, which decided the case on January 18, 1892. That decision, however, sent an unfortunate signal that Japanese immigrants were unlikely to evade the types of pernicious measures imposed on Chinese migrants. While Congress had passed exclusion acts specific to China, it had also moved in 1882 and 1891 to restrict immigration across the board and enacted new categorical bans, for example on those believed to have contagious diseases and "people likely to become a public charge." Nishimura was barred on the latter basis because immigration officials accused her of lying about being married and coming to reunite with her husband. The Immigration Act of 1891 further created strict grounds for enforcement, putting bases for deportation into legislation for the first time and granting control over enforcement to a federal "superintendent." Nishimura filed a writ of habeas corpus, asserting that her detention was unconstitutional and that she was denied her due-process right to defend herself in court. But through Nishimura's case and three others involving Chinese and Japanese immigrants between 1889 and 1903, the Supreme Court made it clear that the federal government's control over entry and, with some qualifications, its deportation of immigrants were not subject to judicial review. These foundational cases established a basis for the Immigration and Naturalization Service and, a century later, Immigration and Customs Enforcement, to wield enormous power over the fate of immigrants, as well as to create a climate of fear and precarity.[9]

While many Koreans and Japanese left Hawai'i seeking better conditions in California and the West Coast, they could not outrun the exclusion movements, which broadened scope to target successive Asian immigrants. On the global stage, Japan commanded more respect from the United States after defeating China and, especially, Russia in war. Yet this simultaneously created a new level of "yellow peril" fear and loathing. The journalist Willard Straight privately confessed to a friend while covering the Russo-Japanese War (1904–5), "For no particular reason, with no real cause for complaint I now find myself hating the Japanese more than anything in the World. It is due I presume to the constant strain of having to be polite and to seek favors from the yellow people." Before the war was over, Straight concluded that the Japanese were "very much less human than the others." He later served as a prominent adviser to President William Howard Taft on East Asian foreign policy, as hostility toward Japan intensified. Because Straight was a wealthy Cornell alumnus and donor, the university named its student union in his honor after he died in the "Spanish flu" pandemic.[10]

The spread of "yellow peril" sentiment, particularly among white labor agitators, took hold domestically, centered in California. In 1905, the Asiatic Exclusion League formed and secured a pledge by San Francisco to force Japanese American students into segregated schools. The following year, a world-renowned Japanese seismologist studying the great earthquake was physically assaulted in San Francisco and Eureka. These international incidents provoked President Theodore Roosevelt to issue his 1907 executive order stopping secondary migration of Asian migrants from Hawai'i and to negotiate the Gentlemen's Agreement in 1908. Japan agreed to end labor migration to the United States, and the U.S. administration forestalled a complete immigration ban by allowing nonlaborers and family members to enter. Roosevelt's approach to Japan was amiable compared to that of his successors. California and other states passed exclusionary measures, such as "alien land laws" preventing Japanese and "aliens ineligible to citizenship" from owning land. In the early 1920s, the Supreme Court affirmed the ban on land ownership and ruled definitively in the case of *Takao Ozawa v. United States* that Japanese were barred from becoming naturalized citizens. Congress capped off the anti-Japanese exclusion movement with the 1924 Immigration Act, targeting Japan with a ban on admission of any "alien ineligible to citizenship."[11]

During the era of "separate but equal," the courts served to articulate the fictive belief that the nation could discriminate against Asians without being racist. The *Ozawa* decision of 1922 offers a prime example. Citing a 1790 law reserving naturalization rights for "free white persons," the U.S. solicitor general argued that the Founding Fathers had intended that citizenship be granted "only to those whom they knew and regarded as worthy to share it with them, men of their own type, white men." He immediately felt compelled to add, "This does not imply the drawing of any narrow or bigoted racial lines." Similarly, the justices of the Supreme Court went out of their way to disclaim any racist intent. In a unanimous opinion, George Sutherland declared, "Of course there is not implied—either in the legislation or in our interpretation of it—any suggestion of individual unworthiness or racial inferiority. These considerations are in no manner involved." The following year, in the *Thind* ruling that immigrants from India were ineligible for naturalized citizenship, the same justice delivered a nearly identical extraneous comment supporting another unanimous decision. Sutherland wrote, "It is very far from our thought to suggest the slightest question of racial superiority or inferiority. What we suggest is merely racial difference."[12]

The evasive language of judges stood in stark contrast to the violence that confronted Asian immigrants rendered vulnerable by the denial of basic rights. As with Chinese in the United States, the Japanese immigrants most subjected to physical attacks—with some noteworthy exceptions—belonged to the working class. The first significant wave of immigrants from Japan came to the Kingdom of Hawai'i in the 1880s as contract workers through an arrangement with the sovereign Native Hawaiian government before it was overthrown by American business interests and annexed to the United States. They worked on plantations, mainly growing sugar, where Chinese had previously worked. Whites were prepared to keep them in their place.

One of the most notorious instances of violence in this era was the lynching of Katsu Goto by a group of white men on October 29, 1889. At the age of twenty-three, Goto had come on the first ship of contract workers from Japan. Arriving with over nine hundred others in February 1885, Goto was assigned to work on a white-owned sugar plantation on the Big Island. Not only did he complete his three-year indenture, Goto managed to save enough money to open a general store in the town of Honoka'a. As the only Japanese-owned store in the area, his business thrived, and Goto was respected by workers from nearby plantations as a leader of the Japanese community.[13]

Two months before his murder, Goto moved next door to a larger building, arousing the ire of a neighboring business owner, Joseph R. Mills. In the eyes of whites, the upstart entrepreneur had refused to stay in his place. Even worse, Goto, remembering his roots on the plantation, helped workers advocate for their rights in a manner that upset the power structure. When a fire broke out on Robert Overend's plantation, the owner blamed Japanese workers for starting it and accused Goto of being the instigator. If he came back to the plantation to meet the workers, Overend warned, Goto would be killed. After Goto defied the warning, he was ambushed on his way home and pulled off his horse. A group of white men connected to Overend and Mills hanged Goto from a telephone pole. Overend was never charged. Mills was one of four white men tried for murder and convicted of lesser manslaughter charges. Two escaped from prison. Following the overthrow, Mills was pardoned by the white planter government in 1894. Only one of the convicted served his entire sentence.[14]

Although such lynchings were infrequent, violence and intimidation, as the late historian Ronald Takaki recounted, were integral to establishing and maintaining power relations on the plantations. Amid paltry wages and onerous working conditions, the task of imposing discipline and speeding up work was delegated to the lunas, or overseers, who typically rode on horseback and issued commands with a crack of the whip. In response, Asian immigrants fought back, often using their hoes to strike the overseers. Okinawan Chinzo Kinjo was furious with a luna he stated had whipped him after confusing him with another worker. Using karate, he managed to subdue the much larger man. Overcome with an urge to kill him with his bare hands, Kinjo was cheered on by his fellow workers until the head luna intervened. "I was at the point of jumping him, risking my whole life in that one blow," he said. "I wanted revenge even to the point of committing suicide."[15]

The harsh conditions continued into the early twentieth century, when the plantations recruited Korean and Filipino immigrants. Creating a more diverse workforce allowed the bosses to pit ethnic groups against each other and to blunt labor organizing efforts. Korean migration to Hawai'i, however, was short lived, ending abruptly after reports of severe economic exploitation and physical abuse reached Korea. In 1905, for instance, Korean workers used their hoes to attack a member of a plantation's security force, whom they charged with killing one of their brethren. A decade later, a Filipino worker cracked the skull of an overseer with a hoe. Resistance, however, could provoke a more forceful response by the authorities. On September 9, 1924, one of the deadliest labor massacres occurred in the town of Hanapēpē on Kaua'i, when local police opened fire on striking sugar plantation workers. Sixteen Filipinos were killed, then hastily covered up in an unmarked grave that was not discovered until 2019. Four police officers died during the conflict, which may have triggered retaliatory violence.[16]

Though the pre–World War II targeting of Japanese American individuals and communities in the continental United States did not rise to the scale of anti-Chinese pogroms, they were repeatedly assaulted during the drive for exclusion. In 1914, four Japanese immigrant coal miners were killed in connection with the Ludlow Massacre in Colorado. Partially as a legacy of Chinese workers' persistence, ethnic Japanese workers were members of the United Mine Workers Association at Rock Springs, Wyoming, one of the very few sites where they or any Asians were accepted into white-led trade unions. But the unique confluence of interests that produced that outcome was not replicated elsewhere. In Ludlow, white coal miners, including a wide array of European immigrants, struck in September 1913. The companies, whose ownership group included John D. Rockefeller, refused to recognize the union and coordinated with Japanese labor contractors to hire around one hundred strikebreakers. Siding with management, the governor ordered in the state militia, which fired on the makeshift camp the strikers set up after being locked out of work and company housing. The militia killed twenty-one people; the majority were family members of strikers, including eleven women and two children. Seeking to avenge these deaths, the strikers went on a rampage, burning down company buildings and camps housing strikebreakers. Among the dozens of fatalities, four Japanese immigrants (Ito Kotaro, Niwa Masukichi, Hino Tetsuji, and Murakami Jobei) burned to death in their shacks.[17]

In July 1921, Japanese farm laborers were rounded up and driven out of Turlock, California, by two connected mobs, each comprising fifty to sixty white men. While no deaths were reported, the laborers were told that they would be lynched if they came back. This was the worst of several mob attacks leading up to the 1924 Immigration Act. At least one similar attack occurred the following year in Toledo, Oregon, where sixty Japanese Americans worked at a sawmill with a handful of Filipino and Korean Americans. A mob of fifty white men, alongside two hundred women and children, violently expelled the Asian workers, who feared they would be killed. But five of the victims fought back in court, winning what author Ted Cox identified as the first federal suit to award civil damages for a violation of resident aliens' rights.[18]

Agriculture was central to early Japanese immigrants' survival, but by the 1920s the growing community—with more family households than other Asian groups—increasingly settled in urban areas. The community both outgrew the Little Tokyo enclaves and hoped to escape the stigma of the segregated ghetto. In Los Angeles, the most economically successful Japanese immigrants sought to move into relatively outlying areas. While the newest subdivisions were strictly governed by restrictive covenants limiting habitation to whites only, ethnic Japanese home seekers followed the path of Black and Mexican homeowners into white neighborhoods where restrictions failed to take root, broke down, or expired. Embattled white residents, feeling sold out by the whites who fled for newer suburbs but lacking the resources to follow them, repeatedly turned to violence and intimidation to keep and drive out nonwhite buyers. Some of the most vivid cases occurred in the East Los Angeles district of Belvedere. In February 1923, a leading merchant and community leader, Mitsuhiko Shimizu, contracted to buy a house from a white seller. Before his family moved in, the Japanese Exclusion Committee pressured the seller to rescind the deal and asked the court to halt it. When those attempts failed, they put up anti-Japanese signs around the house and a large billboard reading, "Japs: Don't Let the Sun Set on You Here."[19]

To make sure they got through to Shimizu, the racist group even commissioned a Japanese interpreter to deliver their message: Belvedere was a sundown town. When Shimizu still refused to budge, the exclusionists set his house on fire. Thankfully, the fire department saved it from total destruction. But the arsonists left behind tar, feathers, and rope to warn that a Klan-style lynching would be next. With authorities failing to come to Shimizu's aid, the Japanese Exclusion Committee held more mass demonstrations near the house—family affairs that drew white women and children. Japanese consular officials, however, prioritized major foreign policy matters; they urged the local residents to take a moderate stance. If no more Japanese Americans moved into the neighborhood, the white leaders would back off the violence. But this was a shaky peace. Mokichi Kawamoto, one of the few remaining Japanese residents, was targeted the following year, starting on June 19, 1924. The exclusion act had passed Congress but would not go into effect until July 1. More racist signs—"Keep Japs Out of Belvedere"—appeared outside his house. That night, a mob of as many as twenty white men and women demanded that Kawamoto get out. When he refused, they dragged him out, beat him, and threatened to lynch him. One of the responding police officers was a leader in the Japanese exclusion movement. Kawamoto finally agreed to move, but the incident was so disturbing it aroused indignation in newspapers overseas in Japan.[20]

Korean immigrants, against their will, found their fates bound up with those from Japan, which asserted a protectorate over Korea in 1905, then moved to formalize colonization in 1910. In response, the United States regarded Korean immigrants as subjects of Japan. In fact, the United States, through a secret binational agreement, sold out Korea, telling Japan it would not oppose its annexation of Korea, so long as Japan did not oppose U.S. colonization of the Philippines. Koreans thus existed in political and sometimes physical proximity to Japanese Americans, leaving them exposed to other violent attacks motivated by anti-Japanese racism. Fiercely committed to independence, however, Koreans in the United States ardently distinguished themselves from Japan, so much so that one of the most publicized acts of violence—and a foundational moment in Korean American history—was carried out by a group of Korean nationalists. Durham White Stevens, a middle-aged white American, came to San Francisco in March 1908, hired as a propagandist for Japan. As recounted by historian Richard S. Kim, a group of four Koreans confronted Stevens at his hotel, led by Lee Hak-hyun, who was commonly referred to by his English name, Earl Lee. They demanded that Stevens account for spreading injurious lies glorifying Japan's brutal occupation of Korea. "We are willing to suffer and die for Corea," Lee told reporters. "Liberty or death is our motto."[21]

When Stevens was leaving town, Chang In-whan, who had been part of the migration of plantation workers from Hawai'i, assassinated Stevens, shooting him twice in broad daylight. "Lynch the Japs! They've killed a white man!" yelled members of a white mob as Chang fled with an accomplice.

"Why would I not kill him? Thousands of thousands of people have been killed through his plan, and as much will be killed if he returns to Corea from the United States," Chang declared in a statement (in Korean) from his cell. "So I shot him for the sake of my country and to sympathize with the people who have already been killed, and to save the people from another killing by Stevens." Although Chang was convicted of second-degree murder and sentenced to twenty-five years in prison, the Korean American community took it as a victory of sorts that his punishment was not harsher. Activists mobilized international support for his defense, and this momentum fueled the creation of the Korean National Association, which was established in 1909. By 1912, it had 116 chapters worldwide pushing for Korean independence.[22]

TRANSNATIONAL SOUTH ASIAN ACTIVISM AND REPRESSION

Just as the United States collaborated with Japan, it aided the British in the repression of Indian independence activists. Although there were notable intellectuals and political exiles among the migrants from India, the most significant grouping came looking first for work. As Girindra Mukerji, a University of California student, pointed out in 1908, their presence was "due to the organized American or Canadian capitalist, demanding labor for upbuilding of railroads and other industries." The push to exclude them stemmed in part from the same narrow approach of white labor organizers toward other Asians. In fact, the Asiatic Exclusion League began as the Japanese and Korean Exclusion League, then broadened its scope to attack Indians.[23]

In the most well-documented pogrom, five hundred or more whites coalesced in a violent mob to drive Indian lumber-mill workers out of Bellingham, Washington. As historian Joan Jensen recounted, Bellingham was a boomtown, though its wealth came from wood rather than gold. Within a few years, the area's population surged to thirty thousand, mostly owing to the in-migration of young men. With India under British colonial rule, migrants came primarily to the United States via Canada, which implemented such harsh restrictions around 1906 that migration from India ceased within three years. Since it was well north of Seattle and near the border, Bellingham was a logical stop. Although most were Punjabi Sikhs, including many veterans of the British military, they were labeled "Hindus," which racists began to hurl as a slur. In late August 1907, white workers organized to demand that the local mills stop employing Hindus past Labor Day. They marched one thousand strong for the holiday. Some white men beat Indians they accused of rude acts in violation of "white womanhood." The next day, when Indian workers continued at their jobs, more isolated assaults occurred. With a citywide force of only nine officers, the local police did nothing.[24]

On September 4, the Wednesday after Labor Day, the agitators issued a new call to "drive out the Hindus." Following a meeting to coordinate the assault, a mob of hundreds set out on a terror spree that evening. They broke into the homes of Indians, wresting them out of their beds and setting fire to their bunkhouses. According to a local journalist, Werter Dodd, hundreds of Indians were "herded along the streets like cattle." They were marched to the city line, and many kept walking all the way back to Canada. Dodd further claimed, "The only Hindus injured were those who leaped from buildings in an attempt to escape." But this directly contradicted a *New York Times* report that "six badly beaten Hindus" were hospitalized. Near the start of the riot, police had arrested two youths, only to quickly release them. The mayor, likely concerned most about the mill owners' interests, initially vowed to protect the Indian community and uphold the law. Nonetheless, only five rioters were arrested, and the mayor let them go without any prosecution. By Friday, most of the seven hundred to more than a thousand Indians in Bellingham and nearby towns had vacated the area. The rest of the Asian population fled too. A group of fifty Japanese Americans with deeper ties to the city took up arms to defend their continued residence. But they too relented. On September 17, five Indians, reportedly the last holdouts in Bellingham, left town after being evicted by their landlord.[25]

"Whether for good or ill," Dodd wrote, "Bellingham has probably solved for herself the Hindu problem just as she solved the Chinese problem several years ago. The Chinese, once having been intimidated, now steer clear of that city." After rounds of lynching and massacres, the anti-Chinese racists had developed a "peaceful method" of exclusion that became the standard used to drive out Indians. For many, the hardships were far from over. Some found their attempts to move to Alaska stymied. One group began boarding a ship in Seattle, only to be forcibly removed. Jensen noted that hostile passengers "pushed them down the gangplank" and "threw one over the rail onto the pier." Two different groups made it to Wrangell and Juneau, Alaska, where they were not allowed to disembark. In November 1907, police stepped aside as a well-armed mob of five hundred in Everett, another lumber-industry site closer to Seattle, drove the "Hindus" back to Canada, only to reencounter the exclusionists they had come to the United States to evade. Vancouver had arguably the largest joint anti-Indian, anti-Chinese, and anti-Japanese rioting of this period.[26]

Although anti-Indian violence was especially prominent in the Pacific Northwest, it followed migrants throughout the United States. In January 1908, eight Indian railroad workers, having completed a job in Chico, were moving to Marysville, California. They were threatened and forced out by a racist mob that robbed them of all their money. In New Orleans, as documented in Vivek Bald's *Bengali Harlem*, a small group of Muslim peddlers from what is now Bangladesh added to the city's multiethnic culture. But this remained a period of intractable Black-white conflict. Abdul Fara was caught in the crossfire. In 1922, Fara boarded a streetcar and took a seat near the tail end of the white section. This enraged Fitzhugh Davis, a white passenger, who grabbed the wooden divider separating "white" and "colored" passengers and beat Fara over the head with it. When Fara sued, the court sympathized with Davis. It was reasonable, the judge assessed, for Davis to get upset at the site of a brown-skinned man in the white section. At the same time, Bald recovered stories of solidarity, including that of Dada Amir Haider Khan, a migrant worker who came to the United States in exile to build the Indian anticolonial movement. The more Khan encountered white supremacists, the more he saw the Black freedom struggle as crucial to the global struggle for revolution. Consequently, he moved to Detroit to join a scattering of Indians in the Black Bottom district—the city's largest African American ghetto—where he organized with Black radicals.[27]

While Oregon was home to less than 10 percent of the eight to ten thousand South Asian migrants who came to North America in the early twentieth century, the small community had an outsized historical impact. Nearly all were male lumber-mill workers who came secondarily from British Columbia and Washington state. Despite Oregon's notoriously anti-Black state origins, it proved initially to be a relatively hospitable place for Indian migrants. To be certain, Harnam Singh was shot and killed on October 31, 1907, just one day after he started a job near Portland. But two white men were convicted of murder and three others of manslaughter. In the expanding economy—the Portland area in particular was booming—capitalists coveted immigrant labor. One white company manager portrayed Hindus as model workers compared to slothful whites. While ostensibly a compliment, this was, as historian Johanna Ogden pointed out, a self-serving characterization to instill competition and division among workers. Simmering racial tensions eventually boiled over. On March 21, 1910, a mob of two to three hundred whites, provoked by a rumor that a mill was about to hire more Indians, broke windows and tore down doors to attack Indians at home and at work in the town of St. Johns—now part of Portland. Although no one was killed, some of the town's one hundred Indian residents were beaten and one was pushed out a second-floor window. In response, some armed themselves for self-defense. Others pressed for intervention by the British consul, whose action spurred the indictment of mob leaders and complicit city officials. The main instigator, Gordon Dickey, tried to deceive both the Indian community and the court, when he claimed he engaged the mob only to protect the immigrants. But Kanshi Ram testified that Dickey broke into his home, put a gun to his head, and threatened to kill him, all while a police officer was robbing him. The outcome was a mixed decision. While Dickey was convicted of felony riot, his entire sentence was suspended. Charges were dropped against the rest, including the mayor.[28]

Though whites were hardly impacted, the St. Johns riot galvanized the Indian migrant community. Locally, the Indian community had stood its ground—maintaining their jobs and refusing to be driven out. Nationally and internationally, the incident prompted a new level of resistance. Sohan Singh Bhakna called it "a wakeup call and a game changer for Indians working in Oregon and Washington State." In the spring of 1912, Bhakna presided over the founding of the Pacific Coast Hindi Association, which grew out of St. Johns. The following year, the association gathered diasporic activists in Astoria, Oregon, a larger mill town at the mouth of the Columbia River, and laid foundations for the Ghadar Party, founded by a union of Indian independence groups in November 1913. For Indian immigrant activists, consciousness of violence and discrimination in North America fused with their desires to liberate India from British colonialism. In 1914, four hundred Indian passengers aboard the Japanese steamship *Komogata Maru* were denied entry to Canada on the basis of the exclusionary "Continuous Journey" law—a saga that symbolizes the transnational links between oppression and violence. This incident was protested in British Columbia, and the Ghadar Party lifted the Indians' struggle as it rallied its members to return home and overthrow British rule. When the *Komogata Maru* came back to India, colonial police fired on the passengers, killing nineteen and jailing others.[29]

Historian Seema Sohi has given us a deeper understanding of this period through her groundbreaking book, *Echoes of Mutiny: Race, Surveillance, and Indian Anticolonialism in North America*. For a brief period, the West Coast was a space of relative freedom where the Ghadar Party could build membership and spread revolutionary ideas among both students and workers. Ultimately, however, their repression was driven by the transnational context. Ram Chandra, who helped build the Ghadar Party after coming to the United States, argued that the British supported immigrant restrictions "to keep the Hindus at home in order to prevent them from acquiring ideas of political liberty." In 1915, the British began trying dozens of revolutionaries, including many returning U.S. emigrants, through the Lahore Conspiracy Trials, sentencing many to death by hanging and imprisoning many more. In 1917, the U.S. Congress passed a new immigration act naming a "barred zone" to exclude Indians and most Asians. Aiding British repression, the United States also prosecuted Ghadar activists in the "Hindu Conspiracy" trial held in San Francisco from November 1917 to April 1918. Twenty-eight of twenty-nine were found guilty. Ram Chandra suffered an even worse fate: During the trial, he was killed by a fellow Ghadar member, Ram Singh, who in turn was killed by a marshal for the court. This cumulative series of tragic events effectively brought pre–World War II Indian immigration and revolutionary activism in the United States to a violent end.[30]

The small, depleted populations of Indians in the United States were struggling to maintain community, and this was made even more challenging by the Supreme Court's 1923 decision in *Thind v. United States*. Baghat Singh Thind was a revolutionary who worked among Ghadar Party comrades in an Astoria lumber mill. He joined the U.S. Army in July 1918, serving in noncombatant roles during World War I. In December 1918, Thind gained citizenship, only to have it revoked. When he was reapproved for naturalization in 1920, Thind was represented by a new attorney who prevailed by centering the controversial argument that Indians were considered "Caucasian" or "Aryan" by the prevailing race science. Although Thind allowed this assertion to go forward, Ogden recounted that his actual background was far from assimilationist. One British intelligence agent noted he associated with Finnish Americans belonging to the "anarchistic" Industrial Workers of the World, embraced militant labor organizing, and identified with Irish revolutionaries in the Sinn Fein. In any event, the Supreme Court ruled unequivocally that Indians were not "white" and, therefore, were subject to the 1790 Naturalization Act barring nonwhite immigrants from becoming citizens. For those in California and states with "alien land laws," this meant they could not own land, shutting many out of farming. For some, this also meant revocation of citizenship. While Thind later achieved citizenship for a third time, his fellow Ghadar veteran Vaishno Das Bagai struggled to adapt to life as a stateless person, the final indignity coming when he was denied a U.S. passport. On March 16, 1928, he penned a protest letter published in the *San Francisco Examiner*: "We cannot exercise our rights, we cannot leave this country. Humility and insults, who is responsible for this? Myself and American government." It was Bagai's suicide note. "I do not choose to live the life of an interned person," he concluded.[31]

This was the world made by exclusion.

DEHUMANIZING THE ENEMY IN THE GOOD WAR

The Philippine-American War has been deliberately erased from history. World War II, by contrast, comprises the good and triumphant war that Americans are universally expected to remember. With the notable exception of Japanese American incarceration, it was also a time of great democratic advances domestically. The demand for industrial labor and home-front unity provided opportunities for women and for Black, Latino, Chinese, Filipino, and Korean Americans to find work and press for long-sought civil rights. African American leaders called for a "double victory" against fascism abroad and racism at home. With Japan attempting to rally Asian nations and peoples to unite against white racism and Western colonialism, Congress overturned the Chinese Exclusion Act in order to maintain a healthy alliance with China.[32]

World War II caused death and destruction on a scale theretofore unknown to humanity. Germany and Japan bore the brunt of responsibility. Germany invaded the Soviet Union and Poland, where roughly thirty million people, mostly civilians, cumulatively died. Japan's aggression led to fifteen million deaths in China, plus millions more in other parts of Asia, revealing the so-called Greater East Asia Co-Prosperity Sphere to be little more than a brutal smokescreen for Japan's imperial designs.[33]

Concepts of race pervaded all aspects of the war and fueled much of the dehumanization, though not in a consistent manner. In the Atlantic Theater, U.S. leaders sought to counter Hitler's "Aryan" supremacy with an appeal to the "Good Germans" they believed could restore their country to Western democracy. To name the enemy as the "Nazis" meant defining them by their political allegiance and affiliation rather than their race or nationality. In the Pacific War, as historian John Dower argued in *War Without Mercy*, Americans countered Japan's race-war logic with an opposing racial logic. There was no parallel to the "Good German" in Japan, where none were considered redeemable. Whites hated the Japanese more than Germans *before* December 7, 1941. The attack on Pearl Harbor, Dower wrote, "provoked a rage bordering on genocidal among Americans." Japan's rapid expansion into the Philippines and other Western-controlled territories aroused a new form of anxiety, if not hysteria. Stories of the Bataan Death March brought news of the Japanese army's vicious tactics alongside the stupefying implications of American surrender. The routine use of epithets, most commonly *Jap* and *Nip*, defined the enemy as a race of people with a treacherous essence. But anti-Japanese racism quickly morphed into attacks on any Asian in the United States, prompting *Life* magazine to run a December 1941 article titled "How to Tell Japs from Chinese" that was replete with annotated photos and "anthropometric conformations." A Gallup poll in December 1944 found that one in eight Americans wished to exterminate all Japanese people.[34]

Undoubtedly, the fervid rhetoric of a race war fueled discrimination against Japanese Americans. Every member of the community aroused suspicion, leading to attacks ranging from name-calling to job suspensions to physical assault. In February 1942, Dr. Seuss portrayed Japanese Americans in a cartoon as buck-toothed hordes "waiting for the signal" from Japan to arise in sabotage—like regimented members of a sleeper cell. This was published the week before President Franklin D. Roosevelt issued EO 9066 authorizing the mass exclusion and incarceration. A vocal minority of Japanese Americans defied the exclusion order. Hideo Murata, a Japanese immigrant who had served with U.S. forces in World War I, refused to report for incarceration. Instead, alone in a rented hotel room near his home in Pismo Beach, California, he ingested strychnine, a common rodent poison that causes "dramatic and painful deaths." Hotel staff discovered his body the next day, his hand clutching an honorary citizenship certificate.[35]

The most famous case of a Japanese American resisting the exclusion order, Fred Korematsu's challenge in *Korematsu v. United States*, is also one of the most notorious examples in history of the U.S. Supreme Court denying the reality of blatant anti-Asian racism. General John L. DeWitt, the army commander on the West Coast who issued the order, was unabashed in his racism toward Japanese Americans, and his views were central to the frenzied campaign to put them in concentration camps: "In the war in which we are now engaged racial affinities are not severed by migration. The Japanese race is an enemy race and while many second and third generation Japanese born on United States soil, possessed of United States citizenship, have 'Americanized,' the racial strains are undiluted." Race thus accepted as a basis for suspicion, DeWitt insisted that all persons of Japanese ancestry be removed from the West Coast—citizenship be damned. He summed up this sentiment more succinctly when later telling reporters that "a Jap is a Jap."[36]

In fact, knowledgeable figures within the U.S. Department of State and Office of Naval Intelligence had completed detailed studies indicating that the overwhelming majority of Japanese Americans were peaceful and law abiding. The military's evidence that Japanese Americans posed an uncontrolled threat to national security was so flimsy and fabricated, even the famously paranoid FBI director, J. Edgar Hoover, dismissed it as the product of "public hysteria" and "political pressure" rather than "factual data."[37]

When the court ruled on *Korematsu v. United States* in December 1944, three justices in the minority declared the exclusion order invalid. Justice Robert H. Jackson questioned the credibility of DeWitt's "unsworn, self-serving statement, untested by any cross-examination, that what he did was reasonable." Asserting the indispensable role of judicial review, he concluded, "I should hold that a civil court cannot be made to enforce an order which violates constitutional limitations even if it is a reasonable exercise of military authority. The courts can exercise only the judicial power, can apply only law, and must abide by the Constitution, or they cease to be civil courts and become instruments of military policy."[38]

Justice Frank Murphy offered the most forceful and memorable dissent. The exclusion of all Japanese Americans "on a plea of military necessity in the absence of martial law," he wrote, "goes over 'the very brink of constitutional power,' and falls into the ugly abyss of racism." The exclusion order was "an obvious racial discrimination" that flagrantly violated the equal protection and due process clauses, Murphy continued, ultimately resting "upon the assumption that all persons of Japanese ancestry may have a dangerous tendency to commit sabotage and espionage." The government's "military necessity" argument was vested in "misinformation, half-truths and insinuations that for years have been directed against Japanese Americans by people with racial and economic prejudices." To suspend constitutional rights on the basis of "this erroneous assumption of racial guilt" constituted the "legalization of racism." Four decades later, Murphy's dissenting opinion was generally validated by a congressional inquiry that prompted the government's formal apology and payment of reparations to survivors.[39]

Writing for the six-member majority, Hugo Black used far more antiseptic language to justify the government's actions. "Our task would be simple, our duty clear," Black opined, "were this a case involving the imprisonment of a loyal citizen in a concentration camp because of racial prejudice." Indeed, the majority saw only "assembly and relocation centers," deeming it "unjustifiable to call them concentration camps, with all the ugly connotations that term implies." It framed the military's actions as reasonable responses to a perceived danger—a position courts and juries have frequently taken when absolving police of crimes in the deaths of civilians. "Hardships are part of war," Justice Black stated, downplaying the notion that Japanese Americans were suffering in any peculiar manner. In the end, the majority went to great lengths to argue that the case was not about "racial prejudice."[40]

While the concentration camps for Japanese Americans were not the death camps of the Holocaust, there were instances of detainees being shot by military guards, including two who were killed when soldiers fired on unarmed protesters at Manzanar. With mayors Fletcher Bowron of Los Angeles and Fiorello La Guardia of New York publicly warning Japanese Americans that they were not welcome on either coast, bias incidents—some overtly violent—also struck those who were ultimately permitted to leave the camps. Although many of the survivors' most enduring scars were psychological, those were covered up by officials, too. Dillon Myer, a liberal New Dealer who presided over the War Relocation Authority for FDR, offered the most self-congratulatory assessment of the concentration camps. He described them as "an exciting adventure in the democratic method," an experiment that "yielded some excellent results." Because of the government's benevolence, Myer asserted, Japanese Americans were "better off as a result of the evacuation." Assessing the incarceration of Japanese immigrants, his audacity knew no bounds. Myer insisted that "probably at least half had never had it so good."[41]

Following the military's decision to draft Japanese Americans for service, the wartime heroism of the all-Nisei 442nd Regimental Combat Team became a counterweight to prejudice and racism. In July 1946, after a procession down Constitution Avenue, the Japanese American veterans were honored at the White House. President Truman famously declared, "You fought not only the enemy, but you fought prejudice—and you have won." Within the Japanese American community, the veterans were held up as shining models of patriotism. Rejecting that narrative as assimilationist, the Asian American movement generation uplifted the stories of those who were imprisoned for resisting the draft. But the story of the 442nd was always more complicated. They were the most decorated unit of World War II not just because of their bravery, but also for two reasons that have not been discussed enough. First, many were incensed by the racist treatment they and those still incarcerated endured. Nazis became the most acceptable target of their anger: They could kill the foot soldiers of white supremacy while reinforcing rather than renouncing their U.S. citizenship rights. Second, many believed they were treated as "cannon fodder," sent on the most hazardous missions because U.S. commanders like John Dahlquist viewed them as more expendable than white Americans. During fall 1944, more than 850 Nisei were killed or wounded in the harrowing battle to capture France's Vosges Mountains—often because of decisions by General Dahlquist that they and others deemed incompetently made. Most of the casualties and 117 deaths occurred during the two-week rescue of the "Lost Battalion" comprising white soldiers from the 141st Infantry of Texas. "The price is too costly for our men," wrote Masayo Yamada. "I feel this way more because the burden is laid on the [442nd] combat team when the rest of the 141st is not forced to take the same responsibility." Amid their thousands of decorations, the Japanese American veterans received, contemporaneously, only one medal of honor because dozens of nominations were downgraded.[42]

ONLY OUR ENEMIES COMMIT WAR CRIMES

If Japanese Americans—most of whom were U.S.-born citizens—could be viewed with animosity after being regularly welcomed into the homes of white Americans for the service they humbly provided as domestic servants and gardeners, there was little or no room for most Americans to recognize the humanity of Japanese citizens portrayed as merciless combatants in an existential war. Deformed caricatures of slant-eyed, buck-toothed Japanese, as well as subhuman portrayals of racially marked vermin and beasts, pervaded American popular culture as part of the campaign to boost home-front resolve. Many American soldiers made a sport of collecting body parts like ears and gold teeth from the dead. Whatever the Americans did, they were assured "the Japs" had done worse. When U.S. soldiers admitted that their own acts were equally or more heinous, it was fitting payback.[43]

A wartime cartoon in the marines' *Leatherneck* magazine portrayed the Japanese enemy as an oversized louse. In response to the "lice epidemic," the U.S. Marine Corps "was assigned the gigantic task of extermination." To enact "a complete cure," the caption concluded, "the origin of the plague, the breeding grounds around the Tokyo area, must be completely annihilated." This was, in other words, an open call to commit genocide against women and children. While the cartoon was speculative, Edgar L. Jones explained the realities of the war to *Atlantic Monthly* readers in 1946:

> We shot prisoners in cold blood, wiped out hospitals, strafed lifeboats, killed or mistreated enemy civilians, finished off the enemy wounded, tossed the dying into a hole with the dead, and in the Pacific boiled the flesh off enemy skulls to make table ornaments for sweethearts, or carved their bones into letter openers.[44]

While the Allies carried out destructive attacks on civilian areas in Germany, the rhetoric of exterminating and annihilating enemy "Japs" corresponded with a greater willingness to target civilians in Japan. When Japan bombed Chinese cities in 1937, the United States and its European allies roundly condemned its actions as unprecedented. The U.S. Senate passed a resolution castigating Japan for having committed a "crime against humanity" that was "reminiscent of the cruelties perpetuated by primitive and barbarous nations upon inoffensive people." Eight years later, the U.S. military set a new precedent. General Curtis E. LeMay designed the firebombing of Tokyo—one of sixty-six cities the United States targeted from the air. The campaign executed on March 9 and 10, 1945, left the residents of sixteen square miles (in LeMay's words) "scorched and boiled and baked to death." LeMay's aide Robert McNamara admitted, "We burned to death 100,000 Japanese civilians in Tokyo—men, women, and children." Given the density of residents living in wooden structures, this was an entirely foreseeable outcome. LeMay boasted of burning down nearly half of one of the world's largest cities. But he also surmised, "If we'd lost the war, we'd all have been prosecuted as war criminals." Instead, McNamara went on to become president of Ford Motor Company and then secretary of defense overseeing the Vietnam War.[45]

By prosecuting Japanese leaders for war crimes, the United States and its allies sought to establish a stable postwar order guided by the sanctity of international law. Political and military officials were held to account for the massacres, sexual violence, coerced labor, and torture inflicted on civilians and POWs in China, the Philippines, Burma, Indonesia, and elsewhere. Individuals could not get away with the rationale that they were merely following orders or doing work for the state. In the Nanjing massacre alone, an estimated twenty thousand women were raped within the first month, and two hundred thousand people were killed within six weeks. The trials in Tokyo ran parallel to those in Nuremberg, where Justice Robert Jackson offered a memorable opening address. "We must never forget that the record on which we judge these defendants today is the record on which history will judge us tomorrow," he said. "To pass these defendants a poisoned chalice is to put it to our own lips as well." With the United States playing the pivotal role in its creation, the United Nations sought to institutionalize peaceful relations governed by international law in the aftermath of the war. In 1948, the UN ratified the Convention on the Prevention and Punishment of the Crime of Genocide.[46]

But the Tokyo trials were an early sign of the double standard that would prevail in the Pax Americana. As author Gary J. Bass has pointed out, "the victors were too quick to forget" their own words, when they precluded any American from being charged for war crimes. In one stark example, only Japanese leaders were prosecuted for the U.S. firebombing of Tokyo. Following the death of sixty-two Allied prisoners, who were incinerated inside wooden structures during the American attack, their Japanese captors were put on trial because they had survived by staying in buildings that were less flammable.[47]

THE UNENDING HORRORS OF HIROSHIMA AND NAGASAKI

The judges in the Tokyo trials also failed to consider passing any criminal judgment for the unprecedented use of nuclear weapons by the United States: dropping not only the first atomic bomb, on Hiroshima on August 6, 1945; but also the second one, three days later, on Nagasaki. The bombs killed an estimated 129,000–226,000 people, perhaps more. Roughly ten thousand or more Koreans, brought to Japan to do coerced labor, were among the victims. Some died instantly. Others suffered tremendously—their bodies scalded by toxic burns and their organs failing. Traveling at the speed of light, the thermal energy reached a temperature in the millions and incinerated everything at ground zero. Within one minute, the combination of gamma rays and neutrons began to destroy all living tissue it touched. Last came the shock wave and hurricane-level winds that toppled structures. Still more victims died from the aftereffects of radiation poisoning, which the Americans willfully denied. Survivors were left permanently disfigured—maimed and mutilated in a shocking manner never before witnessed.[48]

As a result of the widespread destruction—symbolized for some by the figure of the mushroom cloud and brought home more cogently for others by the permanent shadows of vaporized Japanese civilians baked into walls and sidewalks—the world has since viewed nuclear weapons as a special form of treachery, beyond the pale. A nation can justify developing them only by counterintuitively arguing that the point is to never use them. Those foreign leaders deemed "evil" and "madmen" by the United States have never pushed the button. Albert Einstein deemed his signing of a letter from scientists to FDR recommending the production of atom bombs to be the "one great mistake in my life."[49]

But I wonder, would Americans have changed their view of the bomb if our country had maintained its monopoly over it? How much of our revulsion of nukes is tied mainly to the fear they could be used not just by us but *against* us?

In August 1945, President Truman told the American public that dropping the bomb—a terrible marvel of physics and engineering conceived and implemented by a collective of phenomenal scientists—was necessary to end the war and save "half a million" American lives. Millions of schoolchildren were later taught some version of that rationale by their social studies teachers (I can still hear mine). There is, however, a substantial counterpoint to this inherited common sense. While most of Truman's confidants supported his decision, multiple military leaders of considerable prominence determined that the use of nuclear weapons was not a military necessity. General Dwight D. Eisenhower opposed it and expressed "grave misgivings." Although General Douglas MacArthur was not consulted on the decision, he agreed with Eisenhower that the bomb was "completely unnecessary" to save American lives. Chief of Staff Admiral William Leahy, the president's primary liaison to the military, bluntly registered his disapproval of "uncivilized warfare." The United States, Leahy concluded, "had adopted an ethical standard common to the barbarians of the Dark Ages." By some assessments, Japan was on the verge of defeat. According to this line of reasoning, only the terms of surrender were left to sort out: conditional or unconditional. The latter was an intemperate demand stemming in large measure from the public vitriol whipped up by the memory of Japan's acts, which Americans—

forgetting their own history of genocidal wars on Indigenous peoples—considered uniquely savage. Some historians have argued that the atomic bombs served as the first act of the Cold War, a show of American force meant to stave off the Soviet Union's involvement in Japan and an attempt to deter the superpower rivalry that became inevitable.[50]

The question is whether there is room in this ongoing debate to consider how the moral parameters regarding the use of the atomic bombs may have been shaped by race-war logic and anti-Asian sentiments within the broader U.S. culture. While acknowledging the aforementioned factors, Ronald Takaki insisted that we consider race as a primary factor in the decision to use the atomic bombs. Truman was not, in Takaki's opinion, bigoted to the point of wanting simply to kill as many Japanese people as possible. On the day the bomb fell on Nagasaki, the president wrote in a private letter, "I certainly regret the necessity of wiping out whole populations," adding, "I also have a humane feeling for the women and children in Japan." And yet, Truman ultimately absolved himself of responsibility for this act. It was a tactic he believed was made "absolutely necessary" by the "pigheadedness" of Japan's leaders. He could not remotely conceive of his actions as war crimes or genocide because he viewed the United States as a morally superior nation acting to stop the evil and treachery of its enemy. "When you have to deal with a beast," Truman declared after the attack on Hiroshima, "you have to treat him as a beast."[51]

Takaki argued that an underlying racial prejudice—akin to unconscious bias—shaped Truman's decision to drop the bombs. This bias was not in any way unique to Truman. Anti-Japanese racism was central to mobilizing the U.S. public in "total war" against Japan. Franklin Roosevelt was at least as liberal and humanitarian-minded as Truman, but his underlying bias permitted him to accept the racist rationale for incarcerating Japanese Americans as a dubiously perceived threat to national security. While Truman privately disagreed with FDR's decision—recognizing that the "relocation" centers were "concentration camps"—he also considered the Japanese to be "savages." This was not merely a reaction to Pearl Harbor and Bataan; it was entirely consistent with his use of anti-Asian slurs throughout his life. As evidence of this latent prejudice, Takaki cited a letter Truman penned to his future wife, Bess, on June 22, 1911: "I think one man is as good as another so long as he's honest and decent and not a nigger or Chinaman." His uncle, who fought for the Confederacy in the Civil War, hated the "Japs" and Chinese. "So do I," Truman confirmed. "It is race prejudice I guess. But I am strongly of the opinion that negroes ought to be in Africa, yellow men in Asia, and white men in Europe and America." Racial bias—even when not driven by hatred or animus—distorts reality and warps a sense of what is reasonable or permittable. Indeed, those who are more highly educated, intelligent, and sensitive to criticism are often more effective at generating rationales, for themselves as much as for the sake of others, to justify racist acts.[52]

With such considerations overshadowed by the joy and relief of V-J Day celebrations, the U.S. public stood overwhelmingly with President Truman. A survey in the immediate aftermath of Hiroshima and Nagasaki found that 85 percent of Americans supported using the bomb. Nearly one in four who were polled in December 1945 wished that "many more" bombs had been used. By this time, the national and international misinformation campaign was already in high gear. In his first public address about the bombing of Hiroshima, Truman cited Japan's war crimes to justify using a weapon of mass destruction. In so doing, he wrongly described the city of Hiroshima as "a military base." In fact, the areas most impacted by the bomb were primarily residential and commercial. As a result, fewer than 10 percent of those killed in Hiroshima were military personnel. The high rate of civilian deaths was consistent with the U.S. strategy to break the will of the Japanese people. When the bomb hit Hiroshima, most school-aged children had the misfortune to be outside. It killed 84 percent of children who were unsheltered within a four-mile radius. While the second bomb was originally slated to hit a factory producing weapons, poor weather conditions shifted the target to Nagasaki.[53]

Was one bomb not enough to break Japan's will? The U.S. military apparently struck Nagasaki without even notifying the president in advance and had a third bomb ready to go until Truman finally stopped the madness. Compared with the uranium-235 bomb dropped on Hiroshima, the 4.5-ton plutonium bomb that hit Nagasaki produced 75 percent greater force. At Shiroyama Primary School, all but forty of the school's 1,324 students were killed. A local doctor collected some of the most horrific stories from children in Nagasaki. Hearing the plane coming, a boy named Fujio was the first to rush into a shelter. He was blown against the back wall by the bomb's impact. After letting some time pass, he peeked out the door to find bodies littered across the ground and buildings everywhere on fire. With the wounded hobbling and crawling to the shelter, Fujio rejoiced when first his brother and then his sister arrived. One of the last to make it was his mother. Fujio hugged his blood-soaked mom. "I will never forget how happy I was," he recounted. But the bomb's grim reality soon set in. His father never turned up. Then, he could do nothing but watch as his family and other survivors "died in agony one after another." First sister. Then mother. Then brother. Gone.[54]

Instead of hearing from these victims and survivors, the public was mainly fed lies and distortions in an indoctrination campaign tightly controlled by the U.S. military. The key correspondent for *The New York Times* was an ambitious science reporter named William Laurence, who won the Pulitzer Prize for his coverage of the atomic bomb and became known thereafter as "Atomic Bill." In flagrant violation of his professional ethics, Laurence was placed on the army's payroll as the Manhattan Project progressed in 1944. The reports he wrote for the War Department were published nearly verbatim by newspapers across the nation. Embedded with a flight crew for the bombing of Nagasaki, Laurence wrote of feeling "awestruck" by the sight of the mushroom cloud erupting in real time: "It was a living thing, a new species of being, born right before our incredulous eyes." Amid this wonder and amazement at what had been achieved, there was no room to consider the impact on humanity. "Does one feel any pity or compassion for the poor devils about to die?" Laurence flippantly asked. "Not when one thinks of Pearl Harbor and of the Death March on Bataan."[55]

The misinformation campaign kicked into high gear after Japanese doctors detected a "radiation reaction" among bomb survivors within ten to thirty days. The visible signs included red spots, bruises, and skin lesions, as well as hair loss and swollen gums. On top of widespread pain and thirst, symptoms ranged from high fever and diarrhea to bloody vomiting and nasal hemorrhaging. Some lost feeling in their limbs. Over the next few years, many with no previous signs of illness or injury developed cancer. The U.S. military went to great lengths to censor and deny the obvious evidence and firsthand accounts of radiation poisoning. Mindful of the 1925 Geneva Protocol, which the U.S. had initiated, banning chemical and biological warfare, the Manhattan Project's director, General Leslie Groves, insisted that the bomb was a conventional weapon. Taking the cue, "Atomic Bill" Laurence published a story in *The New York Times* on September 12, 1945, citing "leading scientists" with the War Department. Claims that postimpact radiation exposure caused death or illness, Laurence brazenly asserted, were outright lies.[56]

In fact, Robert Oppenheimer and other members of the Manhattan Project were aware of research findings on the harms that radiation posed for humans from enduring effects of both the initial radiation exposure and radioactive fallout. As historian Sean Malloy notes, they ignored or minimized these concerns as they focused on speeding completion of the project. It took a Nisei with the bilingual fluency and bicultural competency of Dr. James Yamazaki to lead American research and reporting on the deleterious effects of radiation, especially on children and fetuses. A veteran of combat in Europe, Yamazaki went to occupied Japan in 1949 as a researcher for the U.S. Atomic Bomb Casualty Commission. Having endured racism growing up in Los Angeles and while serving in the army, he was moved to challenge and overcome bias where he saw and experienced it. Yamazaki found that radiation caused spontaneous abortions, stillbirths, and birth defects. Longevity studies found extremely elevated risks of leukemia and breast cancer. The problems spread to Micronesia in the Marshall Islands, one of Japan's former colonies that fell under U.S. control after the war. Yamazaki revealed that fallout from hydrogen bomb testing caused radiation sickness and birth defects for the Marshallese, particularly those on Rongelap Island. While these were officially deemed accidents, Yamazaki became more resolved to stop all use of nuclear weapons as a crime against humanity.[57]

Lacking any concern for the potential Japanese victims of the bomb, American leaders covered up the bomb's enduring impact as best and as long as possible. The Manhattan Project's Groves launched a sham investigation with orders to "prove there was no radioactivity." One of the few journalists to challenge the official U.S. position was Charles H. Loeb, a member of the Black press. In October 1945, Loeb wrote in the *Atlanta Daily World* of the "considerable argument" between Japanese and U.S. officials regarding the lingering effects of "radio activity." Without directly flaunting army censors, he cast doubt on the investigation by describing a group of fellow journalists as having "returned completely flabbergasted" from a two-day army briefing in Hiroshima. Confronted with mounting evidence, Groves shifted racist tactics, testifying before the Senate in November 1945 that Japanese reports had vastly overstated the scale of radiation casualties. But, in a trademark imperial posture, his gall remained unmitigated. "As I understand it from the doctors," Groves said, "it is a very pleasant way to die."[58]

FOUR

How Asian Women Become Targets of Violence

In August 2019, Robert Aaron Long checked into the Maverick Recovery "treatment" center in the suburbs of Atlanta to overcome what he came to believe was a "sex addiction." He stayed five months, yet afterward, he could not resist returning to massage parlors for sexual gratification, especially those where Asian women worked. Though he denied harboring any fetish, the pattern was so noticeable that those around him questioned whether he had "an Asian thing." In his desperate quest for absolution, Long sought a "cure" for his addiction not from a licensed medical facility, but from a controversial faith-based center. According to *The Washington Post*, Long told Tyler Bayless, his roommate at that facility, that he was "living in sin" and "walking in darkness."[1]

Over the preceding decades, imperialists and white nationalists had often justified racist violence as an expression of American manhood. Long's mass-murder spree in March 2021 would add to the history of American men invoking reactionary ideas of gender and sexuality to rationalize violence against Asian women. His parents and church leaders had instilled in him a Christian nationalist model of masculinity that he had failed to fulfill. He had internalized the notion that his patronage of massage parlors was not merely a sinful act; it constituted a betrayal of God's will that mandated retribution.

Long's mounting sense of failure and torment grew into an intense self-loathing. Bayless characterized him as "the kind of guy who would hate himself for masturbating." He despised himself to such a degree that his former roommate said he would call him into his room just "to hear him confess his sins." According to Bayless, Long returned from a massage parlor on at least one occasion declaring that he was suicidal. But he rejected

Bayless's insistence that he get psychiatric or psychological treatment, maintaining he was "uninterested in therapy that was not specifically related to the church." While causation is difficult to establish beyond a shadow of a doubt, the evidence points to a definite correlation. Long's rejection of medical care, in favor of "spiritual counseling" of unproven medical validity, correlated with his move toward homicidal rather than suicidal behavior.[2]

Roughly a year before the murders, Long admitted himself as a "patient" into another "evangelical treatment facility" called HopeQuest. Already drawing national attention for its "conversion therapy" and "ex-gay" rehabilitation, the facility offered an even more intensive program to cure "sex addiction."[3] While experts on sexuality would not in any way deem regular viewing of pornography or hiring of sex workers as necessarily unhealthy or a problem, Long concluded that he had failed another treatment. He turned back to his parents for guidance, including his father, who was a lay leader at their church. The night before the shooting spree, however, his parents—apparently fed up with their son's inability to end his "sex addiction"—kicked him out of their house. Permissive gun laws allowed Long to buy a 9mm handgun the next day, just hours before he targeted the spas.[4]

Ultimately, Long decided that others would have to pay for his sins, with their lives instead of his. He first targeted Young's Asian Massage, where he murdered four people and wounded a fifth victim. The HopeQuest facility stood at the end of a cul-de-sac on Crossroads Drive in Cherokee County. Young's Asian Massage was located nearby on Highway 92, just before the turnoff for HopeQuest. The proximity strongly suggests that Long's revulsion toward the massage parlors became an extension of the self-hatred generated by his failure to cure his "addiction." From there, Long drove to Atlanta, where he killed four more people—all Asian women—in two more spas. That these murder sites were nearly thirty miles from the first round of shootings solidifies the racial connection.[5]

Recall when the Cherokee County Sheriff's Office promoted Robert Aaron Long's contention that the shootings were "not racially motivated": This claim was predicated on the notion that Long had acted solely in response to his "addiction to sex." The authorities repeated the fallacy that racism and sexism are mutually exclusive, when both should be seen—as the Combahee River Collective stated—as part of interlocking systems of oppression. Indeed, the mass production and distribution of guns, which allowed Long quick and easy access to deadly arms, is rooted in racist ideas of fear and masculinist notions of protection. The binary opposition of race and gender surfaced again in the mixed conclusions of the prosecutors. In Cherokee County, the district attorney ruled out charging Long with race-based hate crimes because only two of the four murder victims were Asian. Instead, the DA intended to pursue gender-based hate counts, but dropped the matter after Long pled guilty to the murders and was sentenced to life in prison. In Fulton County, however, where all four killed were Asian women and Long pled not guilty, prosecutor Fani Willis sought the death penalty while pursuing convictions for hate crimes based on "actual or perceived race, national origin, sex and gender."[6]

Delving deeper into historical context moves us beyond determinations of individual culpability. Reverend Chul Yoo ministered at Crabapple First Baptist Church during Long's early teenage years. "We are silent on this racism and misteach what the Bible says," he stated. "It doesn't say that girls are at fault for being a temptation." The notion that Asian women in massage parlors are a source of sin to be eliminated feeds on a legacy of colonialism that has stereotyped Asians as heathens who need to be either saved through missionary work or subdued through conquest. "There's no doubt racism is happening in the U.S.," said Reverend Michelle Ami Reyes, vice president of the Asian American Christian Collaborative, which began in 2020 as a vehicle to promote antiracist advocacy, particularly within evangelical communities. "There's also no doubt that the fetishization of Asian women is normalized, even in church. And there is no doubt that there is a history in evangelical Christianity of promoting ideas of female purity," Reyes added.[7]

Scholars and analysts of evangelical "purity culture" identified connections between racism, toxic masculinity, heteronormativity, and Christian nationalism as underlying factors in the Atlanta shootings. Historian Kristin Kobes Du Mez noted that purity culture is rooted in imagery of heroic masculinity—which, in American mythology, presumes white male superiority. Its adherents are taught, as Robert P. Jones of the Public Religion Research Institute has noted, "that men are biologically hardwired for arousal and women are simultaneously morally dangerous and morally responsible for behaving in ways that keep those male desires in check." In *Preparing for War*, Bradley Onishi described purity culture as "a projection of all the gendered, racial, and societal fears that White Christian nationalists harbor onto the canvas of teenage flesh." It was foundational to the drive to restore traditional marriage, gender roles, and racial hierarchy.[8]

As an Asian American scholar of evangelicalism, Onishi brings a perspective that combines research and personal experience. "Evangelicals," he points out, "see themselves as 'not of this world' because their true home is in eternal paradise with Jesus and God the Father. The 'world' is an evil enemy, given over to sin and licentiousness." Beyond looking inward, the New Religious Right emerged in the 1970s with a more politicized response to the social movements of the 1960s. Cast in an "apocalyptic tone," it advanced a Christian nationalist mission "to take America back for God and the people they deem worthy of holding power in his name." As a former youth adherent, Onishi acted like a "model minority" evangelical, keeping quiet about racism. His sense of belonging came from being drafted as a soldier into a "civil war" being fought to restore a mythical social and political order controlled by "real Americans." Onishi's insights raise the disturbing possibility that Long was not influenced so much by extremism, but by an ambient "culture warrior" mentality that acquired a mass following.[9]

When we consider how and why Asians have migrated to the Americas, and the primary factors that have shaped Asian Americans' experiences in the United States, we must further analyze race and racism in conjunction with militarism, labor exploitation, ableism, xenophobia, and the policing of borders. This is the point that Kimberlé Crenshaw and scholars of "intersectionality" have stressed to highlight the factors that compounded to increase the vulnerability of the Atlanta shooting victims. On top of being immigrants, women of color, and working class, they are deemed to work within "illegal and immoral sites." Being marked for surveillance and deportation by law enforcement restricts their ability to turn to the authorities for protection.[10]

In this chapter, it should become clear why we must move beyond a narrow interpretation of motivation to connect the many social influences behind tragedies like the Atlanta shootings. The sexual objectification of Asian women by Americans can be traced back to the conscription of prostitutes to serve male laborers in the nineteenth-century American West. During the twentieth century, American imperial expansion in Asia generated a rise in sexual violence against Asian women amid the routinization of sex work on a mass scale surrounding U.S. bases. Militarism and the demonization of Asian enemies also shaped racist notions of masculinity that figured prominently in the domestic resurgence of anti-Asian violence from the 1970s to 1990s. Collectively, these histories point to the integral role that sexism plays in anti-Asian violence and why any meaningful effort to confront anti-Asian racism must address sexual violence and misogyny.

In the wake of the Atlanta shootings, numerous commentators pointed to the Page Act of 1875, a precursor to the Chinese Exclusion Act of 1882, as proof of a deeply rooted history of discrimination against Asian women in the United States. The law particularly stigmatized Asian women as prostitutes and subjected them to violence. As most of the nineteenth-century Chinese migrants were male laborers, women were vastly outnumbered by men. Racialized demographic and employment patterns disrupted gender norms in the American West. As historian Robert Lee has argued, the dominant culture stereotyped Chinese Americans as a deviant "third sex." Racism and a dearth of white women led Chinese men to do domestic work typically performed by women. At the same time, Chinese women were hired or coerced to work as prostitutes for men of all races. In response, white women and children often participated in exclusion drives and pogroms, purportedly carried out in defense of (white) families from these perceived threats. Some white women, pledging to do their own laundry as a moral duty, called for Chinese household servants to be fired and excluded.[11]

Reflecting the rise of Western influence in the wake of the Opium Wars, Chinese prostitutes came to America particularly from Hong Kong and Canton. Many young women were sold by their families or lured under false pretenses into the profession. Some were kidnapped outright and had no idea where they would end up. Life was doubly difficult. White society was rife with xenophobic hostility, limiting the mobility of women who often remained cloistered within Chinatowns and labor camps. At the same time, Chinese American owners and operators of illicit enterprises—from smugglers to pimps—were often ruthless and abusive. Though typically contracted to work four to six years, many women did not survive that long. Some were beaten to death. Some killed themselves. And some were abandoned and left to die after contracting sexually transmitted diseases that rendered them worthless to their exploiters.[12]

Chinese immigrant prostitutes became a source of public scrutiny. Viewing the practice as a violation of moral order, white Protestant women reformers in San Francisco set up a rescue mission in the 1870s to save Chinese women, whom they described as "refugees from a slavery worse than death." But the Chinese were irredeemable in the eyes of the American Medical Association, which proclaimed them a public health menace rooted in "thousands of years of beastly vices, resistant to all the efforts of modern medicine." Exclusionists such as Congressman Horace Page of California seized on the public outcry for political gain, creating high barriers to entry for Chinese women, who were forced to prove they were not prostitutes. The Page Act barred most from coming to the United States.[13]

As scholar Tamsin Kimoto notes, the long-standing degradation of Asian immigrant prostitutes led some community leaders, in a form of respectability politics, to focus more on issues of racism alongside a generalized discussion of sexism that eschews the topic of sex work. In challenging this dichotomization, which arose in responses to the Atlanta shootings, Kimoto points to the specific language in the Page Act that prohibits "the importation into the United States of women for the purposes of prostitution." That is, the objectification of Asian women caused them to be reduced in the eyes of Congress to products banned from importation. The dehumanization of Asian women as "purely sexual objects," Kimoto concludes, must thus be recognized as a key source of anti-Asian violence. This means countering the erasures that too often silence accounts of sexual violence against Asian women or bracket them off from awareness of anti-Asian violence as a racist phenomenon.[14]

Recounting the tragic rape and murder of artist Theresa Hak Kyung Cha on the cusp of potential breakthrough success, Cathy Park Hong, author of *Minor Feelings*, cites this story as a prime example of erasure. Cha received posthumous renown for her avant-garde writing and mixed-media artistry that disrupts linear narration in ways that reflect the traumatic effects of war, violence, and oppression. Yet, even while recognized as a brilliant artist taken from the Earth far too soon, Cha has never been embraced as a martyr of anti-Asian violence like Vincent Chin, whose death preceded hers by only four months. One of Cha's close friends told Park that Cha's murder failed to attract media attention because she was "just another Asian woman."[15]

"More disturbing," Hong writes, "is that no one admits that Cha was also raped," even when acknowledging she was the victim of a homicide. She thus points to the gendered nature of anti-Asian violence as a twofold problem. One study found that somewhere between 21 and 55 percent of Asian American women have experienced physical and sexual violence. The range of indeterminacy is so wide because Asian American women are possibly the least likely group of survivors to report being assaulted. A history of gaslighting survivors—in mainstream society and within ethnic communities—has conspired to promote this pattern of repression.[16]

Central to this erasure lies the fact that much of America's history of sexual violence has been hidden from the U.S. public, confined to overseas military bases and their immediate surroundings. To exert influence throughout Asia, the United States has established and maintained bases throughout the region since the twentieth century. While these bases played an integral role in the U.S. wars in Korea and Vietnam, the troops remained decades after hostilities ended. At the turn of the twenty-first century, some one hundred thousand U.S. troops were stationed in Japan, Okinawa, and Korea. Given this substantial presence and investment, such bases, though often resented by citizens of the host nations, became a key source of economic subsistence for thousands of local residents. Adjacent to the bases, "camptowns" emerged to cater to the recreational needs and desires of U.S. servicemen in the Philippines, Okinawa, South Korea, Thailand, and Vietnam. For male U.S. soldiers, they served as sites of leisure, entertainment, and drinking—not always but typically tied to the business of prostitution. American military leaders argued that the provision of sexual outlets for servicemen is a fundamental need. Local women were thus objectified as necessary resource inputs, and the function of R&R for GIs was akin to the refueling of planes and ships. Feminist activists and scholars, including Gwyn Kirk and Carolyn Bowen Francis, have argued that relations between U.S. men and Asian women are stained by the "sexist attitudes and hyper-masculine culture" at the core of militarism. Suzuyo Takazato, a women's rights activist and founder of the group Okinawa Women Act Against Military Violence, characterized the military as "a form of structural violence" that perpetuates sexism and misogyny. "Teaching humanity in the military is a gross contradiction," Takazato declared at a 1995 protest. "The military is a place for teaching brutality." Legally, the U.S. government established Status of Forces Agreements with host countries that perpetuated forms of extraterritoriality redolent of the unequal treaties. Moreover, the system has nowhere near the will or capacity to investigate and hold offenders accountable for the complaints that would arise if women were fully empowered to confront rape and sexual assault.[17]

In *Sex Among Allies: Military Prostitution in U.S.-Korea Relations*, social scientist Katherine H. S. Moon provides an in-depth examination of the camptown phenomenon. In 1997, Moon noted that the cumulative number of Korean women who had engaged in sex work tied to the U.S. military presence had surpassed one million. While they were not necessarily coerced into sexual slavery, as occurred under Japan's occupation, women experienced an unduly oppressive environment in the camptowns. Historian Ji-Yeon Yuh called them "America's comfort women," stereotypically "treated as play-things easily bought and easily discarded." For example, the "American Town" near Kunsan Air Force Base was built during the dictatorship of U.S. ally Park Chung Hee in the late 1960s and early 1970s. It was a walled city completely owned and controlled by a corporation that permitted only invited Americans to enter as patrons. The company took 80 percent of the revenue that Korean women sex workers earned, then charged them for rent and other supplies. Women in the profession were routinely assessed a fee to enter work and fined for missing work, including when they were sick or on their period. Because many borrowed funds for initial expenses, camptown workers often ended up in a "debt bondage system."[18]

Sexualized images of submissive Asian women stood at the core of these commoditized relations in an Orientalist fantasy. A military newspaper, *Pacific Stars and Stripes*, described the *kisaeng* party as the "ultimate experi-ence" in a 1977 account: "Picture having three or four of the loveliest crea-tures God ever created hovering around you, singing, dancing, feeding you, washing what they feed you down with rice wine or beer, all saying at once, 'You are the greatest.' This is the Orient you heard about and came to find." Such imagery only reinforced the racist and sexist views inherent among many U.S. soldiers. For Americans, assignment in Germany was considered more favorable and catered to military families. Those stationed in Korea were generally younger and single. For Koreans, the camptowns became disreputable sites where low-income, rural women and "fallen women"—divorcées, survivors of rape, and mothers of children born out of wedlock—turned for work after being scorned by mainstream Korean culture. Some were lured to the camptowns with false promises of education or better jobs. Others were forced in by being sold or through an "initiation" by rape. Once there, Moon observed, they became "irreversibly tainted" by their sex work and relations with non-Koreans, cast as pariahs unable to return to "normal" society. This precarious condition rendered camptown women especially vulnerable to physical violence and psychological abuse.[19]

Aside from being stereotyped as props in American movies, camptown sex workers, Moon argued, were erased from the history of the Korean War. Some became visible to Americans by immigrating as military wives—these women's primary possibility of escape from the camptowns for a new life. As Ji-Yeon Yuh documented, many of the one hundred thousand Korean military brides who had migrated during the four decades since the onset of the war established foundations for entire families to come to the United States. As such, they deserve to be recognized as pillars of the postwar Korean American community. Still, while many of the marriages were healthy and long lasting, an estimated four out of five ended in divorce. Furthermore, many Korean women were abandoned by the American men who impregnated them, leaving their Amerasian children to grow up severely stigmatized. In the worst cases, women workers in camptowns have been savagely beaten and killed, including the notorious 1992 murder of sex worker Yun Geum-I by a white enlisted man, Private Kenneth Markle. The victim was found with a coke bottle inserted in her vagina and an umbrella lodged in her anus. Yet this horrific crime, as Korean American writer Marie Myung Ok Lee has noted, barely registered with the U.S. public. In 2000, U.S. serviceman Christopher McCarthy beat and strangled to death Kim Sung-hi, a bar hostess in the Itaewon red-light district of Seoul, after she refused his demand for what the army called "abnormal sexual activities." Such incidents have generated staunch resistance movements in Korea and elsewhere, as activists cite heteropatriarchal abuse as symptomatic of an imperialist system and culture.[20]

The history of Okinawa provides another example of how an American culture steeped in racism, militarism, and misogyny was defined and shaped on bases in Asia. Its Indigenous history as the Ryukyu Kingdom predated Japanese annexation in 1872. But the islands, referred to Americans then as "Lew Chew," became a target of Commodore Matthew Perry when he returned in 1854 to secure his goal of opening up Japan to U.S. commerce. With Perry's interests piqued by the discovery of coal, he left a crew of men in Lew Chew as he proceeded to Taiwan. According to U.S. sources, a man identified as "Board" was one of three Americans who broke into an Okinawan home to steal sake. The drunken Board then climbed over a wall to intrude upon another local residence. There he sexually assaulted a woman at knifepoint until her screams provoked the ire of neighbors. A group of men grabbed Board and threw him to the ground. While Board managed to flee, the villagers pelted him with rocks. Attempting to run away, the inebriated American reportedly fell into a body of water and drowned. Perry felt obligated to demand an investigation into the death and a conviction by the local authorities. Still, he would not allow the violent incident to interfere with his primary mission. In July 1854, Perry secured his coveted treaty opening Lew Chew to American interests. The commodore's scribe felt compelled to add, "He was also particularly careful to send a handsome present to the poor woman who had been the subject of Board's outrage."[21]

With their islands coveted as a strategic site for trade and militarism, Okinawans challenged Japanese rule until 1945, followed by U.S. control in the postwar era. Near the end of World War II, they came under fire from both Japanese and American forces, losing a ghastly one-third of their population (140,000 deaths). Then the United States confiscated land for permanent bases and displaced thousands of residents, compounding the existing poverty and social problems. As the activist Takazato stated in 1994, "Okinawan women who survived the battlefield assault faced a new battle in postwar years: the sexual assault that continued through U.S. military occupation and the U.S. civilian administration." While the U.S. military offered various forms of assistance, Americans stationed there committed rape and other acts of violence against Okinawans from practically the onset of the occupation. Okinawans also reported a rise in sexual assaults, including cases of sex workers being strangled to death, during the Vietnam War, when Americans, some afflicted with what would now be diagnosed as PTSD, went there for R&R breaks.[22]

In September 1955, the "Yumiko-chan Incident" sparked the first notable anti-American protests in postwar Okinawa. Tragically, five-year-old Yumiko Nagayama was discovered in a garbage dump. She had been raped and murdered, with a gaping knife wound evident from her stomach to her anus. Sergeant Isaac Jackson Hurt, a thirty-one-year-old white man from Kentucky, was court-martialed, convicted, and sentenced to death for the crime. This was no isolated incident. Hurt had previously been convicted of assault and attempted rape, which he fraudulently concealed when he enlisted. Hurt brazenly insisted, nonetheless, that he was a political prisoner—one who was "sacrificed to appease the dissident political elements" in Okinawa opposed to U.S. bases. Prominent politicians, including Senate majority leader Lyndon B. Johnson, made him a cause célèbre, leading President Dwight Eisenhower to reduce his death sentence to forty-five years without parole. With additional support from President Gerald Ford, Hurt ultimately left Leavenworth prison on parole, unbeknownst to most Okinawans.[23]

The United States did not relinquish control of Okinawa until 1972—and, even then, only through a "reversion" to Japanese rule with a Status of Forces Agreement (SOFA) maintaining the bases. Social conflicts on and around the bases continued, with local protests ramping up against the U.S. and Japanese governments. From 1972 to 2015, according to Okinawan police, U.S. military personnel and their family members murdered twenty-six and raped 126 Okinawans. The latter number is almost certainly a severe undercount, because most rapes were not reported or prosecuted, owing to sexist social and legal structures, internalized oppression among Okinawans, and extraterritoriality provisions in the SOFA granting Americans effective immunity. These problems received more exposure following an international incident that prompted over ninety thousand Okinawans to protest on October 21, 1995, demanding curtailment of the U.S. military presence. Three American men in their early twenties—two in the marines and one in the navy—kidnapped a twelve-year-old Okinawan girl and bound her with duct tape. The nightmarish episode began when Marcus Gill recognized that he lacked funds to hire a prostitute. He then told the other two, "Let's go rape a girl," later adding that "it was just for fun." An imposing figure, six feet tall and 275 pounds, Gill sexually violated the much smaller girl while pummeling her in the stomach and face. Though the other two denied it, Gill stated they had joined in a gang rape. They left the girl bloodied and unconscious. Although the girl, thankfully, survived, the notoriety of this case overshadowed a brutal murder that had taken place just three months earlier, when a U.S. serviceman beat his Japanese girlfriend to death, striking her in the head twenty times or more.[24]

Despite some reforms and concessions by the U.S. military, both the bases and the tensions on Okinawa persist. In fact, a new wave of mass protests erupted more recently following the murder of Rina Shimabukuro, whose badly decomposed body was found in a suitcase, spawning another international incident. In May 2016, Kenneth Gadson, an American contractor and ex-marine married to a woman from Okinawa, stabbed Shimabukuro in the neck and clubbed her on the head to subdue her—thereby enacting a longstanding rape and kidnap "fantasy." Gadson acknowledged a history of mental illness and said that he repeatedly thought of killing himself and others. Yet he had managed to pass background checks and gain necessary security clearances for his work over many years. Gadson was tried in the Japanese legal system only because he was off duty at the time of the murder. He was convicted and given a life sentence with hard labor.[25]

Gadson, like the three convicted of the 1995 rape, is an African American man from the South. On one level, that seems incidental to the crimes that were committed, as the violence, misogyny, and dehumanization of

Okinawans exhibited in these acts are generally reflected in offenses perpetrated by American military personnel, rather than being unique to Black servicemen. On another level, however, race complicates our analyses in several ways. First, institutional racism and implicit bias within the U.S. military can lead to alleged crimes by Black men becoming relatively more recognized and exposed. This can be traced back to the early years of the occupation, when U.S. officials deliberately scapegoated Black men as perpetrators of sexual violence. Second, anti-Black prejudice among Okinawans and "mainland" Japanese can consciously or unconsciously generate greater indignation when Black men are the offenders. Third, Black-Okinawan relations have formed a counterculture outside the bases. Although there is a stigma attached to Okinawan women who date American men, author Akemi Johnson found many who were particularly attracted to Black men, which they also affirmed as an act of rebellion. Her interviewees also included African Americans who deemed life in Okinawa to be relatively free and liberated in comparison to the United States. Mixed-race Okinawan Americans, long stereotyped as the offspring of forced and illicit relations, have also worked to break down the prejudices and structure produced by intersecting histories of oppression.[26]

Finally, we need to recognize the historical countercurrent of Black-Okinawan solidarity. Anti-Black racism in the United States and anti-Okinawan discrimination in Japan increased the precarity of both groups, making them more likely to meet in the marginalized spaces governed by military occupation. In the 1970s, this developed into political alliances, as the Black Panther–inspired "Bush Masters"—made up of disaffected Black soldiers and veterans resisting the segregation and discrimination inherent in the U.S. imperial base culture—fused their activism with Indigenous anti-imperialist movements. The most overt display of joint resistance erupted in the Koza Uprising. After midnight on December 20, 1970, an American driver struck an Okinawan man on the streets of Koza, the nightlife district tied to Kadena Air Base. A crowd of men and women gathered in protest, growing to as many as two thousand strong. Tempers on the island were already near boiling from a similar incident several months earlier in Itoman, where a drunken U.S. solider ran over and killed an Okinawan woman pedestrian with no accountability. When U.S. military forces tried to put down the Koza Uprising with tear gas and fire hoses, the crowd resisted further, throwing rocks and Molotov cocktails—even burning some cars and buildings on the U.S. base. It was the first violent rebellion against the

American base presence in Okinawa. But Okinawan protesters consciously insisted that African Americans would not be the target of their ire, setting a model for how disparate groups, whose social positions were anything but equal, found ways to identify with each other's struggles.[27]

AMERICAN NIGHTMARES

Given the deleterious effects of imperialism, it is understandable that many Asian women, especially those from former U.S. colonies, would seek to migrate to the metropole. In the most tragic instances, though, the end of the dream of becoming American was only more violence. Raised in the Philippine province of Masbate, Susana Remerata saw an opportunity to meet American men when she registered for the *Asian Encounters* catalogue in spring 1990. Run out of Bellingham, Washington, the service promised its male clientele "pretty single Asian women who want to meet you!" A bona fide beauty queen, Remerata attracted dozens of "pen pals." Her mailbox overflowed with nearly one hundred letters per week. She agreed to marry Timothy Blackwell, a white man more than twenty years her senior. To the media, Susana would be known as a "mail-order bride." Writer Alex Tizon described the friction inherent in these unions: "The men enter into a power relationship in which it's easy for them to be the absolute power. The women leave their communities, land in a foreign culture often with no money or contacts, and are, at least in the beginning, totally dependent on their new spouses."[28]

The marriage foundered almost as soon as it began. Just one day after their wedding, Blackwell yelled at his new wife for causing them to miss a ferry in the Philippines. She alleged that he choked her, too. Against her mother's warning, Remerata next moved to the United States with Blackwell. But the couple split within two weeks. When Susana reported being assaulted, including another choking, Blackwell was arrested. Having spent thousands of dollars, Blackwell now felt duped. Instead of a clean break, he moved for annulment so that she would be deported. Remerata's attorneys countered by invoking a "battered-wife" claim for permanent residency. These charges and counter-charges prompted a contentious trial. Remerata, now eight months pregnant with another man's child, testified about the physical abuse she had endured. Blackwell described her as a "disease" that he regretted bringing into the country. Though closing arguments were set for March 2,

1995, we will never know the trial's outcome. Shortly before returning to the courtroom, Blackwell approached Remerata in the hallway with a 9mm semiautomatic handgun. At close range, he methodically killed his estranged wife and her fetus. Then he gunned down Phoebe Dizon and Veronica Laureta Johnson, two friends who had testified on her behalf. Blackwell was convicted and sentenced to life in prison. But the most important legacy has been carried on by the victims' families and the activists who formed API Chaya, a community organization supporting survivors of domestic violence, sexual assault, and human trafficking. For three decades, they have held an annual candlelight vigil around the anniversary of the shootings, dedicated to honoring the victims and envisioning "a just and equitable world free of violence and oppression."[29]

On March 7, 2024, API Chaya held its twenty-ninth annual vigil honoring the victims of the 1995 courthouse shootings. One of the featured speakers was Cindy Domingo, who lost her brother, Silme, in the labor union murders tied to the Marcos dictatorship. She spoke to that year's theme, *Kapwa*, a Tagalog word signifying togetherness, and made the critical connections that are central to this book: between past and present; local and global; Asian and non-Asian. First, she invoked the memory of immigrant workers, particularly those who died in the 1911 Triangle Shirtwaist Factory fire—most of whom were Italian and Jewish women. Domingo then spoke about the ongoing wars and violence taking lives around the world in Gaza, Ukraine, and Ethiopia. "It has been the interconnectedness that has kept our movements alive," she said.[30]

The program closed with a performance by Roger Rigor, who served as Remerata's interpreter. "To be vigilant, to be militant, is not violent," he proclaimed. "Militancy against violence is the most human thing we can all do."[31]

ASIAN AMERICANS AND THE METOO MOVEMENT

While media representation of Asian American women has undoubtedly increased, their stories often remain in the hands of others. Even the groundbreaking first season of the *Serial* podcast in 2014 had a glaring omission that was scarcely discussed by its many fans or by critics. Although the investigative series' crucial attention to police misconduct—including Islamophobic racial profiling—undoubtedly built momentum to overturn Adnan Syed's murder conviction, not a single episode or segment addressed patterns of violence against Asian American women that might have factored into the murder of Hae Min Lee. The impropriety of the police prematurely fixating on Syed as a suspect comes into much sharper focus when contrasted with the detectives' quick acceptance of the flimsy alibi provided by Lee's significantly older white boyfriend. No investigation was attempted by the police—or by journalists—into how race might, even potentially, have colored this roller-coaster courtship. Even Sarah Koenig and Julie Snyder, the coproducers of *Serial*, acclaimed as a model for investigative journalism, missed this low-hanging fruit that anyone who has taken an "Intro to Asian American Studies" class would have detected immediately.

Given these developments, it is no surprise that Asian American women have broken through the silence primarily through self-advocacy and grass-roots organizing, including at the forefront of the MeToo movement. Two biracial Asian Americans, Chanel Miller and Emma Sulkowicz, stepped into this media spotlight, though much of the public may not have been aware of their ancestry. In 2019, Miller courageously announced to the world through the publication of her book, *Know My Name*, that she was "Emily Doe," the survivor of the felony sexual assault by Stanford student and swim team member Brock Turner that left her "terrified" of her own body. Turner, a white male, was convicted. This itself is a sadly rare occurrence in a society in which rapes routinely go unreported by survivors, who justifiably fear their complaints will be minimized and their conduct put on trial. The controversy stemmed from the lenient sentence—six months in prison and three years of probation—handed down by Judge Aaron Persky, a white male who went out of his way to empathize with Turner. Citing the law's willingness to consider probation when "a defendant is youthful and has no significant record of prior criminal offenses," Persky invoked an exception in "the interest of justice" to the prohibition on probation applicable to Turner's conviction. The judge particularly stressed that Turner "was genuinely sorry for all the pain that he has caused to [Miller] and her family."[32]

Sharply disagreeing, Miller found Turner's apology performative and self-serving. After she allowed *BuzzFeed* to publish it in full, her statement at Turner's sentencing became a true phenomenon, a cultural touchstone. Miller responded:

> Unfortunately, after reading the defendant's report, I am severely disappointed and feel that he has failed to exhibit sincere remorse or responsibility for his conduct. I fully respected his right to a trial, but even after twelve jurors unanimously convicted him guilty of three felonies, all he has admit-

ted to doing is ingesting alcohol. Someone who cannot take full accountability for his actions does not deserve a mitigating sentence. It is deeply offensive that he would try and dilute rape with a suggestion of "promiscuity." By definition rape is the absence of promiscuity, rape is the absence of consent, and it perturbs me deeply that he can't even see that distinction.

The judge summed up Miller's sentiment in two sentences: "[Miller] has stated that he hasn't really taken responsibility for his conduct. And I think at one point she basically wrote or said that 'He—he just doesn't get it.'" Then, Persky reiterated his assurance that Turner's remorse was "genuine." And in the American system of justice, the judge was given the final word— at least in the courtroom.[33]

Miller's decision, not only to speak out but also to break her anonymity, was clearly a retort both to her assailant and to the judge, whom many saw as biased in the rapist's favor. But she exposed deeper levels of gaslighting in her memoir. For instance, after interviewing Miller and her assailant, the court-assigned probation officer took her words out of context to support a recommendation for a lenient sentence, praising Turner for expressing "sincere remorse and empathy for the victim." To add insult to injury, the probation officer mislabeled Miller's race as "white," erasing her Chinese ancestry. "This single check mark was a testament to how little time she'd taken to know me," wrote Miller, "making the assumption I was white over the phone without bothering to ask." Drawing from personal experience and the collective wisdom of survivors, she delivered a powerful repudiation of those who would question why victims are reluctant to report assault, when the process extracts a demanding level of time and emotional labor with no assurance of a positive outcome or fair process:

> This is not about the victims' lack of effort. This is about society's failure to have systems in place in which victims feel there's a probable chance of achieving safety, justice, and restoration rather than being retraumatized, publicly shamed, psychologically tormented, and verbally mauled. The real question we need to be asking is not, *Why didn't she report*, the question is, *Why would you?*[34]

Sharing the disgust she felt reading "the graphic details of my own sexual assault" in an article that proceeded to report Turner's swimming times, she further testified to the severely warped character of our media coverage and public discourse. In doing so, Miller delivered a cogent message on the pervasive manner in which privilege operates. "The fact that Brock was an athlete at a private university should not be seen as an entitlement to leniency," she stated, "but as an opportunity to send a message that sexual assault is against the law regardless of social class."[35]

Miller further recounted surviving the Isla Vista murders while attending college at the University of California, Santa Barbara, in May 2014. The deeply disturbed killer, Elliot Rodger, wrote a manifesto and posted internet videos detailing his hatred of women he perceived to have scorned him as an incel (involuntarily celibate). He shot and killed two women near a sorority house, then a man in a deli mart. But Rodger's misogyny fused with self-hatred of his life as a biracial Chinese American. Of the six he killed, the first three were Chinese American men he stabbed to death in his apartment. While not physically impacted by the rampage, Miller detailed the psychological trauma it caused. In 2021, Miller lauded and joined the Stop Asian Hate demonstrations, which caused her to discuss with Asian American friends how their past experiences with racial slights were "always somewhere in the conversation" but had "never been the center" until now.[36]

Chanel Miller's distinct voice was part of a chorus of survivors that empowered others to come forward. Kelly Yang filed a formal complaint of sexual assault as a Harvard Law student in 2005, though she publicly disclosed her experience only in May 2020. To get a campus hearing, she was forced to waive her right to file a criminal complaint. She was next required, Yang wrote, "to sit in a room in front of my attacker and listen for hours as he called me a liar." Not only was the man found not guilty, but Yang found herself the subject of a university investigation for "malicious prosecution" that threatened to strip her of the diploma she spent three years earning. "The law school," she stated, "told me that I could make the whole thing go away if I just dropped the charges." Yang's "traditional Chinese parents" urged her "to consider backing down." But she proceeded despite these mounting pressures. Incredibly, the faculty now voted on whether Yang's sexual assault complaint should cost her a degree. After Harvard found her "not guilty," she was finally eligible to graduate. But not before a paternalistic faculty member got in one last dig. "Congratulations!" they stated. "You get to graduate! Let me give you a bit of advice. Move on!" Her faith in the law shattered by these events, Yang left the field and is now a *New York Times* best-selling author writing fiction to empower young women, including stories of sexual assault.[37]

Although survivors of all ages have been coming forward with powerful stories, there has clearly been a generational uprising against the imperative to keep quiet. For Emma Sulkowicz, who identifies as gender nonconforming and uses *she* and *they* pronouns, this began several years before the MeToo movement went viral in 2017. As a student at Columbia University, Sulkowicz famously carried a mattress on her back for an entire school year. Standard dorm-issued. Fifty pounds. Extra-long. She made sure everyone noticed in class and around campus. It was a symbol of the weight Sulkowicz carried going to school with a man she reported had raped her in April 2013. It was a performance, but not a stunt. While reporting often presented this as a classic both-sideist case of indeterminacy, Sulkowicz charged the university with running a sham investigation process that was biased against survivors. Her case brought national attention to struggles of survivors subsumed within Title IX procedures they see as Kafkaesque and designed mainly to protect the interests of the institution. "When I was raped, I was screaming 'no' and struggling against him. It was obviously not consensual, but he was turned on by my distress," Sulkowicz wrote in a May 2014 *Time* magazine article.[38]

Despite Sulkowicz's testimony, Columbia absolved Paul Nungesser, the man she charged with rape. Buoyed by the result, he turned around and filed his own Title IX lawsuit against Columbia for allegedly failing to protect him as a victim of a smear campaign by Sulkowicz. "Rapist," Nungesser charged, was a gender-based epithet stigmatizing him as a man. Men's rights activists pilloried Sulkowicz in publications, as well as rampantly and anonymously through social media trolling. After carrying the mattress across the stage at graduation, Sulkowicz found posters with her image reading "Pretty Little Liar" and "#RAPEHOAX."[39]

A reporter wanted to know, "Is it worse to be raped or is it worse to be raped by the media?"

"It's worse to be raped by the media," Sulkowicz answered.[40]

Columbia's president, Lee Bollinger, graciously and customarily shook the hand of every graduate. But when Sulkowicz approached with three friends carrying the mattress, he turned his back. University officials, who had failed in their attempts to convince Sulkowicz not to bring the mattress on stage, denied there was any act of spurning by Bollinger: He just couldn't shake hands with the mattress in the way. Video footage suggests otherwise. "I think the school is pressured to find him not guilty," Sulkowicz concluded, "because up until now Columbia could just push these things under the rug and no one would know. But that means the Columbia administration is harboring serial rapists on campus. They're more concerned about their public image than keeping people safe."[41]

"We understand the pain that motivates our Asian and Asian-American community members' call for increased policing, but we nevertheless stand against it."[42] In the aftermath of the Atlanta shootings, a New York–based organization called Red Canary Song issued this declaration with a set of demands from Asian massage-parlor workers. When women are victims of violent crime, it is understandable that they and others seek to bring safety to their environments. In the dominant culture of the United States, danger has often been associated with street life. Police are seen as the solution to restore law and order. While random acts of street violence may create the most sensational media coverage, this chapter has shown that there are patterns that must not be ignored, including state violence, acquaintance rape, and work-related violence.

Red Canary Song emphasizes that safe and sustainable working conditions are vital to the health and well-being of sex workers and spa workers. Most crucially, they called for the decriminalization of sex work and the right of workers in sex industries to organize. As scholar and organizer Elena Shih found from interviews, police raids carried out in the name of rescuing victims of sex trafficking often make Asian massage workers feel more vulnerable. Even when no evidence of trafficking is found, workers can be arrested for failure to show a proper license or subjected to detention and deportation if they are unauthorized migrants. Such businesses can also come under disparate scrutiny and receive sanctions for code or zoning violations. These onerous conditions cause mental and physical health problems.[43]

Preceding yet another avoidable tragedy, authorities arrested massage worker Song Yang for prostitution three times in Queens, New York. In 2016, Yang accused a man, who said he was an undercover officer, of coercing her to give him oral sex at gunpoint and under threat of arrest. In addition, she told family members that she was pressured to become a police informant to "report on other masseuses." Yang refused but feared retaliation for doing so. The situation was redolent of the precarious state in which workers like Yang toil, particularly in Flushing, where the presence of sex-related businesses with Asian immigrant women workers soared during the 2010s. On November 25, 2017, after vice squad cops came to arrest her again, Yang fell from the fourth floor of an apartment building and died. Though the circumstances of her death were unclear, Yang's family was dissatisfied with explanations from the police and suspected they somehow "forced her to die."[44]

The infamous February 2019 raid on the Orchids of Asia Spa in Palm Beach, Florida, foregrounded the inequities inherent in anti-trafficking enforcement. Headlines flashed that Robert Kraft, the billionaire owner of the New England Patriots, was arrested for solicitation. All charges against Kraft, however, were dropped. Meanwhile, spa workers were subjected to arrests, asset seizures, and deportations. As the authors of a February 2022 report, "Un-Licensed: Asian Migrant Massage Licensure and the Racialized Policing of Poverty," asserted, "The consequences of such raids always fall disproportionately on migrant women, who are especially vulnerable due to their economic and immigration status."[45]

Organizer Elene Lam and the Toronto-based group Butterfly—allied in advocacy with Red Canary Song—have challenged what they deem to be over-policing. In 2016, massage parlors and their employees were the target of nearly one in four investigations by the Toronto police. Based on surveys of Asian immigrant workers—most from China—in spa and wellness centers, Butterfly further asserted that more than one in three stated they had been "abused or harassed" by code inspectors or police officers, including some incidents of physical or sexual assault. Yet their lack of trust in police meant that they rarely reported these abusive acts or robberies to the authorities.[46]

Red Canary Song's open letter drew hundreds of organizational endorsements in its campaign to prompt a paradigm shift in our thinking and response to the hardships of sex workers and others in sex-related industries. It is imperative, they declared, to end the stigmatization of those, mostly women, who perform this work. They called on the community to "stand in solidarity with us and all immigrant and migrant massage workers and sex workers" by recognizing their five demands:

1. Pay attention to the life and work safety of massage and salon employees!

2. Asian massage workers and businesses come from the community and give back to the community!

3. The legal working rights of Asian massage workers must be protected!

4. The lives of Asian massage workers must not be lost in vain!

5. The legal profession of massage work should be respected and protected by US society![47]

The statement echoed with the voices of Asian women who live a life of danger in the shadows, resisting a totalizing form of objectification and asking the public to recognize their common humanity. Their voices broke through the silence surrounding gendered violence and its embeddedness within a system of oppression governed—in the words of Dr. Martin Luther King Jr.—by racism, militarism, and materialism.

FIVE

The Violence Beyond Vietnam

With the struggles over civil rights intensifying in April 1963, Dr. Martin Luther King Jr. and the Southern Christian Leadership Conference launched a campaign to break the spine of the Jim Crow system. Their prime target was Birmingham, Alabama, which they deemed "the most segregated city in America." A stunning breakthrough in visibility and momentum came on May 2 with the advent of the "children's crusade." Led by youths ranging from elementary school to college aged, over one thousand demonstrators were arrested in a mass show of defiance against the authorities that sought to outlaw protest. At the center of these efforts stood Sixteenth Street Baptist Church. But this exposed its congregation to retaliation.

On the morning of September 15, 1963, as the intense showdown in Birmingham persisted, four African American girls were freshening up in the church's basement lounge before joining the Sunday service. Addie Mae Collins, Carole Robertson, and Cynthia Wesley were fourteen. Denise McNair was only eleven. They were unaware that a group of Klansmen had planted a bomb in the back of the building, just below a stained-glass window depicting Jesus. At 10:22 a.m., an explosion ripped through the wall, killing the girls in a horrific massacre that made instant headlines. But the atrocities did not end there. Later that day, two other Black children died in the clashes that followed. Sixteen-year-old Johnny Robinson was shot in the back and killed by police, who claimed he threw rocks at them. Virgil Ware, thirteen, was sitting on the handlebars while his older brother pedaled the bicycle. After attending a segregation rally, two white teenagers rode by on a red motorcycle with a Confederate flag. One shot Ware in the chest and cheek, knocking him off the bike. He died on the spot.[1]

Six dead in Birmingham.

The mass murders shattered the dream that Dr. King had proclaimed just eighteen days earlier at the March on Washington. Standing in front of the Lincoln Memorial, he delivered his most famous address to a quarter of a million attendees. Part of a series of statements beginning with "I have a dream," King envisioned a day when "little Black boys and Black girls will be able to join hands with little white boys and white girls as sisters and brothers." It was a defining moment in U.S. history.[2]

After a summer of rising expectations, these murders demonstrated how much the nation was steeped in white supremacist violence and how many would resort to racial terror to eliminate difference and silence dissent. In his eulogy for the "martyred heroine," Dr. King proclaimed, "They say to us that we must be concerned not merely about *WHO* murdered them, but about the system, the way of life which *PRODUCED* the murderers."[3]

In 1986, the country honored Dr. King with a national holiday. But new signs revealed how elusive his dream of a world free of racism and violence remained. On Tuesday, January 17, 1989, as children returned to school after the King holiday, a gunman consumed with anger at refugees shot at hundreds of students on the playground of Cleveland Elementary School in Stockton, California. Although the Columbine massacre is generally cited by the media as the start of the school shooting phenomenon, this occurred ten years earlier. Reflecting the school's primary demographic, the five children killed—ages six to nine—were Southeast Asian refugees. The shooter, Patrick Purdy, then turned the weapon on himself.

Six dead in Stockton.

When the six Black youths died in a spree of racist murders on a single day in 1963 Birmingham, it would have been hard at that time for the public to imagine anything like that happening to Asians in the United States. The era of rampant exclusion had ended, and a new stereotype of Asian Americans as a "model minority" had significantly taken root. To be clear, racist violence against Asian Americans most certainly did not end with World War II. But there was a sharp decline in documented incidents until anti-Asian sentiments were whipped into a fury during the Vietnam War.

This chapter begins our exploration of the connection between the violence wrought by U.S. imperialism overseas during the Cold War era and the new wave of anti-Asian violence that manifested at home during the 1980s and 1990s. It focuses on the American attitudes, policies, and actions that produced the indiscriminate, mass slaughter of civilians in Vietnam. It further reveals how the devaluing of Asian lives made the U.S. government an accessory to genocide in a wider space of conflict that included Cambodia and Bangladesh and how war crimes in Southeast Asia evolved into hate crimes against refugees. Schools became sites not only of simple bullying, but also of violence, sometimes lethal, toward Southeast Asian American youths.

Had he not been taken from us prematurely, it would be easy to envision Dr. King awakening the nation to see how the murder of children in Stockton exposed our urgent need to build the beloved community, similar to how the murder of children in Birmingham did a quarter of a century earlier. Taken collectively, acts of racist violence were symptomatic of what he called the "giant triplets" at the rotting core of U.S. society: racism, militarism, and materialism. Dr. King's convictions led him to speak out forcefully against the Vietnam War exactly one year before his assassination on April 4, 1967. Delivered at Manhattan's Riverside Church, his monumental "Beyond Vietnam" speech is better known by the wake-up-call moniker "A Time to Break Silence." Dr. King spoke "as a child of God and brother to the suffering poor of Vietnam" on behalf of "those whose land is being laid waste, whose homes are being destroyed, whose culture is being subverted." Just as he linked white supremacy and terror from Vietnam to America, his call for "a radical revolution of values" can serve as a basis for cross-racial and international solidarity in the ongoing struggle against racist violence.[4]

"LIFE IS CHEAP IN THE ORIENT"

As the 1960s progressed, Dr. King increasingly warned the nation that it was losing its soul. With the historic events of 1963, he declared that the "Negro Revolution" had reached a new stage, foreshadowing the landmark passage of the 1964 Civil Rights Act and 1965 Voting Rights Act. But then he witnessed the urban rebellions in Watts and dozens of other cities, corresponding with the entrenched poverty, police brutality, and white populist bigotry that defined systemic racism in places outside the South. While Dr. King understood and, in many ways, validated the new Black militancy, he feared that continued rebellions would provoke the rise of a "fascist state" in America. "They'll treat us like they did our Japanese brothers and sisters in World War II," he surmised. "They'll throw us into concentration camps like the Japanese."[5]

With President Lyndon B. Johnson's war on poverty dying a sordid death on the battlefields of Southeast Asia, Dr. King focused his crusade for non-violence on the Vietnam War, going far beyond a call for peace to upbraid the U.S. government as "the greatest purveyor of violence in the world today." This massive diversion of resources toward war and militarism over basic human needs was leading down the road of "moral and spiritual bankruptcy." Embracing the long Vietnamese struggle for independence, he excoriated the United States for its murderous atrocities and assaults on civilians, its sponsorship of political repression, and its policies rooted in lies and racism. His antiwar stance prompted MLK ostracization not only by LBJ and the white liberal establishment, but also by less courageous civil rights leaders.[6]

Dr. King increasingly drew connections—as Malcolm X did—between the Black freedom struggle and Third World decolonization. The Vietnam War was but the most glaring sign of how the United States, owing to the overlapping interests of its political leaders and corporations, stood on "the wrong side of a world revolution." In *The Jakarta Method*, author Vincent Bevins documents the pivotal American role in creating "a monstrous international network of extermination" that drove a series of dirty wars waged in the name of anticommunism. Its goal was to snuff out the rising expectations emanating from the "Spirit of Bandung." In 1955, representatives of twenty-nine countries in Asia and Africa that comprised more than half the world's population came together in Bandung, Indonesia, for a historic declaration of Afro-Asian unity against colonialism and white supremacy. It was a sign of international leadership in the Third World liberation movement by the large, and predominantly Muslim, Asian nation and its president, Sukarno. Primarily through the covert operations of the CIA, the United States responded by coordinating the repression of leftists and the promotion of the friendly military dictator Suharto, who took control of Indonesia in 1965. These events furthered the pernicious influence of the CIA, which had orchestrated the overthrow of governments in Iran (1953) and Guatemala (1954) and backed the military coup in Brazil (1964). But Indonesia was more populous than those countries, and American leaders prioritized strategic interests there more than in Vietnam. As such, the United States maintained a firm alliance with Suharto as his murderous regime killed between five hundred thousand and one million Indonesians and forced another one million into concentration camps.[7]

The U.S. intervention in Vietnam drew more notice mainly because covert operations morphed into a massive deployment of troops. Alongside Laos and Cambodia, Vietnam had been colonized by the French. When it was overtaken by Japan during World War II, the Vietnamese liberation forces led by Ho Chi Minh fought alongside the Americans. Upon liberation, they issued their own Declaration of Independence, citing the U.S. Founding Fathers as inspiration. But this went totally ignored by the United States. American Cold War objectives supported the reinstallation of French colonial rule, and then the installation of anticommunist rulers in the South after the Vietnamese ousted the French. President Johnson escalated the conflict in August 1964, using the so-called Gulf of Tonkin incident as a pretext to declare that the North Vietnamese had initiated attacks on Americans. By lopsided votes of 416 to 0 and 88 to 2 in the House and Senate, respectively, Congress granted LBJ carte blanche to invade Vietnam and operate throughout Southeast Asia in the name of "peace and security." Undermining his liberal domestic agenda and terminally damaging his presidency, he escalated the draft and boosted troop levels in Vietnam above 535,000 by 1968. Imperialist presumptions of U.S. hegemony over Asia were bolstered by the racist logic behind the "domino theory," repudiating the notion that independent Asian nations could think for themselves rather than be controlled by the Soviet Union.[8]

As the war raged on, U.S. military leaders not only disagreed with Dr. King's opposition to the nation's foreign policy; they also refused to place the lives of Vietnamese and Asian people on anything remotely close to an equal footing with those of white Americans. Instead, they reproduced the deeply rooted pathology informing decades of U.S. militarism and systemic white supremacy. Through his extraordinary research, Nick Turse has documented how this pathological dehumanization routinized war crimes and terror in Vietnam. The fundamental message of Turse's book *Kill Anything That Moves: The Real American War in Vietnam* cannot be repeated or emphasized enough:

> Murder, torture, rape, abuse, forced displacement, home burnings, specious arrests, imprisonment without due process—such occurrences were virtually a daily fact of life throughout the years of the American presence in Vietnam.[9]

To be clear, these were not isolated incidents or rogue acts by enlisted men; rather, "they were the inevitable outcome of deliberate policies at the highest levels of the military." The U.S. public is understandably moved by Maya Lin's Vietnam Veterans Memorial, with its minimalist design, foregrounding the names of over fifty-eight thousand Americans etched into a black granite wall for eternity. But we must not overlook the tremendous scale of loss for the Vietnamese people. An estimated 3.8 million died because of the war. While most were combatants—on the side of North or South—an alarmingly high number of civilians were killed. The North Vietnamese reported sixty-five thousand or more civilian deaths. Drawing on available sources, Turse has estimated 195,000–415,000 civilian deaths in the South, plus over one million casualties, owing to the war's direct and indirect effects. Koreans tragically understood how it felt for a country with a fraction of the population and resources possessed by the world's greatest superpower to endure losses on such a horrific scale. But these figures dwarf the number of Americans killed in all wars throughout U.S. history. Of course, U.S. forces were not solely responsible for these deaths and casualties. However, the U.S. military never bothered to count the number of Vietnamese civilians killed. Indeed, it systematically and repeatedly covered up massacres and destroyed records.[10]

What kind of mindset made it possible to repeat the wanton murder of civilians in the Philippines, Japan, Korea, and Vietnam? In contrast with Senator Beveridge's verbose oration, General William Westmoreland succinctly expressed his views in the Academy Award–winning 1974 documentary *Hearts and Minds*, on the Vietnam War: "The Oriental doesn't put the same high price on life as does a Westerner. Life is plentiful. Life is cheap in the Orient."[11]

The film's director, Peter Davis, explained over twenty years later that the quote was indispensable to his antiwar film. But he recognized that it came across as so sensational that he would be accused of distorting the general's words or taking them out of context. The first time Westmoreland made the statement on camera, the general himself yelled "Cut!" as if he were directing. He asked to reshoot the scene because he felt he had not expressed himself properly. Given a second take, "the general began saying exactly the same thing" until Davis ran out of film and had to interrupt the shoot again. Thus, Westmoreland was given a third take to make sure his true sentiments would be captured. He tripled down on the statement in the most comprehensive way, and that take was used in the film.[12]

Throughout U.S. history, military figures have been some of the most candid of the nation's leaders in exhibiting racist and genocidal discourse. Commanders like Andrew Jackson and George Custer explicitly stated that their purpose was Indian removal and domination. The twentieth century brought modern forms of warfare with advanced technologies—increasing the capacity to kill not just soldiers on the battlefield, but also civilians in their homes. During the Cold War and especially the Vietnam War, military officials and civilian commentators commonly used the euphemistic phrase "collateral damage" to characterize the deaths of civilians, ostensibly the necessary cost of implementing strategies to target combatants in a just war. But behind the messaging, the commanders knew the implications of the orders they gave. They also understood that convincing soldiers to carry out these deadly orders required dehumanizing the enemy—and allies, in the case of Korea and Vietnam. Yet American culture scarcely acknowledges the fact that millions of Asians have been killed as a direct or indirect result of U.S. military actions, let alone the long pattern of horrendous war crimes that was normalized and swept under the rug.[13]

I suspect that even Americans who are strongly opposed to war and imperialism often know few of the details or the full extent of American atrocities in war. I confess to being floored by Turse's devastating and deeply researched accounts of war crimes in Vietnam, which he obtained by digging through military records that had been suppressed. Turse also interviewed U.S. veterans, who repeatedly confirmed that they were ordered to carry out directives to kill "everyone" with little to no regard for civilians, women, or children. The message came across clearly to the soldiers: Vietnamese people "were less than human." GIs regularly went into the field saying, "Kill 'em all and let God sort 'em out." One recalled the enemy being defined as "anything with slant eyes who lives in the village." Veteran Wayne Smith stated, "The drill instructors never even called the Vietnamese, 'Vietnamese.' They called them dinks, gooks, slopes, slants, rice-eaters, everything that would take away humanity."[14]

Like the ubiquitous use of slurs such as *Jap* and *Nip* during World War II, the racist epithet *gook* crossed over from GI talk to common parlance within American popular culture. Its use went unquestioned to such a degree that John McCain, considered one of the most honorable men to have graced the Senate chambers, repeatedly used it in conversation with reporters as a leading candidate for president, while recounting war stories on his "Straight Talk Express" campaign bus in 1999 and 2000. For months this went largely unnoticed, until the *San Francisco Chronicle* drew attention to McCain's brazen language in the run-up to the pivotal South Carolina primary in mid-February 2000. (That same day, *The New York Times* made only fleeting reference to McCain's use of *gooks* in an account buried on page 25.) McCain eventually agreed to cease using language he belatedly acknowledged as "bigoted and offensive." The senator's initial response, however, was defiance. "I hate the gooks," McCain told reporters querying him about using the epithet. "I will hate them as long as I live." His stance had gone unchanged for three decades. "I will call right now, my interrogator that tortured me, a gook," McCain said.

"These interrogators and prison guards were cruel and sadistic people who deserve the worst appellations possible." He then reiterated his stance yet again for effect. "Gook," he said, "is the kindest appellation I can give."[15]

More than a term of derision, *gook* came to have operational usage by American forces. To rationalize conduct that flew in the face of international humanitarian law, they put into practice what became known as the "mere-gook rule." In other words, they could eschew moral agonizing about the victims because they were merely "gooks." Ostensibly, U.S. leaders provided a rationale underlying this sadistic mentality. As Turse has pointed out, the former auto executive Robert McNamara, who became secretary of defense under JFK and LBJ, pushed for accelerated kill counts as if he were speeding up an assembly line. His goal was to eliminate the Viet Cong's combatants faster than they could replace them. Reaching this "crossover point" was the key, in McNamara's eyes, to winning the war. In practice, this translated into commanders producing skyrocketing body counts by ordering and tolerating whatever measures were necessary to obtain them.[16]

After watching its resource and firepower advantages repeatedly being neutralized by the Viet Cong's guerrilla warfare tactics, the U.S. military turned toward "pacification" strategies, reminiscent of the Philippine-American War. Consequently, civilians increasingly came under fire. The goal was to take and hold control of territory by using literal scorched-earth tactics—burning down villages and agricultural fields—to depopulate areas. Thousands of "pacified" refugees were forced into squalid camps lacking sufficient food and care. While these were effectively concentration camps, other Vietnamese people in the South suffered worse fates. American soldiers found that the surest way to inflate kill counts was to massacre civilians and mark them down as "VC" for Viet Cong. Roy Bumgarner became one of the war's most decorated marines by killing more than fifteen hundred Vietnamese people. But he was eventually exposed for wantonly murdering civilians he had recorded as "VC" kills. Bumgarner's Vietnam exploits built on a storied military career that had previously taken him to China during its civil war, to the Philippines during the Huk Rebellion, and to Korea for two tours of duty. The common theme: confronting enemies who were doubly dehumanized because they were Asians and suspected communists.[17]

Aerial attacks further magnified the scope and scale of the damage and terror. Since the Viet Cong lacked any air force, the U.S. military sought to exploit this discrepancy with a massive bombing campaign. It used twenty-six times more ammunition per soldier in Vietnam than it had in World

War II. A single plane dropping cluster bombs could send 7.5 million steel shards ripping through every living thing across an area nearly one square mile in surface. On top of billions of pounds of conventional munitions, U.S. forces used four hundred thousand tons of napalm and over seventy million pounds of Agent Orange and other herbicides. Capable of burning through flesh and bone, white phosphorus was even more destructive than napalm. Here lay the bonanza the military industrial complex had lobbied to achieve, and Vietnam served as its testing ground for product development and marketing. With routine use of racist epithets, a U.S. pilot praised the "backroom boys at Dow" (the chemical corporation) for its lethal impact. "The original product wasn't so hot," he said, because "if the gooks were quick they could scrape it off." So they added polystyrene and "Willie Peter" (white phosphorus) "to make it burn better."[18]

The combined impact on Vietnamese villages and their inhabitants was devastating. Air force captain Brian Wilson, charged with assessing bomb damage, characterized these attacks as "the epitome of immorality." He recounted a typical air strike that ended "with two napalm bombs which would just fry everything that was left." Wilson found sixty-two dead in the incident, particularly "women between fifteen and twenty-five and so many children—usually in their mothers' arms or very close to them—and so many old people." This stood in total contradiction to the official record of 130 Viet Cong killed.[19]

One must read *Kill Anything That Moves* from cover to cover to grasp the full extent of Turse's research. American soldiers shot at civilians for fun and sport, laughing aloud while they were terrorizing, maiming, and killing human beings. As in the Pacific War, they mutilated victims and cut off body parts to claim as trophies. While ears were most frequently taken, occasionally U.S. soldiers mounted heads on pikes and paraded them around. The war was no doubt vicious on all sides, and the Vietnamese guerrillas often unleashed severe and uninhibited attacks to harm and kill the Americans who invaded their land and homes. The U.S. public has become deeply familiar with the stories and scenes of U.S. prisoners of war being tortured and brutalized by their communist captors. Nevertheless, to keep this in perspective, roughly eight hundred Americans were detained, whereas U.S. and South Vietnamese forces held as many as three hundred thousand civilians and combatants. Torture became routine, usually administered by South Vietnamese trained by the CIA. In 1968, a counterintelligence expert with the U.S. Marines provided Congress an account of some of the interrogation tactics used in the CIA-designed Phoenix Program. For example, electronic devices were attached to the genitals of women and men to "shock them into submission." One woman suspected of being sympathetic to the Viet Cong was held in a cage until she starved to death. Another subject had a six-inch dowel pushed deeper and deeper through his ear until he perished.[20]

Exposés of war crimes in Vietnam dismantled the long-standing myth that war promotes civilized manhood. Instead, the total dehumanization of the Vietnamese rendered women easy, disposable targets. Atrocious, reprehensible sexual and misogynistic violence became all too common. Perpetrators were rarely reported or disciplined. Soldiers coined the phrase "double veterans" to recognize peers who raped Vietnamese women before murdering them. In February 1968, army medic Jamie Henry witnessed a massacre by a company in the 35th Infantry. Henry recalled seeing at least one naked young girl being dragged out of a hut, a sign of rape that he characterized as "pretty SOP": standard operating procedure. Next, after piling up bodies, "five men around the circle opened up on full automatic with their M-16s." They slaughtered nineteen women and children in one round.[21]

Everything came together at My Lai on the morning of March 16, 1968: a massacre of approximately five hundred civilians by Charlie Company, 1st Battalion, 20th Infantry; the murder exclusively of women, children, and the elderly; rape and sexual violence; and a cover-up that went high up the chain of command. Herbert Carter, who served in Charlie Company, refused to fire on civilians but witnessed the massacre firsthand. Carter remembered seeing a woman in tears after her small child had been shot. "She came out of the hut with her baby," he testified. An enlisted man "shot her with an M16." When the woman fell, she dropped her child to the ground. The solider then "opened on the baby with his M16 and killed the baby too." Others were herded into large groups, where Lieutenant William Calley ordered that they be gunned down. The army's official record documented a "battle" in which 128 enemy combatants were allegedly killed. That it also noted that only three weapons were recovered should have immediately alerted army officials that a one-sided massacre had occurred. But it took more than a year for Ron Ridenhour's whistleblower letter to break the silence, and even longer for the media to take notice. And still, My Lai was far from an isolated incident. In May 1970, an anonymous "Concerned Sergeant" wrote to General Westmoreland noting his awareness of "a My Lai each month for over a year." In fact, on the same day as the My Lai massacre, 230 Vietnamese were massacred by Bravo Company in My Khe.[22]

Turse collected powerful testimonies from survivors in Vietnam, too. He went to the hamlet of Quang Nam, where fifty-two were killed by U.S. soldiers in June 1967. Ho Ngoc Phung described finding the dead body of his pregnant cousin: "Her belly had been split open and you could see the baby." At Phi Phu, he was shown a small monument memorializing villagers who were forced into a trench and massacred by Americans. Elsewhere, Phan Thi Dan reported having horrific flashbacks from her discovery of bodies with "no heads." Describing a different massacre from 1970, Ho Thi "suddenly broke down, sobbing convulsively" for more than twenty minutes.[23]

LOOKING LIKE THE ENEMY AGAIN

Many of Turse's central findings are corroborated by the accounts of Asian American veterans. As the antiwar protests escalated, activists in the Asian American movement spread testimonies by Asian American soldiers who broke the silence regarding the racism they endured and witnessed up close. These appeared in independent newspapers like *Gidra*. Vietnam veteran Norman Nakamura commented that American GIs routinely assaulted and abused Vietnamese civilians with impunity. They took "security in the knowledge that other GIs consider these people as 'Gooks'" and that they would not be "subject to Vietnamese law." In 1970, he recalled seeing a Vietnamese mother in tears after a U.S. driver ran over and killed her child. Yet he also heard drivers say that "it is better to run over a 'Gook' than a chicken" because killing a chicken required compensating its owner for the value of the eggs it would have laid. Nakamura believed racism undermined the prospects for U.S. victory. "It seems ridiculous and hypocritical to be antagonizing the very people you are supposed to be aiding," he wrote. Other Asian Americans echoed his tune. In a reported case of mistaken identity, a Chinese American on patrol was shot in the back in a friendly-fire incident. He was destined for a Vietnamese hospital until he proved he was American.[24]

Author Toshio Welchel offers a deeper look into the lives of Japanese American veterans in the 1999 oral history book *From Pearl Harbor to Saigon*. Some volunteered out of a sense of patriotic duty. Some acknowledged that the failed pursuit of assimilation left them self-hating and directionless. The racist treatment began on American soil during basic training, most commonly in the marines. Sent to Quantico for training in 1966, Don Mitsuo was ordered to dress like a stereotypical Viet Cong combatant.

Japanese Americans like him were dragged in front of their platoons by drill instructors, who spouted degrading lines like "This is what your enemy looks like. I want you to kill it before it kills you." But the attacks went beyond playacting. "I was beaten up by two drill instructors one night while everybody was asleep," David Hakata recounted. "They took me into their room and beat me up, for what I don't know; they did that routinely."[25]

Matters only devolved after they arrived in Vietnam. One after another, Welchel's interviewees recalled that U.S. soldiers not only called Vietnamese people—allies and foes—"zips, gooks, slopes, and zipper-heads" routinely; they also called their Asian American peers slurs like *gook*, *Jap*, and *chink*. Raymond Imayama, who served in the marines from 1968 to 1969, was the only Asian American in his unit. His sergeant taunted him for one week straight, spouting racist drivel while making slant-eyed gestures. Pushed beyond the limit, Imayama whaled on the sergeant when the opportunity arose, punching him repeatedly "like a machine" until he was pulled off the man and subsequently transferred to another unit. Knowing they had to repress their anger, many turned to drugs as an escape and were scarred by trauma. But they watched white soldiers get drunk and take their anger, frustrations, or even boredom out on Vietnamese civilians with impunity. They also witnessed the abuse of women who worked as prostitutes or "hooch maids" to survive. Melvin Wadachi, whose tour of duty in the army spanned 1969 and 1970, observed Americans in a helicopter shooting at Vietnamese civilians just "for the hell of it." On his last day of service, Wadachi burned his uniform in disgust. Nearly all left Vietnam with a stronger consciousness of American racism. Some became activists after coming home. Born in the Poston concentration camp during World War II, Miles Yakao was serving in the army when he was jumped by "a big, giant, white boy," who punched him while screaming, "You fucking gook." It did not take long for him to conclude, "This is really a bullshit war." Yakao told a group of other soldiers, "When I get out of here, I'm going to go back and join the anti-war protesters."[26]

Repulsion toward the Vietnam War, and particularly the virulently racist dehumanization of the "gook" enemy, spawned a new generation of Asian student and youth activists. Mike Nakayama, a marine veteran, came home from Vietnam with a Bronze Star and two Purple Hearts. To stop others from signing up, he worked with high school students to organize walkouts against the war. At California State University, Long Beach, Nakayama joined the Asian American Student Alliance and fought for ethnic studies. His actions were part of a broader awakening. Rejecting the imperative to assimilate that lay at the heart of the "model minority" stereotype, formerly disparate ethnic groupings—Japanese, Chinese, Filipino, and Korean Americans—came together in the panethnic Asian American movement. They were inspired by the radical challenge to white supremacy issued by the Black Power movement and other social movements of the late 1960s and early 1970s. As scholar-activists Michael Liu, Kim Geron, and Tracy Lai have noted, antiwar protests served as the "starting point" from which these young Asian radicals "expanded their vision to root out racism and imperialism globally in search of a better world." They did not merely criticize the war as a misallocation of resources or unnecessary sacrifice of American GIs. Asian American activists denounced the wars in Southeast Asia as instances of "genocide" that perpetuated a historical pattern that ran through Hiroshima and Nagasaki.[27]

ACCESSORY TO GENOCIDE

Although my focus has been on the systemic nature of violence, there are times when one must highlight the escalated role of individuals at critical moments in U.S. history. Henry Kissinger deserves special mention for the hand he played in facilitating genocide. While tens of thousands of civilians in Asia died under fire from the U.S. military, tens of thousands more died from American arms supplied with Kissinger's signature neglect for humanity. In *The Blood Telegram*, Gary J. Bass recounts how three hundred thousand or more Bengalis became the sacrificial lambs of U.S. foreign policy because President Richard Nixon and Kissinger, his national security adviser, viewed Pakistan's dictatorship under General Agha Muhammad Yahya Khan as an indispensable Cold War ally. The "Blood telegram" refers to a dissent cable, the first of its kind, sent by Archer Blood, the State Department's consul general in Dacca, to his superiors in Washington, D.C., on April 6, 1971. Blood described the wanton murder of Bengalis, as part of the Pakistani military's crackdown on protest and dissent in the Eastern section that was then seeking to secede—ultimately becoming the independent nation of Bangladesh. Thousands of innocent people were massacred. Some were executed by firing squads. But the Bengalis elicited no sympathy because they were allied with the government of India, which Nixon and Kissinger saw as too cozy with the Soviet Union. General Khan was a reliable anticommunist partner who was also critical to cementing America's ties with red China.[28]

"Why would we give a damn about Bangladesh?" Kissinger asked.

"We don't," Nixon answered.[29]

But at least twenty members of his administration cared enough to risk objecting. "Unfortunately," they wrote, "the overworked term genocide is applicable." Many of the State Department's experts on South Asia endorsed the dissent cable and called on Nixon to change his stance. The Bengali resistance, they asserted, was pro-American. Worried more about bad publicity than human lives, Kissinger became "furious." Calling the reports of genocide a hoax, he and Nixon insisted that the deaths had resulted from internal conflicts among the Bengalis. Archer Blood was now persona non grata. But the United States was more than complicit, for it had supplied the Pakistani military with the F-86 Sabre jets, M-24 Chaffee tanks, guns, and ammunition used to commit the genocide. In fact, later in 1971, Nixon and Kissinger continued to supply arms to Pakistan—secretly using Iran and Jordan as proxies—despite clear warnings from advisers within the State Department, Pentagon, and White House that doing so was an illegal violation of the congressional arms embargo.[30]

When today's U.S. college students wonder how their government can so cavalierly be complicit in, or even actively sponsor, genocidal military action in Gaza, this longer pattern of iniquity and erasure must be recognized. According to Bass, Kissinger began lying about the Bengali genocide almost as soon as it started. Although his records are in the Library of Congress, Kissinger ensured that researchers will not see them until he has been dead for five years. Alas, while that countdown has finally begun, one will still need proper clearance to view documents Kissinger had classified. With the genocide warranting scarcely more than a footnote in their voluminous writings and speeches, neither Kissinger nor Nixon offered any critical reflection on their actions. "Few Americans today remember anything about these atrocities, let alone about Nixon's and Kissinger's support for the government that was committing them," Bass concluded. "In this forgetting, Americans have absorbed some of Nixon's and Kissinger's contempt for Bangladesh. Faraway, poor, brown—the place is all too easily ignored or mocked."[31]

During this same period, centered on Nixon's presidency, the United States bombed Laos and Cambodia heavily in its broader efforts to target the Vietnamese communists and their cross-border operations. As with Vietnam, Americans viewed Laos and Cambodia as stereotypically backwards, Third World nations that were better off under French colonial rule and would be a threat if allowed to act independently. Typifying this mentality that rendered millions as mere pawns under U.S. Cold War strategy, *Time*'s Stanley Karnow characterized Laos in 1961 as "so primitive that the currently flavored adjective 'underdeveloped' would be an unwarranted compliment." Following France's withdrawal in 1954, the Americans distrusted nonaligned governments in both countries and ultimately refused to support international agreements declaring their neutrality. The CIA acted to rig elections and aid the overthrow of governments. In the case of Laos, it launched a secret war fought mainly by ethnic minority Hmong under General Vang Pao. In the words of historian Seth Jacobs, Laos became "the testing ground for counterinsurgency and nation-building programs." All the while, U.S. air forces subjected it to "the heaviest sustained bombing in history." To put this in perspective, U.S. pilots dropped more tonnage of bombs on Laos between 1968 and 1972 than it did in all operations during World War II. Civilians in areas controlled by the communist Pathet Lao suffered enormous casualties. These actions only served to delay the rise of a communist government until 1975, at which time the Hmong clans connected to Vang were subjected to severe persecution. Thousands fled with ethnic Laotians to Thailand, as one-fourth of the country sought refuge. From California, Vang became a leader-in-exile of a protracted effort to topple the Pathet Lao.[32]

Simultaneously, secret and illegal U.S. bombings destabilized Cambodia economically and politically. Historian Ben Kiernan has argued that this was "probably the most important single factor" precipitating the rise of the genocidal Khmer Rouge regime led by Pol Pot. The United States supported the overthrow of Prince Norodom Sihanouk's neutral government in 1970, believing that coup leader Lon Nol would be a more reliable anticommunist ally. Nixon clandestinely bombed Cambodia in defiance of Congress. By August 1973, he had altered his deceit, telling the media he was targeting only areas "totally occupied by the North Vietnamese Communists." In reality, the U.S. bombings killed as many as 150,000 Cambodian civilians. "The bombers may kill some Communists," a Cambodian from a targeted area said in 1973, "but they kill everyone else, too." The Khmer Rouge exploited rural resentment and fear of continued U.S. bombings. A report by the army acknowledged in 1973 that "the civilian population fears U.S. air attacks far more than they do Communist rocket attacks or scorched-earth attacks."[33]

Two weeks before the fall of Saigon, the Khmer Rouge took power in April 1975. The U.S. government then became complicit in the ensuing genocide. Pol Pot's vision of a socialist utopia entailed social engineering on a cruelly inhumane scale. Urban residents were forced into rural labor camps set up to persecute political opponents and purge intellectuals of hostile ideas. People died by the tens of thousands from malnutrition, from uncontained and untreated illnesses, from being worked to death, and from executions. Kiernan estimates that 1,671,000 Cambodians died in just four years under the Khmer Rouge. As he had been in the case of Bangladesh, Kissinger was unmoved. Vietnam was the enemy, and containing Soviet influence was his main goal. Now promoted to secretary of state (while continuing as national security adviser), Kissinger was unbothered by Cambodia's repression, so long as it was "aligned with China rather than with North Vietnam." In November 1975, he characterized the Khmer Rouge as America's "friends." The heralded statesman accentuated his point: "They are murderous thugs, but we won't let that stand in our way." While candidate Jimmy Carter pledged to uphold global human rights and compared Pol Pot to Hitler, his presidential administration did little to distance itself from Kissinger's stance toward the Khmer Rouge. In fact, after Vietnam intervened to topple Pol Pot in 1979, Carter's foreign policy team continued to provide support for the Khmer Rouge, reinscribing the tired adage that the enemy of my enemy is my friend. The Reagan administration generally followed suit. Amid a devastating famine, the United States refused to recognize the Vietnam-backed government or provide it with humanitarian aid. Congressman Stephen Solarz of New York criticized this disregard as emanating from "implicit racism."[34]

THE MASSACRE AT CLEVELAND ELEMENTARY

As the dehumanization of Asians at the core of U.S. foreign policy diffused broadly through the American public, it motivated hostility toward the resettlement of Southeast Asian refugees. Such hostility formed one of the primary factors underlying the massacre at Cleveland Elementary School in Stockton, California, on January 17, 1989.

Four victims were Cambodian Americans: Sokhim An, age six; Ram Chun, age eight; Oeun Lim, age eight; and Rathanar Or, age nine. One was Vietnamese American: Thuy Tran, age six. Around 11:30 a.m. in the morning, they were on the playground with three to four hundred of their peers, when a twenty-four-year-old white man named Patrick Purdy arrived, destined to break this daily routine. As a former attendee, he was well familiar with the location. Clad in blue jeans and black boots with a camouflage jacket and olive drab flak vest covering his torso, Purdy drove up to the school in a 1977 Chevrolet station wagon. After parking and exiting the vehicle, he lit it ablaze with a Molotov cocktail he had rigged with a gasoline-filled beer bottle. Purdy next entered the school grounds armed to the teeth. He brandished a variant of the AK-47 semiautomatic rifle he had purchased for $349.95 the prior summer from a gun and jewelry shop in a small town east of Portland, Oregon. He kept two pistols, a bayonet, and multiple rounds of ammunition in tow.

Witnesses said Purdy calmly took up a position on the west side of the yard beside a four-classroom portable building. Shooting from the hip, he fired sixty-six rounds from a rotary ammunition clip across the length of the asphalt playground. With bullets ricocheting off the blacktop surface, children on the yard screamed and ran in terror. The wounded hopped and crawled their way toward shelter and safety. Enacting the steps California students instinctively knew through repeated earthquake preparedness drills, children in the portable classrooms dropped to the floor and covered their heads. Meanwhile, Purdy moved to the opposite side of the building and emptied the remaining nine rounds. He then reloaded a "banana clip" and unleashed the whole of its thirty rounds in the direction of the kids on the playground.

Within a short span of perhaps three minutes, Purdy killed five young children. He wounded thirty other students and a teacher. As he paused during his shooting spree, the blare of sirens signaled the imminent arrival of police officers. Purdy reached into his jacket pocket for a 9mm semiautomatic pistol. Pointing it to his right temple, he ended his life on the playground of Cleveland Elementary.[35]

The mass shooting made breaking news, especially in the Central Valley region of California. This opened a new front in the war over racial discourse and interpretation. As the *Sacramento Bee* reported, "Local television stations sent news crews scrambling in search of answers after Tuesday morning's tragic attack on a Stockton elementary school, but nobody was able to answer the big one: Why?"[36]

Law enforcement served mainly to obfuscate. "Why did he do this?" Captain Dennis Perry, the lead investigator for the Stockton police, said the day after the shootings. "We may never know." Purdy's murder-suicide left the police dumbfounded. "He did not leave us a message," said the chief investigator for the Stockton Police Department. "Without that we'll never know exactly why he did what he did. In a way, he beat us because we'll never know." The repeated emphasis on the questions we can "never" ask a deceased person, however, evaded responsibility for what we can and should investigate and discern. In fact, Purdy had made a string of racist comments. One prior arrest report from April 1987 even indicated that he was found with "an Aryan Nation type book on guns and killing." The deputy reporting this finding retracted it when interviewed for the attorney general's report, saying he found no reference to the Aryan Nation or white supremacists. Because the police did not retain the book, however, it remains unclear what its actual contents were.[37]

In contrast to the nonplussed officials, the city's Southeast Asian American communities felt directly targeted by the Cleveland Elementary shooter. Children of Southeast Asian refugee families comprised two-thirds of the students who were shot, a proportion roughly equal to their representation among the nearly one thousand students enrolled at the school. It was one of three in the district where administrators had concentrated most of the refugee children seeking bilingual education. Hoping to restore a sense of normality, school officials held class the next day following the shootings. More than three-fourths of the students stayed home.[38]

Asian American parents made it clear that they feared for the safety of their children. Many Cambodians in Stockton lost six to nine close relatives to war and genocide in their homelands. In fact, some mothers of the shooting victims had lost their families in Cambodia, and their children in Stockton were from new families they had started after remarrying in the United States.[39]

Perhaps well intentioned but uninformed, non-Asian school and community representatives tried to allay their anxieties by downplaying race as a motivation for the massacre. "Nobody knows why," a teacher at a social services agency near the school told a class of Cambodian Americans. Purdy "was an alcoholic" and "a very unhappy person."[40]

The quote appeared in a *New York Times* article by one of the gray lady's iconic veteran journalists, Robert Reinhold. With a penchant for Armani suits and Gucci shoes embodying "his measured subdued style and air of perpetual calm," Reinhold was known by peers as a "meticulous and insightful reporter." His *Times* obituary characterized him as "a role model for a generation of national correspondents." Writing three days after the massacre, Reinhold assessed in his own words, "There was no evidence that Mr. Purdy had any special animosity toward Asians."[41]

Cleveland Elementary School's principal, Patricia Busher, appealed directly to the parents. "Please bring our children back to school," she announced from the balcony of the Park Village apartments, an overcrowded, rundown complex that was home for seven hundred Asian families, including the families of two of the murdered children.

"I thought that he's going to come here too," said thirteen-year-old Och Sao.

"It is safe. We do not have to be afraid anymore," the principal concluded with the assistance of a translator. "They will never stop their fear if you keep them at home."[42]

The fears of the Asian American students and their parents, however, were well founded. Three months before the shootings, forty cars at the Park Village had their tires slashed in what some suspected was a hate crime. Within forty-eight hours of the massacre, local reporters had uncovered witnesses who heard Purdy complain about Southeast Asian refugees competing for jobs with white workers, about the threat of the "Commies" taking over, and about how he outright "hated" Vietnamese Americans. *The Sacramento Bee* tracked down a former coworker who stated on the record that Purdy was "seething with rage" at Asian immigrants and refugees he accused of getting governmental aid and job training at the expense of opportunities for whites.[43]

Purdy's grandmother, a retired cannery worker, pushed back against these reports. "As far as I know, he was not prejudiced," she told the Associated Press. "We're not a prejudiced family. We weren't raised that way." She was "shocked" and could not fathom why her grandson would commit such a crime.[44]

The Stockton police swatted down any suspicion that the shootings were motivated by anti-Asian hatred or resentment, but they did so from an entirely different angle. "Through his lifetime, Mr. Purdy developed a hate for everybody," surmised Perry, the police captain. "As far as dislike for any one race, that is not a pattern that shows up." He further asserted that Purdy had sprayed gunfire over the entire playground, wounding children of other races and ethnicities besides Southeast Asians.[45]

"Whoever he happened to be talking about on a particular day, he didn't like," Perry continued. "He might not like Vietnamese. But if the next day . . . he was talking about the Lebanese, he probably didn't like them either. And the day after that he would talk to you about the police and he didn't like them either."[46]

The logic the police investigator used was contorted, if not outright fallacious. Why was it necessary for the shooter to *only* hate Asian Americans or Southeast Asian refugees in order for this to be considered an act of anti-

Asian violence? And are we to conclude that there would only be evidence that he was targeting Southeast Asian refugee children if he deliberately identified those who were of a different race and paused the AK-47 fire whenever he came across a non-Asian student?

Asian American community members and civil rights activists insisted there was more to this story that needed to be examined. The most extensive investigation was conducted by the office of California's attorney general, John Van de Kemp. In October 1989, the state released findings that repudiated the initial conclusions of the police. "Purdy focused on Southeast Asians in Stockton as the target of his homicidal plans," wrote Nelson Kempsky, the chief deputy attorney general and lead author of the report titled *Patrick Edward Purdy and the Cleveland School Killings*. "He blamed all minorities for his failings, and selected Southeast Asians because they were the minority with whom he was most in contact."[47]

There was a long trail of bias and bigotry in Purdy's past. He had regularly used the "n-word" and made racist comments about African Americans to family and friends. In line with the "English-only" campaigns of the 1980s, he scorned those who spoke other languages and directly confronted people in public, declaring they were only allowed to speak English in America. Furthermore, the state's investigation substantially bolstered the early reports that Purdy resented Southeast Asian refugees for taking away jobs from white Americans and getting what he perceived to be special treatment from the government.[48]

Multiple witnesses who worked with Purdy in early 1988 heard him complain that the United States was "letting all the Vietnamese and communists into the country." America was being "overrun" by refugees, giving away its jobs to them, plus free money to live on before they started working. While attending vocational classes at a local community college, he claimed there were five Vietnamese for every white student in his class. By December 1988, Purdy had purchased multiple weapons and made multiple statements indicating he was committed to carrying out the massacre. At this point, evidence of his anti-Asian racism became more pointed and more pronounced. On January 3, 1989, he entered a bar in Stockton wearing a fatigue jacket and told the bartender he owned an AK-47. Purdy motioned with his arms like he was firing multiple rounds, and he complained to the bartender that Vietnamese "boat-people" were taking over everything and getting government handouts. As he left the bar, he proclaimed, "You're going to read about me in the papers."[49]

Two days later, Purdy was seen in his car parked outside Cleveland Elementary. In the week before the shooting, he was twice seen in the evening at Lincoln High School. The timing was significant, because after 4:30 p.m. the school served as a cultural center and K–12 school for Cambodian language speakers. Thus, Purdy was likely assessing and selecting his target.

Finally, on the morning of the shooting, Purdy spoke with another guest at a motel where he was staying. When that guest griped that the early 11:00 a.m. checkout time had been imposed by the "Hindu" manager, Purdy answered, "The damn Hindus and boat people own everything."[50]

The investigators, to be certain, found other relevant details to explain Purdy's antisocial attitudes and behavior. He came from a broken home. His parents separated when Purdy was a toddler, and each of their lives was marked by severe instability. Young Patrick lived with his mother and witnessed her suffer from abuse by his stepfather. Constant conflicts resulted in Purdy being banished from home as a teenager, followed by bouts of homelessness and substance abuse. A series of arrests began at the age of fifteen, when he was charged with solicitation as a sex worker in West Hollywood. He bounced around from job to job, city to city, and ultimately acknowledged to a therapist that he was suicidal.[51]

Two things were thus simultaneously true. First, there were multiple, interrelated factors that led up to Patrick Purdy committing mass murder at Cleveland Elementary School. Multiple forms of intervention would, therefore, have been necessary to stave off his homicidal tendencies. Second, *there is no doubt that this was an act of anti-Asian violence.*

We should be mindful of the specificities that render this a unique event, particularly for the victims and their families. Nevertheless, we must do so without treating it as an isolated incident. While Purdy may have been a lone gunman, he was not alone in his views. The attorney general's investigation found that "Purdy received reinforcement in his prejudices from many of those with whom he was in contact in Stockton," including "acquaintances and co-workers." It further cited evidence that other Stockton residents viewed Southeast Asians as "an unwelcome intrusion" and felt threatened by their presence, "even without a rational basis for that feeling." Although he may not have expressed a consistent or systematic worldview, Purdy's grievances—about "Commies" threatening freedom-loving Americans, about the foreign-born speaking languages other than English and taking away jobs, and about white men being pushed aside by the government in favor of minorities—were all standard fare for the not-so-subtle dog-whistle politics of the new right. Indeed, two U.S. presidents from California, Richard Nixon and Ronald Reagan, played the most pivotal role in mobilizing white resentment in response to rising racial and ethnic diversity for tremendous electoral gains as part of the historic political realignment that overturned the New Deal order and augured a widening economic divide.[52]

The California attorney general's report concluded with two recommendations that have become standard fare in the aftermath of mass shootings: more gun restrictions and increased attention to mental illness. But it devoted its longest passage to a relatively novel idea: a call for ethnic studies curricula to be implemented from kindergarten through twelfth grade to reduce "the amount of violence motivated by bigotry in California." The report credited the attorney general's Asian and Pacific Islander Advisory Committee for this proposal and excerpted the report that body had released just one month before the school shooting. Combined with the call for ethnic studies education, the naming of the shooting as an act of anti-Asian violence reflected the influence of community leaders advising the attorney general. Asian American activists spent much of the 1980s developing this line of argumentation and advocacy in response to a spree of violent, racist attacks. The most notable incident was the murder of Vincent Chin, on which we will now focus our attention as we begin part 2.[53]

PART TWO

How the Murder of Vincent Chin Remade Asian American Identity and Politics (1980s–Present)

SIX

Martyr in the Motor City

"It's because of you little motherfuckers that we're all out of work."

Racine Colwell, a performer in the Fancy Pants Club, swore under oath that she heard Ronald Ebens yell those words at Vincent Chin, who was out with friends for his bachelor party on the night of June 19, 1982.

Vincent Chin had an easygoing side. A poet and book lover, he was particularly fond of authors James Michener and James Clavell, both known for epic works set in Asia. On his infrequent days off, he would drive north of town to spend the day fishing at Cass Lake. But he also carried a strong sense of dignity, and something that night set him off.[1]

What began as a verbal altercation escalated into a physical confrontation, first inside the adults-only club, then on the streets of Highland Park, Michigan, a small city located within the geographic center of Detroit. It ended with Ebens repeatedly beating Chin in the knee, torso, and head with a Louisville Slugger baseball bat while his stepson, Michael Nitz, restrained him. The two assailants, both white men, hunted down and ambushed Chin in the parking lot of a McDonald's restaurant, where he and friend Jimmy Choi had fled for safety. Vincent tried to escape by running out into Woodward Avenue, but Nitz corralled him. The savage beating occurred in the middle of the region's most prominent north-south thoroughfare and in full view of two police officers who were moonlighting as security guards.[2]

"I didn't mean it," Ebens told the cops. "I am sorry."[3]

A paramedic who arrived on the scene soon after would later tell the FBI that Ebens was more bombastic. "That's right I did it," he recounted Ebens saying. Then Ebens pointed at Choi and declared, "If I had it my way, you would be there too."[4]

Chin was nearly brain dead. Four days later, after his loved ones agreed to take him off life support, he passed away in a hospital bed. Family and friends who had planned to attend Vincent's wedding stayed instead for his funeral. In the months that followed, Ebens's infamous words would become known to scores of people across the nation, crystallizing the sense of alarm Asian Americans felt as reports of anti-Asian hate and violence surged. The accusation that Asian Americans were taking jobs from whites served as a haunting reminder of how Chinese and Asian immigrants a century prior were stigmatized as "coolies."

But there was a crucial twist in the narrative. Asians in the nineteenth century were scorned by Americans as "cheap labor"—immigrants from geopolitically weak countries whose state of impoverishment led desperate migrants to venture overseas. By the 1980s, Japan, a once vanquished foe that became a junior partner of the U.S. empire, was simultaneously admired and loathed as America's economic rival. In 1975, the U.S. trade deficit with Japan stood at $2 billion. By 1982, it was $16 billion and rising. Between 1980 and 1982, the share of Americans with an unfavorable view of Japan more than doubled, from 12 to 29 percent. Nowhere was this truer than in the midwestern "Rust Belt," where Asian American representation was scarce and where deindustrialization produced widespread economic dislocation. Under such conditions, as scholar Robert Lee has argued, the conditional acceptance of Asian Americans by whites as a high-achieving "model minority" could easily revert to the stereotype of Asians as a threatening "yellow peril" or "gook" enemy.[5]

Historian John Dower has suggested that "war hates and race hates" tied to the Pacific War never disappeared; they were simply transferred to other politically useful outlets like Korea and Vietnam. During the 1980s, they rebounded back on Japan. Between 1978 and 1981, American auto employment plummeted from 760,000 to 490,000 jobs industry wide. This quick unraveling caught the United Auto Workers union with its guard down, increasing the sense that the American middle class was vulnerable and that established institutions could no longer guarantee its economic security. Japan's export-driven economic growth threatened to upend the hierarchical order established during the postwar American occupation. Now the specter of "unfair" Japanese competition prompted a backlash from Americans whose long memories of the "sneak attack" on Pearl Harbor shaped the new discourse of a transpacific "trade war."[6]

The Vincent Chin tragedy is underlain with bitter ironies and even absurdity. Vincent was a U.S. citizen of Chinese ancestry whose father, C. W.

Hing Chin, served in the U.S. Army during World War II. His veteran status allowed him to bring his wife, Lily, to the States as a military bride at a time when Asian immigration was severely restricted. Adopted as a young child from China, Vincent grew up entirely in the Detroit area, where he faced the same distressed job market as his white assailants.[7]

Even if one felt justified in fighting a "trade war" with Japan, there was no valid reason for anyone to make Chin a casualty of it. This constituted the point where references to economic anxiety became guided by the logic of racism. Ebens, a Chrysler foreman, and Nitz, a laid-off autoworker, had strong connections to the U.S. auto industry at a time when its corporate leaders, workers, and political champions were leading the charge against purportedly unfair Japanese competition.

Some were more careful than others when choosing their words and targets.

Referring to the atomic bombing of Hiroshima, Bennett Bidwell, a member of Chrysler's board of directors, told a Detroit radio host that he would "charter the Enola Gay" to strike back at Japan.[8]

In a March 1982 meeting of House members, John Dingell Jr.—the longest-serving congressman in U.S. history—racialized the specter of global competition with his remarks decrying "the little yellow people." There was "an embarrassed silence," *The New York Times* reported, followed by several gasps in unison of "What?"

"The little yellow people," Dingell repeated. "You know, Honda."

One of those in the room who was taken aback was future vice president and Nobel Peace Prize recipient Al Gore. Yet his retort did little to challenge his colleague's flagrant othering of Asians. "Those little yellow people," Gore stated, "have built a plant in my district that is giving jobs to a lot of white and black people."[9]

Younger generations may know Dingell from his retirement, when he became a social media hero of the "Resistance" to Trump. Six decades before that, he had attained the congressional seat long held by his father. In August 1941, months prior to the outbreak of war with Japan, John Dingell Sr. had called for the federal government to round up ten thousand Japanese Americans in "concentration camps" and hold them as "hostages" for leverage. The following year, my grandfather became one of those hostages, taken by the FBI to an Immigration and Naturalization Service internment camp for "enemy aliens." In time, my mother's remaining family members were ordered to a mass incarceration site run by the War Relocation Authority.[10]

The recurring conflation of Asian Americans, as perpetual foreigners, with overseas enemy combatants has been an overriding feature of anti-Asian racism. So too has been the stereotype that "all Asians look alike." Whether committing microaggressions or overt assaults, perpetrators rarely concern themselves with accurate determinations of ethnicity or national origin.

The horrific, senseless violence of Chin's murder is not the main reason we remember him today. After all, on February 27, 1984, Khamseng Praphnvana, a refugee from Laos, was beaten to death by a baseball bat in a similar manner on the streets of St. Louis. "There was nothing racial about it," a police detective quickly concluded without offering evidence of a substantive investigation to support this assertion. When I searched Praphnvana's name, first on Google and then with a subscription-based newspaper database, only a single, solitary hit came up.[11]

Vincent Chin became a household name mainly because the justice system failed and community activists publicized the case. Ebens and Nitz did not deny responsibility for the beating that caused Chin's death. But prosecutors allowed them to avoid standing trial for murder by pleading guilty to manslaughter. Judge Charles Kaufman then sentenced Ebens and Nitz to just three years of probation and ordered them to pay a $3,000 fine plus $780 in fees.

"They ruined my life, my future," said Chin's fiancée, Vikki Wong. "How can you commit murder and get away with nothing? It's not fair. All I can do is scream to myself—for him and for me."[12]

Thousands of Asian Americans shared Wong's outrage at the leniency of these sentences, prompting the rise of the "Justice for Vincent Chin" movement, a history-making development that reverberated through Asian American communities far beyond Detroit.

"We must tell the American people this is wrong," Lily Chin declared.[13]

As she crisscrossed the nation to tell her son's tragic story, the movement helped push the federal government to try the killers for civil rights violations. Defining Chin's murder as a case of racism, this movement popularized the use of the term *anti-Asian violence*.

Ebens (but not Nitz) was found guilty for the first and only time by a Detroit jury. Although he was initially sentenced to twenty-five years in prison, Ebens successfully appealed on procedural grounds for a new trial and change of venue. He was cleared of all charges in Cincinnati by a mostly white jury that had been screened to exclude those who had had interactions with Asian people. Moving to civil court, Lily Chin won a ruling for $1.5 million from Ebens, who moved to Nevada to take advantage of homestead laws protecting his estate from payment. Henceforth, Ronald Ebens would be known colloquially as the man who got away with murdering Vincent Chin.[14]

In concert with Ebens's words about "motherfuckers" taking away would-be American jobs, Chin's dying words, "It's not fair," became etched into the collective memory of Asian Americans, too.

THE SIGNIFICANCE OF BLACK DETROIT HISTORY

I moved to Detroit at the turn of the twenty-first century, primarily to be close to the scholar-activist elder Grace Lee Boggs. In 2002, I helped coordinate a three-day commemoration for the twentieth-year remembrance of Vincent Chin's death. Our events drew more than five hundred attendees, demonstrating the degree to which Asian Americans and people from diverse backgrounds continued to learn and draw inspiration from Chin's story. During my more than fifteen years living in and around Detroit, I saw and participated in a resurgence of Asian American activism in the region that harkened back to the original Justice for Vincent Chin movement. What became absolutely clear was that we needed a deeper engagement with Detroit's history, especially its Black history, if we are to understand the broader meaning of Chin's story for the pursuit of social justice.

While it is correct to characterize the Chin case as a civil rights matter—legally and politically—it is imperative that we understand it in the larger context. The civil rights movement was centered on Black freedom struggles, especially in cities that, like Detroit, became majority Black. And the right-wing campaign to reverse the gains of the civil rights era was significantly driven by anti-Black racism. We will see how such factors complicate our analysis of the events that took place during the 1980s, when Asian Americans forged their way into discussions about race tied to "multiculturalism" and Jesse Jackson's vision of a "Rainbow Coalition." These historical analyses, in turn, carry major implications four decades later for interpreting the Chin case and movement for justice.

Aside from the activism that initially sparked concern about Chin's murder, the primary awareness-raising vehicle about it has been the Academy Award–nominated documentary *Who Killed Vincent Chin?* (1988) by Renee Tajima and Christine Choy. Masterfully constructed, the film presents a *Rashomon*-style narrative that cuts back and forth between the voices of Chin's mother and his friends; Chin's assailant Ronald Ebens, with his lawyers, family, and friends; and third-party witnesses to the attack. Viewers see the shock on the faces of the witnesses, while the despair of Chin's mother contrasts with the alternately stoic and indignant faces of Ebens, his wife, and Michael Nitz. This emotionally powerful film has certainly reached exponentially more people than the original Justice for Vincent Chin movement it chronicles. In other words, it is largely the film's narrative that has galvanized Asian American political consciousness and sustained Chin's legacy.

Still, one work can cover only so much ground. Editorial choices must be made for various political and practical reasons. As I engaged community-organizing work among Detroit's majority Black population, I came to see how the Chin case was a part of the city's history and politics in a more profound and complex manner than I had initially understood. For most viewers of *Who Killed Vincent Chin?*, Detroit tends to function in the story primarily as metaphor—a symbol of American economic woes that provides the context for an analysis centered on racial scapegoating. Detroit's landscape is represented in the documentary film by repeated scenes of urban abandonment. These scenes, paired with news reports about the extent of layoffs and unemployment, paint a picture of a city in deep crisis. During an era of soaring gas prices amid recession, Detroit's Big 3 automakers are observed floundering in the face of foreign, especially Japanese, competition. This is the critical backdrop to the overarching theme of "Japan-bashing" and anti-Asian violence as a form of scapegoating. The voices of Detroit-area political and labor representatives speak directly to the threat posed by "the Japanese" while imploring consumers to "buy American." The filmmakers then employ dramatic music to accompany public displays of metro Detroit residents emphatically smashing Japanese import cars with a sledgehammer.

Our analysis must pay much greater attention to the multiracial context in which the Chin murder and subsequent court case transpired. Geographically, the conflict and murder occurred in a city, Highland Park, that lies within the heart of Detroit and, like the surrounding city, is predominantly Black. Correspondingly, anti-Black racism and Black civil rights activism shaped the social and political background of the Chin case. Without studying Black history, we cannot understand how white racist violence became so pervasive, and permissible, in Detroit.[15]

Although the story of Vincent Chin has become a prototypical case of white racism toward Asian Americans, African Americans figured prominently throughout its central events. Many of the firsthand witnesses and bystanders to the altercation at the Fancy Pants Club and the subsequent murder were Black. These include Starlene, the dancer on stage when Ebens first reportedly confronted Chin, and Jimmy Perry, who said Ebens offered him twenty dollars to "catch the Chinaman." Less well known, a Black woman driving past the Fancy Pants told FBI investigators that she saw Chin fleeing his assailants and tried to warn him they were after him. After watching Ebens swing the bat at Chin's head, police officers Morris Cotton and Michael Gardenhire arrested him. Beyond these initial examples, we will see that a range of Black figures played integral roles as Ebens and Nitz were charged with federal civil rights violations.[16]

But there is also a broader social and historical context we need to consider. The Chin case is substantively a study of whiteness—especially toxic white male masculinity—and the effects of systemic patterns of racism that emerged in Detroit over years and decades leading up to his murder. And for most of that time, whiteness was defined primarily in relation to Blackness. Despite heralded examples of white Detroiters committed to civil rights and racial equity, white identity was too often intertwined with anti-Black racism. Up to the civil rights era, overt discrimination was a common factor in the construction of racial boundaries. Violence and the ever-present threat of violence further played an integral role. As much as the story of Vincent Chin centers on overt violence, however, it also symbolizes certain trends in racism that became more prominent after civil rights laws took effect and blatant racism became less publicly acceptable. It behooves us to understand how racism has been perpetuated through patterns of avoidance and denial.

To complicate our analysis of the Vincent Chin narrative, we must analyze conflicts over place and space by seeing the connection between competitive and aversive modes of racism—what historian Thomas Sugrue has called the white "fight or flight" reaction to the prospect of racial integration. Before World War II, Detroit city proper was over 90 percent white, and it remained home to a total population of roughly two million as late as the 1950s. Though economically prosperous, Detroit as a majority-white city proved anything but peaceful. In the 1920s, the Ku Klux Klan had a large following and its chosen candidate nearly claimed the mayor's office. During World War II, as Black southern migrants sought jobs in the booming factories that were serving as FDR's "arsenal of democracy," whites vehemently opposed the integration of factories, schools, and neighborhoods. Racist whites deployed intimidation routinely. In 1943, they unleashed an anti-Black riot that rivaled any such disturbance nationwide. Scores of African Americans were attacked by white mobs. Most of the thirty-four people who died were Black Detroiters killed by the police.[17]

Entrenched racism, especially in the form of rampant brutality by the predominantly white police force, stalled the pursuit of Black advancement, prompting the next uprising in 1967. White observers generally called it a "riot," but many Black Detroiters saw it as a "rebellion." The scenes of inner-city destruction became indelibly linked to anti-Black stereotypes that characterized the city and its residents as lawless. In fact, more than three-fourths of the forty-three people killed were Black, again primarily by authorities and often motivated by rank prejudice. After the National Guard was rushed in from outside the city, one soldier brazenly proclaimed, "I'm gonna shoot anything that moves and is black." Another guardsmen claimed he mistook a cigarette being lit in a residence for sniper fire. He responded by gunning down Tanya Blanding, a four-year-old Black girl, with a machine gun. In the notorious Algiers Motel incident, three Black teenagers—Carl Cooper, Aubrey Pollard, and Fred Temple—were detained, tortured, and killed, possibly execution style, by police.[18]

Subsidized in a discriminatory manner by government policies such as Federal Housing Administration and Veterans Administration mortgages, white flight to the suburbs gained momentum after World War II, then accelerated in the aftermath of the 1967 uprising. As the populations of the nation's largest cities grew increasingly nonwhite, civil rights and voting rights laws, affirmative action programs, and the loosening of immigration restrictions augured a new era of diversity and multiculturalism. But the political and economic power of the suburbs grew, too, as they often became sites where segregated white spaces were recreated. By 1982, Detroit's mass depopulation and the region's stark Black/white segregation were dramatic. Nearly 90 percent of African Americans in the metropolitan area lived in the city of Detroit. Nearly 90 percent of whites lived in the suburbs. White opponents of integration essentially conceded the city, which some came to regard as a "foreign country." They shifted focus to maintain social control through regional, state, and national politics.[19]

BETWEEN BLACK AND WHITE

"Being different is what makes it difficult," said Detroit police officer Mark Bando, a Japanese American, when interviewed by the *Detroit Free Press* in the aftermath of Chin's murder. Bando described the conundrum he experienced in the starkly divided city. "If you were the only Caucasian in a black neighborhood, they'd terrorize you. If you were the only black in a white neighborhood, same thing. If you're Oriental around here, you don't fit in anywhere."[20]

Although Grace Lee Boggs had been part of an Asian American movement collective and other Asian Americans had joined or supported Black-led activist groups and campaigns, Detroit's small Asian American population had generally stayed on the margins of local politics. In order to gain release from the concentration camps, Japanese Americans who came to the city during World War II were more or less required to pledge that they would quietly assimilate. Government action scattered and disrupted the Chinese American community, too. During the postwar era of "urban renewal," the city's original Chinatown was bulldozed to make way for the Lodge Freeway. Similar redevelopment projects displaced the Black business district on Hastings Street and the residential district in Black Bottom. In the 1960s, the municipal government helped seed a "new" Chinatown in the lower Cass Corridor district, where it also concentrated homeless shelters and "red light" activities. Though elders can be seen there in *Who Killed Vincent Chin?*, the growth of the new Chinatown stalled as longtime residents and newer immigrants settled in the suburbs.[21]

Vincent Chin lived with his mother in a relatively liberal and tolerant city north of Detroit called Oak Park. Like most of suburban Detroit, Oak Park sprouted up during the postwar era as an almost exclusively white bedroom community. But to a greater degree than just about any other suburb in the area, Oak Park's civic leaders came to embrace the concept of racial integration, working cooperatively with civil rights leaders on several occasions beginning in the 1960s. Still majority white, this middle-class suburb would have been viewed by Asian Americans as a relatively welcoming place.[22]

By contrast, Ronald Ebens, Michael Nitz, and their friends inhabited the type of suburban spaces where right-wing populism surged in opposition to the rise of civil rights and Black power in cities like Detroit. Ebens and Nitz lived in East Detroit, which is depicted in *Who Killed Vincent Chin?* with scenes of modest ranch-style houses on quiet tree-lined streets. That city boomed to reach nearly fifty thousand residents between World War II and the 1960s, yet it counted only thirteen Black residents in 1970 and twenty-six in 1980.[23]

Although an incorporated municipality and not a district within the major city, East Detroit was immediately adjacent to Detroit. As sprawling development proceeded to ever more distant places, its proximity to what had become the Blackest big city in the United States coincided with a renewed sense of defensiveness among its now stagnating white population. While some of these white residents of the blue-collar suburbs may have fought to retain their well-paying, unionized jobs in urban factories, they otherwise scorned Detroit. A campaign of racism by disavowal surfaced during the 1980s and early 1990s, animated by the call to change East Detroit's name to "Eastpointe." Though succeeding by majority vote in 1992, the move was a largely unsuccessful marketing ploy to connect the town to the wealthy Grosse Pointe cities. The underlying sentiment was unmistakable.

"We need to rid ourselves of being associated with the crime and slum image of Detroit," George Lawroski, the leader of the renaming campaign, told the *Detroit Free Press* in 1987. "I don't care what the name is, as long as it's not Detroit," he added. "If my name were Hitler, I'd want to change that."[24]

Lawroski was alluding to the common image of the inner city as a space of lawlessness beyond the pale. This pernicious trope led to skyrocketing rates of mass incarceration and severe racial disparities tied to differential sentencing for possession of crack versus powder cocaine. In fact, the illegal drug economy that devastated so many Detroit neighborhoods was in large measure designed for suburban consumption. One report covering the period between 2000 and 2002 revealed that 60 percent of those arrested for drug-related offenses in Detroit came from outside the city. The greatest concentration of drug deals took place along the city's outer borders.[25]

The inner-city strip clubs located at Detroit's entry points were similarly set up to serve suburban men. Vincent Chin and his friends most often frequented the clubs on the northern border, located along 8 Mile Road—the highway cited by rapper Eminem as a symbol of this notorious social and racial divide. On the night of his murder, Chin and his friends first went to Mocombo's Go-Go Club on 8 Mile. But after ordering a couple drinks, they decided the place was too crowded. The Fancy Pants Club, where they ended up, was located farther from the suburbs, in Highland Park, a city that had once enjoyed an abundance of auto industry jobs and stable middle-class households. Vincent and his best friend, Gary Koivu, had grown up there during those more prosperous times. By 1980, Highland Park's median income stood at just $13,180, trailing even impoverished Detroit by roughly 25 percent. The city where Henry Ford's "Crystal Palace" had given birth to the modern assembly line in 1913 was now home to many who had been abandoned by white flight and capital flight.[26]

We need to know Detroit's history of race and class segregation, conflict, and oppression to understand how Vincent Chin and Ronald Ebens came to their tragic meeting. On the surface, it was a perfect storm of bad circumstances.

If only the Golden Star restaurant had been packed with customers when Vincent asked his boss for the night off . . .

If only the club on 8 Mile had been less crowded . . .

If only Vincent had not brought a flask of vodka when they considered moving to the no-alcohol Fancy Pants Club . . .

If only he and Choi had gone inside the McDonald's rather than sitting outside, where they thought their white friends could better see them . . .

If only those friends had found them before Ebens and Nitz did . . .[27]

The speculation can go on endlessly.

If only Jack Morris—the Detroit Tigers' future Hall of Fame pitcher—did not have arguably the worst start of his career . . .

If only the Milwaukee Brewers had not scored ten runs and made the game a blowout by the fourth inning . . .

If only Ebens and Nitz had not turned on the radio and canceled their plans to go to the ballgame after hearing it was a blowout . . .[28]

But more significant patterns underlie these circumstantial facts. In *Who Killed Vincent Chin?*, friend Rich Wagner says he regularly went to the Fancy Pants and various topless bars with Ebens and other "married and very family-oriented people" for "a night out" with "the guys from the plants." Such venues were far less likely to do business in predominantly white suburbs, where NIMBY politics cast them as nuisances. These "family-oriented" men instead crossed the border to inner-city places—more economically dependent on illicit activities—with a "what happens in Vegas stays in Vegas" mentality lubricated by alcohol.

Despite the license such suburban men take when partying in the inner city, Ebens had convinced himself—even after killing Chin—that he was different than the stereotypical Detroiter. "Detroit," he declares near the end of *Who Killed Vincent Chin?* "It's got the reputation 'murder capital of the world.' It's like, and I didn't even do it on purpose. You know, I didn't walk up and shoot somebody."

The image of the upstanding white suburban "family man"—contrasted with dangerous or lawless "others"—is bathed in mythological innocence: One is intentionally violent, while the other is a victim of circumstance. Such thinking goes a long way toward explaining why privileged white men are generally presumed innocent—literally in court and figuratively in other social situations—while people of color, if not outright presumed guilty, are much less likely to receive the benefit of the doubt.

To what extent did suburban whites like Ebens use anti-Detroit language as a dog-whistle form of racism in public, while talking about racism more explicitly behind closed doors? Appearing once again in *Who Killed Vincent Chin?*, Rich Wagner invites us to ponder that question. "Ron's not that way," says the self-identified friend of Ebens. "He's not the type of person that's outward prejudiced. You always might have some little comments or something when you're alone, but he wouldn't go into a bar or public place and really make the kinds of gestures and things that were said during that time."

In support of Ebens, Wagner effectively admitted that he had heard his friend make racially biased or derogatory remarks in private. Nonetheless, he remained convinced (though he was not an eyewitness) that Ebens would never have made "prejudiced" comments toward Vincent Chin in the Fancy Pants Club. "I'm no racist!" Ebens adamantly insists in *Who Killed Vincent Chin?* "I've never been a racist. I've never had anything against anybody in this whole world. And with God as my witness, that's the truth."

We need to weigh the significance of this mythological innocence for our times, when right-wing populism in response to economic restructuring and demographic change has surged further and when a white male vigilante like Kyle Rittenhouse can be hailed by millions as a hero for killing two protesters. Although we can debate for eternity whether Ebens is telling the truth or whether he personally is a racist, it is more productive to understand both the obstacles that must be overcome in order to bring civil rights charges against white anti-Asian assailants and the prevailing factors that would lead a jury of their peers to side with them.

BUILDING A CIVIL RIGHTS CASE

The title *Who Killed Vincent Chin?* challenges viewers of the film to look beyond the immediate act of murder. Because Ronald Ebens admitted in court that he swung the bat that struck Chin, this is not a whodunnit film. Instead, it directs our attention toward what social justice activists and educators at the time would have called institutionalized racism, as well as to the conscious and unconscious biases that may have shaped the thoughts and actions of the killers, bystanders, justice system, media, and jurors.

The sentencing in March 1983, rather than the killing nine months earlier, sparked a national protest movement. Judge Charles Kaufman allowed Ebens and Nitz to avoid jail time by paying a small fine and serving three years on probation. But the differential treatment began soon after the beating. Morris Cotton, a rookie officer who knew racist policing from personal experience in Highland Park, recalled that "it was devastating" to watch Ebens waltz out of the station. His lieutenant took Ebens for an "outstanding citizen" caught up in a "fair fight." As Cotton recounted to author Paula Yoo, "They pulled up, hid behind a pole, and waited with a baseball bat. How was that self-defense?" The scenario reeked of racial bias to him. "I locked up Black people for smoking marijuana, and they were letting the white guy go," he stated. "That really bothered me."[29]

The inconsistencies continued at the arraignment two days after Vincent's death. Judge Kalem Garian was shocked to learn that police had released Ebens and Nitz without cash bond for second-degree murder charges. This would normally have signaled that the police had a weak or nonexistent case. Nevertheless, Garian inexplicably approved "a very, very low" $5,000 bond. A different judge, who presided over the preliminary hearing, told prosecutors that even second-degree murder charges were insufficient for a "willful, deliberate, premeditated killing" that was consistent with first-degree murder. But the principle of prosecutorial discretion prevailed. All this time, the press largely ignored the case. "Everybody walked away from that case, and just let it go through the courts," reporter John Castine admitted. "This is a murder you should've wanted to know more about."[30]

Once Ebens and Nitz pled guilty to manslaughter, Kaufman could have sentenced them to a maximum of fifteen years in prison. Some critics accused him of anti-Asian bias resulting from his detention as a POW by the Japanese military during World War II. But the judge, who led a civil rights support group, self-identified as "a liberal in the avant garde of liberals." When the outcries erupted, Kaufman was stunned and offended. "In all my years, I have never received such vilification," he retorted. "This was just another case. This wasn't anything unusual."[31]

The judge did not need to be motivated by hate or spite to produce a decision clouded by bias. Neither Vincent Chin's family nor any witnesses, including the police officers who made the arrests, were notified of the sentencing hearing. Indeed, though the prosecutor's office stated that this was par for the course, it was galling to Chin's supporters that no one from the prosecution showed up. As a result, the judge listened only to the defense attorneys, who characterized their clients as upstanding and responsibly employed, family-oriented men. They were caught in a brawl only after "Mr. Chin threw the first punch." Ignoring witness accounts indicating that the killers had stalked Chin, their lawyers asserted that Ebens and Nitz were driving to the hospital and came across Chin by chance.[32]

The defendants' self-justifications rang true to the judge. "These weren't the kind of men you send to jail," Kaufman said after the sentencing. "These men are not going to go out and harm somebody else. I just didn't think that putting them in prison would do any good for them or for society. You don't make the punishment fit the crime, you make the punishment fit the criminal."[33]

Even if the judge truly did not negatively stereotype Chin, his lenience in sentencing may have resulted from his positive stereotyping of the killers.

Meanwhile, friends of the Chin family and other members of the Asian American community of metro Detroit began to mobilize. On March 31, 1983, more than one hundred people representing more than twenty community organizations founded the American Citizens for Justice (ACJ), bringing together a diverse and panethnic grouping that included Chinese, Japanese, Filipino, and Korean Americans. In May 1983, they rallied five hundred or more supporters in downtown Detroit, setting the Justice for Vincent Chin campaign in motion. Kin Yee of ACJ called it the largest political demonstration by Asian Americans in Detroit history. The protesters demanded that Ebens and Nitz be resentenced in the interest of justice. But the prosecutor's office disagreed. It affirmed that the sentences fell within normal bounds. There was "no legal authority" to reconsider them.[34]

Having reached a dead end with the county court, ACJ shifted tack to push for federal civil rights charges against Ebens and Nitz. The Civil Rights Act of 1968 would apply if a case could be made that the killers willfully interfered on the basis of race, color, religion, or national origin with Chin's right to engage in one of six federally protected activities, including patronizing a public facility. There was precedent for this strategy, as the Justice Department sometimes intervened when local courts in the South failed to prosecute or convict cases of Klan violence, including the murder of Viola Liuzzo, a white Detroiter who had traveled to Selma to march for civil rights. This "dual prosecution" strategy did not amount to double jeopardy because the defendants were facing different charges. Still, it was exceedingly rare.

Federal guidelines indicated that it was to be deployed only when a serious breakdown had occurred with the state prosecution or when a state conviction resulted in a sentence that evidence demonstrated needed to be enhanced.[35]

The already high bar was elevated further because ACJ could not find a precedent for such charges when the victim was Asian American. Helen Zia, one of ACJ's activist leaders and spokespersons, noted that "some of the most liberal activist attorneys" in the Michigan chapters of the ACLU and the National Lawyers Guild flat out declined to assist. (The latter was overruled by its national organization.) A prominent constitutional law professor from Wayne State University, Robert Sedler, asserted that "Asian Americans cannot seek redress using federal civil rights law." Sedler added, "Asians are considered white." One must wonder if the professor had not read the cases of Takao Ozawa and Bhagat Singh Thind, who were denied the right to naturalized citizenship because the court insisted they were *not* white.[36]

Although the FBI agreed to open an investigation into the Chin murder, federal officials were similarly reluctant to affirm that civil rights laws protected Asian Americans. In fact, the matter remained in doubt through the appeals court ruling, when the three-judge panel dispositively affirmed, "Orientals come within the broad constitutional protections of the Fourteenth Amendment even though the original thrust of the amendments was primarily motivated by concern for the rights of black persons."[37]

Eventually, Zia recounted, federal prosecutors were more willing to pursue charges after confirming that Vincent, a transnational adoptee from China, had become a naturalized U.S. citizen. Given that Asian Americans were a tiny and nearly invisible sector of the Detroit population, we can better appreciate why it was essential for ACJ to garner multiracial support for the Justice for Vincent Chin campaign. Their plan took a step forward on May 18, 1983, when the City of Detroit's Human Rights Commission passed a resolution condemning the "travesty on the justice system" that had occurred with the lenient sentences. Appointed by the city's first Black mayor, Coleman A. Young, its members—with roughly equal Black and white representation—feared that Judge Kaufman had granted "a license for others to kill." The Justice for Vincent Chin campaign ultimately garnered support from a diverse body of organizations that included the NAACP, the Archdiocese of Detroit, the Roundtable of Christians and Jews, Latino-Americans for Social and Economic Development, and the Anti-Defamation League.[38]

Black allies were crucial to ACJ in building an effective coalition centered in Detroit. This required framing Chin's murder as part of a pattern of hate attacks against minoritized groups more broadly. Hailed by Helen Zia as "a dependable supporter at ACJ events," Horace Sheffield Jr. proved pivotal to the advancement of this argument. Appearing on camera in *Who Killed Vincent Chin?*, Sheffield directly connects the "brutal murder" of Chin to the history of racism that "many of us have experienced." He concludes, "Freedom is indivisible." With a reputation as a longtime activist and former director of the Detroit NAACP, Sheffield can symbolically be seen as putting the clout of Detroit's Black civil rights community behind ACJ. As the campaign is shown to be spreading nationally, the filmmakers cut to Jesse Jackson speaking before another well-attended Justice for Vincent Chin event, situating Chin and the concerns of Asian Americans within the rubric of the Rainbow Coalition. "These attacks on Asian Americans," Reverend Jackson once declared, "are no different than the atrocities of the Ku Klux Klan against Blacks in the South." In November 1983, the campaign reached a new milestone, when a federal grand jury indicted Ebens and Nitz for acting to "injure, oppress, threaten and intimidate Vincent Chin . . . because of his race and national origin."[39]

Through the presentation of these prominent Black voices, the filmmakers portrayed Chin as a victim of what federal prosecutors called "a modern-day lynching" using "a bat instead of a rope." Reviewing the court records, it becomes clear that the prosecutors felt compelled to demonstrate that Ebens was bigoted toward African Americans. It is, of course, entirely possible for a white person to harbor anti-Black racism but not commit civil rights violations against an Asian American. But the prosecutors likely thought that such a line of argumentation would sway Black jurors. Moreover, in the face of the defense's continued insistence that Asian Americans were not protected by federal civil rights laws, prosecutors may have assumed that no jury would convict a white defendant unless they could prove he was anti-Black.[40]

This strategy largely worked in the first federal trial, which was held in Detroit. Fortunately for the prosecution, the trial was assigned to Judge Anna Diggs Taylor, a Black woman with a background in civil rights law. Jurors received Ebens's testimony with notable skepticism. The defendant was certain that race played no role in any of the events in question. Witnesses testified that they heard him use the epithets *Nip* and *chink*. Ebens countered that he had never used either slur in his entire life. (Under cross-examination, he admitted he had used *Jap* and *nigger*.) But when asked about details of that night, Ebens claimed, almost uniformly, that he had no recollection. Indeed, he testified that he had no memory of beating Chin with the bat. Although they acquitted Nitz, the jurors found Ebens guilty of violating Chin's civil rights. While the jury cut through layers of embedded racism to make its groundbreaking findings, its ruling could not withstand the broader societal biases working against it.[41]

GETTING AWAY WITH MURDER

When the conviction against Ebens was overturned on appeal, it exposed the catch-22 bind that ACJ had faced. Bringing the federal charges against Ebens and Nitz required convincing the Reagan administration's Department of Justice to discern that Asian Americans were protected by civil rights law and that this specific case was worth prosecuting. As Helen Zia noted, this required—as in the case of civil rights cases generally—public awareness and political organizing. Unfortunately for ACJ and the Chin family, the tactics necessary to bring about the indictments of Ebens and Nitz provided the defendants with grounds for both a successful appeal and a change of venue.

First, the appeals court ruled that the trial should have excluded testimony by Willie Davis, a Black Detroiter who prosecutors expected would provide smoking-gun evidence that Ebens had a history of bigotry. When first tracked down by FBI agents, Davis stated he distinctly remembered being harassed and threatened by Ronald Ebens, circa 1973, in a bar called Jo-Jo's on Detroit's East Side. "What's this black son-of-a-bitch doing in the bar?" Davis alleged Ebens said. "You're in the wrong place. I know what you niggers are doing. You're looking for white women." Ebens had been a regular at Jo-Jo's, then bought the bar and renamed it "Ron's Place." Taking the stand, however, Davis became a reluctant witness and could only recall being threatened by a "man named Ron" who matched the general physical profile of Ebens. Prosecutors asserted that Davis had changed his story after being intimidated by the defense.[42]

Second, as part of ACJ's investigation into the murder, attorney Liza Chan had interviewed numerous witnesses, collecting the pivotal testimony from Racine Colwell documenting Ebens's statement about "you little motherfuckers" putting Americans "out of work." But the defense focused on recordings, obtained through discovery, that Chan made with Chin's friends, who gave varying accounts about whether and when they heard Ebens use racist language. The appeals court ruled that the trial judge had erred by not allowing the defense full use of these recordings.[43]

Third, the publicity that ACJ and its allies generated through its awareness-raising campaign ultimately led the court to approve Ebens's request for a change of venue. Despite lamenting the "public excoriation" of Judge Kaufman, the appeals court had grudgingly affirmed Judge Taylor's original decision to keep the trial in Detroit. The Detroit jurors had been thoroughly screened. Of the 158 in the pool, 90 percent knew something about the murder of Chin and half were immediately dismissed for prejudice. Both sides approved of the jury that was seated without exhausting their peremptory challenges. But Judge Taylor herself ordered that the retrial be moved to Cincinnati. The first trial in Detroit had garnered so much additional media coverage that seating another impartial jury was now impractical.[44]

In part or in whole, these rulings likely made the difference between guilt and acquittal for Ebens. We will never know what was going on in the minds of each juror, but we can examine underlying patterns. Civil rights cases can be difficult for prosecutors and plaintiffs to win because, even when they admit that a defendant has committed a heinous act, defense attorneys have various tactics for denying that the motivation for the act was discriminatory. This is particularly true when they tap into an existing culture of white denial. In northern states like Michigan, whites often clung to the false belief that racism was only a southern problem. What would it mean for Ebens to get a true jury of his peers? Political scientist Stanley Greenberg surveyed whites who lived in the same blue-collar suburbs just outside of Detroit as Ebens. Many, he wrote, "rejected out of hand the social-justice claims of black Americans." More specifically, "They felt no sense of personal or collective responsibility that would support government anti-discrimination and civil rights policies."[45]

Though it was not apparent to viewers of *Who Killed Vincent Chin?*, Starlene was called as a reluctant defense witness. She told FBI investigators that "she did not hear racial remarks made by either the white males or the Oriental males." (She inaccurately described Chin, Choi, and their two white friends as a group of "Oriental males.") In fact, her Blackness was highly relevant to the defense. "She felt as though the white males were not prejudiced," the FBI agent noted, "as she is black and if anyone would have been shown prejudice it would have been her."[46]

But we must also consider the converse of the situation above. Legally, it is entirely possible that someone who does not exhibit any prejudice toward African Americans could commit civil rights violations against an Asian

American. One could and should go a step further and recognize that a white man like Ebens could be sexually turned on and make encouraging comments about Starlene as a topless dancer yet still harbor racist attitudes toward African Americans as a group, as well as toward Starlene as an individual Black woman. Nonetheless, for storytelling purposes, a discourse that was literally and figuratively black-and-white could work in Ebens's favor.

Once the original evidence of Ebens's anti-Black racism was excluded, his defense team could zero in on rebutting the charge that he had committed an anti-Asian civil rights violation—a task made eminently easier by the fact that even progressive attorneys had doubted that civil rights laws applied to Asian Americans. From 2000 to 2014, I taught hundreds of the so-called best and brightest students in southeastern Michigan, and far less than 1 percent of them had ever learned anything meaningful about Asian Americans throughout their entire K–12 education. Now, shift the location to Cincinnati, where Asians comprised less than 1 percent of the metropolitan region and the Asian population was only one-fifth the size of Detroit's. And in the 1980s, the potential jurors had attended school as early as the 1910s and 1920s. The chance of the average juror having any consciousness of discrimination against Asian Americans falls to just about nil.[47]

Living in East Detroit, Ebens asserted that he had no connection to Asian Americans. "Do you see any Asian-Americans around here?" Ebens asked a reporter after his acquittal. "I don't even know them. I don't know what their plight is. I've never been around them." Despite citing his lack of interaction with Asian Americans as evidence of his innocence, Ebens most likely had chosen to live in a place constructed to be nearly all white by design. Asians comprised only 0.5 percent of that city's population as late as 1990.[48]

Ebens's lawyers maintained that the entire claim of anti-Asian bias was fabricated. Such purportedly false claims, they argued, "cheapen the legitimate claims of racial discrimination and racial violence." In practice, all they needed to do was cast reasonable doubt. They played recordings for the jury that, they argued, revealed attorney Liza Chan coaching Chin's friends to say they heard Ebens use specific racial epithets. "I'm not accusing people of perjury," defense attorney Frank Eaman said, "I'm just saying their memories were helped." He believed the tapes proved pivotal.[49]

And perhaps he was right. But countering that perspective is the anonymous juror from the Detroit trial interviewed in *Who Killed Vincent Chin?* She said that the jury found Racine Colwell to be the most credible witness and discounted the testimony of Chin's friends. To repeat, Colwell never testified that she heard explicit racial slurs, but she was confident that Ebens said, "It's because of you little motherfuckers that we're out of work." This suggests that a key difference between the two trials was that jurors in Detroit were more prepared to see the racist overtones in that remark than those in Cincinnati. Whites in Ohio shared much of the anti-Japan sentiment found in Michigan—some slit tires and threw rocks at cars on the lots of Japanese-brand dealerships—while having little or no exposure to the antiracist education carried out by the multiracial coalition of supporters in the Chin movement.[50]

Is it more fair and objective to hold a trial in a location where the population is less racially diverse and knows or cares far less about an alleged racist crime? The same questions arose when the police officers who killed the Black teenagers in the Algiers Motel, mentioned earlier, had their state trial moved from Detroit to the 99 percent white town of Mason, Michigan. Their federal conspiracy trial was relocated to Flint, but all the Black members of the jury pool were excluded on the grounds that they would inherently identify with the victims. In both cases, juries found the officers not guilty. After four Los Angeles Police Department officers were caught on video repeatedly beating Rodney King, their trial was sent to the distant city of Simi Valley, home of the Reagan Library and known for its conservative, pro-police orientation. The predominantly white jury declined to convict any of the four officers in 1992.[51]

What might appear fair and balanced on the surface, in court, can simply reproduce and reinforce systemic racism.

THE POSTINDUSTRIAL "MANHOOD" PROBLEM

"Chin was defending not his race but his manhood," lawyer Frank Eaman told jurors.[52]

Here lay another central argument of Ebens's defense team. The lawyer elaborated on this point in *Who Killed Vincent Chin?* "Ron Ebens is guilty of having too much to drink, being a macho man who wouldn't back down from a fight and wanted to avenge . . . his stepson," said Eaman. "He's guilty of letting himself go too far and killing somebody with a baseball bat—a serious crime no doubt. He's not guilty of doing this because of racial animus or racial feelings or racial bias or racial prejudice. It so happens the person he was involved with was Chinese."

Inadvertently, this passage helps us understand why racist violence often involves men attacking other men. When we break down the logic of Ebens's defense team, it is specious but straightforward: If the conflict between Ebens and Chin was rooted in gender, then it could not be motivated by race. As scholars and activists going back decades have argued, however, race and gender—as well as class, sexuality, disability, and all structures of difference—operate in an overlapping rather than mutually exclusive fashion. When we dissect Ebens's gendered comments, they correlate with the actions of a white man trying to put an Asian man in his place, particularly when one points out the obvious: The altercation began in a strip club where men were competing for the attention of topless female dancers. Ebens called Chin a "boy" and "little fucker." He later characterized Chin's friend Jimmy Choi as a "little pest."

Of course, he would never admit such a connection. "This black girl dancing was a knockout, OK?" Ebens told the *Detroit Free Press*. "Now if you think Mike and I are going to be sitting there making comments about the car industry with her dancing there, well, you got to be some kind of wimp. I mean, get serious." He wants us to believe he would never allow racial comments or concern with industrial jobs to get in the way of a true performance of masculinity. Anyone who thinks otherwise is a "wimp." After Ebens claimed he was "upset at Chin for discriminating against the black dancer by giving her the smaller tip," the reporter sarcastically characterized him as "acting as sort of a one-man civil rights commission at the Fancy Pants." But Ebens pushed things even further. In conjunction with his elation at having been acquitted, he sarcastically remarked, "About all that's left to charge me with now is rape." Rape would, in his view, be just as obviously bogus a charge as the civil rights violations were. His quip betrayed a cavalier attitude about both sexism and racism, as unsubstantiated charges of rape—notably against white women—have been at the center of lynchings and persecution of men of color.[53]

To unpack this exchange, we must understand how race, class, gender, and sexuality were inextricably bound together for white men in the industrial era. During the middle decades of the twentieth century, marking the height of American industry and empire, the "common man" was heralded by patriarchal and heteronormative culture as a provider and protector of the family. As feminist author Susan Faludi argued in her 1999 bestseller *Stiffed: The Betrayal of the American Man*, these "bedrock concepts of American manhood" were rooted in an industrial culture in which men worked with their hands, were household breadwinners, and fought gallant wars on behalf of the world's undisputed economic titan. The privileged notion of "manhood" as provider and protector, especially in the case of white men, licensed both domestic violence within the patriarchal household and state violence when the "common man" wore a police or military uniform in public. Ebens and his defense team tapped into these dominant tropes when they asserted that he was defending both Starlene and his stepson from Chin.[54]

But the deal was undone. Once global finance capital reigned supreme, deindustrialization brought about a "categorical shift" in reality: The market share of American manufacturers plummeted, women demanded workplace equality, and wars from Korea onward brought neither victory nor honor. After soaring during the post–World War II period, the real wages of U.S. men began to decline in the 1970s. "A social pact between the nation's men and its institutions was collapsing, most prominently but not exclusively within the institutions of work," wrote Faludi. "The boy who had been told he was going to be the master of the universe and all that was in it found himself master of nothing." Previously defined by character and internal fortitude in a "society of utility," the new version of so-called manhood became a commoditized spectacle in a world defined by "ornamental culture." Faludi concluded, "As men's utilitarian qualities were dethroned, as their societal roles diminished, violence more and more came to serve as the gang leader for a host of rogue masculine traits."[55]

While the violence Ebens committed, ostensibly in the name of protecting others, was all too real, the notion of manhood that Ebens's defense attorney invoked was entirely performative. And does anyone doubt that the patrons of strip clubs are performing an alter ego as much as the dancers on stage?

Theorists of performance like Judith Butler, renowned for her queer approach to the study of gender and sexuality, emphasize that sex, gender, and race are not biological facts. There is no concept of "male" or "female" that exists independent of the way society defines these terms. Rather than representing fixed essences, such identities are produced and reproduced through the actions we take to give them meaning. For instance, by foregrounding and parodying the illusory and malleable notion of gender, drag performers are giving us the truest account of how concepts of gender and sexuality are constructed. It is necessary to point out, however, that individuals cannot construct or change social categorizations by themselves. We live within systems in which dominant structures manifest power and oppression.[56]

The would-be Golden Age of American industry, capitalism, and empire was rooted in assumptions of white dominance—so too were hegemonic notions of manhood. Indeed, all were interconnected. The jobs, neighborhoods, schools, and institutions that sustained these notions of manhood were almost uniformly restricted to whites. The flipside is that both foreign and American men of color—unless they remained in a subordinate position—could quickly be taken as threats to white "manhood," particularly as the acceleration of globalization, immigration, and racial integration coincided with deindustrialization.

Inside the Fancy Pants Club, Ebens experienced an immediate and localized version of this "crisis of manhood." And his failed performance came on a public stage. The preponderance of evidence indicates that Chin won the fight. Furthermore, by the way Ebens belittled Chin, we can presume with some confidence that he never expected this anonymous and slight-framed Asian American man, weighing all of 149 pounds, to physically confront him.[57]

In *Who Killed Vincent Chin?*, Ebens scoffs at what he characterizes as ACJ's opportunistic use of the Chin murder to address the "alleged plight" of Asian Americans. "The only ones I had ever met are the ones in the Chinese restaurants," he says, "and they were always nice and I was always nice to them." His recollection of real-life Asians was limited to "nice" persons whose job it was to serve him, an image in line with a stereotype of Asian Americans as docile. But Chin was an actual Chinese restaurant worker who defied the "model minority" image by fighting him.

As such, Ebens felt compelled to describe the fight in a manner that affirmed his white masculinity. Chin came over, he says in the film, and "sucker punched" him. In other words, Chin did not fight like a real man. He lodged the equivalent of a so-called sneak attack, reminiscent of Japan's bombing of Pearl Harbor and its trade war. After both parties were removed from the club, says Ebens, Chin persisted in challenging him, saying, "Come on you chicken shits, let's fight some more." This is when Ebens went to get the bat, unwilling to fight Chin barehanded and perhaps rationalizing this disparity through his contention that Chin's purported "sucker punch" had first violated the prevailing rules of war and "manhood."

Ebens describes what finally pushed him completely over the edge: "We seen Vincent and Jimmy [Choi] standing in front of McDonald's. They were sitting there laughing. All I could think was 'They're laughing. They really put one over on us.'"

He says he cannot explain what happened next. It was as if an "audible click" went off in his head just before he administered the blows. But he wanted everyone to know that it was not in his nature to be racist or violent.

"I am not the way I've been made out to be," he told the *Detroit Free Press*. "I'm easy, you know. I'm a pushover. I'm a pussycat." He was not the kind of bellicose guy that "just goes down clearing the streets of Asians." In fact, there were hundreds of Americans, mostly white and "family-oriented" men, who did just that in wars with Japan, Korea, and Vietnam.[58]

When interviewed by the FBI, Ebens's ex-wife vouched that he was "not a violent person." But there was, she indicated, a notable exception. After filing for divorce, she returned home, where Ebens was unexpectedly waiting for her. Since they had already separated, she told him to leave. Ebens then punched her in the mouth. In truth, she said, Ebens was a "hot-tempered" man. The confidential psychiatric report produced for the court prior to sentencing went further: "Behind the easygoing demeanor that this defendant attempts to portray lies an extremely hostile and explosive individual when confronted with stressful situations."[59]

There are clear parallels to these "stressful situations." Ebens had his sense of white manhood thrown into crisis by a white woman and an Asian American man. And his "easygoing demeanor" quickly turned into a violent outbreak. In both cases, regardless of what we can know or conclude about his individual motive, Ebens's behavior reflected a hegemonic culture of toxic white masculinity that has for too long permitted, or even rewarded, perpetration of such violence. That is why our takeaways must necessarily depart from those of the judicial process.

To prove motivation in civil rights and hate crime cases, one must often produce smoking-gun signs of hatred or bigotry, usually through evidence that overt racial epithets or ethnic slurs were used. But beyond the courtroom, the use and tolerance of offensive language is most commonly a symptom—not a cause—of systemic racism and oppression. When individuals perform identities, it is not necessary for them to utter the epithets to sustain and reinforce the underlying structures of power. Indeed, much of the power of these structures lies in their ability to make the oppressor and oppressed conform to them by habit and custom without anyone having to say or draw attention to the fact they are doing so.

It is abhorrent to scapegoat Vincent Chin or any person for the unemployment and economic problems created by a system governed by transnational corporations. But it is short-sighted to fixate on Ronald Ebens, Judge Kaufman, or any individual if we want to confront or transform these systems of power.

SEVEN

White Grievance and the Rise of the Counterrevolution

From the day he killed Vincent Chin through the end of his trials, Ronald Ebens repeatedly refused to give extended interviews to the press. For five years, he turned away scores of journalists, deeming them "a bunch of jerks" and saying "to hell with them." In *Who Killed Vincent Chin?*, Ebens can be seen berating a group of Japanese reporters for trying to "put words in my mouth."

Following countless phone calls to him and his lawyers, he finally opened up to a thirty-three-year-old writer for the *Detroit Free Press* in 1987. "This is your chance to tell your side of the story," the reporter impressed upon Ebens.[1]

So who was the persistent young journalist who scored this major interview? His name was Michael Moore.

Yes, *that* Michael Moore. He was not yet famous (*Roger and Me*, his breakout film about the impact of GM's downsizing on Flint, came out the following year) and there is no verbal mention of him in *Who Killed Vincent Chin?* Nearly four decades later, prompted by the Atlanta spa shootings, Moore jogged his memory of that time. The activist filmmaker described the Ebens story as one of the most important he has ever told, noting that he was moved to pursue the interview not only by the miscarriage of justice he had witnessed, but also by Ebens's strident refusal to acknowledge that the killing was racially motivated.

"I wanted him to say the things that he really wanted to say," Moore recalled in March 2021, "things that he had held back on." It had taken months of back and forth with Ebens and his lawyer before they met. "I was surprised he did not have his lawyer present," he said, "and it was just he and I sitting in his living room for an hour or two."

"And he let loose. I was surprised at how bold he was," Moore acknowledged—though, having known many white men in Michigan, he immediately added, "but then again not."[2]

One can just picture the iconic Moore egging Ebens on with an early test run of his regular-Joe brand of interviewing. And his piece conveyed this in words. "If he [Ebens] got through all of this without a scratch," Moore wrote, recalling the mass protests and serial trials, "what harm can an interview do?"

This was phrased as a rhetorical question. Whether or not Moore posed it directly to Ebens, he convinced the killer to let his guard down. Apparently pleased with the interview, Ebens said goodbye to Moore, shaking his hand firmly with one hand and giving him "a big, friendly squeeze" with the other. "Now, I don't look like some killer, do I?" Ebens asked.

August 30, 1987: The cover of the Sunday magazine of the *Detroit Free Press*, the region's most widely read newspaper, blared: "THE MAN WHO KILLED VINCENT CHIN: By Michael Moore." Featuring pictures of Ebens and Chin, the cover quoted Ebens as saying that Chin "was looking for trouble and got it."

Ebens would eventually find company among legions of regretful Moore interviewees. Feeling comfortable, justified, and entitled to reveal both his prejudices and his sense of self-righteousness to a seemingly sympathetic white male, he put forward without any reservation his charge that he was the victim of so-called reverse racism.

Inside, Moore's story bore another headline, "THE WAGES OF DEATH." It opened with his characterization of Ebens as "elated" that the "system has worked to his advantage."

"That's it, it's over!" declared Ebens in the aftermath of his federal acquittal. "Done. Finished. Over! Yeah!"

Moore wrote, "He can barely contain his excitement, sounding like a fan whose baseball team has just won the pennant," a not-so-subtle reference to the Louisville Slugger murder weapon.

Later in the interview, Moore evoked from Ebens the exact sort of self-contradictory statements that thousands of viewers of *Who Killed Vincent Chin?* would come to see as thinly veiled racism. "Everybody has some racist feelings," Ebens stated, "you, the Chinese, everyone. I can't honestly say I harbor any feelings against any ethnic group, OK? That doesn't mean I want to live with them, OK?"

This was no dog whistle. A person who does not want to live with or near others because of their ethnicity fits the textbook definition of a bigot.

While Ebens and Nitz were found not guilty by the American justice system, they are still being judged in the court of public opinion. One of the most enduring tragedies of *Who Killed Vincent Chin?* is that we never get to hear Vincent's voice or any audio or video recording of him. Instead, the person taking up much of the screen time is his killer. The filmmakers' editorial decision helps us see how white denial functions at the center of systemic racism. Indeed, we need to go a step further to see how both the murder of Chin and the acquittal of his killers were driven by a deep sense of white grievance and victimhood in the face of perceived threats from "others" and corruption from within. Foreign and nonwhite rivals were deemed a threat to the traditional order. The implementation of civil rights laws was cast as harmful to white men.

When screening *Who Killed Vincent Chin?* for a new audience, it is always breathtaking to see and hear the visceral responses of those who are just learning about this tragedy. One of the most common reactions is, "Why have I never learned about this before?" An Asian American student at the University of Michigan once told me, "I feel like my whole education up to this point has been a lie."

The urgency of the film for these viewers most frequently translates into rage at Ronald Ebens. For all the power of Lily Chin's uncontrollable sobbing and steadfast determination to avenge her son's death, or Helen Zia's dauntless arguments against racism and calls to organize, it is Ebens's utter remorselessness and brazen claims that he is being unfairly persecuted that often prove most memorable and most infuriating. Viewers do a double take when Ebens laments the one night he was detained in a local jail, agonizing over how "there is no blankets, there is no mattress, there is no pillows, there is nothing there but a steel cot and that's what you get through the night on." But they recoil in disgust when Ebens, searching for words to explain what led him to batter Chin, concludes, "It's just like this was preordained to be."

How can we best appreciate the significance of this story in the aftermath of Donald Trump's presidency and his constant appeals to white nationalism, toxic masculinity, xenophobia, and so-called reverse racism? With China replacing Japan as the rival to U.S. economic hegemony, Asian Americans have served as convenient scapegoats once again. But in light of the perpetual victimhood espoused by Trump and his supporters, it becomes easier to see how Ronald Ebens saw himself—rather than Chin—as the true martyr. The white male grievance that Ebens harbored has fueled the rise of the MAGA counterrevolution.

This chapter connects the history of anti-Asian violence to the right-wing resurgence in the aftermath of the civil rights movement and the Vietnam War. First, the agitation of the Nixon, Reagan, and Trump years pushed white people like Ronald Ebens, especially but not only men, to see themselves as victims of a government and society that had been captured by the radical left. These "culture wars" against the so-called excesses of the 1960s served as a strategic front in the drive to sway working-class and middle-class whites to embrace a neoliberal agenda that shifted the balance of power back to big business and finance capital.

Second, while many on the right espoused libertarian ideals of freedom, the far right's actual political appeals fed on hostility and demonization. Casting Southeast Asian refugees as the embodiment of societal corruption and the illegitimacy of the federal government, a new wave of white nationalist groups sprang up. It pushed the boundaries of mainstream political discourse into areas previously deemed extreme while inciting overt racism and violence. As their populations grew during the 1980s and 1990s, Southeast Asian refugees were repeatedly targeted with intimidation and violence, problems compounded by their settlement in economically challenged areas where social tensions were already high. At the same time, some of the most critical instances of anti-Asian violence involved refugees, who were veterans and survivors of armed conflict, resisting or using deadly force against their tormentors.

Third, whereas minoritized groups perceived a hostile backlash to the pursuit of equality, white nationalists asserted they were defending the American way of life and armed themselves to the teeth in preparation for civil war. What one side called racist violence, the other framed as self-defense. Although the right invoked the image of Asians as a "model minority" out of political expediency, in actuality many Asian American communities were treated as an alien threat.

The tragic result was that there would be many more victims of anti-Asian violence following the murder of Vincent Chin.

"COLOR-BLIND RACISM" AND THE COUNTERREVOLUTION

When Michael Moore came to the home of Vincent Chin's killer for an interview, Ebens was quick to point out that East Detroit was *not the east side of Detroit*. "No way," he protested. "We're like Roseville." Although Ebens worked in a Detroit plant, he did not reside in the city. Indeed, Ebens lived in the suburban county that came to symbolize hostility to civil rights during the 1980s.[3]

To ensure that this telling statement does not pass as a side comment, we need to examine the political role that cities like East Detroit and Roseville—both situated to the north and east of Detroit, in Macomb County—played in the rise of "color-blind racism." As noted previously, these residents of white blue-collar suburbs coveted highly compensated, unionized jobs in Detroit plants, but they often had no desire to live in the now Black majority city. While the inner city and university campuses became seedbeds for the New Left, these suburbs made by white flight provided a base for Richard Nixon's "Silent Majority" and the emergence of the New Right. They called school busing "forced integration"—an attack on the sanctity of the family and individual freedoms. They rallied under the banner of "law and order" for militarized policing, mass incarceration, and expansive gun ownership. But justice for some came at the expense of suffering for others.[4]

An overarching culture of white grievance arose to condemn the perceived threats of liberal governance and left-wing activism, leading much of the white middle and working classes to switch their votes to the Republicans, who had long been known as the party of big business. The GOP not only dominated most of the presidential elections between 1968 and 1988; they also shifted the national debate and policy toward a pro-corporate agenda that gutted government programs of the New Deal era. Seen in context, Ebens's portrayal of himself as a white victim of Asian American protesters and federal prosecutors emblematized the advance of the New Right social movement in the age of Reagan.

By 2008, the nation seemed miraculously to have turned the corner. Barack Obama's election filled his supporters with the audacity of hope. Within eight months of his inauguration, however, Grace Lee Boggs warned that we were in a moment of "great danger" that was "much more comparable to that of Germany in the Thirties than to anything that the American people have experienced up to now."[5]

What could explain this disjunction?

The threat, Boggs asserted, came from the "counterrevolution" aiming to roll back social progress and impede the true potential of a democratic nation. "Rooted in race, and the search for the American Dream, it began at the end of World War II when white people moved to the suburbs to escape blacks in cities like Detroit," she explained. "Taking with them their schools, their businesses and their taxes, they impoverished the cities and attracted the attention and money of extreme right-wingers like the Koch brothers." The economic crisis of the Rust Belt and the decline of America's "global dominance," Boggs noted, signaled "the end of the American Dream." In response, suburban places like Macomb County became "increasingly reactionary"— rife with resentful voters who believed that the White House belonged to the white race and clamored to take their country back.[6]

As the counterrevolution laid the groundwork for Donald Trump's call to "Make America Great Again," a "new" form of racism coincided with the rise of a right-wing economic and political framework known as "neoliberalism." A reaction to the progressive advances of the 1960s, the neoliberal agenda prioritized the drive to dismantle the nation's safety net, eliminate government regulations, and boost corporate power. With Wall Street's portfolios and influence dramatically expanding, companies sought to cut labor costs and protect profits through automation, outsourcing, union busting, and casualization (i.e., gaining flexibility by replacing permanent, full-time employees with temporary and part-time workers). While some members of the United Auto Workers maintained good wages and benefits, they enjoyed a relatively privileged status that became the exception rather than the standard for workers nationwide. Whereas workers' productivity and their incomes had both nearly doubled between 1948 and 1973, the typical U.S. worker's income suddenly stagnated, despite the continued growth in productivity. But the effects were highly uneven. Wages for the wealthiest Americans shot up while workers at the bottom saw their incomes decline. When adjusted for inflation, the federal minimum wage peaked in the 1960s. And although the gender gap still exists, women's wages have risen while men's wages have fallen. The most significant, protracted wage declines occurred between the late 1970s and mid-1990s, a period that coincided with a surge in reports of anti-Asian violence.[7]

To rationalize the new disparities, right-wing proponents of the "culture wars" drummed up white middle- and working-class fear and resentment directed at foreign competition, immigrants, inner-city crime, civil rights, and feminism. Coming on the heels of the rebellions of the 1960s, the recession of the late 1970s marked the end of the New Deal era, which had coincided with unprecedented growth and prosperity for Macomb County and its blue-collar residents. Between 1940 and 1970, the county's population soared from 107,638 to 625,309. It drew thousands of factory jobs away from Detroit yet remained virtually all white. In the early 1960s, with Macomb

County residents generally crediting Democratic policies and politicians for these gains, it was "the most Democratic suburban county in the country." By 1970, however, the "whitelash" against civil rights was well afoot. The county's largest city, Warren, aroused national attention and scorn when its residents vocally rejected a multi-million-dollar federal grant for housing and economic development because acceptance required signing a pledge of non-discrimination. When former Michigan governor George Romney, now secretary of Housing and Urban Development under President Nixon, came to Warren to explain that this was a "win-win" offer, he was physically chased away by a white mob yelling "Hell no!" Much like those who denounced school busing programs, these whites revolted against what they deemed "forced integration."[8]

By the 1980s, Detroit and its suburbs were fighting for pieces of a shrinking pie. Deindustrialization, automation, and outsourcing now consumed the entire region. Between 1979 and 1982, Macomb County lost 21 percent of its manufacturing jobs, raising the unemployment rate to 15.3 percent by March 1981. The erosion of what the white middle class had come to know as the "American Dream" went hand in hand with the fracturing of the New Deal coalition. In 1984, white residents of Macomb County embraced Ronald Reagan's reelection to such a degree that political scientist Stanley Greenberg drew principally on data and private interviews with this specific population in attempting to make sense of the Reagan Democrat phenomenon. These white middle- and working-class voters did not simply stop voting for Democratic candidates; they blamed liberalism as the cause of both their personal woes and the ills of the nation writ large. "For these white suburban residents," Greenberg found, "the terms *blacks* and *Detroit* were interchangeable. The city was a place to be avoided—where the kids could not go, where the car got stolen, and where vacant lots and dissolution have replaced their old neighborhoods." Virulent anti-Detroit and anti-Black sentiments were two sides of the same coin.[9]

In the public discourse of the New Right, however, it was possible to separate these noxious stereotypes of Detroit as a majority-Black city from the problem of racism, which whites, especially outside of the South, were more likely to associate with the old hatreds and absolute forms of denigration and exclusion that occurred under slavery and Jim Crow. In a 1990 interview, for instance, when asked about the views of his white suburban peers, Macomb County commissioner and public relations executive Richard Sabaugh stressed that "the attitude isn't as much racist as one of fear," implying the legitimacy of the latter but not of the former. "People don't see every black as bad," he said, as if that were a requirement for racism to exist. "But the image of Detroit is of a decaying, crime-ridden city headed by a mayor who makes racist remarks. We view the values of people in Detroit as completely foreign. To us it's like a foreign country and culture."[10]

When discussing a complaint that the East Detroit police had failed to hire African Americans, Ronald Ebens told Michael Moore that affirmative action was necessary only in "some place like down in Alabama where they have been passed over just because they were black." He believed that affirmative action had led "to the other extreme where they [Black workers] are promoted over the white guy who has a higher score and stuff, and I don't think that's right at all." Sociologist Eduardo Bonilla-Silva has described this post-1960s development as "racism without racists." Whites have willingly embraced dog-whistle and institutionalized forms of "color-blind racism," while vehemently denying that they are openly racist or even complicit in systemic racism. If there was nothing racial in depictions of Detroit as a "foreign country," then it was no stretch to see Japan-bashing as an acceptable form of American patriotism.[11]

Quixotically, some on the right were more than ready to invoke Vincent Chin as a "model minority" victim in a twisted attack on affirmative action and so-called liberal handouts. Reagan's appointee to chair the U.S. Civil Rights Commission, Clarence Pendleton, highlighted the case in a 1985 interview. "Look at that guy Chin, Vincent Chin in Detroit," he said. "He got beat to death just because of his pigment." Pendleton was a Black conservative who argued that "so-called black leaders" comprised the "new racists" who were keeping African Americans dependent on quotas and government programs as a modern form of slavery. He invoked the racist murder of Chin in his portrayal of Asian Americans as people who never complained but who succeeded in the "bootstraps" manner. "They made it, didn't they," Pendleton declared. "But they didn't ask for no government help. They didn't ask for no bilingual education. They didn't ask for no government programs." In reality, aside from ACJ pushing the federal government to intervene in the Chin case, Chinese American activism led to the Supreme Court's *Lau v. Nichols* decision establishing the right to bilingual education, and Japanese Americans were leading a push for reparations from the U.S. government that would be signed into law by Reagan.[12]

Ever since the landslide Republican victories of the 1980s, progressives have been struggling to develop a political response that addresses the concerns of minoritized groups without falling into a narrow framework of "identity politics." When we take a closer look, a deeper connection between race and class can be seen at the heart of the Justice for Vincent Chin coalition. Helen Zia has stressed that "cross-racial partnerships with key Black organizations and leaders in Detroit and nationally" proved to be "instrumental in ACJ's multiracial, multicultural outreach efforts." National leaders like Jesse Jackson and Detroit's Horace Sheffield saw fighting all forms of racism and discrimination as crucial to building a multiracial coalition, including white blue-collar workers, to continue the progress of the labor and civil rights movements. Jackson's Rainbow Coalition strategy explicitly sought to build unity between diverse civil rights supporters and trade unions by challenging corporate power. During the 1988 presidential campaign, Jackson won the Michigan Democratic caucus with 55 percent of the vote, consciously offering autoworkers a progressive path forward. Sheffield had a history of fighting racism within the plant and organizing autoworkers through the left-leaning United Auto Workers Local 600.[13]

They sent a clear message: When workers scapegoat racial minorities or foreigners, they are doing the work of the bosses and capitalists. Black leaders like Jackson and Sheffield advanced solidarity with Asian Americans to achieve justice not only in the Chin case but through a broader movement addressing the new facets of oppression and inequity in the age of neoliberalism.

BRINGING THE WAR HOME

No one is born in their homeland wanting to become a refugee; my family had to flee Viet Nam because of the militarism and destruction that America brought upon us, and that view of us as an enemy followed my uncle to death's door.

This statement was issued by the niece of Thong Hy Huynh during the 2021 surge in anti-Asian violence. In May 1983, Huynh was one of the first Vietnamese students to attend Davis High School in the college town of Davis, California (west of Sacramento), which was then predominantly white. Week after week, he and a handful of refugees endured harassment from a much larger group of white students. Words turned to fisticuffs. Huynh's friend Bon Chau scuffled with one of the white boys. James "Jay" Pierman left to retrieve a large "military-type" knife. When he returned,

Pierman stabbed Huynh to death. Although she did not see the lethal attack, teacher Grace Kim had observed Pierman bullying Vietnamese students on an almost daily basis without reprieve. Outside agitators from the xenophobic "White Student Union" lionized the killer. Yet his attorney insisted that Pierman was "not a racist." He had even dated a Korean girl one time! Backing up the narrative of the defense, the school's principal stated, "I'm not aware that it was a racially sparked incident." This may have factored into Pierman's conviction for manslaughter rather than murder. Huynh's family and friends, however, were outraged that his killer was sentenced to a mere six years in juvenile detention. In the mind of his niece, there was no doubt that "anti-Asian discrimination" had motivated the murder: "To refute this is to deny the ugly existence of racism that has pervaded through centuries of systemized white supremacy; to turn a blind eye is a political statement in and of itself."[14]

Thong Hy Huynh's murder was part of an appalling trend that was sweeping the nation. Vietnamese and Southeast Asian refugees bore far more than the brunt of the cyclical xenophobia that surges with each new wave of migration or economic dislocation. They became convenient targets of the anger, frustration, and resentment that hung in the air following the Vietnam War. The intense debates and protests over the war shattered the repressive consensus of the 1950s and left irreparable tears in the nation's social fabric. Arguably even more palpable than the polarization loomed the ignoble specter of defeat. The dogged resistance of tens of thousands of guerrilla fighters and supportive villagers had forced the domineering superpower to withdraw in shame. In concert with the "whitelash" against civil rights and the so-called crisis of masculinity, war-inspired hatreds and resentments fueled a toxic culture of late imperial grievance.

Around New Year's Day in 1984, James Oliver Huberty moved west from Ohio. Leaving behind a troubled life, the forty-one-year-old white man looked to start anew in San Diego. By mid-July, however, things had begun to unravel once again. He lost his job as a condo security guard and vowed to take revenge—not on his employer, but on the broader society he believed had failed him. On the afternoon of July 18, 1984, Huberty entered a McDonald's in San Ysidro, California, a municipality near the U.S.-Mexico border. The *Los Angeles Times* described him as wearing "a Vietnam-style jungle camouflage suit and carrying three weapons—a pistol, a shotgun and a semi-automatic rifle." Huberty methodically fired his weapons, one by one, at patrons and workers. He emptied each gun, then reloaded and fired again until he was shot and killed by a police officer. The total dead numbered twenty-one. The newspaper called it "the worst mass-slaying in U.S. history." (While the scale of the tragedy was undeniable, that statement seemed to defy historical facts. It was perhaps an estimate of the greatest toll one non-military shooter had ever taken in one incident.) Seventeen were shot inside the restaurant and four in the parking lot and adjacent playground. Nearly all were Latino. Most were children. Witnesses heard him scream, "I killed thousands in Vietnam and I want to kill more!"[15]

Initial media reports named Huberty as a veteran. This proved to be unfounded. Instead of an explicit example of combat-related PTSD, the San Ysidro tragedy served to demonstrate how much the wartime hatred and violence had been internalized by the entire U.S. population. The Vietnam War proved to be the defining event for millions of baby boomers coming of age in the 1960s and early 1970s. While the concept of "bringing the war home" began as a slogan of U.S. antiwar radicals seeking to disrupt the bourgeois social order, it ultimately took root among the far right. As historian Kathleen Belew has documented, a sense of resentment and betrayal fueled the rise of a new "white power" movement. White nationalists and paramilitary groups recruited men who felt that the U.S. government and military had sold them out, resulting not only in defeat on the battlefield in Vietnam, but also in a loss of pride and the loss of the American nation itself. This was the same government, they insisted, that had declared war on white men while uplifting women's rights and civil rights. It was thus incumbent on real men to fight back. Bringing the war home was not metaphorical. Taking advantage of lenient gun regulations, white power groups heavily armed themselves and plotted to overthrow the federal government. But as they recruited their shock troops, these groups did not provoke an immediate showdown with the state. Instead, they chose public targets to win more adherents and inject white nationalist ideas into political debate.[16]

The scapegoating of Asians, centered on animosity toward refugees, became an integral component of white power agitation. One of the principal groups to emerge from this period was David Duke's Knights of the Ku Klux Klan, based in Louisiana, which built broader bases of support in Texas, North Carolina, and Southern California. Reflecting the direct and indirect effects of this racist crusade, hate-related attacks on Asians occurred in all those places. The Texas Klan branch, led by Louis Beam, injected itself into one of the first public conflagrations between whites and Vietnamese refugees. The recession of the late 1970s created hardships for fishermen in

Seadrift, Texas, on the Gulf of Mexico. Diane Wilson—the only female sea captain in the town—saw that toxic pollution from the burgeoning petro-chemical plants was poisoning the waters, with devastating effects on the fisheries. White fishermen, however, focused more on recently arrived refugees as unfair competitors. Many of their leaders joined or allied with the Klan. Like the white labor unions who denounced Chinese immigrants as "coolies" during the exclusion era, they saw Southeast Asian refugees as pawns of more powerful forces in a conspiracy to hold down white citizens. Refugee communities, the Klan insisted, had been infiltrated by the Viet Cong with the aid of the U.S. government. They posed a public health menace and a threat to white womanhood.[17]

Sau Van Nguyen was not drafted by the South Vietnamese marines until the end of the war. That brief service was enough for him to fear retribution by the communists after the fall of Saigon. He fled by boat with family and joined the growing Vietnamese community in Seadrift, on San Antonio Bay near Corpus Christi. There, Nguyen became one of many refugees accused of violating the unwritten rules of the sea by putting crab buckets in places whites had claimed for themselves. Billy Joe Aplin, who had joined the Klan, told friends he wanted to "get rid of all the damn gooks." Racist slurs were commonplace, but sometimes they led to violence. In August 1979, Aplin confronted Nguyen, cavalierly mistaking him for a newly arrived Vietnamese fisherman with whom he had recently quarreled. He slashed Nguyen across the chest with a knife, pushed him to the ground, and beat him. "Leave Seadrift!" Aplin exclaimed. "If you don't, I'll shoot you in the open sea!" Nguyen then shot him twice. Tried for murder, he claimed self-defense and was found not guilty—perhaps surprisingly—by an all-white jury in a sun-down town. Drawing national attention, the Klan descended on Seadrift and called for the Vietnamese community to be driven out of town. Most refugees, comprising more than 10 percent of the town's population, fled in fear.[18]

One hundred and fifty miles away from Seadrift, the white supremacist hatemongering spread to Seabrook, Texas, on Galveston Bay. "The Vietnamese have invaded our country," railed some white fishermen. They burned some of their boats, which the refugees had purchased at inflated prices from whites eager to gouge them. Clad in white robes, they burned crosses too. By exploiting animosity toward refugees, the Klan experienced a surge in membership nationwide. It falsely asserted that the U.S. government was funding the refugees—giving welfare payments to secretly wealthy Vietnamese Americans who were hiding gold bars in storage. An agitational flyer stated, "The government has brought in Vietnamese replacements." It linked the so-called replacement of white local fishermen to the moral panic over whites "being replaced by non-whites all over the United States." Seabrook became a base camp of sorts, where the Klansmen conducted paramilitary training for their coming war with the state.[19]

Perhaps the case most cited by Asian American advocates as the second coming of Vincent Chin occurred in North Carolina. In July 1989, a twenty-four-year-old Chinese American, Ming Hai "Jim" Loo, was assaulted in a Raleigh pool hall by two white men, brothers Lloyd and Robert Piche. Berating Loo and his Vietnamese American friends for the deaths of Americans in the Vietnam War, Lloyd called them "gooks" and "chinks." As in the Chin case, "mistaken identity" would be the wrong way to interpret this encounter. Loo was targeted because the war hatreds and postwar resentments tied to Vietnam fused with panethnic patterns of anti-Asian racism. Though they were escorted out by the manager, the brothers lay in wait for the Asian American group, attacking them when they emerged outside. Robert pistol-whipped Loo on the back of his head, causing him to fall on a broken beer bottle that pierced his eye. Two days later, Loo died from a bone fragment lodged in his brain. Both Piche brothers were convicted. Robert was found guilty of second-degree murder, but Lloyd was sentenced to only six months in prison for misdemeanors. A local group of activists and lawyers formed the American Justice Coalition, successfully pushing for Lloyd Piche's conviction for eight civil rights violations, for which he received a four-year prison sentence.[20]

Although the 2021 Atlanta shootings drew belated attention to the South as a site of anti-Asian violence, one of the most shocking murders occurred in Orange County, the part of Southern California that became the nation's preeminent center of Vietnamese American culture and community. In January 1996, twenty-four-year-old Thien Minh Ly went in-line skating at Tustin High School. For no reason other than racist hatred, Gunner Lindberg beat and killed Ly, viciously stabbing him more than fifty times and saying it felt "better than a drug." Lindberg, a twenty-year-old avowed white supremacist, had recently moved to California after touring the country recruiting for his hate group. In Tustin, he bonded with Christopher Dulaney, a teenager who was convicted of murder for aiding the crime. Lindberg was sentenced to death—the first time that a hate crime had served as the "special circumstance" required to invoke the death penalty in California. Once again epitomizing the cumulative effects of anti-Asian wars and racism, the main evidence was a letter in which the killer referred to his Vietnamese American victim as "a Jap."[21]

Such murders represented the extreme tip of a broader pattern of animosity directed at Vietnamese and Southeast Asian refugees. For those of my generation, born during the Vietnam War but too young to remember it, stereotypes of Southeast Asians primarily came from racist depictions in popular culture—including ostensibly high-art films like *The Deer Hunter*, which preceded the Rambo craze. As the "Vietnam syndrome" inhibited public support for large-scale military intervention, Reagan invaded Grenada and started proxy wars in places like Nicaragua. But for Americans still attached to the racism and xenophobia of the Vietnam War, Vietnamese and Southeast Asian refugees embodied the enemy as the war came home, even if attacking them accomplished nothing more than lashing out at symbols of their cognitive dissonance. To be certain, many Americans felt a need for intercultural exchange and understanding with refugees made stateless by the rise of communist governments that U.S. presidents had labeled enemies of freedom. Privileged citizens of the metropole could not fathom the level of death the refugees had witnessed and the suffering they had endured. But many Americans centered their own grievances in an ethnocentric manner that rendered the refugees as ingrates and parasites.

This anger and resentment, significantly but far from exclusively among white Americans, surfaced for multiple reasons. It began with lingering hatred of the Viet Cong and the communists—never mind the fact that refugees were most likely to be staunch anticommunists from South Vietnam. Another source of resentment came from the notion that America did not owe these Asian refugees anything—or, indeed, that the refugees should pay America back for all "we did for them." This disregarded the facts that the United States had invaded, bombed, and poisoned their lands, producing death, destruction, and displacement. Closely related was the resentment aimed at refugees for allegedly stealing jobs, draining resources meant for citizens, getting special handouts, and being privileged over citizens in need. Nearly half of Americans surveyed in 1980 blamed Southeast Asian refugees for taking jobs away from existing residents. Overarching all these sources of antagonism was historically rooted anti-Asian racism and ignorance. Hence, just as Vincent Chin could become a target of Japan bashing, anti-Vietnamese hatred could potentially strike any Asian American.[22]

Prior to the fall of Saigon, the population of Vietnamese and Southeast Asians in the United States was comparatively sparse. In March 1975, policymakers rather arbitrarily decided on a figure of 130,000 entries for refugees, and these were quickly filled by August of that year. The Vietnamese who first came were the relatively educated and elite members of South Vietnam with the most exposure to Westerners. Being violently uprooted from home and having to adjust to living in a completely foreign country is a necessarily harsh experience. But the first wave, though much larger than U.S. officials anticipated, had the relatively smoothest adjustment. The 1979 escalation of tensions between China and Vietnam produced a new wave of refugees as genocide and famine prompted an exodus of refugees from Cambodia. Factoring in those from Laos as well, the second refugee wave that peaked in the 1980s was much larger but relatively less educated, poorer, and in greater distress. By 1990, the collective Southeast Asian American population reached one million. Nearly 80 percent were foreign born, and over half came as refugees during the 1980s. Reflecting their difficult adjustment, the poverty rates for Hmong (63.6 percent), Cambodian (42.6 percent), Laotian (34.7 percent), and Vietnamese (25.7 percent) Americans vastly exceeded the national average of 13 percent.[23]

Although some socially conscious Americans, including those within churches and volunteer groups, demonstrated tremendous humanitarian sentiments toward Southeast Asian refugees, the United States overall failed to either acknowledge its role in producing refugees or prepare to meet their needs. Increasingly, refugees were resettled with scant resources in urban areas that had been hit hard by economic recession and neoliberal restructuring. Not coincidentally, these places were often working-class white (or non-white) enclaves. The combination of underlying precarity and racist stereotyping and resentment fueled the new upsurge of anti-Asian violence and intergroup conflict that arose during the 1980s and continued into the 1990s.[24]

The United States turned into a different type of killing field for some Cambodian refugees. Khun Nhem and his young children "had to walk day and night through mine fields" to escape to Thailand. While tens of thousands established new lives safe from genocide, Nhem's son Sam was murdered in the courtyard of the Watuppa Heights housing project in Fall River, Massachusetts. Only twenty-one years old, Sam and his fiancée had just welcomed a baby boy. His family was enjoying a New England clambake on a warm Saturday evening in August 1993. When Sam went to observe a fight that had broken out, a man named Harold Robert Latour exclaimed, "I'm gonna knock that gook out!" Latour then beat Sam and kicked him in the head so viciously that he died later in a hospital. Although the defense claimed there was no racial motivation, Latour was convicted of second-degree murder and racial intimidation. Though Khun Nhem was devastated, he refused to be displaced again. "I don't like it here, but I don't want to move," he told *The New York Times*. "I miss my son so much that I don't want to leave the place where he last lived. We are the victims. Why should we move?"[25]

Nhem's victim-impact statement further exemplified Southeast Asian refugees' troubled quest for home. "I thought I could rely on the United States for safety," he said. "I thought it would be a safe place for my family."[26]

HOW THE RIGHT COVETS "MODEL MINORITY" ASIANS

Coterminous with the resettlement of Southeast Asian refugees came an unprecedented wave of immigration by highly educated Asian professionals. Alongside renewed migration from China, the Philippines, and Korea, transnational migration from India, which had been clamped down by restrictive laws of the early twentieth century, rose exponentially following the 1965 Immigration Act. In *The Karma of Brown Folk*, Vijay Prashad links the emergence of Indian Americans as a "model minority" to a process of "state selection" fostered by the preference categories at the center of the new law, which favored those in STEM fields. From 1966 to 1977, 83 percent of immigrants coming to the United States from India were prioritized for entry under the professional and technical workers category, including a combined eighty-five thousand engineers, doctors, and PhDs in science.[27]

We have seen how rising populations of working-class Asian immigrants and refugees were cast as the "perpetual foreigner" and as the stereotypical *problem*. At the same time, certain shifts in immigration policy and demographic patterns over the past half century have made Indian American professionals increasingly the face of the "model minority" and the stereotypical *solution*. These ostensibly "good" and "bad" stereotypes have worked in concert to promote the divisiveness and resentment at the heart of the counterrevolution, pitting white workers against nonwhite immigrants, then pitting the latter against other nonwhite groups.

Following Donald Trump's selection of JD Vance as his running mate in July 2024, the *Wall Street Journal* published an op-ed titled "J. D. Vance and the Indian-American Dream," by Tunku Varadarajan of the American Enterprise Institute. The piece was timed to coincide with the unprecedented spotlight shined on Vance's wife, Usha, a highly educated corporate lawyer and a daughter of immigrants from India. "Indian-Americans have achieved a breathtaking amount in this country in a couple of generations," wrote Varadarajan. "What's impressive is both the range of their success and that they have succeeded entirely on their own steam. No ethnic or racial favors have come their way from schools, colleges or government."[28]

Teachers of Asian American studies could be forgiven for thinking the *Journal* had simply changed some identifiers and reprinted William Petersen's 1966 *New York Times* article "Success Story, Japanese-American Style"—one of the most cited texts in the field and a prototype for the "model minority" stereotype:

> Barely more than 20 years after the wartime concentration camps, this is a minority that has risen above even prejudiced criticism. By any criterion of good citizenship that we choose, the Japanese Americans are better than any other group in our society including native-born. They have established this remarkable record, moreover, by their own almost totally unaided effort.[29]

The rise to prominence of Indian Americans like Usha Vance, Kash Patel, Jay Bhattacharya, and Vivek Ramaswamy, who are all linked to Trump—adding to a list of GOP figures that includes Bobby Jindal and Nikki Haley—has reinforced the notion that Indian Americans now embody the conservative representation of the "model minority" more than any other ethnic group. Through such distorted narratives, Asian Americans have become pawns of the culture wars. Like William Petersen, Varadarajan name-dropped exceptional individuals while citing aggregate data for educational attainment, household income, and professional employment that he asserted confirmed the success story—Indian American style. One slight variation: Petersen cited low arrest rates, whereas Varadarajan cited low divorce rates, as purported evidence of stable family life. Both promoted a pull-yourself-up-by-your-bootstraps response to the existence of racism. Petersen wrote of Japanese Americans, "Every attempt to hamper their progress resulted only in enhancing their determination to succeed. Even in a country whose patron saint is the Horatio Alger hero, there is no parallel to this success story."[30]

Varadarajan seemingly discovered a new parallel: "What Indians don't specialize in is grievance," he wrote. "There is, instead, a quiet determination among Indian-Americans to take full advantage of being in a land that gives them a range of opportunities unavailable in their country of ancestral origin." Indian Americans are the "model minority" successor, he asserted, as the "one group that holds fast to its belief in the American Dream." Such comments exude a palpable right-wing eagerness to find Asian Americans—willing or unwilling—to bolster ideological attacks on antidiscrimination measures and other liberal and progressive social policies. The broader purpose is to exacerbate fissures and conflict between Asian American and Black, Brown, and Indigenous communities. Of course, Varadarajan concealed the irony of linking a supposed "bootstraps" model of success to a Trump-Vance campaign fueled by high-octane doses of grievance. Instead, he laid out the terms by which "model minority" Asians could become junior partners in the MAGA counterrevolution: "I'm an ethnic Indian immigrant to the U.S., in the process of becoming an American, but I don't write this to be self-congratulatory. Instead, I do so to point out that contrary to claims of 'systemic racism' and pervasive 'white privilege,' America has been a place where this ethnic minority has blossomed."[31]

That newfound visibility, however, aroused fears that these brown-skinned newcomers were advancing at the expense of whites and doing so with special assistance from the powers that be. When Varadarajan states that some Indian Americans are "unapologetic about their drive to thrive" and "rightly scornful of those who would say that America is a place that thwarts people on the basis of race," that may be true. But it continues to remain true that other Americans have used violence and intimidation in response to viewing them as an alien threat.[32]

As author and community organizer Deepa Iyer has documented, turban-wearing Sikhs and South Asians from diverse backgrounds were swept up in the post-9/11 bias incidents tied to racism and Islamophobia. On September 15, 2001, a Sikh American named Balbir Singh Sodhi was minding his gas station in Mesa, Arizona, when he was killed in an unprovoked shooting by Frank Roque. That same day in Dallas, neo-Nazi Mark Stroman went "hunting A-rabs" to avenge a fictional sister he claimed had died in the World Trade Center. He killed Pakistani immigrant Waqar Hasan and Vasudev Patel, an Indian Buddhist. Rais Bhuiyan, a gas station attendant from Bangladesh, survived a shooting and subsequent near-death experience. Seeking atonement, he tried but failed to stop Stroman's execution. Within the first week following the 9/11 attacks, South Asian Americans Leading Together tracked 645 incidents of violence and discrimination against Arab, Muslim, and South Asian Americans. But as with the Vietnam War, the violence has long since lingered. On the morning of August 5, 2012, Wade

Michael Page, a white supremacist and army veteran, gunned down six people in the Sikh Temple of Wisconsin, a gurdwara in the town of Oak Creek, near Milwaukee. On February 22, 2017, Adam Purinton came across two Indian immigrants at a bar and grill in a suburb of Kansas City. Srinivas Kuchibhotla and Alok Madasani went there regularly to decompress over shots of Jameson after a day of work at the Garmin GPS company nearby. Purinton called them "terrorists" and scolded them, saying, "Get out of the country." After going home to retrieve a semiautomatic pistol, he shot and killed Kuchibhotla and wounded his friend. He told others he had shot "two Iranians."[33]

Another mass shooting occurred at the FedEx facility in Indianapolis on April 15, 2021. Brandon Hole, a nineteen-year-old white male and former employee, shot and killed eight people, four of whom were Sikh Americans. Citing the premeditated nature of the shooting, the Sikh Coalition called on the authorities to investigate it as a hate crime, arguing that Hole "had knowledge that the warehouse was primarily staffed by employees of the Sikh faith." The organization further asserted that the shooter "specifically aimed at the Sikh employees and made a concerted effort to avoid non-Sikhs." While the FBI acknowledged that Hole had Nazi and white supremacist content on his computer, it deemed the crime unmotivated by hate or bias. The agent in charge cited toxic masculinity and mental illness as underlying factors. Coming within a month of the Atlanta shootings, this was another instance that called for a contextual analysis transcending individual motivation and culpability. The Sikh Coalition's Amrith Kaur charged that the police and FBI should have been "far more forthcoming and transparent."[34]

Civilian deaths and casualties have sadly proven all too common in the global war on terror. Brown University researchers estimate that more than 408,000 civilians have been killed in Afghanistan, Pakistan, Iraq, Syria, and Yemen "as a direct result of the post-9/11 wars," in addition to 3.6–3.8 million indirectly related deaths. While ISIS and the Taliban bear much of the responsibility for civilian deaths in Afghanistan, Amnesty International concluded that the United States had failed to take accountability for the thousands it killed. Because the U.S. military relies largely on self-policing, commanders can block an investigation from proceeding. As such, criminal prosecutions for war crimes or murder of civilians are exceedingly rare. When the human rights organization examined ten incidents involving at least 140 Afghan civilians killed, it found no prosecutions of any kind. Only six occurred during the five-year stretch from 2009 to 2013. Retired Lieutenant General Douglas Lute, who served as deputy national security advisor during that period, acknowledged in 2023, "We virtually never held anyone accountable for civilian casualties."[35]

These contrasting images of Indian and South Asian Americans as either high-achieving model minorities or threatening, faceless hordes were part of a broader framing that scholar Mahmood Mamdani has called "good Muslim, bad Muslim." During President George W. Bush's war on terror, the "bad" Muslims were those said to have committed, supported, or sympathized with terrorism. The state marked them for death, detainment, or deportation. Simultaneously, this framing mandated the expectations for being recognized and accepted by the U.S. nation-state. As Japanese Americans learned during World War II, being a law-abiding citizen was not sufficient to avoid repression. That led scores of Japanese Americans, including those who had been incarcerated, to sign up for military service, with many paying the ultimate price. Mamdani outlined the terms of agreement governing the post-9/11 era:

> The president seemed to assure Americans that "good Muslims" were anxious to clear their names and consciences of this horrible crime and would undoubtedly support "us" in a war against "them." But this could not hide the central message of such discourse: unless proved to be "good," every Muslim was presumed to be "bad." All Muslims were now under obligation to prove their credentials by joining in a war against "bad Muslims."[36]

The state thus deployed a "model minority" framework when commissioning South Asian and Muslim Americans to actively support the war on terror, but the pressure for Asian Americans to conform to the dominant culture's expectations goes much farther. The central purpose of "model minority" discourse for the counterrevolution is buttressing the ideological pillars of capitalism and white supremacy. Therefore, as much as the stereotype has served to efface or deny the existence of anti-Asian racism and discrimination, the white proponents who assembled and disseminated these stereotypes since the postwar era have been relatively unconcerned with how Asian Americans are viewed and treated. Rather, their primary motivation has been the racialized denigration of African Americans as a collective problem. Just as the "model minority" stereotype denies the history and ongoing effects of white racism, it makes hyper-visible any image of Black assailants disrupting the peace. This came to a head with the 1992 Los Angeles rebellion and the so-called Black-Korean conflict.

In March 1991, the entire country watched the extended video footage of Rodney King, a Black motorist pulled over by the LAPD, being wantonly beaten. For many African Americans, it was incontrovertible proof of the racism they had experienced for decades from the LAPD, still under the leadership of the notorious Daryl Gates. The longtime police chief felt so untouchable that he made brazenly offensive comments about Black and Latino residents on the record. After I moved back to Los Angeles that summer, I saw the King video replayed over and over again on news programs. In the media-driven metropolis, it felt like everyone was talking about it. But another video soon competed for public attention. It showed Soon Ja Du, a Korean immigrant liquor store owner, shooting Latasha Harlins, a fifteen-year-old Black girl, in the back of the head, killing her. Similar to a store boycott in Brooklyn that took off in 1990, regular protests in Los Angeles accused Korean immigrant merchants of disrespecting Black customers.[37]

Du, whose trial proceeded ahead of that of the officers who beat King, was convicted of voluntary manslaughter. As with the death of Vincent Chin, many Americans felt she had committed murder. But in the eyes of a white conservative jurist and some like-minded Asian Americans, Soon Ja Du was a victim of anti-Asian violence. Rejecting the prosecutor's recommendation of sixteen years, the newly appointed judge, Joyce Karlin, sentenced Du to five years of probation, plus community service and payment of Harlins's funeral expenses. Karlin's public comment painted Du as a hard-working "model minority"—a victim of circumstance. Her store and others in the area had been subjected to a series of robberies. After Du had grabbed Harlins and accused her of stealing a bottle of orange juice, Harlins had punched her. "I find the defendant committed the crime under great provocation and duress," the judge said. While some Korean Americans appreciated Karlin's sympathetic tone, her sentence ensured that a new wave of outrage would sweep through the city. Calls for "Justice for Latasha" spread far and wide, sometimes accompanied by renewed calls to boycott stores operated by Korean Americans. Already devastated by years of disinvestments, systemic racism, and abusive policing, South Central LA was a tinder box ready to explode.[38]

On April 29, 1992, when jurors failed to convict the four officers on trial for beating Rodney King, the citywide uproar fed on this existing sentiment. The fissures that surfaced in response to the trial of Soon Ja Du multiplied exponentially. Dozens of Korean American stores—especially convenience stores selling liquor—were burned down, reinforcing the sense that they were targeted by interethnic violence. With the leftist model of Third World unity seemingly in tatters, the right wing seized on the moment to sway Asians to the counterrevolution. One of the most prominent conservative voices was Shawn Steel, who later served as chair of the California GOP and whose wife, Michelle, won a key congressional swing seat for the Republicans in 2020 and 2022. "The black community has never been attacked by mobs of white people in California the way Koreatown was deliberately ransacked," Steel wrote in the English edition of the *Korea Times*. Aside from the hyperbolic language of white innocence, Steel's geography was completely off. Koreatown was not part of South Central LA, where the damage began and was most widespread. Steel took particular aim at Korean Americans who embraced structural analyses of the situation and multiracial approaches to social justice: "Why blame the American culture and not those who did the damage? Why identify with the black leftist thinking to call the looting a 'rebellion' and to praise the vicious thugs who beat innocents?"[39]

Many factors, however, defied Steel's simplistic portrayal of the 1992 uprising as an outbreak of anti-Asian hate necessitating greater policing of "thugs." When we look at the sixty-plus victims who were killed, the vast majority were either Black or Latino. Much of this occurred through the policing of a "bread riot" that highlighted class divisions, as poor people in a city with yawning gaps in income grabbed diapers and other essentials when the opportunity was presented. Korean merchants—many operating stores in economically depressed urban neighborhoods—were often targets of convenience. In other cases, corporate stores and even Black-owned businesses were also ransacked. Moreover, Korean Americans harbored mixed feelings about the law enforcement. Many believed they were sacrificed as the police chose to defend whiter and wealthier parts of the city. Vigilantism also led to one of the biggest tragedies of the disturbance. After hearing a live radio broadcast for help, eighteen-year-old Edward Jae Song Lee went to a Korean restaurant whose roof was reportedly occupied by Black rioters. There, he was shot and killed. Yet, as Lee's mother tragically learned, her son was shot by fellow Koreans, who had been wrongly identified as Black. In this muddled context, Korean Americans also chastised the mainstream media for turning interpersonal conflicts into ethnic and racial warfare. Reflecting a range of ideologies, tens of thousands marched through Koreatown demanding "justice."[40]

For a time, it looked like Steel's counterrevolutionary posture would dominate California politics. I recall that period in history from firsthand experience living and organizing in Los Angeles and statewide. After serving for twenty years, LA's first Black mayor, Tom Bradley, was replaced by a white Republican, Richard Riordan, in 1993. At the state level, Governor Pete Wilson won reelection in 1994 by seizing upon the burgeoning xenophobic sentiments that fueled the landslide passage of Proposition 187, which sought to deny services to undocumented immigrants. Anticrime measures also multiplied as investments in prisons greatly outpaced those in education. Following a ban on affirmative action within the University of California system, the voters extended the ban statewide when they passed Proposition 209 in 1996 and kickstarted another right-wing trend nationwide. Next, they outlawed bilingual education and same-sex marriage. But the attacks bred resistance. Younger generations who mobilized mass opposition to these measures can now be found in the seats of government, as well as leading schools, unions, and community organizations across the state. And surveys of Asian Americans showed a sharp move to the left from the early 1990s through 2012. Though inequity is still omnipresent and the situation remains in flux in the era of Trumpism, California became the center of progressivism, in large measure because its nonwhite demographic majority actively sought to become a political majority. By developing a more complex response to interethnic conflict that stressed root cause analysis, cross-racial alliances, and grassroots organizing, Asian American activists played an integral role in turning the tide.

In the aftermath of the 1992 uprising, Asian American organizers rededicated themselves to building infrastructure and solidarity among working-class communities. The Little Tokyo Service Center partnered with Korean Americans to convert liquor stores into laundromats, seeking to meet a social need and eliminating a nuisance flagged by residents in inner-city neighborhoods. Formed shortly before the 1992 uprising, Korean Immigrant Workers Advocates (KIWA) has since been a preeminent voice for working-class solidarity. I was part of a group of UCLA student activists who wanted to get more involved off campus. Because we recognized a need to challenge the self-interested positions of some ethnic business and political leaders, we met with cofounder Roy Hong, who welcomed us to volunteer. We first helped in KIWA's campaign to obtain grants for workers from the Korean American Relief Fund. Millions in donations, particularly from South Korea, had come in to aid the recovery from *sa-i-gu* or "4/29" (Korean American terms for the period of unrest), but initially the managers of the fund restricted applications to business owners. We next supported immigrant sweatshop workers challenging wage theft from runaway shops. Through that work, we met a recent Harvard Law School graduate, Julie Su, who shunned a lucrative corporate path to take a public interest fellowship. Su joined a team of lawyers and advocates, including Thai Community Development Corporation, supporting dozens of Thai immigrants from an El Monte garment shop outside of LA. In a landmark case, they received residency and redress, after they were found living and working behind barbed wire in slave-labor conditions. In 2023, Su was named acting secretary for the U.S. Department of Labor. Meanwhile, KIWA has become *Koreatown* Immigrant Workers *Alliance*, reflecting its mission to organize the multiethnic workforce, heavily Latino, that sustains the district's businesses.[41]

These grassroots activists know that the "model minority" stereotype is not driven by altruism. It only renders Asian Americans more vulnerable to attack. And the ostensible safety it offers resembles the operation of a protection racket. Even those who can buy into it can be thrown under the bus for the sake of other forms of political expediency. The "good" minorities can never split themselves off from the "bad." Amid a citizenry stocked to the brim with firearms and invoking "stand your ground" laws against perceived intruders, the slippage between "good" and "bad" can amount to the difference between life and death.

THE SHOT HEARD 'ROUND JAPAN

"We are here for the party," said Yoshi Hattori. A sixteen-year-old exchange student from Nagoya, Japan, Yoshi was excited to attend his first Halloween party on the night of October 17, 1992. Enamored with American popular culture, Hattori was assigned to Baton Rouge, Louisiana, where he lived in the home of Louisiana State University professors Richard and Hollie Haymaker.

"We are here for the party," repeated Yoshi, clad in the blinding white tuxedo he had rented to dress up as John Travolta's Tony Manero from *Saturday Night Fever*. He rang the bell, but no one came to the door. Still, the Halloween decorations signaled that the other partygoers must be inside.

The jubilant teenager was totally unprepared for what came next. The Haymakers' son, Webb, belatedly realized that he had driven to the wrong house. They were looking for the homestay of another Japanese student, at 10311 East Brookside. Instead, Yoshi was standing at 10131 East Brookside. Bonnie Peairs saw someone outside, whom she later described as "oriental, Mexican or whatever." She reported being fearful of the "darker colored" stranger at her doorstep.

"Get the gun!" Bonnie yelled to her husband, Rodney, who came out to the carport branding his Smith and Wesson .44 Magnum revolver.

"We are here for the party!" Perhaps Yoshi thought that Rodney Peairs was also in costume, or maybe his vision was impaired without his contacts. Yoshi walked closer. Peairs claimed that Yoshi was speaking a foreign language and made him "scared to death."

BANG!

Peairs shot Yoshi straight in the chest. Webb screamed for the neighbors to call 911. An ambulance came, but Yoshi passed away before it reached the hospital.[42]

Anyone who has read this far in the book can guess what transpired next. Peairs, a thirty-year-old white man, insisted he was only standing his ground and that this incident had nothing to do with race. Family members, however, said he "constantly used racial slurs," as did his father, the local president of David Duke's National Association for the Advancement of White People. With sheriffs agreeing he had acted in self-defense, Peairs was released without being charged. He was later tried for manslaughter rather than murder, and even this came only after pressure from the Louisiana governor and the Japanese consul. After three hours of deliberation, a jury consisting of Second Amendment supporters—screened by the defense to ensure they were "concerned about the current level of crime"—found him not guilty.[43]

Historian Andrew McKevitt, author of *Gun Country*, advises us to push back against the media narrative that took hold. Yoshi was portrayed as a victim of "cultural difference": first, in the immediate sense, because he may not have understood when Peairs yelled "freeze"; and second, in the broadest sense, because pervasive gun ownership is a foreign concept in his home country. Instead, McKevitt argues that the underlying cause of Yoshi's death was racialized fear. Yoshi was an ambiguous other in the eyes of Bonnie and Rodney Peairs. But Rodney's possession of five guns and his readiness to use them in an objectively nonthreatening situation was rooted in the explosion of gun sales that occurred in the United States after the defeat of Germany and Japan. Between the end of World War II and 2020, gun ownership grew tenfold in response to consumer marketing that exploited anti-Black fears of urban crime and disorder, patriarchal ideas of male guardianship, and Cold War–era notions of patriotism and individual rights as America fought hot and cold wars against "totalitarian" regimes. These interconnected notions made owning guns a symbol of freedom that was especially rooted in "the white logic of safety and security." Pervasive ownership of firearms became a central feature of the counterrevolution.[44]

That Yoshi's story inspired McKevitt to write his book, however, is a sign of how his memory served a greater cause. Following the Vincent Chin playbook, Asian American advocates called for civil rights charges, but the U.S. Attorney for the region declined. Hattori's parents, Masaichi and Mieko, got a glimmer of redress in civil court, which ordered Peairs and his insurer to pay them $653,077.85 in damages plus legal fees. "There was no justification whatsoever that a killing was necessary for Rodney Peairs to save himself," the judge stated.[45]

Uninterested in keeping the money for their own use, the Hattoris donated all of it to the cause of gun control. In a little over a year following Yoshi's death, the Hattoris collected nearly two million Japanese signatures petitioning the United States to restrict guns. While Japan was comparatively devoid of gun violence, Yoshi was one of thirty thousand annual gun deaths in America. The Haymakers also dedicated their lives to gun control, launching Louisiana Ceasefire and advancing the national Coalition to Stop Gun Violence. To be certain, the gun lobby fought back and did not hesitate to tap into the nation's ingrained xenophobia. A direct-mail fundraising appeal from the Second Amendment Foundation warned on the envelope: "JAPAN LAUNCHES 'SNEAK ATTACK' ON YOUR GUN RIGHTS." Its founder, Alan Gottlieb wrote, "My father didn't risk his life in World War II to have Japan or any other country dictate away our Bill of Rights."[46]

A faint silver lining to the growing casualty list of anti-Asian violence could be found in increased support for gun control. After the Cleveland Elementary School shootings in 1989, California passed an assault weapons ban that same year. Its sponsor in the state senate, David Roberti, credited its one-vote margin of passage to the awareness of the young children who were massacred. After Governor George Deukmejian, a Republican, defied his former supporters in the National Rifle Association and signed it, California proceeded to enact 107 additional gun control laws, more than any other state in the nation, between 1991 and 2023. While multiple factors shaped the national legislation, the advocacy by the Hattoris and Haymakers built momentum for the 1993 Brady Handgun Violence Prevention Act, which instituted background checks and a waiting period. Though it expired after ten years, the landmark federal Assault Weapons Ban came the following year.[47]

Another break in the clouds emerged in 1994. The mayor of Baton Rouge, Tom Ed McHugh, moved to create a public memorial site honoring those lost to gun violence. He invited Richard Haymaker to be part of the commission, which approved the inclusion of a plaque with Yoshi Hattori's picture. "He came in friendship," it would read. This was a modest proposal that would recognize a Japanese youth born three decades after the U.S.-Japan alliance became a centerpiece of American foreign policy. Yet it drew public ire. Opponents were upset to see Yoshi's name mentioned in the vicinity of a historical museum and World War II ship named for Admiral Isaac Kidd, who was killed in Japan's attack on Pearl Harbor. Frank Masanz, a veteran of World War II and former commissioner of the Louisiana Naval War Memorial, insisted that the site should only recognize "the victims of Japan's innumerable misdeeds."[48]

Even in death, an innocent Asian victim comprised an alien threat. This was the perversion at the heart of the counterrevolution, for which racism justifies aggression carried out in the name of self-defense and maintaining law and order.

EIGHT

Naming and Confronting Hate Crimes

In September 1987, *The Jersey Journal* published a story headlined "Bigot Brags of Racial Attacks" with a photo of a disturbing handwritten letter. "Look! Let's cut out the small talk," warned the anonymous authors. "We will go to any extreme to get Indians to move out of Jersey City."

They claimed to represent a two-year-old organization called the "Dotbusters": a name steeped in hatred toward Hindu women who wore Bindis on their foreheads. The letter contained unabashed boasting of random assaults on innocent passersby: "If I'm walking down the street, and I see a Hindu and the setting is right, I will just hit him or her." The authors planned "more extreme attacks" in advance, including "breaking windows" and "crashing family parties" to terrorize Indian Americans in their homes.[1]

While the dissemination of a violent, racist screed is always cause for alarm, it is not always immediately clear if the perpetrators' intent is purely to intimidate or if they are concretely engaged in physical violence. In the summer of 2020, for instance, I moved with my family to the Dallas–Fort Worth area. Not long after, a similar letter turned up in the mailboxes of homeowners in Irving, Texas. I was aware that northern parts of the city, located near tech employers, had seen an exponential rise in Asian immigrant residents. In some elementary schools, Asians, especially Indian and South Asian Americans, comprised as much as 90 percent of the student body. "American citizens in IT industry and other professional fields have lost their jobs to many Indians and Chinese," the letter proclaimed. "We asked you to leave the country without further delay. We will have no choice but to shoot mercilessly at work place, in community, on pool or on playground."[2]

Less than three years later, a neo-Nazi gunman of Latino ancestry murdered eight people at an outlet mall in Allen, a suburb north of Dallas. The victims included an Indian American woman and a Korean American family. Like Irving, Allen is experiencing rapid demographic transformation, though this incident seemed only to be part of a broader pattern with the prior death threats.[3]

In the case of the Dotbusters, at least one violent crime was directly linked to one of the letter writers. In August 1987, two white men broke into the home of Bhered Patel in the middle of the night. Finding him sound asleep and defenseless, they beat him with a metal pipe. The assault conformed to the racist letter in one key regard. The authors disclosed that they found Indian Americans to victimize by searching the phonebook for the address of people named "Patel." Authorities arrested James Kerwin, a twenty-one-year-old white man, and determined he was responsible for both the letter and the unprovoked attack.[4]

This chapter provides a case study of the Dotbusters episode, as well as racist incidents across multiple states that provoked Asian American awareness in the 1980s and 1990s. It charts the progress of activism to combat anti-Asian violence in the wake of the Justice for Vincent Chin movement. As the Chin case motivated and shaped a new wave of community activism, it also created a quasi-template for advocacy. The first step was drawing attention to the overlooked problems of Asian Americans. A shocking anti-Asian murder or attack provided a teachable moment to do consciousness raising regarding the history of discrimination and racism. The second step involved challenging the typical notion that such attacks were isolated incidents or not racially motivated. Hence, community activists invoked the concept of "anti-Asian violence" to connect the dots between people, places, and historical periods.

At the same time, naming the problem as anti-*Asian* violence paved the way for a third step—employing and expanding the panethnic coalitional framework created by the Asian American movement during the 1960s and 1970s. Highlighting the scourge of the Dotbusters helps us see how Indian and South Asian Americans united across class lines and played an increasing role within panethnic formations originally rooted among East Asian Americans.

The fourth step entailed issuing calls to bring the assailants to justice. This involved attracting media attention and mobilizing community support—from Asian Americans and non-Asian allies—to pressure the authorities to arrest, charge, convict, and sentence perpetrators. As a corollary to this step, when activists deemed the actions of district attorneys to be ineffective or insufficient, they pressed the federal government to bring civil rights charges.

Although these efforts seem to have produced a growing number of successful prosecutions, most Asian American organizers believed that the best tangible method to institutionalize progress in the fight against anti-Asian violence was passing new and enhanced laws to combat hate crimes, bias incidents, and ethnic intimidation. The road to federal hate crimes legislation proved long and winding, but New Jersey moved to the fore of state-level action, owing partly to concerns voiced about the Dotbusters.

Legislative victories, however, proved to be incomplete and, in some cases, pyrrhic. Consequently, when increased awareness of anti-Asian violence during the pandemic created urgent momentum to pass a new law, Asian American community activists were found on opposing sides of the COVID-19 Hate Crimes Act.

BUSTING THE DOTBUSTERS

In its inaugural newsletter, the newly formed Committee Against Anti-Asian Violence sounded the alarm in response to the "surge of racial violence against Indians" that had erupted in the New York metropolitan area from mid-1987 through 1988. While the murder of Vincent Chin has been definitively tied to the Japan-bashing outbreak in the 1980s, these incidents pointed to a broader trend of anti-Asian xenophobia outside of the Rust Belt. Indian immigration rose in concert with rising demand for employees in STEM fields and service industries. Many settled in North Jersey. From 1960 to 1980, New Jersey's Indian American population grew seventeenfold, from just 1,699 to 29,510 people. By 1990, Indians comprised the state's largest Asian ethnic group, numbering nearly eighty thousand, with the greatest concentrations residing in Hudson and Middlesex counties.[5]

Violence became a disturbing sign of intolerance to this new and growing presence. In popular memory, the string of attacks arising in this period has been attributed to the "Dotbusters." In fact, only the beating of Bhered Patel was officially linked to the Dotbusters' letter. That meant that a more pervasive sense of racist antagonism underlay the menace. Far from keeping quiet, many Indian Americans protested loudly and publicly while condemning systemic racism.[6]

Around 2:00 a.m. on September 24, 1987, Kaushal Saran, a doctor from India who was a naturalized citizen, was ambushed on an active business strip in Jersey City. A group of men in their late teens or early twenties beat him with a baseball bat until he fell into a partial coma. Unlike Vincent Chin, Saran survived. But amnesia and permanent brain damage would preclude him from stable employment. Both the Jersey City Police Department and the Hudson County Prosecutor's Office conducted investigations without producing any indictments. Following in the footsteps of ACJ, Indian and Asian American community advocates pushed for federal civil rights charges, turning to the recently appointed United States Attorney for New Jersey. They learned he was a graduate of Princeton and Yale named Samuel A. Alito Jr. "If it appear[s] in any case that justice is not being done at the county level," said the future Supreme Court justice, "then we will proceed at the Federal level if we've got the evidence to do so."[7]

Alito, however, never followed through with any formal action regarding Saran's assault, and it took the FBI four years to even open an investigation—and the Justice Department nearly five years to indict three defendants. The court filing arrived in September 1992—just days before the statute of limitations ran out. By then, Alito had moved on to the Third Circuit as an appellate judge. In the meantime, one of the suspects, Mark Evangelista, found work patrolling the streets as a Hudson County police officer (a pre-employment background check had turned up nothing of note). Alito's former deputy, Michael Chertoff—now best known for his later roles as special counsel for the Whitewater investigation and as second head of the Department of Homeland Security—filed the charges, which carried a maximum twenty-year sentence.[8]

"We're absolutely pleased," Dr. Lalitha Masson, head of the Hoboken-based National Organization for Defense of Indian Americans, told *The New York Times*. "But it's shameful it took so long. We're still very angry with the Jersey City police and the Hudson County Prosecutor's office. They didn't do anything; they always made excuses."[9]

Prosecutors sought to tie the defendants to the Dotbusters letter. Thomas Kozak confessed to the crime and implicated two codefendants. But defense counsel claimed the confession was coerced. By June 1993, all three defendants were either acquitted or had their charges dropped, owing to a hung jury. Accepting the federal prosecutors' efforts as sincere, Judge Joseph E. Irenas scoffed at the negligence of the local authorities. The police had failed to take or record statements from the officers who responded to the assault, the thirty to forty witnesses who saw it, or the firefighters whose station was right next to the scene of the crime. Further hampering the prosecution was the beating's enduring impact on Saran, whose loss of memory prevented him from testifying in detail about what had happened.[10]

Kozak was the first to be acquitted. Saran was appalled. "This is frustrating," he stated. "Kozak has admitted to kicking me, and left me there to die. Kozak, in his own words, said Asian Indians are not Americans. What more does the jury need?"[11]

Several days after Kaushal Saran was beaten, another Indian American died from injuries received in an altercation with a group of teenagers. Navroze Mody was a thirty-year-old Wall Street professional living in Jersey City. He was leaving a Hoboken bar when a group of teenage girls taunted the bald man with names like "baldie, Kojak and glowhead." Mody, who may have been at least a bit inebriated, reportedly pushed one of the girls. This prompted four youths to emerge from a car. Claiming that Mody adopted a combative karate stance, they beat him repeatedly in purported self-defense. Mody fell twice. First, he hit his head on a fire hydrant. Next, the back of his head struck a cement ledge. He was taken to the hospital, where he died three days later from cranial and cerebral injuries.[12]

The series of events horrified Indian American community members in the same manner that Vincent Chin's murder had aroused Asian Americans. By October 1987, community leaders mobilized over five hundred people to march through the Journal Square district chanting, "We want justice."

"We are taught to be nonviolent," Devraj Patel told *The New York Times*. "But if the attacks keep on, we have to fight back."

While Jersey City's mayor denounced the attacks, the *Times* had no trouble finding whites who openly supported them.

"It's white people against the Hindus," said one white male youth.

"I just don't like them," added a second. "I can't stand them."

While the boys denied being part of a Dotbusters hate group, both readily admitted that they had "harassed Indians."

The interviewees did not mince words. "Anti-Indian violence has always been a part of Jersey City," professed a twenty-four-year-old truck driver. "That's always going to be."

In a variation on the theme of Asians taking away jobs from whites, the trucker voiced the popular urban legend that Asian immigrants received unique and preferential treatment from the U.S. government at the expense of American-born citizens. Also afflicting Southeast Asian refugees, such misinformation bolstered right-wing populism: "These people come over here and get $10,000 to start a business," he claimed. "That's not right. And we have to work and fight all our life."[13]

In mid-December 1987, around 150 Indian Americans and their allies braved the cold to demonstrate on the steps of the Hudson County Courthouse. "End racism now!" they chanted. "We want justice!"

Such calls for justice can be instinctual. What exactly do they mean in practice?

In response to Navroze Mody's death, demonstrators demanded that the four teenaged defendants be tried as adults. Prosecutors agreed.[14]

But the jury rejected the murder charges, as well as the lesser charges of manslaughter and aggravated manslaughter. The youths were ultimately found guilty of assault. Three of four defendants were convicted of "aggravated assault." Because they were tried as adults, they received the maximum (ten-year) prison sentences for which they were eligible.[15]

Many Indian American protesters felt that the sentences were too lenient—a sign of disregard for both the victim and his ethnic community. They further objected to the prosecutor's failure to put forward any bias-related charges. A senior staff attorney for Jersey City said there was no evidence that Mody's attackers knew he was "an ethnic Indian." Hudson County District Attorney Paul DePasquale was more circumspect. It was safe to assume, he said, that two of the defendants "didn't like Asian Indians." But without any overt references to the victim's race or nationality, the district attorney insisted, there was no basis for bias-related charges. Most of the incidents being portrayed as "anti-Indian," DePasquale maintained, were "simple assaults" and "street fights." Another complicating factor was the ethnicity of the defendants, who were Puerto Rican Americans. That did not in any way preclude the possibility that they had acted out of bias. It did, however, mean that the case did not fit the same pattern of Dotbuster attacks in which the assailants were presumably non-Hispanic whites.[16]

Navroze Mody's father, Jamshed, was livid. "The justice system completely stinks," protested the elder Mody, a retired real estate agent. "My son was murdered because he was Indian."[17]

Expressing a widely held feeling among some Asian Americans, Mody believed that African American civil rights advocates had proved more effective because they took a stronger stand than Indian Americans. He cited their response to the death of Michael Griffith, a young Black man who was killed in an act of racist terror in December 1986. Griffith was struck by a car on the Belt Parkway in Brooklyn while fleeing a white mob wielding tire irons and baseball bats. "The black community received justice in the Howard

Beach case," said Jamshed Mody. "I wish the Indian community would rise to the occasion and show them we mean business."[18]

With Al Sharpton leading vocal protests, the killing of Michael Griffith drew major attention from the community, politicians, and media. Governor Mario Cuomo named a special prosecutor, and the case set a new precedent when the judge precluded the defense from arbitrarily excluding Black jurors with peremptory challenges, a common practice until then. Despite claiming the incident was a street brawl over turf rather than race, three white youths were convicted of assault and manslaughter, though not of murder.[19]

In April 1989, Mody pursued a private civil rights lawsuit in federal court. He sought damages from the four youths, their parents or guardians, the City of Hoboken, and leaders of the Hoboken Police. For the Mody family and other community activists, the most significant development was a finding that two of the youths had assaulted two additional Indian Americans, Syed Hasan and Vikas Aggarwal. Both men, students from Stevens Institute of Technology, had been accosted at a Hoboken restaurant two weeks before the attack on Navroze Mody. Because they were targeted at random and not robbed, Mody's father was convinced that it was a bias-related crime. One suspect had reportedly told friends he had "beat up two Indians."[20]

But Hoboken Police detective Thomas Cahill simply let these suspects go. Though he claimed that Hasan and Aggarwal had declined to file a complaint, in fact he did not have the right phone number for Hasan or the correct address for Aggarwal. Moreover, the police admitted that they did not need a complaint from the victims to arrest the suspects. Mody's father thus accused Cahill and the Hoboken Police of callous disregard and negligence leading directly to the death of his son. Had these youths been taken off the streets, he asserted, they would never have encountered Navroze. Despite these glaring lapses of accountability, Mody's case proved to be an uphill fight. The judge granted a motion to end the trial prematurely in the defendants' favor. In effect, the court told Jamshed Mody that he lacked any substantive evidence to warrant further consideration of his complaint. Mody appealed and lost again.[21]

Although this was a civil rather than criminal case, there was a key similarity with the trial of Ronald Ebens and with other civil rights cases. It was not enough to demonstrate that the defendants—through an active assault or failure to prevent an assault—had caused harm, even physical or deadly harm. Rather, the court implied, the plaintiff needed "direct evidence" that the youths "attacked Navroze Mody because he was Asian Indian." This meant that any disregard for the Indian American victims based on systemic racism, unconscious bias, or a lack of cultural competence was unlikely to sway the judges or jury. Even more troubling for the Mody family's case, the Third Circuit's three-member panel—one Nixon and two Reagan appointees—further implied that the plaintiffs were required to prove that the police and city did not simply permit or allow the attacks to occur but that they also shared "a racial hatred of Asian Indians with those persons or groups in the community that were perpetrating the vicious assaults."[22]

How might that be possible? The court's example was stark:

> It would be different if Mody had shown the police uttered racial slurs against Asian Indians or produced other evidence of an atmosphere of disparagement towards Asian Indians among the police that was knowingly tolerated by the Hoboken officials responsible for police conduct, or presented evidence of a consistent police pattern of conduct that required Asian Indian assault victims, but not victims from other discrete minorities, to file criminal complaints before suspects would be apprehended.[23]

Their twisted logic is so breathtaking it is difficult to say which requirement raises the bar higher: the demand for evidence that police used explicit anti-Indian slurs or the demand that Mody prove a pattern of negligence by the police toward Indian Americans *that was not also exhibited* toward "other discrete minorities." In either case, the court seemed to be telegraphing to the authorities the steps they could take to conceal evidence of discrimination or even get away with discrimination once it was exposed.

The broader takeaway is this: Civil rights laws are extremely important policy tools that are the result of decades of sacrifice and struggle in the United States. But they do not guarantee protection. Indeed, considerable energy can be spent—by victims' advocates and the government—without achieving the desired result, as occurred in the cases tied to the deaths of Vincent Chin and Navroze Mody. Proving motivation is a tremendous burden based on legal standards; however, it poses a greater challenge for marginalized groups whose history, experience, and perspectives are not well known to the average judge and juror, who may not be "outwardly prejudiced" but who, in fact, likely harbor deeply ingrained stereotypes they cannot admit to themselves.

On the night of April 8, 1988, Thanh Lam was minding his own business in the working-class Boston neighborhood of Dorchester. He was approached by a white male teenager with a five-foot-long stick. In the epitome of a hate crime, the young man walloped Lam on the head while calling him a "Vietnam fucking shit." He struck him with such force that the stick broke in half. Lam had no idea who this stranger was or why he chose to assault him in such a violent manner. He would learn that his assailant was named Mark Wahlberg and that his brother was attaining fame in the "boy band" New Kids on the Block. Seeing a police officer coming, Wahlberg fled the scene as Lam lay on the ground unconscious. He then came across Hoa Trinh, another man minding his own business, and socked him in the eye. Trinh assisted the police with the arrest of Wahlberg, who remained defiant and unrepentant. He continued to rant about "slant-eyed gooks." While staring down Lam, he told the officers, "You don't have to let him identify me, I'll tell you now that's the mother-fucker whose head I split open." Although arrested for attempted murder, Wahlberg pled guilty to assault. Sentenced to two years in prison, he was released after just forty-five days.[24]

By 1993, "Marky Mark" Wahlberg was a bona fide celebrity. While profiting from the sale of artless pseudo-rap songs in the wasteland of corporate radio, he also reached the status of an icon through advertising, his body displayed on billboards and signs for Calvin Klein underwear. And nowhere was his shirtless physique more prominent than in Manhattan—where the Committee Against Anti-Asian Violence (CAAAV) happened to be headquartered. The activist group promptly began a guerrilla culture-jamming campaign, printing fifteen hundred "neon orange bumper-size stickers" that read

Marky Mark: CONVICTED RACIST.

CAAAV organizers posted these stickers over images of Wahlberg's bare torso to alert the public. As well as attacking Lam and Trinh, Wahlberg had assaulted twelve-year-old Jesse Coleman in 1986 while yelling, "Kill the nigger, kill the nigger," in addition to a separate homophobic attack.[25]

As the cases piled up, Asian Americans grew appalled by the failures and limitations of the justice system, but galvanized by the awareness the Justice for Vincent Chin movement had raised. In cities across the nation, activists mobilized through existing grassroots organizations and formed new ones focused on the problem of anti-Asian violence. One of most prominent and enduring groups to emerge from this historical moment was CAAAV. While the Chin case was still active in 1986, multiple groups—including the panethnic Asian American Legal Defense and Education Fund (AALDEF, modeled on the NAACP LDF) and ethnic-specific groups—came together first as the Coalition Against Anti-Asian Violence. Proceeding as an independent committee as of 1988, CAAAV prioritized "victim advocacy" by pushing for greater responsiveness from the police, enhanced bias crime classification, and education to get at the sources of prejudice and hate. It demanded accountability for the deaths of Navroze Mody and other Asian Americans killed or harmed in the region. Between 1988 and 1991, its newsletter devoted considerable attention to the Dotbusters, as well as to suspected hate crimes in the deaths of Paul Him Chow (a gay Chinese American "bludgeoned to death" in Manhattan but not robbed) and Henry Kwok Kin Lau (an immigrant from Hong Kong, stabbed to death on a Brooklyn N train by an attacker who yelled, "Hey eggroll").[26]

With its call to "Jail the Racist Killers," the Chin campaign provided a playbook of sorts for holding the justice system accountable by demanding swift retributive action through local law enforcement and federal civil rights charges as a backup or enhancement to criminal prosecution. In contrast with the political fissures over enforcing and expanding civil rights laws during the Reagan era, there was unquestionably stronger and more broad-based support for getting tough on violent crime. As Chin's story spread to the national media, some connected the demands of his supporters to broader "war on crime" measures. In April 1983, under the headline "The $3,000 License to Kill," a *Washington Post* editorial cited Judge Kaufman's lenient treatment of Ebens and Nitz as proof that two reforms were "badly needed." First, survivors and the families of the deceased should have the right to speak in court prior to sentencing. When Michigan adopted this right to victims' impact statements, it was colloquially dubbed the Vincent Chin rule. Judges, especially those standing for election, were mindful, going forward, not only of the words of victims' families but also of the public's response to such statements.[27]

Second, the *Post* called for stricter sentencing guidelines, reducing judicial discretion by creating mandatory minimum sentences for those convicted. The following year, the state's high court responded. According to Roland Hwang, a Michigan-based attorney and longtime leader of American

Citizens for Justice, "partly, as a result of the Vincent Chin case, the Michigan Supreme Court promulgated a mandatory minimum sentencing guideline." In 1998, the state legislature followed suit, enacting guidelines to "reduce sentencing disparities." As these anticrime measures advanced locally and nationally, they increasingly drew bipartisan support.[28]

In hindsight, it should be abundantly clear that advocacy for "tough on crime" measures played a pivotal role in the nation's shift to the right. In response to the protests and rebellions of the 1960s, Nixon had championed "law and order" as the core rallying cry of a resurgent GOP. Long before he entered electoral politics, Donald Trump pushed this agenda to boost his public profile. In 1989, five Black and Latino youths were accused of raping and attempting to murder a white female jogger in Central Park. Exploiting the occasion, Trump took out full-page newspaper ads blaring "Bring back the death penalty and bring back our police!" But hard evidence exonerated the "Central Park Five." Their convictions were vacated in 2002. To settle their civil rights complaint, New York City paid them $41 million. Trump has never apologized for his rash response.[29]

When the Democrats reclaimed the White House after George H. W. Bush's single term, the Clinton administration reinforced the bipartisan embrace of the war on crime. Following sweeping defeats of presidential nominees cast as liberals in 1984 and 1988, moderate Democrats were determined to counter the party's reputation as soft on crime. Guided by Stanley Greenberg's surveys, Governor Bill Clinton, during his 1992 run for president, explicitly signaled a move to the center in order to reclaim the votes of Reagan Democrats in places like Macomb County, Michigan. In office, he signed the momentous Violent Crime Control and Law Enforcement Act of 1994, which is more commonly and controversially known as the 1994 crime bill, which, with the Senate majority in Democrat hands, Joe Biden cowrote and championed. Figuratively speaking, Senator Biden answered Trump's demands in the notorious "Central Park Five" ad, boasting of "60 new death penalties," "70 enhanced penalties," "100,000 cops," and "125,000 new state prison cells." The law further instituted the "three strikes and you're out" rule requiring life sentences (California passed a similar state law that year by voter initiative) and set "truth in sentencing" guidelines that restricted early release and parole. Following the prevailing political winds, Hillary Clinton issued her infamous call, two years later, to crack down on youths she deemed "super predators," whom the First Lady proclaimed had "no conscience, no empathy."[30]

In the South, three notable examples of vigorous prosecution and sentencing in response to the murders of Vietnamese Americans occurred during the early 1990s. "God forgive me for coming to this country," pleaded fifteen-year-old Hung Truong. "I'm so sorry." In the hours after midnight on August 9, 1990, Truong, who had moved to Houston with his father a decade earlier, reportedly said these words while begging a group of self-identified skinheads to stop pummeling him. Two of them had yelled "white power" before chasing him down. Truong's friends called paramedics, who determined he was well enough to walk away on his own. That proved a tragic miscalculation. Staying with a friend, Truong suffered from catastrophic injuries and died shortly after he was rushed to the hospital later that morning.[31]

Denouncing the murder as part of a pattern of racist violence, Asian American community organizers in Houston gathered around fifty protesters at City Hall. Although a fraction of the size of the Justice for Vincent Chin demonstrations, participants saw this event as an awakening within the Houston community. They were supported by prominent Black political leaders, such as then councilmember Sheila Jackson Lee. This cross-racial advocacy likely shaped the receptive response from authorities. A homicide detective said that Truong's killing "can't be anything but a racial crime." The district attorney called it a "senseless" and "racially motivated" killing. Known both for prior conflicts with Asian Americans and for virulent anti-Black hatred, Derek Hilla was convicted of murder and sentenced to forty-five years in prison. Kevin Allison admitted to assaulting the victim because he was Vietnamese. The jury found him guilty of involuntary manslaughter, and he received the maximum ten-year sentence. Truong's father stated that he was satisfied with the outcome.[32]

In August 1992, the families and friends of Luyen Pham Nguyen, a nineteen-year-old Vietnamese refugee, were reminded of the tragic lesson that any racial altercation carried murderous potential for Asian Americans. The University of Miami premed student attended a party in Coral Springs, a suburb of Fort Lauderdale, Florida. While the town is now majority Hispanic, Black, and Asian, it was then predominantly white. After being called an ethnic slur, Nguyen voiced his objection and left the party. According to the police, he was followed by a group of men who "chased him down like a hunter chases down an injured deer." Ultimately, around fifteen white men piled on, beating Nguyen until he stopped breathing and was taken to a hospital. His assailants had broken a cervical vertebra with a kick to his neck. They also severed an artery. Like Vincent Chin, Nguyen was put on life support and died a few days later.[33]

"He never got any chance to fight back," Luyen's mother, Thang Nguyen, told the judge. "How can they do this to my son? Is it because they hate my son so much because my son is different?"

Put on trial for murder, Bradley Mills was but one of the assailants reported to have made racist comments. Flagged by Nguyen's friend as the instigator, he was convicted of second-degree murder. While Florida guidelines recommended a maximum twenty-two-year sentence, Judge Richard D. Eade found that insufficient. Citing the brutal nature of the beating and his past juvenile record, the judge ordered Mills to serve fifty years in prison. "Excuse me?" Mills blurted out to the judge. "In that case, you might as well give me the electric chair!"[34]

Four of the other six who were charged pled guilty to or were convicted of second-degree murder, one was found guilty of lesser charges, and one was acquitted. These convictions and sentences were significantly harsher than those delivered to Ebens and Nitz. While Asian American advocates could claim that justice was finally being served, the irony was cruel. More Asian Americans had to be killed to give the system additional chances to prove that it valued their lives.[35]

A third victim of this era, who was killed between the murders of Hung Truong and Luyen Pham Nguyen, has gone largely unnoticed by Asian American historians. The story of Thanh Nguyen, who was shot and killed in Dallas, challenges us to consider how the politics of remembering shape our awareness of anti-Asian violence. It may have gained less traction because it was cast more as a story about homophobia than about racism.

On the night of October 26, 1991, Nguyen, a twenty-nine-year-old Vietnamese refugee, bought fast food with his companion, Hugh Callaway. They went to Reverchon Park, an integral part of the Oak Lawn district, known as the city's "gayborhood," to eat their takeout. In a culturally conservative state where sodomy laws criminalized homosexual acts, Oak Lawn was a relatively safe space for the LGBT community. But the park—a reputed cruising spot for gay men—became a target of antigay youth violence. Two years earlier, a high school kid from the suburbs had bragged about torturing and killing two men there in a "fag-bashing" spree.[36]

Only nineteen at the time, Corey Burley was with two friends a couple years older when they identified Nguyen and Callaway as easy marks for a robbery. Burley pointed a gun alternately at their heads. "My homies," Burley recalled in an interview with filmmaker Arthur Dong for the 1997 documentary *Licensed to Kill*, "start beating up on them." This was "not nice guy beating up." They were "busting 'em up real good." Burley shot Nguyen in the stomach, then aimed at Callaway, who was hit twice but turned just in time to avoid a fatal wound. Nguyen tried to flee, but he collapsed and died near the shooting site.[37]

The violence reached the point of no return, Burley admitted, after one of his friends egged him on: "Go ahead and shoot 'em. It ain't that hard to do." He took it as a dare. While pointing a finger of contemplation to his head, Burley told Dong that he was not consciously thinking about killing a fellow human being. "It's just like on impulse," he stated. "You do it because more or less you want to see what's gonna happen."

In this sense, his actions conformed to Hillary Clinton's depiction of incorrigible young men acting without conscience. Deliberating for only an hour, the jurors felt no sympathy for Burley. They convicted him of capital murder and he was sentenced to life in prison. While this specific case was not prioritized by national Asian American advocacy groups at the time, it showcases in hindsight some of the tensions that surfaced within the hate crimes discourse. When it was first reported, a detective with the Dallas Police Department determined that the motive was robbery. Was he confounded by the fact that the murder victim was Asian? If so, was that because he was gay? Or because an Asian male and a white male were attacked by Black males? Such complexities had rarely been discussed, let alone competently dissected, in mainstream American society. Yet there was unmistakable evidence of bias. During the assault, the assailants called both victims "fag." Callaway said they called Nguyen "gook." Senior officials in the police department said the detective had "misunderstood the situation." They confirmed that it was a "hate crime." As civil rights coalitions expanded over the course of the next decade, Asian Americans would increasingly work with Black and LGBT groups, especially to address hate crimes.[38]

At the same time, proponents of restorative justice have asked us to weigh how the emphasis on more incarceration and longer prison terms has impacted the broader society. Corey Burley was locked up for life, a harsher sentence than that imposed on the killers of Hung Truong and Luyen Pham Nguyen. Was he a worse offender than these white men? Were he and others similarly convicted beyond rehabilitation at the age of nineteen or twenty?

It can be excruciatingly difficult for those who have been victimized, especially when their loved ones have been murdered, to believe that offenders and incarcerated persons can be restored to the community. In the case of hate crimes, the call to lock up assailants can bring a sense of safety to those directly harmed, but it also constitutes a call for social justice on behalf of oppressed groups or protected classes. That makes stories of redemption even more meaningful. In January 1985, Jean Kar-Har Fewel, an eight-year-old orphan from Hong Kong, was kidnapped and sexually assaulted in Chapel Hill, North Carolina. In a crime that shocked the town, Jean was lynched, and her lifeless body was discovered hanging from a tree. Tom Fewel and Joy Wood, who were in the process of adopting the girl, asked the jury not to impose the death penalty on her convicted killer. While Fewel could not forgive him, he had befriended another man on death row, Steven Van McHone, learning more about absolution through deep exchanges. He sent pleas to the governor to commute McHone's sentence to life in prison.[39]

More recently, an anonymous Asian American man, who was attacked at a public transportation stop in Portland, Oregon, asked that the judge allow his assailant to enter a restorative justice program. In December 2020, Daniel Hutchins asked the man, "Are you Chinese?" and then punched him in the face. Hutchins pled guilty to a second-degree bias crime. As an alternative to incarceration, he apologized to the victim and underwent an accountability process managed by the Oregon Chinese Coalition. The goal of such programs is to restore the offender to a right relationship with the community, reducing the rate of recidivism and diverting resources from the prison industrial complex to essential human needs.[40]

In choosing to interview Corey Burley, Arthur Dong pointed to the broader purpose of *Licensed to Kill*, which seeks to understand the mindset of an array of men convicted of murdering victims they perceived to be gay. Dong felt a need to present "the perpetrator's point of view" to dissect how homophobia has been normalized in the upbringing of boys in America.[41]

Having grown up as a Black child in a housing project, Burley spoke of seeing "wrong everywhere." He said he had been a "coward" and a bullying victim until he decided to become the aggressor. After turning the tables on his neighborhood bullies, Burley later stalked gay men, robbed them, and stripped them of their clothes, knowing that the victims would be too ashamed to report the incident. While he did not have any out gay male acquaintances, he developed stereotypes about them from the media. "We had it embedded in our head that they were weak," he added. "We could get away with it, and they wouldn't put up a fight."

Countering the initial determination of the police, Burley candidly acknowledged that robbery was not the primary motive. "It really wasn't for the money," he said. "It was more or less just to do it." Interviewing him behind bars, Dong explained that Nguyen was a refugee of the Vietnam War. "He came to escape the war and got killed by nonsense." Burley replied, "I really didn't mean to take this person's life."

"When I was growing up, I wanted to be bad," Burley reflects at the end of the film. "I didn't want to be no cowards and stuff like that. So I built myself up, pumped myself up to be bad. But look where it's got me. I'm bad, but I'm locked up. I'm doing time, a lot of time."

Following the well-publicized murder of Matthew Shepard in October 1998, Dong was asked to comment on the push to expand hate crime laws. He described such laws as "useful in sending a strong message to the public that this is not a type of crime to be tolerated." At the same time, he added that his film aimed "to get to the roots of the problem." The goal, Dong asserted, should be stopping homophobic violence "from the very start, as opposed to doing something about it after the fact."[42]

While opponents of hate crimes understandably pushed for stricter accountability, some civil rights advocates began to question the emphasis on longer, mandatory, and enhanced sentencing. Too often in court, Black and Brown men were portrayed as the "super predator" offenders rather than being seen as those whom laws are designed to protect. As cracks in the anti-crime consensus of the 1990s have emerged, we are challenged to consider the fallout. In Detroit, most of those impacted directly and indirectly by the "Vincent Chin rule" and other victims' rights measures have been working-class African Americans rather than white perpetrators of racist violence. As of 2009, one in twenty-five adults in Motown were under correctional control—draining nearly $400 million annually in funds from the embattled city as scores of schools were closing and public services were cut. With their communities under siege by mass incarceration, women of color–led organizations began to advance restorative and transformative justice approaches to domestic and intimate partner violence, arguing that increased policing and incarceration had created more problems than they solved.[43]

These kinds of complications came to the fore as concern for victims of anti-Asian violence amplified calls to criminalize hate. Given the uneven outcomes in the application of the law, Asian American activists joined with other civil rights organizations to push for changes in the law itself.

Joseph Ileto was not scheduled to work on August 10, 1999. But that Tuesday morning, he woke up, put on his postal carrier's uniform, and set out under the summer sun to deliver mail to San Fernando Valley residents on the route of a sick colleague. Working for the United States Postal Service was one of two jobs the thirty-nine-year-old Filipino immigrant held while attending college. His father had passed away only a few months earlier, and he was helping sustain a household that included his mother and three younger siblings. Helping others was in Joseph's nature. When he heard the garbage truck coming, he would go to the curb and assist the workers emptying his cans. When he was approached in the middle of his shift by a white man in his late thirties asking to mail a letter, Joseph instinctively reached out to him. The man would later be identified as Buford Furrow.[44]

Unbeknownst to Joseph, Furrow was a neo-Nazi who had once belonged to the Aryan Nations, one of the largest white power groups to emerge after the Vietnam War. Raised in the Pacific Northwest, he amassed an arsenal of weapons before driving down to Los Angeles. Furrow said he was haunted by "the decline of the white race" and "wanted to send a message to America by killing Jews." That morning, he unloaded seventy rounds in a span of less than thirty seconds on unsuspecting summer-camp participants and staff at the North Valley Jewish Community Center. The gunfire struck five people, including a middle-aged receptionist, a teenaged girl, and three boys between the ages of five and six. Like Patrick Purdy at Cleveland Elementary, Furrow intended to commit mass murder. By the grace of God and access to emergency medical care, all the wounded survived the attack.[45]

After stealing a car during his escape, Furrow pulled over when he spotted Joseph. His terrorist work was incomplete. In the eyes of the white nationalist, the postal carrier was a "target of opportunity" because he was either Asian or Latino and a federal government employee. Furrow pulled out a Glock 9mm semiautomatic pistol. Then he gunned down defenseless Joseph in broad daylight.[46]

The mass shooting caused breaking news. Pledging to end such vile attacks, state and national leaders came to the area to pay their respects. They offered heartfelt vows to combat anti-Semitism and expressions of empathy with the Jewish community center members. Despite being the sole murder victim, however, Joseph was getting lost in the shuffle. At one commemoration, his family sat in the front row for a press conference by California governor Gray Davis. They listened intently as Davis decried the problems of bigotry and uncontrolled gun sales. But they were stunned when he failed to acknowledge their presence or—save an impromptu gesture as the event was shutting down—even mention Joseph's name.[47]

Fearing that their beloved "Jojo" was not just gone but also forgotten, the Ileto family was doubly distraught. They had sat through the entire press conference without saying a word. Now they felt compelled to stand up and speak out wherever possible. They joined a march against violence and hate in the historically white San Fernando Valley, then a Black-led march through South Central Los Angeles and a national march led by Jesse Jackson. Alongside their mother, Lilian, Joseph's younger brother Ismael and sister-in-law Deena became leaders in the movement against anti-Asian violence and hate crimes.

Before the shootings, they had never paid much attention to politics or been immersed in activist campaigns or protests. Now they were crisscrossing the country for activities several times a week, continuing steadfastly in the face of hate mail and death threats. "Don't wait until something happens to your loved ones," Ismael said. "That's what we did. We stayed out of trouble and we just depended on other people. But it's a lot harder to stand behind a podium to share the story about losing a loved one. Be outspoken about it and speak up."[48]

One of the principal goals of the Iletos and other activists in this period was implementing anti-hate legislation. In response to Furrow's crime spree, Congressman Brad Sherman, whose district included the North Valley Jewish Community Center, explained why such laws were necessary. "Hate crimes injure not only the individual victim and his or her family," said Sherman, "but can sow the seeds of fear and intolerance throughout the region and sometimes throughout the country." At the time of Joseph's death, however, the most up-to-date federal hate crimes prevention bill had passed the Senate but stalled in the House. In April 2000, Joseph's family joined victims of the Jewish community center and the families of Matthew Shepard and James Byrd Jr., the Black victim of a Texas lynching, to meet with President Clinton to break the stalemate. They were building on an effort that began in the 1980s.[49]

Though used colloquially to encompass a range of acts, *hate crime* has a specific legal meaning. Whether committed against persons or property, the crime in question must have been motivated by animus toward a protected class (e.g., based on race, religion, or national origin). Parsing the specifics of its actual application and how the motive is determined can be challenging. The use of racist slurs, for example, may be highly offensive and hurtful without being a crime; and acts of discrimination may be illegal without specifically falling under hate crime laws. A hate crime can also be part of a broader set of criminal charges or used to enhance other charges. Finally, hate crime provisions vary by jurisdiction, and some jurisdictions have none.[50]

Activists confronting anti-Asian violence and hate crimes pushed for several forms of legislation. At the most basic level, they sought requirements that the government classify and record statistics on bias incidents. In 1985, with Democrats and civil rights organizations providing the base of support, Congress took up bills for the Hate Crimes Statistics Act. "I can tell you quite confidently," stated Norman Mineta, "that Americans of Asian ancestry are deeply concerned that the violence that is occurring to us because of our ethnic background is reaching alarming proportions in both frequency and degree. Furthermore, we are concerned that our Federal Government is not vigorously enforcing the civil liberties that we possess as citizens and residents of the United States." Representatives Mineta and Barbara Kennelly both invoked Vincent Chin's murder in supporting the legislation. After considerable debate, including initial opposition to the inclusion of "sexual orientation" as a designated category, the law finally passed in 1990.[51]

Beyond seeking greater documentation, advocates pushed for laws that made hate crimes a prosecutable offense. The horrific murders of Shepard and Byrd in 1998 aroused national attention and demands for action. Other white supremacist attacks hit members of multiple groups, solidifying the importance of multiracial solidarity. In July 1999, neo-Nazi Benjamin Smith went on a shooting spree across the state of Illinois, murdering Won-Joon Yoon, a Korean American graduate student at Indiana University, and Ricky Byrdsong, an African American who had previously been head basketball coach at Northwestern University. Smith also shot and wounded a second Black man, a graduate student from Taiwan, and six Orthodox Jews. The following year, in a tragically similar spree, Richard Baumhammers, another white male, killed his Jewish neighbor, an African American, and three Asian Americans—including two restaurant workers and a grocery store clerk—in Pittsburgh.[52]

It took until 2009, however, for Congress to pass the Matthew Shepard and James Byrd Jr. Hate Crimes Prevention Act. Prior to this, federal prosecution could occur only if the victim was engaged in a federally protected activity when the crime occurred. Furthermore, hate crimes now encompassed acts based on a wider range of victims' actual or perceived backgrounds: race, religion, national origin, gender, sexual orientation, gender identity, and disability. The "tough on crime" sentiment was most reflected in new laws that called for more severe charges and enhanced sentences for underlying crimes related to bias and hatred. The 1994 crime bill for example, included an amendment that increased the penalty for crimes of hate.[53]

At first glance, the Hate Crimes Prevention Act appears to have been highly effective at achieving the aims of its sponsors. According to federal data for the ten-year period (2010–19) following its passage, over 90 percent of those charged with hate crimes were convicted. Nearly all were imprisoned, and the sentences averaged more than ten years. But when we look more deeply into the numbers, we find that the Hate Crimes Prevention Act led to fewer than six convictions per year. This is largely because only a small fraction of the incidents deemed worthy of investigation were referred for prosecution. The low rate of prosecution, high rate of conviction, and lengthy mean prison sentence—when taken together—are signs that prosecutors have been highly selective. They seem to invoke the hate crimes act for the most serious violations, when there is "smoking gun" evidence that the suspect exhibited overt signs of hate, such as making distinct reference to the identity of the victim or using an epithet. It is thus an open question as to how effective the law has been in deterring racist and bias-related attacks or how satisfied the victims are with the resolution of the many incidents that were never prosecuted.[54]

While the passage of federal laws was pending, some activist campaigns achieved quicker success at the state level. New Jersey was one of the first states to enact an antibias law, through the Ethnic Terrorism Act of 1981, which in practice applied mostly to the defacement of buildings and structures. In no small measure because of public concern about the Dotbusters attacks and advocacy by the Indian American community, New Jersey passed one of the nation's most aggressive laws enhancing hate crime sentences with the Ethnic Intimidation Act of 1990. Misdemeanors could now become indictable offenses. Notably, the law gave judges the latitude to make bias crime determinations at sentencing based on "preponderance of evidence" and without needing a jury to decide "beyond a reasonable doubt." A police chief highlighted its impact on juveniles, whom he fretted would previously get a "slap on the wrist" but now could be put under correctional control.[55]

The effects of these laws remained uneven, too. A cat-and-mouse game developed as legislators and prosecutors grappled with writing and implementing laws that would withstand judicial review. Deferring to a 1992 U.S. Supreme Court opinion, New Jersey's high court, citing violations of the First Amendment, overturned the law that made expressions of hate illegal. But it upheld the indictment of a man who painted "Dots U Smell" on the home of a Pakistani American family in East Brunswick because the underlying crime of harassment constituted action beyond speech. After the Supreme Court overturned another hate crime law enhancing sentences for lack of due process in 2000, New Jersey passed a stand-alone law for the crime of "bias intimidation."[56]

In the aftermath of Thanh Nguyen's murder in Dallas, civil rights advocates successfully advocated in 1993 for passage of a Texas hate crime law with enhanced sentencing. Much of the momentum came from outrage generated when the white supremacist murderer of Donald Thomas, a Black man, was given a ten-year probation sentence following a trial with an all-white jury. Thomas had been in his front yard in Arlington when the killers drove by and shot him for sport.[57]

While the enactment of these and other state laws provided a long-sought victory for activists, some called for a paradigm shift in their approach to anti-Asian violence. Given that the Committee Against Anti-Asian Violence was one of the longest-standing organizations to focus on the issue, its new orientation was particularly noteworthy. In fall 1992, CAAAV announced that having conducted a self-study, its work would be moving to a new stage. Beyond its initial focus on victim's advocacy, the organization would expand to develop tenant and worker organizing. "We concluded that community organizing, economic justice issues, and a commitment to address race, class, and sex biases within our communities were necessary to expand our ongoing efforts to prevent anti-Asian violence." By the mid-1990s, CAAAV redefined racist violence as "the repression, exclusion, and disciplining of people of color by the state in order to control labor in the interests of capital accumulation, as well as to consolidate a white, male, heteronormative citizenry." Ultimately, it removed "anti-Asian violence" from its name and became known as CAAAV: Organizing Asian Communities.[58]

Jospeh Ileto's family understood that the passage of hate crimes legislation was only one part of a broader movement that required changing hearts and minds. Their mission was articulated by a cousin who made an acrostic message from the letters of Joseph's name: Join Our Struggle, Educate to Prevent Hate. Instill Love, Equality, Tolerance for Others. Toward that end, they established the memorial Joseph Ileto Hate Crimes Prevention Fellowship in conjunction with the Asian Pacific American Legal Center of Southern California to advance work that increases education and advocacy in the arena of hate crimes prevention.[59]

During the COVID-19 pandemic, the eruption of anti-Asian incidents made it clear that existing hate crime laws were not an adequate deterrent. The Asian American community was divided, however, on whether more such laws and sterner enforcement were the answer.

THE COVID-19 HATE CRIMES ACT

On March 14, 2020, near the outset of the first pandemic lockdowns, Jose Gomez III, a nineteen-year-old Hispanic-presenting man, saw Bawi Cung and his two small children enter a Sam's Club in Midland, Texas. Viewing the family as a "threat," Gomez yelled, "Get out of America!" Cung had migrated from Burma five years earlier and worked at Walmart. But Gomez perceived the family as Chinese—the group he blamed for spreading COVID-19. Grabbing kitchen knives from a store shelf, he cut Cung across his face. In what he confessed was attempted murder, Gomez then "slashed open" Cung's six-year-old son from his face to the back of his head. Cung feared the attacker would kill his whole family. Store employee Zach Owen, totally unarmed, risked his life to subdue the assailant, who stabbed him. Grateful for the bystander's intervention, Cung later remarked, "God sent Zach to protect my family right there at the right time." For the authorities, this was an obvious act of hate. Gomez confessed to hate crime charges and was sentenced to twenty-five years in prison.[60]

While these kinds of attacks put the community on edge, the Atlanta shootings produced a new mandate to address anti-Asian violence. In May 2021, President Joe Biden signed into law the COVID-19 Hate Crimes Act, based on bills sponsored by Senator Mazie Hirono of Hawai'i and Representative Grace Meng of New York. The two Asian American women Democrats had partnered in the immediate aftermath of the Atlanta spa shootings to advance legislation. Proponents saw the act's passage as a key step toward holding law enforcement and governmental agencies accountable to Asian American communities. The new law mandated that federal, state, and local officials properly record and spread public awareness of hate crimes against Asian Americans. In a vital step toward overcoming invisibility, Congress not only acknowledged thousands of reported cases of anti-Asian discrimination and incidents related to COVID-19; it also specifically flagged racism as the primary source of these attacks. The legislation provided resources and measures to assist with data collection, public education, and cultural competency training. These were largely incremental reforms, not introducing the sorts of criminalization measures, such as mandatory minimum or enhanced sentencing, found in prior hate crime bills.[61]

In an age defined by political polarization, the COVID-19 Hate Crimes Act received a rare level of bipartisan support. It passed with a greater than three-hundred-vote margin in the House of Representatives and by a vote of ninety-four to one in the Senate. Expressing serious concern, Susan Collins of Maine called the bill's passage "an unmistakably strong signal that crimes targeting Asian-Americans and Pacific Islanders in our country will not be tolerated." This was the type and scale of recognition that Asian American advocates had sought for decades. Casting the only Senate vote against the new law, Republican Josh Hawley of Missouri was pilloried by his hometown paper. "Sen. Josh Hawley, last seen encouraging a riot at the U.S. Capitol, now thinks America is too tough on hate crimes," declared an editorial in *The Kansas City Star*.[62]

The right-wing senator, however, was joined in opposition by over a hundred self-identified Asian American and LGBTQ organizations. "While we wish we could celebrate the historic visibility of anti-Asian violence and racism, which is as old as the colonization of the Americas," read a collective statement opposing the law, "the COVID-19 Hate Crimes Act contradicts Asian solidarity with Black, Brown, undocumented, trans, low-income, sex worker, and other marginalized communities whose liberation is bound together." Their primary objection lay in the law's centering the role of law enforcement and its failure to recognize "that police violence is also anti-Asian violence." Consistent with the spirit of militancy that erupted during the protests of the police killing of George Floyd, the joint statement asserted that bolstering policing and criminalization would not increase safety; it would only bring more harm. Contrary to the COVID-19 Hate Crimes Act's broad support, the George Floyd Justice in Policing Act—which proposes to outlaw controversial police practices like the use of chokeholds and no-knock warrants—repeatedly stalled after initial passage in the House.[63]

Writer Jay Caspian Kang questioned whether progressive critics like these were out of touch with much of the Asian American community. A sense of "viral outrage," he asserted in *The New York Times*, had erupted from scenes of elders being "shoved to the ground by Black assailants." In one of the highest-profile incidents, Vicha Ratanapakdee, an eighty-five-year-old Thai immigrant, died from an assault captured on video in San Francisco in January 2021. Antoine Watson, a nineteen-year-old African American, was arrested and jailed for murder. Citing the lack of any robbery, Ratanapakdee's family insisted, "This is a hate crime." Watson's public defender, however, pointed to mitigating factors. Attorney Sliman Nawabi said his young client had suffered a mental-health breakdown after he "lost his job and support structure during the pandemic." More than four years later, the case remained pending.[64]

As with the Atlanta spa massacre and the murder of Vincent Chin, the closer one looks, the clearer it becomes that while individuals may have committed these attacks—often picking up cues from anti-Asian rhetoric spouted by politicians or heard in the media—the problems underlying them are systemic in nature. In New York City, at least six attacks during the pandemic involving an Asian victim and a Black suspect occurred in broad public view and received prominent media attention. All took place in Manhattan. Three victims died. Yao Pan Ma—a Chinese immigrant who had lost his job but could not obtain unemployment benefits—was collecting cans in East Harlem. The middle-aged man, who weighed only 114 pounds, was blindsided by a man who kicked and stomped his head repeatedly. Maria Ambrocio, a Filipina nurse, died from injuries after being knocked down in Times Square by a man who was dashing through crowds after stealing a cell phone. Michelle Go, a Chinese American finance professional, was waiting on a subway platform when a man emerged from nowhere to push her into a train. Three others were wounded. Noel Quintana had his face slashed with a box cutter while riding a subway. Vilma Kari was hospitalized from brutal kicks to the body and head in Times Square by a male assailant who yelled, "You don't belong here." Incredibly, Katie Hou was attacked by a man who asked for her sign while she was leaving a Stop Asian Hate demonstration.[65]

The effects of these attacks were unmistakable. They devastated the victims and their families. They created a wave of anxiety and vulnerability that overtook a wide swath of the community. By foregrounding the societal effects of anti-Asian dehumanization, they galvanized thousands to take action and spread consciousness. In none of these cases, however, did the assailants exhibit clear objectives. In this regard, they stand apart from other campaigns—like the white labor groups that pushed for Chinese exclusion or the Klan-adjacent fishermen who tried to drive Vietnamese refugees out of Galveston Bay—that had discrete political motives and goals. The Manhattan attacks, by contrast, were vicious but uncoordinated. Most of the assailants were homeless. Most also had a long and serious record of run-ins with the police. Brandon Elliot, whose beating of Vilma Kari was caught on security video, killed his mother at age nineteen and was incarcerated for sixteen years. Elliot had an extensive history of serious and well-documented mental health problems.[66]

The New York Times characterized Martial Simon, who killed Michelle Go, as caught in an "endless circuit of hospitals and jails, outpatient psychiatric programs and the streets." The Haitian immigrant lived a relatively happy and productive life until he was struck by schizophrenia and became increasingly delusional. As this tragic story exposed, there is a lack of compassionate, effective treatment for people on the social and economic margins of society, even those who need and seek care. Adding more cops is no panacea. After a February 2021 stabbing of unhoused persons near transit stations, Mayor Bill de Blasio added hundreds of additional officers to patrol the subway system. Still, thirty New Yorkers were pushed onto tracks that year. When Go was killed, there were two officers on the platform unable to prevent the attack. "Real change comes with meaningful preventive measures," Go's father wrote in *The New York Times*. "This requires, among other things, adequate and continued funding for housing, treatment and other programs."[67]

As exemplified by the "model minority" discourse, conservatives counter that progressive policies ignore cultural factors, especially the role of stable families, in preventing crime. Their arguments trace back to a 1965 study, *The Negro Family: The Case for National Action*. Better known as the "Moynihan Report," it was written by Daniel Patrick Moynihan, a flamboyant scholar who became New York's senior senator. Moynihan argued that low-income African Americans were stuck in a "tangle of pathology" tied to an excess of absent fathers and out-of-wedlock births. His controversial thesis, however, is of little service to addressing overarching patterns of anti-Asian violence and hate incidents. As Asian American studies professor Janelle Wong reported in June 2021, despite the sensational attention given to crimes with Black suspects, perception does not match reality. In cases where the perpetrator could be identified by race, the overwhelming majority of assailants were white.[68]

Public perceptions might change if other cases, in which privileged whites who grew up with two parents targeted Asians, were highlighted. One such hate attack occurred on the streets of Manhattan in March 2021. Maria Ha and Dan Lee, an Asian American couple, were falsely accused of stealing a taxi from an older white woman. "Go back to communist China," she told them. The woman's parents had been part of elite society, hobnobbed with the wealthy and powerful, and owned a five-hundred-acre dairy farm upstate. In fact, her father was the late Senator Moynihan. Caught on video, Maura Moynihan quickly changed her story, stating she had "devoted most of my life to working with and for Asian people." The incident "had nothing whatsoever to do with any bias or racism or anti–Asian American prejudice," Moynihan insisted, going so far as to claim she was the actual victim of "awful" verbal assaults by Lee.[69]

In the end, these tragedies require us to broaden our analysis of anti-Asian violence. The most violent incidents by non-state actors seem to be happening especially in places where people feel a combination of economic hardship, social discrimination, and psychological distress. In the age of neoliberalism, the big city is both increasingly diverse and intensely competitive. The erosion of the safety net leaves residents feeling caught in a rat race and a zero-sum game. Given that violent crime is overrepresented in these distressed and often majority nonwhite sites, it should not surprise us that we have seen more interethnic conflict and violence going along with continued attacks by whites. Still, we should not overlook the fact that African Americans are far more likely than whites or Asians to be victims of homicide and violent crime. During the pandemic, murders surged (though still far from the 1990s peak), reaching 21,500 nationwide in 2020. Nearly half of the victims were Black. Yet research indicates they are less likely to be acknowledged or humanized as victims in the news media.[70]

The critics of the COVID-19 Hate Crimes Act called for investing in "community alternatives" to support those most vulnerable, such as "non-coercive mental healthcare infrastructures," "neighborhood-based trauma centers," and "community food banks." These community-based measures can advance multiracial solidarity by promoting safety through self-reliance and collective empowerment. Such thinking beyond criminalization measures is a pivotal step toward expanding our consciousness past the limits of the hate crimes framework. Advocacy for individual victims and cases can be a worthy endeavor; nevertheless, social justice outcomes cannot be held to the whims of a specific jury or whether a prosecutor like Samuel Alito is convinced a perpetrator had racist motives. While these new laws were received by many as a critical step forward, we need to look more closely at the problem of police misconduct—one that is too often dissociated from debate over Asian American concerns.[71]

———

NINE

When the Police Cause More Harm

About half an hour past midnight on May 27, 1991, fourteen-year-old Konerak Sinthasomphone was seen by witnesses running—naked, bloodied, and confused—outside the Oxford Apartments in Milwaukee. Struggling to keep his five-foot-three-inch, 110-pound frame upright, he fell to the ground near the corner of North 25th and State Streets.[1]

Konerak had come to the United States as a refugee from Laos, a nation torn apart by American bombing campaigns during the Vietnam War and the secret proxy wars that engulfed much of the region. After fleeing to Thailand and spending a year in a refugee camp, his family resettled in Milwaukee with the aid of a Catholic charity around 1979. A working-class family with limited means, the Sinthasomphones presumed that their new home would be a safe haven.[2]

Two young Black women, cousins Sandra Smith and Nicole Childress, saw the teenaged boy running in a state of distress and immediately sensed that something was seriously wrong. They found him in an alley looking bruised and beaten. Smith saw scrapes across multiple parts of his body and blood running down his inner thigh. He seemed young—she guessed he was eleven or twelve years old—and looked ethnically "Chinese" but had trouble speaking. In fact, Konerak had been taken captive from the Grand Avenue Mall on his way to soccer practice the prior afternoon. Now, he was fleeing for his life.[3]

Smith and Childress, both eighteen, saw an older white man pursuing Konerak. "Stay away from that boy," Childress yelled. Konerak, she sensed, was struggling and reaching out to her for help. A confrontation ensued.[4]

The women had it all wrong, the man replied. The boy was his "friend," and he was coming to take him home. But something seemed terribly off. The white man called the Asian boy by several different names, then held him in a headlock as he tried to break free.[5]

As Smith sought to protect the boy, Childress dashed to a phone booth to call 911. "I'm on 25th and State," she hurriedly explained to the operator. "And there's this young man, he is buck-naked and he has been beaten up. He is very bruised up. He can't stand. He has no clothes on. He is really hurt."[6]

"You got a man down," the police dispatcher relayed. "Caller states there's a man badly beaten and is wearing no clothes, lying in the street. 2–5 and State. Anonymous female caller. Ambulance sent."[7]

The sheriff's department received a separate call: "Subject male dragging a naked male who looked like he was beat up severely."[8]

Two white male police officers, thirty-four-year-old John Balcerzak and twenty-eight-year-old Joseph Gabrish, soon arrived on the scene. The man who claimed to be Konerak's friend now insisted the boy was his gay lover, was nineteen years old, and went by the name of "John Hmong." He claimed that "John" got drunk and left the apartment they shared while he was away. None of this was true. Yet the police sent the paramedics away and left the endangered boy alone in the would-be suspect's custody. They believed every word from the mouth of a fellow white man, roughly their same age. He struck them as "polite"—"just like a neighbor."

It was all a joke to the officers, whose assessment betrayed a lethal combination of racist and homophobic stereotypes. "The intoxicated Asian naked male (laughter in background)," they were recorded saying in their squad care, "was returned to his sober boyfriend (more laughter)." One of the officers later added, "My partner is going to get deloused at the station." They laughed harder.[9]

Their dereliction of duty ensured that Konerak's torture and agony would resume. Within half an hour of the police leaving the scene, he was dead: the thirteenth murder victim of notorious serial killer Jeffrey Dahmer.

Following the brutal murder of Vincent Chin, Asian American activists channeled outrage over Judge Kaufman's lenient sentence for Ronald Ebens and Michael Nitz into calls to "Jail the Racist Killers." In practice, this led to demands for more effective policing, hate crimes legislation, and enhanced prison sentences. Konerak Sinthasomphone's death, however, provides a stark example of why many Asian Americans do not trust the police and have pushed alternatives to criminalization. During the Asian American movement, activists framed the police as agents of oppression who used violence to attack student organizers on strike for ethnic studies or resisting the eviction of elders from the International Hotel. A younger generation of activists has also come of age—influenced by the Black Lives Matter (BLM) movement—rejecting conventional approaches to criminal justice. In cities on both coasts and in the Midwest, they have organized using the hashtag #Asians4BlackLives, which began as a "rapid response affinity group." In December 2014, Asian Americans supported BLM demonstrators in a multiracial action to shut down Oakland police headquarters. "Solidarity is about relationships forged through political struggle that seek to challenge forms of oppression," they stated.[10]

At first glance, the rate of "AAPI" fatal encounters with the police appears to be significantly lower than that of other racial and ethnic groups. But when researchers examining the period 2013–19 disaggregated the data, they found that the rate of police killings of Pacific Islanders in the United States was comparable to that of African Americans. While the rates for Asian Americans were lower overall, Southeast Asians were killed at more than three times the rate of East Asians and South Asians.[11]

Beginning with a closer look at events surrounding the murder of Konerak Sinthasomphone, this chapter draws attention to the role of police misconduct in anti-Asian violence. Not only were the police officers wantonly negligent in Sinthasomphone's death, but they also resumed their careers without any official discipline sticking—a sign of systemic bias favoring the police. I then examine another shocking killing—that of a Hmong American teenager—just outside Detroit a quarter of a century after the death of Vincent Chin. The story of Chonburi Xiong, however, remains relatively unknown, because he was killed by the police and was not seen as a perfect victim. Families with loved ones taken by state violence have struggled to raise awareness of the problem, especially in cases compounded by ableism and the lack of a humane response to mental health crises.

THE LEGACY OF KONERAK SINTHASOMPHONE

As he had with other victims, Jeffrey Dahmer lured Konerak Sinthasomphone to his apartment on the pretext of paying him to pose for seminude photos. He first drugged the teenager with a Halcion-laced drink, before sodomizing him. He then drilled a hole in Konerak's head and poured in hydrochloric acid, intending to keep the boy in a "zombie-like state." Somehow, while the chronic drinker Dahmer went out for beer, Konerak had enough wherewithal to escape.

Instead of rescuing the boy, the police delivered him right back to the murderer's lair, failing to notice the blood dripping from the hole in his head or the decaying flesh and bones Dahmer kept in his apartment from prior victims, including a full corpse in the bedroom. Dahmer proceeded to pour more hydrochloric acid into Konerak's brain, this time with fatal results. The boy's family, however, had no idea where he was. They were left with nothing but the gut-wrenching anguish that comes from seeing your child go missing and feeling helpless to do anything about it. Their painful resolution came two months later, when Dahmer was finally captured in the same apartment where Konerak was murdered. By this time, the serial killer had ended the lives of four more victims—all in a similarly gruesome manner.

This horrific scene is tragic testimony to American racism at its depths of depravity: a white male serial killer presumed innocent and deemed credible in the face of glaring evidence to the contrary; a defenseless Asian American boy, left to suffer and die by men who had taken a vow to serve and protect the public; two young Black women intervening to save a stranger's life, only to be threatened with arrest by the police.

To be certain, Dahmer's homicidal mentation was the primary driver of the tragedy. However, young Konerak—and at least four other men—would likely be alive today if not for a series of decisions and actions by the authorities, rooted in racial bias and callous disregard.

For starters, the police officers failed to perform a basic background check on Dahmer. Had they done so, they would have found that he was a registered sex offender on probation for second-degree sexual assault of a thirteen-year-old boy. (When the police executed a search warrant of Dahmer's apartment for that arrest in 1988, they looked right past a skull that was covered by a towel.) And quite astonishingly, the police would also have learned—through the type of routine, simple check performed on Black motorists pulled over for alleged traffic violations—that this earlier victim, whom Dahmer had served prison time for molesting, was Konerak's brother. Instead, they took Dahmer at his word and never bothered to verify Konerak's identity either.[12]

Furthermore, if his sentence for the sexual abuse conviction had not been lenient, Dahmer might never have met Konerak. In an era when mass incarceration was devastating urban Black communities, Dahmer was released in

March 1989 after completing a ten-month sentence that fell well short of the prosecutor's recommendation of five to six years. The judge hoped to encourage Dahmer to enter treatment for sex offenders. In fact, Dahmer's probation officer never went to his apartment.[13]

Moreover, the police went out of their way to silence and discredit the voices of the women who had pleaded with them to aid Konerak. It was nothing more than "a domestic squabble between two homosexuals" in the summation of the officers. "We tried to give the policemen our names, but he just told us to butt out," Sandra Smith recounted. "I said, 'What are you going to do about this? This is a boy.'" Childress said they were told to "get lost" or face arrest.[14]

When Smith arrived home, her mother, Glenda Cleveland, found her in tears. Cleveland called the police to express concern about Konerak's well-being. After failing several times to reach anyone involved, she was finally connected to Officer Balcerzak. She insisted that the person her daughter saw in distress was a child, and she feared for his safety in the custody of a man who came across as a predator. Five times in this conversation, Cleveland referred to Konerak as a "child."

With each response, Balcerzak became more adamant. He was "positive" the boy was an "adult."

"Are you sure?" Cleveland asked.

"He's with his boyfriend in his boyfriend's apartment," Balcerzak declared, as if homophobic stereotypes about sexual orientation precluded the possibility of violence and abuse. "I can't do anything about somebody's sexual preferences in life."

"Well no, I'm not saying anything about that," Cleveland retorted, "but it appeared to have been a child, this is my concern."

"Ma'am, I can't make it any more clear, it's all taken care of," the defiant and insouciant police officer said.

"It's all taken care of," he would repeat at least one more time. His unwarranted certainty sustained a deadly arrogance.[15]

A few days later, Cleveland saw a missing-child photo of Konerak in the news and called the police yet again, receiving no response. She next called the FBI, to no avail. When Dahmer confessed, it became clear that eleven of his victims were African American. Lauding Cleveland as a hero, many in Milwaukee's Black community castigated the police for their fatal disrespect for Black testimony. As Jesse Jackson declared while meeting Cleveland, "Police chose the word of a killer over an innocent woman."[16]

Konerak's death was a combined product of anti-Black and anti-Asian racism. Although Asian Americans comprised a marginal presence within the city, they were subjected to policing by the notorious Milwaukee Police Department, which retained and promoted officers with a merciless pattern of brutality against African Americans. For two decades, the infamous Harold A. Breier ruled the department with an iron first. His reign began during the 1960s, when the police routinely harassed and arrested civil rights activists in the name of keeping the peace. Between 1975 and 1979, twenty-two people died in police custody. In 1981, Milwaukee police officers beat Ernest Lacy, a Black man, to death and refused to call for medical assistance while they watched him dying. As in other instances, Breier insisted that his men acted in accordance with procedure and found no reason for discipline. By the time he stepped down in 1984, racism and corruption were deeply entrenched. In the aftermath of the Dahmer scandal, the mayor commissioned a review that found there were 206 citizen complaints against the police, including eighty-three for excessive force. Only fourteen received a hearing, and the cops prevailed in thirteen.[17]

The Sinthasomphone family invoked this pattern of misconduct when it filed a civil rights lawsuit against the City of Milwaukee and the three police officers who had returned Konerak to Dahmer's death grip. Still, the plaintiffs faced an uphill climb. As has been shown in all too many cases, judges and juries hold police officers in high regard and are frequently reluctant to punish them for acts that communities of color view as abusive or discriminatory. One of the primary obstacles that plaintiffs must overcome is the premise that the police are entitled to "qualified immunity." On that basis, Judge Terence Evans dismissed much of the Sinthasomphones' case in federal district court in 1993, precluding the family from bringing any claims based on a violation of due process.[18]

While Evans's ruling was all too common, the reasoning behind it was stunning. The police officers, he opined, could not have known "the inevitable horror which would follow their actions." But the judge was just warming up. "No one could have clearly known or suspected that Dahmer was a monster who killed and cannibalized his victims." It was, he calculated with hyperbolic precision, "at best a billion-to-one shot" that releasing Dahmer and returning Konerak to his apartment would lead to murder. "The police were not, constitutionally, required to know or appreciate that the billion-to-one shot would come up on top."[19]

Evans contrasted the "difficult" issue in this case with one in which the "danger is clear and obvious," citing the example of an officer who returned possession of a car to an intoxicated person who caused a deadly crash two hours later. "On the other hand," the judge concluded, "one does not inevitably know that getting a naked person off the streets, taking him to an apartment where his clothes and near-naked pictures of him are present, and leaving him there with a person who convincingly presents himself as a friend will result in death and dismemberment."[20]

In the opinion of the judge, the bias the officers had exhibited—in sympathy with Dahmer, as against Konerak and the two women who intervened—served as an acceptable defense. It was, he opined, reasonable for the police to assess that there was no "clear and obvious" danger to Konerak's well-being. This required Evans to overlook the same evidence the police had ignored.

First, the boy was more than just a "naked person" on the street. He was bruised, bloodied, drugged, and had a hole drilled into his head. In other words, there were clear signs of trauma and abuse. When the FBI interviewed the serial killer about the night of the murder, Dahmer said he felt he was on the verge of being caught. In fact, he was relieved that the police took only a cursory look at Konerak and did not take him to the hospital for a thorough medical examination.[21]

Second, the fact that Konerak's clothes and half-naked photos were in the apartment was entirely insufficient to establish his identity or place of residence. Would the police have investigated further if they had found Dahmer with a naked fourteen-year-old white girl, unable to speak for herself? The photos would have triggered suspicion that the girl was a trafficking victim.

Third, the judge blithely accepted that Dahmer "convincingly" presented himself as a friend, disregarding the police officers' dismissal of the bystanders' testimony and the failure to investigate the odious stench in Dahmer's apartment.

Finally, there is the point that Glenda Cleveland stressed repeatedly to the police: Konerak was not an adult; he was a boy. He looked younger than his age—as many Asian Americans stereotypically appear to non-Asians. To conclude that the police made a "reasonable" decision, the judge also had to reject implicitly the assertions of Smith and Childress, who declared that any reasonable, unbiased person could see that Konerak was a child in distress.

With the dismissal of their critical due process counts, the Sinthasomphones ended up settling their stripped-down case. The judge did allow their case for "denial of equal protection" to go forward. Civil rights cases are challenging to win, even when the defendants are not police officers. The family's lawyers, however, prevailed in a crucial ruling. As such, their claim did not entirely rest on proving discriminatory intent by the officers. Evans sustained their complaint on the basis of the Milwaukee Police Department's historical record of discriminatory "customs and practices." In other words, he allowed consideration of systemic, institutional racism. Thus, the plaintiffs did not necessarily have to demonstrate that any of the officers were bigoted. The entire department and, by extension, the city could be held liable because it failed to properly train officers to deal with minoritized populations, discipline or remove officers with a record of racial bias, or hire and promote officers from diverse backgrounds with the sensitivity to handle distress calls properly. Although this was not a class action lawsuit, the Sinthasomphones could effectively put the system on trial. On top of the obviously bad publicity a trial would have generated for Milwaukee and its political leaders, this may have been a significant factor in the city's willingness to settle by 1995. The family received $850,000, though no amount of money could compensate for their trauma and heartbreaking loss.[22]

The issue, however, was far from settled in the eyes of Officers Balcerzak and Gabrish. The police chief fired both for "gross negligence." In a fifty-six-page document detailing their misconduct, the Board of Fire and Police Commissioners sustained this decision. Believing they did everything proper, however, both officers appealed their terminations. They found a highly sympathetic audience in Judge Robert J. Parins of the Wisconsin Circuit Court. In May 1994, Parins found the termination of the officers "so disproportionate to the violations found by the Commission and approved by the Court in light of all the circumstances as to be shocking to one's sense of fairness." In this instance, *astonishing* may not sufficiently convey the disbelief one must feel in reading this opinion. The judge was not content to make a dispassionate ruling in favor of the officers. He went out of his way to express "shock" at how unfairly he felt the officers had been treated, given the "busy and stressful" nature of police work. In the minds of many with decision-making authority, it is simply too much to ask for racial awareness or cultural competency.[23]

Balcerzak and Gabrish resumed their careers in law enforcement. In fact, they had the audacity to file their own joint civil rights lawsuit in July 1995 against the police chief and other defendants in municipal government. Their terminations, they argued, had been based on "racially motivated reasons." Claiming they were the parties deprived of due process, they asserted that they had been "singled-out for discipline because of their race, Caucasian, in violation of the Equal Protection Clause." Balcerzak and Gabrish asserted that they were scapegoated "to appease the minority community." The police chief had recommended their terminations, they alleged, "regardless of any and all evidence" in order "to avoid minority rioting or adverse political repercussions." Broadening their scope, they charged that the City of Milwaukee "had discriminated against white police officers in virtually every aspect of employment." All their claims were dismissed in federal district court. When they appealed, the court affirmed the dismissals, opining that "the plaintiffs failed to present evidence of racial bias."[24]

As we witness the "Blue Lives Matter" counterprotests asserting that white policemen are victims of "reverse" discrimination and anti-police bias, we are moved to ponder how much these rulings left these officers and their supporters with a lasting sense that they had been victimized and denied redress. The police chief admitted that some officers, upset by the Sinthasomphones' lawsuit, made harassing calls to the family after the murder. But the principals got more than a second chance professionally. Leaving Milwaukee in 1997, Joseph Gabrish became founding chief of the police department in Trenton, Wisconsin. In August 2019, he was named interim police chief of Grafton, Wisconsin, after being the only candidate interviewed for the job. John Balcerzak went back to the Milwaukee police force and was so respected by his fellow boys in blue that he served as head of the police officers' union for four years.[25]

The infamy of Balcerzak and Gabrish received newfound attention in September 2022, when Netflix released the dramatized miniseries *Dahmer*. While it was too late to save Konerak's life or alter the course of the officers' careers, it was never too late to reshape the narrative. The show was a signature production of superstar director Ryan Murphy, who signed a landmark deal with the streaming content provider worth up to $300 million. Particularly known for gay-themed material, Murphy insisted that his goal as a white male showrunner was to shed light on the racism and homophobia that pervaded the serial killer's spree. To his credit, he shined a spotlight on the police negligence underlying Konerak's murder. Most dramatically, the end of one episode featured a dramatic reading of Glenda Cleveland's call, when she pleaded with the dismissive Balcerzak to take action.[26]

Despite these laudable features, Murphy's *Dahmer* sensationalized an already lurid story in ways that created new problems. Instead of Dahmer coming across Konerak while he is walking to soccer practice, the Netflix show portrays the boy initiating the contact. Even worse, Murphy depicts the fictional Konerak hanging out in front of a liquor store, where he is seen flagging down Dahmer to help him buy booze. After describing his tastes in liquor, the fictional Konerak then goes willingly back to Dahmer's apartment to drink with him. Finally, despite all evidence indicating that this was a tragic coincidence, the fictional Konerak tells Dahmer, who does not recognize him, that he accepted his offer to pose for pictures because he knew Dahmer was arrested for doing the same thing with his brother.

When this scene is viewed in the context of the entire series, Murphy seems intent on using his dramatic license to highlight Dahmer's appeal to his victims. *How could this deranged, homicidal man keep drawing young men to his squalid apartment? There must have been some queer—as in both deviant and homosexual—attraction that will pique the interest of viewers.*

True to expectations, *Dahmer* was a huge hit for Netflix, holding the number one spot for all streaming shows for three weeks. Following *Squid Game* and the fourth season of *Stranger Things*, it was only the third show in Netflix history to surpass one billion viewing hours within sixty days.[27]

But when one knows Konerak's actual story, to suffer through the Netflix version is to recoil in horror at such an inexcusable form of exploitation. Murphy's attempt to infuse sexual tension into Konerak's relationship with Dahmer led him to cast, in the fictional Konerak role, an actor who was nineteen or twenty years old. Moreover, the actor is a real-life karate champion, making him appear even more imposing than the boy who witnesses thought was as young as ten. In this way, Murphy upends the fundamental point the bystanders made to the police: The idea that Konerak was Dahmer's adult boyfriend defied credibility.[28]

In the end, Murphy's creative license undermined his ostensibly noble intentions. The ultimate effect was to expand the misrepresentations surrounding Konerak's murder to an exponentially larger audience, thereby elevating profiteering to new and shameless heights.

THE POLICE KILLED CHONBURI XIONG

In September 2006, I was helping run a program for teenagers called the Detroit Asian Youth (DAY) Project. Participants came mainly from working-class immigrant and refugee communities. Most attended schools that were majority Black. To have a chance at a decent education, they had to overcome school closures, teacher shortages, rancid school food, and budget shortfalls.

Some of us had volunteered with Detroit Summer, a multicultural youth leadership program started by James and Grace Lee Boggs with fellow activists in 1992. While that organization drew especially upon African American participants, we started DAY Project in 2004 as a companion program to locate and connect with Detroit's sparsely populated Asian American community. At the time, it was the only panethnic Asian American activist group in the city of Detroit. We clicked first with a small but concentrated population of Hmong Americans living in the Osborn neighborhood within the city's northeast corner. Many of the youths had lived their entire lives in the city but had never visited downtown. None had taken any K–12 classes that touched remotely on Asian American studies, but they taught us as much or more than we taught them.

Shortly after school was back in session, we met on a Saturday morning for the first time since the end of our summer program. I casually asked the youth participants, "What's new?"

We were going around the circle when Ben, quietly and reluctantly, spoke.

"My uncle died," he said. Ben was around fifteen, but his uncle was only eighteen.

We all gasped. "What happened?" several of us asked, seemingly in unison.

"He was killed by the police," Ben replied, setting off alarm bells in our heads. "It's in the news."

Through talking further with Ben, reading the brief news accounts, and consulting with the family's attorney, I learned that Ben's uncle, Chonburi Xiong, had lived with his parents in Warren, Michigan. Four police officers entered their basement, where he slept, and fired forty shots. They struck him twenty-seven times in his bed. It was self-defense, they asserted—Xiong had pointed a pistol at them first; he was a troubled youth who had had multiple run-ins with the law. The police action had been prompted by his parents calling 911 to report a domestic incident.

Officers entered the Xiong home, the Macomb County Prosecutor's Office concluded, with "probable cause to believe that Mr. Xiong posed a significant threat of death or serious bodily harm to themselves, his family and the surrounding neighborhood." As such, "the use of deadly force was justified." No criminal charges were filed against the officers, who were also cleared of any disciplinary action following an internal investigation.[29]

Chonburi's family, however, told a different story. I learned this firsthand through an interview with his father, Pang Blia Xiong, and a family friend who served as an interpreter. In common with many Hmong and Southeast Asian Americans, the Xiong family's connections to the United States were rooted in war and trauma:

> My name is Pang Blia Xiong. I was born in a small farming village in Laos on December 31, 1956. I did not have much of a childhood because my country was torn apart by war. When the Americans came to Laos, they asked our people, the Hmong, to help fight the communists. I did not know much about America, but my parents told us it was our duty to help the Americans. My father was a Hmong military leader who was killed in combat in 1969. That same year, I joined the army at the age of thirteen. Although I feared for my life at every moment during the war, I managed to survive.
>
> But after the communists took power in 1975, everybody who sided with the Americans became an outcast in Laos. My family fled to the woods to survive. For four years, we were constantly running to avoid the gunfire from communist soldiers. Sometimes, we went for days without food. Many people from my village died—men, women, children, and elders. My family was lucky to escape many close encounters.[30]

DAY Project received great support for our work from the parents of Hmong American youth. In the most immediate sense, they saw this as an opportunity to keep their kids out of trouble, enhance their education, and expand their life opportunities. But in a deeper sense, Hmong parents strived to give their children the safe and promising childhood that war had stolen from their generation. Pang Blia Xiong survived nine years in the Ban Vinai refugee camp, crammed in with others in substandard housing. While the Thai government accepted hundreds of thousands of refugees, it also sought to contain its burden and limit friction with Vietnam and Laos. Thus, to deter additional migration, provisions in the refugee camps were kept to a bare minimum. Xiong met his wife in the camp. Chonburi was their first child, born in 1988 as they were planning to move to the United States. "In our culture," he said, "the first-born son is especially important because he will be the one to carry on our family name and heritage." In Detroit, Xiong worked factory jobs for auto parts suppliers and became a naturalized citizen.[31]

The Eastside of Detroit, however, was a difficult place to raise a child of any race in the 1990s. Schools, libraries, and parks faced crises and shutdowns. Violent crime rates soared amid the drug wars and crack epidemic. In his research on Cambodian Americans in the Bronx, Eric Tang, a scholar who draws on his experience as a community organizer, offers a sense of the hardships that Southeast Asian refugee youths encountered in this era. Survivors of harrowing threats to their lives and well-being were resettled into distressed urban neighborhoods, often exposed as a small minority group within predominantly Black and Latino areas. Initially seen as "easy marks" vulnerable to bullying and physical attacks, the youths learned to "fight back to earn the respect of their tormentors." Acting to survive within the underground economy of the "hyperghetto," some turned to drug dealing and robbery. Subjected to racial profiling, refugee youth became targets of the same aggressive policing and state violence hitting Black and Brown communities.[32]

Although they were unfamiliar with Warren, the Xiong family moved to the city in 2003, crossing the 8 Mile border and historical racial divide made famous by Eminem. Like many working-class families, they hoped to find a safe neighborhood and good schools. And they were not alone. The city that had long resisted racial integration was now undergoing rapid demographic change. Between 2000 and 2010, Warren's white population declined by nearly twenty-two thousand, while its Asian population rose by about 50 percent and its Black population nearly quadrupled. (Next to Warren, the population of Ronald Ebens's former home, Eastpointe, turned majority Black by 2010.) These citywide figures severely understate the magnitude of change in the southern part of Warren, which borders Detroit. The city's leadership, however, remained predominantly white. Reports of friction in schools and with police circulated among Black and Asian American residents. "For nearly three years, we always considered our neighborhood safe, and we trusted the Warren police," Xiong said. "We never imagined that our son, Chonburi, could be killed by police officers in our own home."[33]

The Xiong family contested public reports that they deemed inaccurate and called for a more even-handed account. First, Chonburi had fired a gun in the house, but at the ceiling—not at the police—and long before the police arrived. Second, the family had called for help the day before their son was killed. By the time police arrived that day, Chonburi had driven off. He later came home without incident. Thus, when the police returned the next day, the conflict had already subsided. Third, police entered the home without a search warrant or arrest warrant. Though they claimed that the family invited them in, Xiong's parents disputed that point. Since their English was limited, it is easy to imagine miscommunication if an urgent, heated exchange occurred without a translator.[34]

Finally, the authorities disregarded what was perhaps the most troubling fact. Because of his past record, Chonburi was required to wear an ankle monitor. This meant that the police could tell when he came and went from the house. If the officers believed they had probable cause to enter the Xiong home and use deadly force because Chonburi posed a "threat of death or serious bodily harm" to his parents, then it was grossly negligent of the police to allow him back into the house, when they could have interceded beforehand.[35]

Pang Blia Xiong appealed to those in positions of authority and to the wider community:

> I ask everyone who is a parent, "If you lost your child in this manner, wouldn't you be searching for answers? Wouldn't you do everything you could to see if your child's death could have been avoided?" My wife and I have filed our complaint because we want the court and the public to take a closer look at the facts of this case.

Once again, there is no evidence that police used racist epithets or were motivated by hatred of Asian or Hmong Americans when they killed Chonburi Xiong. But the inconsistencies call for us to raise some thorny questions. Would the police have addressed this matter with different assumptions had the Xiongs been a white, middle-class family in a neighborhood that was predominantly white? Would they have exhibited more cultural competency if Xiong's parents had been fluent in English? We need to look at pattern and practice over a protracted period to best assess structural bias. But we should also scrutinize comments about this particular case. "The only thing the officers needed was the justification to shoot one time," said city attorney, John J. Gillooly. "The 27 bullets don't matter."[36]

Such logic is deeply troubling, for it completely disregards the requirement that police use proportional force—a concept that much of America learned about in the aftermath of George Floyd's murder. Did the police have a compelling argument for why, after the first shot hit Chonburi, twenty-six more shots were required? That Chonburi never fired back would complicate that argument, as would his family's assertion that the medical examiner found evidence indicating that most shots struck him in the side and back. What cannot stand is the city attorney's stance that if one shot is justified, an infinite number is automatically justified. This would ignore police standing over an obviously dead body and continuing to fire in an act of sadism or ritual mutilation.

While we should, of course, pay attention to the outcomes of trials and investigations, we must also be concerned with the level of care that is taken in the justice process. As the cases of Ebens and Nitz demonstrated, process and outcome are interrelated. Helen Zia was asked to compare the responses to the killings of Chin and Xiong. "It took a huge community outcry to find out what happened, to get interviews of the eyewitnesses at the scene in the Vincent Chin case," she told Detroit's *Metro Times*. "It may take that kind of outcry here too."[37]

In fact, the awareness raising we did around the Xiong case was a direct legacy of the Justice for Vincent Chin movement. In 2002, I helped initiate and coordinate a three-day commemoration to mark the twentieth anniversary of Chin's murder. We attracted national media coverage and a local audience of five hundred people. By design, the sessions, sponsors, and audience reflected a concern with multiracial coalition building. But we also saw more Asian Americans turn out than we expected, probably the most for any Asian American–sponsored social justice event in Detroit since the Chin case. To build on this momentum, we organized a conference called "Bridges to the Future" to strategize next steps in Asian American community activism and empowerment. The plan for DAY Project grew directly out of that summit.

The cross-racial activist ties we previously established proved vital to the Xiong justice campaign too. Through my work with Grace Lee Boggs, I developed a close relationship with Ron Scott, a former Black Panther leader, who provided advice based on his extensive work leading the Detroit Coalition Against Police Brutality. Our campaign garnered support from the Michigan ACLU and the Macomb County branch of the NAACP, whose president, Ruthie Stevenson, declared, "We're all in this together. Any injustice to one is an injustice to all of us." In condemning the Xiong killing, Black leaders expressed interethnic solidarity, while drawing attention to a broader pattern of abusive policing that deeply affected their community. Complaints about the Warren police department escalated again in April 2009, when officers killed Robert Mitchell, a sixteen-year-old Black youth, who was a passenger in a car stopped by police for expired tabs. He died after being shot with two taser darts to the chest.[38]

Our call to support the Xiong family also resonated with Hmong American activists in other parts of the nation, especially the Twin Cities, which have been the major site of Hmong political empowerment. Community leader and performer Tou Ger Xiong helped spread the word and lent his voice to the cause. Coming to Warren to perform for a benefit event, he connected the Xiong killing to recent struggles against anti-Asian racism and violence in Minnesota and Wisconsin. An uproar erupted in November 2004 after Chai Soua Vang, a Hmong shaman and National Guard veteran from St. Paul, killed six white people who accused him of trespassing on their property while hunting near Rice Lake, Wisconsin. To the prosecution it was an open-and-shut case. The jury convicted him of six counts of first-degree murder, and he was sentenced to six consecutive life sentences. But Vang said he acted in self-defense after a member of the white party cursed at him, called him racist slurs, and shot first.[39]

Amid signs of a generalized anger at their community, Hmong Americans, noting they had long been subjected to racist harassment by hunters in the region, feared reprisals. In contrast, as reported by *The New York Times*, whites in Wisconsin claimed that complaints of white hunters spreading anti-Asian racism were "exaggerated." A bookstore manager in Rice Lake said, "You hear talk now about racism, but I don't see it." Official notice came from the state's Department of Natural Resources, which reported it was "unaware of tensions between Hmong and white hunters." Its spokeswoman elaborated, "We've had our ear to the ground since this happened, and we're not picking up on that at all." Hmong Americans were aghast at this lack of sensitivity. Their anxieties proved tragically warranted, when another hunter, Cha Vang, was killed in January 2007 by a man previously convicted of painting "K.K.K." and a racist slur on the walls of a cabin he robbed.[40]

Because of this national awareness and support, the police killing of Chonburi Xiong is commonly mentioned alongside other prominent Hmong American cases. The public scrutiny may have helped his family gain a settlement in its civil lawsuit for an undisclosed sum. "We hope that we can all work together," his father said, "and that we can all work with the police and government authorities to ensure that all people are treated fairly. We deeply miss our son, and we do not wish to see any other parents suffer as we have."[41]

Those who worked on the campaign have upheld a commitment to fulfill the Xiong family's goal of fairness for all. Stephanie Chang first volunteered for DAY Project as a college student. After working as an urban community organizer, she was elected to the state house of representatives in 2014. Four years later, she became a state senator. In a sign of how her reputation for service and integrity cuts across racial groups, Chang first won election to a district based primarily in Detroit that was majority Black and less than 1 percent Asian. To promote Asian American political empowerment and civic engagement, she mentored emerging leaders through programs tied to two community groups, Rising Voices and the Michigan chapter of Asian and Pacific Islander American Vote. While no such groups existed at the time of the Xiong justice campaign, new efforts at voter registration and education made it possible for a candidate like Mai Xiong to win election as the first Hmong American state representative in Michigan. Though she is not directly related to Chonburi, we met Mai through the Xiong justice campaign, which became a springboard to her involvement in political activism. She now represents a Michigan legislative district that includes both Warren and Detroit. It is approximately half white, 40 percent Black, and 4 percent Asian.[42]

While DAY Project, like many other grassroots activist organizations, began with a handful of folks sitting around a table to share their concerns and dreams, adult and youth participants have gone on to work in social justice organizations and cultural institutions throughout Detroit. They are building cross-racial solidarity while addressing issues such as gentrification, food justice, and education. Their work highlights the power of consciousness raising. As the civil rights movement proved, the most meaningful forms of education often occur outside of formal institutions through "freedom schooling" programs like Detroit Summer and DAY Project.

THE QUEST FOR SAFETY AND ACCOUNTABILITY

In February 2021, dozens of Asian American organizations in the San Francisco–Oakland Bay Area issued a joint statement aiming to "imagine what real safety could look like for our people." They sought to build a future "that is grounded in accountability, justice, and care for each other." The coalition issued three demands for "culturally-relevant and trauma-informed investments":

1. Ensure victims and survivors of all backgrounds and language abilities receive full supportive services so they can recover and heal.
2. Expand intervention- and prevention-based programs and invest in basic needs and community-based infrastructure that we know will end the cycle of violence and keep all of us safer.

3. Resource cross-community education and healing in Asian American and Black communities that humanizes all of us rather than demonizes or scapegoats any community of color.[43]

The focus on care has come further to the fore as police killings of mentally ill Asian Americans have exposed systemic ableism. On December 23, 2020, the family of Angelo Quinto, a Filipino American, called 911 out of concern that the thirty-year-old veteran was suffering from a mental health crisis. Instead of getting assistance, they assert, he was violently restrained. An officer held his knee on his neck, as Quinto pleaded, "Please don't kill me." After nearly five minutes, he fell unconscious; blood was dripping from his mouth. When he passed away in the hospital a few days later, activists jumped into action. Quinto's death eerily reminded his family and supporters of George Floyd's murder. With the backing of 170 groups, they created the multiracial Justice for Angelo Quinto coalition. Next came what they called a series of lies and deception. The county coroner, who lacked board certification in forensic pathology, ruled the cause of death to be "excited delirium syndrome"—implying a sudden onset of aggression and death based on an overdose of prescription drugs. It was a spurious diagnosis, similarly invoked by the officers who killed Floyd. According to the American Medical Association, there is a disturbing pattern of "excited delirium" being used to justify excessive police force. It is "disproportionately cited in cases where Black men die in law enforcement custody." An independent autopsy commissioned by Quinto's family found no sign of drugs and determined that the cause of death was asphyxiation.[44]

Scarcely a week later, nineteen-year-old Christian Hall was killed by state police on the other side of the country, in rural Pennsylvania. The prosecutor for Monroe County characterized his death as a "classic suicide by cop scenario." But the belated release of evidence exposed this falsehood. An adoptee from China raised by a Black father and Filipino American mother, Christian suffered throughout his childhood from depression and reactive attachment disorder. He made a 911 distress call from a highway overpass, where he was confronted by officers who claimed they shot him in self-defense. A video recording, however, revealed what the cops failed to disclose: Christian had his hands in the air for fourteen seconds prior to the deadly shooting. Pennsylvania's Asian Pacific Islander Political Alliance has worked with Hall's family, the NAACP, and a multiracial coalition of local organizations to hold the police accountable.[45]

Evidence indicates that the surge of anti-Asian racism during the pandemic aggravated mental health crises. Researchers Sasha Zhou, Rachel Banawa, and Hans Oh examined surveys of Asian American and Pacific Islander college students conducted during fall 2020. They found that "over a quarter reported experiencing COVID-19 related racial/ethnic discrimination." More than two-thirds of those respondents had experienced at least one "clinically significant mental health condition," including elevated rates of depression, anxiety, binge drinking, non-suicidal self-injury, and suicidal ideation. These findings have been corroborated by broader surveys of Asian American adults.[46]

After losing their loved ones, the Quinto and Hall families share a common mission to prevent further police killings and abuse. They want others in their position to be able to call a 988 hotline, rather than 911, to ensure that a mental health professional is the first responder instead of armed officers. Sadly, this could not happen soon enough for the family of Victoria G. Lee in Fort Lee, New Jersey. On July 28, 2024, Lee's brother called 911 to report that she needed an ambulance for a mental health emergency. Instead, police arrived and broke through her apartment door. When Lee stepped toward them holding a pocketknife, she was shot and killed—a near replay of the police killing of Yong Yang in Koreatown Los Angeles less than three months earlier. "Even if it is negligence," said her father, K. Y. Lee, "it is almost no different from intended murder." With several African Americans having been killed under similar circumstances in the area, the Paterson chapter of Black Lives Matter demonstrated solidarity with the Lee family. Organizer Zellie Thomas stated that the group was fighting "not just for the safety of Black people, but for the safety of everyone."[47]

Christian's mother, Fe Hall, emphasized that the police are not trained caregivers. In her son's case, a heavy policy response likely created more confusion and fear. "Bullets should not be the first resort," she said. But the advocacy of Quinto's family and supporters has begun to achieve long-needed reforms to police practice. In September 2021, California passed the Angelo Quinto Act, banning the police from using restraints that cause positional asphyxia. Two years later, the enactment of AB 360 barred the use of "excited delirium" as a cause of death by police and coroners.[48]

Families of Asian American police brutality victims have also challenged members of the community to oppose all acts of unjustified police violence. Some of the most widely documented incidents have taken place in New

York City, where charges of police brutality were at the core of one of the largest protests in Asian American history. On April 26, 1975, Peter Yew, an engineering student, was detained by police of the all-white Fifth Precinct for disputing their "mishandling" of a group of Chinatown youths who had amassed following an accident between white and Chinese American drivers. While the police claimed that Yew assaulted them, Yew retorted that he was dragged and beaten by the cops without justification. On May 12, when Yew appeared in court, a protest led by the young radicals in Asian Americans for Equal Employment (AAFEE) drew between twenty-five hundred and five thousand people calling for the charges against Yew to be dropped, for the officers to be charged instead, and for precinct captain Edward McCabe to resign. "This is something that should have been done a long time ago," Chinatown shopkeeper John Hung told *The New York Times*. "So far, the Chinese always keep their mouths shut, and they are always oppressed by other people. Now the young people cannot take any more, and the old people join them. It's really amazing."[49]

Yew's allegations of a police beating sparked a prairie fire among Chinatown youths, who took mounting umbrage over a crackdown on organized crime and gang activity that they asserted was licensing police abuse and racism. Many had been caught up in "stop and frisk" searches they deemed illegal and discriminatory. Even worse, in a late-night tragedy at the Jade Chalet restaurant on December 3, 1974, officers of the New York Police Department (NYPD) clashed with local residents and killed bystander Tsu Yi Wu. "The cops here don't understand the people or our culture," said twenty-three-year-old activist Jean Tam. "We don't want gambling any more than any other community, but the cops use that as an excuse for brutality. To them every Chinese kid on the street is a potential gang member and every Oriental is an illegal alien who can be harassed."[50]

Fretting that their authority over Chinatown was being eclipsed by the militants, the established leaders of the Chinese Consolidated Benevolent Association endorsed a larger community-wide protest, which became a day-long general strike. On May 19, Chinatown businesses closed so that owners, workers, and patrons alike could join the demonstration. "Elderly women, young mothers carrying children in their arms, well-dressed businessmen and young people in jeans, marched six and eight abreast until they ringed the five-block triangular City Hall Park," wrote Deirdre Carmody in the *Times*, which reported there were ten thousand participants. Estimates by activists were double that count. Regardless, the impact registered almost immediately. Within five days of the protest, Captain McCabe was removed from precinct leadership. In early July 1975, the grand jury dismissed Yew's charges and indicted the officers he alleged had beat him. The NYPD agreed to commission Chinese American officers to patrol the neighborhood on foot and without guns.[51]

While these reforms placated moderate Chinatown leaders in the merchant class, they did not eradicate the broader problem for Asians or other New Yorkers of color. On March 24, 1995, Qinglan Huang was horrified to learn that her younger brother, Yong Xin, had been shot by a police officer in Brooklyn. Though she rushed to Coney Island Hospital to see him, she was instead taken to the station, where the police informed her that Yong Xin, only sixteen, was dead. His friends testified that he had his back to officer Steven Mizrahi, who had slammed him into a glass door that shattered. He was not resisting, they insisted, when he was shot in the back of the head. But Mizrahi, who mistook Huang's pellet gun for a handgun, countered that his firearm discharged accidentally while Huang was facing him and tussling. Qinglan was retraumatized when she learned that the NYPD officer would not be indicted. Though her boss at that time advised her not to comment, she willingly spoke out. "This is not the end," she told *The New York Times*. "Our family is going to do everything to fight for justice for Yong Xin."[52]

The Committee Against Anti-Asian Violence (CAAAV) worked with the Huang family and organized support with Yuri Kochiyama and other activist groups. The activists situated Huang's murder within the rightward shift prompted by the inauguration of Mayor Rudy Giuliani in 1994. Giuliani's emphasis on "law and order," according to scholar Vivian Truong, played into the anxieties of whites as they were becoming a minority in the city. Adopting the "broken windows" theory of hyper-enforcement, the NYPD cracked down on minor and nonviolent infractions in the name of preserving public safety but particularly to promote gentrification. In response, CAAAV shifted organizing strategies to support Asian Americans who found themselves in the crosshairs of the NYPD, especially immigrants on the economic margins such as sex workers, street vendors, and working-class youths. To support the Huang family's quest for justice, CAAAV organized a multiracial coalition with community partners who were alarmed that the war on crime was effectively a war on poor and nonwhite New Yorkers. They would join with these partners four years later to protest the tragic police murder of

Amadou Diallo, an unarmed African immigrant who was fired on forty-one times after reaching for his wallet.[53]

Nearly two decades later, when Akai Gurley was killed in a Brooklyn housing project by a stray bullet callously fired down a stairwell by an NYPD officer, thousands of Chinese Americans from many corners marched and demonstrated vocally in New York and other cities. Most of these marchers, however, supported Peter Liang, the rookie cop who also said he fired his gun accidentally when it struck Gurley. And some Liang supporters consciously presented themselves as continuing a legacy of struggles for justice that ran from the era of Chinese exclusion through the movement for Vincent Chin. Unlike Mizrahi and many white officers in high-profile cases of African Americans killed by police, Liang was convicted of second-degree manslaughter and official misconduct. He was scapegoated, his supporters asserted, because whites in power sacrificed a Chinese American to appease their Black critics. Qinglan Huang, however, rejected their assertions and condemned the police again. Though conceding that the NYPD may have had reason to scapegoat Liang, she did not waver from calling for accountability. "Whatever the charges he's facing is exactly what he did," she said.[54]

One of the most enduring images of Black-Asian solidarity came from Minneapolis, following the police murder of George Floyd. "We have to join hands with them," Youa Vang Lee told a crowd of protesters in June 2020. The fifty-nine-year-old Hmong American woman had insisted that younger activists in the community tell her how she could join the marches for Floyd. In 2006, her son Fong Lee was shot in the back eight times by Minneapolis police officer Jason Andersen. Although the shots were caught on video, an internal investigation ruled that the killing was justified, and the grand jury failed to indict. When Lee's family sued in civil court, an all-white jury rejected their claim. Despite the prolonged trauma, Fong's mother remembered the solidarity that Black activists showed. "Here's what I saw with Fong," she said. "Black people were with us the whole time, morning or night." Now Lee, a modest assembly line worker, wanted to let Floyd's mother know she felt her pain. Her speech went viral, providing moral clarity at a time when Hmong and Asian Americans were in anguish after learning that a member of their community, Tou Thao, was one of the officers involved in Floyd's murder. At a Hmong 4 Black Lives rally, Lee implored people of all races and backgrounds "to speak out and to support those voices that have been taken away from us." She declared, "This fight is a fight for humanity."[55]

For most of the decade following the emergence of the Black Lives Matter movement, I have lived in Seattle. I have seen BLM, combined with growing numbers speaking out about anti-Asian attacks, make a notable difference in the public discussion of police brutality and racist violence. While neither of these problems has disappeared, there is growing recognition of the need for greater transparency and accountability. This is partly the result of reforms within the government and media. Mostly, however, it reflects people at the grassroots level expanding social consciousness and feeling more empowered to stand up to injustice. Some recent stories, while unquestionably tragic, demonstrate the multiple ways Asian Americans continue to break through the silence.

Tommy Le was excited to walk through graduation on June 14, 2017. The twenty-year-old Vietnamese American student had just completed his career link program at community college, when he was spotted at an apartment complex in Burien, a working-class city south of Seattle. Someone had called 911 to report that he had been attacked by a man, possibly experiencing a mental health incident, who wielded a knife. Several King County Sheriff's deputies arrived on the scene. They said they tried to tase Le but to no avail. Deputy Cesar Molina, later claiming he feared for his life, then fired six shots at Le. The bullets struck Le three times with fatal force. But the story eventually unraveled. Le was not holding a knife, the sheriff's office admitted, but rather a pen. In fact, an independent review found that he may have been empty-handed. More troubling, while one shot hit Le in the wrist, Molina shot him twice in the back. This meant that Le was either running away, falling down, or already on the ground when hit. Clear determinations could not be made because the sheriff's office failed to preserve evidence properly, through either negligence or deliberate tampering. After nearly four years of fighting in court and in public debate, Le's family settled its civil suit for $5 million.[56]

On the night of August 29, 2022, Zhen Jin, a school bus driver, heard banging on the front door of the condominium where she lived with her elderly uncle, in suburban Kenmore to the north of Seattle. Her neighbor, Burton Hill, was extremely drunk and furious. He accused Jin of leaving chicken bones lying around the complex to make his dog choke. Jin denied harming the dog. But her uncle, a blind and hearing-impaired Palestinian immigrant in his eighties, wanted the dog on a leash because he feared walking the grounds while it was loose. Agnes Miggins, Hill's domestic partner and president of the homeowners' association, belittled the elderly man's concern and mocked his accent. "One down, one to go," she said, referencing the recent departure of another Chinese American woman resident, who alleged that Miggins racially harassed her. As the argument escalated, Hill shouted a misogynistic slur and twice called Jin a "fucking chink." He told her he would get the HOA to "kick you the fuck out of this place." But Hill was more than a belligerent neighbor. He was also a Seattle police officer who walked around the building premises armed. "You're going to jail," Hill threatened Jin. Although she was terrified, Jin did not take this bullying lying down. She brought a recording of the incident to the Chinese Information and Service Center, a local nonprofit organization that had established an Anti-Bias/Anti-Hate Program in response to the attacks during the pandemic. Its staff could receive complaints in nine different languages. They worked with Jin to forward her complaint to Seattle's Office of Police Accountability. The process took around eighteen months—and all the while, her hostile neighbor patrolled the streets. Although Jin reported living in "extreme fear for her safety and her life," she did not back down. In March 2024, Hill was terminated as a police officer.[57]

Meanwhile, in November 2019, Kevin Dave received a $7,500 bonus to start his new job as an officer of the Seattle Police Department. Shortly after, Jaahnavi Kandula came to Seattle from Bengaluru, India, during the COVID-19 pandemic, to pursue a master's degree in information systems. The two met in January 2023 under the most tragic of circumstances. Kandula was walking through a crosswalk several blocks east of the Space Needle. Responding to a 911 call for a possible overdose, Dave was speeding through the dense business district. He plowed into her with his Ford Explorer SUV. The distressed officer was cited only for a traffic infraction. But this was not his first incident. During his probationary period with the Tucson police in 2013, Dave was fired for substandard performance, including a "preventable collision." After that, a Seattle detective discovered, he was pulled over for "likely driving drunk" yet approved for hire following a standard background check. Kandula died from her injuries. Her family memorialized her as a "brilliant student" with "an innate ability to connect with people from all walks of life." But there was much more to the story.[58]

In the months following the incident, a Seattle Police Department employee came across a recording that the police union's vice president, Daniel Auderer, made shortly after Kandula was struck. He laughed uproariously while talking to the union's president, whose replies were inaudible. "She is dead," Auderer said, referring to Kandula. "Just write a check [for] $11,000." Still cackling, he continued, "She had limited value." When the recording made national news, Auderer stated that his words were "not made with malice." They were taken out of context, he insisted. He only intended to mock personal injury lawyers who sue for damages. There were other signs, however, that he discounted the significance of what had transpired. Auderer said, wrongly, that Dave was "going 50" miles per hour. "That's not out of control," he commented. "That's not reckless for a trained driver." In fact, Dave was going seventy-four miles per hour, and an investigation determined that he would not have hit Kandula if he had been doing fifty. And Auderer went further: "I don't think she was thrown 40 feet, either," he said. Kandula's body was found 138 feet from the collision site. Auderer was eventually fired, and Kandula's supporters continued protesting to demand that prosecutors reopen an investigation into Dave's conduct.[59]

When I heard the recording of the cop setting the "limited value" of Jaahnavi Kandula's life at $11,000, my first thought was that we have not come far since Judge Kaufman placed a $3,780 sticker price on the life of Vincent Chin four decades ago. In fact, once we adjust for inflation, $11,000 in 2023 turns out to be worth even less than $3,780 in 1983. Yet, when I look around, I see so many signs of the degree to which Asian American antiviolence activism has grown in scope, scale, and vision. On September 1, 2024, I joined with hundreds outside Tacoma's Northwest ICE Processing Center, a private prison contractor, for the Liberation Obon ceremony. I grew up celebrating Obon as the Japanese Buddhist festival honoring the deceased. Here, the chanting, folk dancing, and food recalled ancestors from Japanese American concentration camps in conjunction with a tribute to those who have died in Immigration and Customs Enforcement (ICE) custody. A multiracial group led by Latino and Japanese American organizers demanded the prison's closure. Using cell phones, they broadcast speeches by current detainees separated from their families, while honoring Charles Leo Daniel, an immigrant from Trinidad and Tobago who died in that prison earlier in the year following an extended detention in solitary confinement.

The expressions of unity were powerful to witness. They also drew attention to the concerns that Asian American activists have raised about ICE long before Trump became president. In February 2006, ICE moved to deport Zhenxing Jiang, a Philadelphia restaurant operator and mother of two U.S.-born children. She was pregnant with twins. In the 1990s, Jiang and her husband came to the country without papers. They applied for asylum but were denied. In ICE custody, Jiang miscarried—losing both fetuses, she argued, because of abuse and neglect by ICE officers. Local and national supporters raised awareness of her situation and called for her release. Over a year later, the U.S. government backed down, and Jiang was granted asylum.[60]

Alongside the Philadelphia Hoyu Chinese American Association, the organization at the center of Jiang's struggle for justice was Philadelphia's Asian Americans United. The campaign exemplified its broad approach to addressing anti-Asian violence, which transcended protesting injustice and worked to build healthy and sustainable communities. Our search for solutions must now draw insights from these activists in the City of Brotherly Love.[61]

TEN

Building Community in the Face of Violence

In 1992, a group of white men boasted that they were on a crusade to beat up people they hatefully referred to as the "slant-eyes" in Southwest Philadelphia. They targeted a Southeast Asian refugee community that had resettled in a city beset by redlining, anti-Blackness, biased policing, capital flight, and segregation by race and class. One of the white men described to a *Philadelphia Magazine* reporter how he and fourteen others dragged Asian Americans at will from local streetcars. "We'd kick the shit out of them," he declared. "Really hurt them bad. When I felt the tire iron smashing his head, it really felt good."

These vigilantes saw themselves as shock troops in a neighborhood race war with an Asian community many simply referred to as "gooks."

"I got one for David," proclaimed the white man wielding the tire iron. "When I went to David's funeral, I felt great. I thought I'd done something good."[1]

He and his peers took it upon themselves to deliver a collective punishment to the Asian community. They claimed they were acting to avenge the death of David Reilly, an eighteen-year-old white male killed in Southwest Philadelphia's McCreesh Playground on August 3, 1991.

It was easy to see why Reilly's death shocked the public, generating breaking news and headlines while eliciting deep sympathy for the victim and his family. Reilly was a high school basketball star from an underprivileged, low-income neighborhood—a white boy playing a Black man's game. And he soared in the hometown of Rocky, whose underdog story served as the ultimate model of the Great White Hope during Reilly's childhood. The newspapers reported that a "gang slay" had led to Reilly being "hacked to death with a meat cleaver." In this "white-Asian feud," Reilly, who "had friends of all races," was cut down as he tried to break up a fight and prevent further violence. Amid flaring tempers and calls to avenge their son, Reilly's parents immediately and repeatedly insisted there be "No Retaliation."[2]

Without attacking the victim or his family, Asian American community activists asserted that the media was presenting a one-sided account and missing the bigger picture. The police and the corporate media, they insisted, had ignored the long pattern of violence, harassment, and intimidation Asian Americans had endured in Southwest Philadelphia. It was fear and vulnerability after repeated assaults under the banner of white power that led the Asian youths to wield knives early that morning. The bias of law enforcement was so evident that an innocent Vietnamese American man, who had absolutely no connection to the altercation, was originally arrested and detained for nearly two months. Subsequently, the police arrested seven Southeast Asian youths, who were portrayed as members of a "gang" acting in a conspiracy. On this basis, the prosecution was able to find six of them guilty without ever establishing who had stabbed Reilly. One was convicted without any indication that he had even touched a weapon.

What Asian American activists referred to as the "McCreesh Playground Incident" came at a notorious moment in a city beset by racism and strife. The hope and promise tied to the election of Philadelphia's first Black mayor, W. Wilson Goode, had quickly eroded. The most enduring sign of state violence came in May 1985, when the city's police dropped a bomb on a West Philadelphia rowhouse—just a couple miles north of McCreesh Playground— to target the Black militant MOVE organization, at the direction of the mayor. Because the authorities allowed the fire to spread, it destroyed sixty-one homes on two city blocks. Tragically, eleven people, including five children, burned to death. Across the nation, right-wing politicians scored repeated gains with voters by portraying cities under liberal or Democratic governance as violent sites of chaos and disorder. Amid these titanic battles of right versus left and white versus Black, Asian Americans were challenged to find their voice and their place as they sought to craft a proactive and inclusive vision of justice for all.[3]

For Asian Americans United (AAU), organizing against anti-Asian violence marked a turning point for what had been a mostly volunteer organization operating out of a small office in Philadelphia's Chinatown. When Asians had been killed and victimized in recent years, their lives did not receive anything close to the daily coverage and banner headlines that the McCreesh Playground conflict generated. Indeed, the police and media had gone out of their way to deny that such acts were racially motivated. But AAU's work also exemplified a paradigm shift that Asian American community activists began to make during the 1990s—transcending the focus on prosecuting hate crimes associated with the advocacy for Vincent Chin. The notion of racist violence as a "random occurrence" striking victims who happen to be in the wrong place at the wrong time resonates most with relatively privileged Asian Americans, for whom such attacks comprise an aberration in their otherwise secure living environments. With the McCreesh Playground killing, AAU was challenged to do public advocacy to reframe a narrative in which Asian youths were portrayed as vicious murderers because they fought back.

For working-class Asians, like those in Southwest Philadelphia, patterned racist violence, including police brutality, can shape everyday life experiences. For AAU activists, confronting these harsh realities entailed moving beyond criminalizing hate to reframe justice as a call for community empowerment. Safety could best be achieved by affirming the rights and dignity of Asian immigrants and refugees; by securing fair wages and conditions for low-income workers and tenants; by improving schools and creating more liberating models of public education; and by working to transform the structures of power through awareness-raising campaigns and civic engagement. Overarching all these efforts, AAU understood that Asian American advances could best be achieved by demonstrating solidarity with other communities of color and building multiracial coalitions through broad-based campaigns to resist gentrification, end police brutality, and create a more livable city for those who have been historically excluded and marginalized.

The McCreesh Playground campaign thus extends beyond traditional methods of seeking justice for victims of anti-Asian violence that rest mainly on claims to equal protection under liberal, judicial institutions and remain within parameters of thought and action deemed acceptable by the state. The activists developed an alternative reading of the incident that explained how systematic forms of exclusion precluded Asian youths in Southwest Philadelphia from seeking conventional forms of redress. They successfully built not only a discourse but also a practice of opposition. Such work rested on its ability to define Asian American identity as one of resistance—an identity through which college-educated activists could share common ground with inner-city youths. This also served to link veteran activists of the 1960s and 1970s with younger activists of the 1990s and to promote cross-racial ties to the struggles of other minoritized communities. In this way,

AAU established a model for how organizers can struggle to build community in the face of seemingly ceaseless, senseless violence.

HOW VIOLENCE SHAPED THE BOUNDARIES
OF RACE AND PLACE

The roots of racist violence and vigilantism run deep in the City of Brotherly Love. In *How the Irish Became White*, historian Noel Ignatiev asserts that anti-Black violence, particularly in the form of race riots, proved indispensable to the creation of the white supremacist social order in Philadelphia and other northern cities during the antebellum era. Predominantly indigent laborers, Irish immigrants were once considered members of a lower race subordinate to American-born whites. They became targets of nativism and discrimination. Through mob violence, the Irish earned their way into whiteness by proving their value to those seeking to uphold systems of oppression. As Philadelphia industrialized over the course of the nineteenth century, white privilege became equated with keeping nonwhites in their place. The coauthors of the book *Philadelphia: Neighborhoods, Division, and Conflict in a Postindustrial City* demonstrate how fraternal bonds of whiteness constructed "ghettoes of opportunity" surrounding bustling factories between the mid-nineteenth and mid-twentieth centuries. Meanwhile, most African Americans were left to fend for survival in "ghettoes of last resort."[4]

The city's southwest side developed in the early twentieth century as a streetcar suburb of densely constructed rowhouses, populated mainly by descendants of Irish and Italian immigrants enjoying stable factory employment. Until the civil rights era, these outlying suburbs extended the breadth of racial segregation throughout most U.S. cities by reserving new housing for whites. By the 1970s, however, the rules of the game had changed. Corporations moved to cut costs, increase efficiency, and weaken the power of labor unions. This produced a series of coordinated shifts in production: from domestic to foreign, from Northeast to Sunbelt, from cities to suburbs, and from humans to robots. From 1955 to 1975, Philadelphia lost 75 percent of all manufacturing jobs citywide. The decline continued for sixteen straight years from 1969 to 1984. Philadelphia's total manufacturing employment fell from 252,500 to 108,400.[5]

Correspondingly, Southwest Philadelphia's population began to plummet. The American Tobacco Company shut down its plant, Purex left, and

General Electric scaled down its workforce from five thousand to 450. Meanwhile, the second Great Migration saw large numbers of African Americans from the South moving into Philadelphia. White flight to the new suburbs left a vast supply of affordable housing, which African Americans quickly occupied. From 1960 to 1970, the Black population of the neighborhood tripled, from 11 percent to 33 percent of the total population. During the 1960s and 1970s, Kingsessing, the section closest to the inner city, went from nearly all white to all Black. By 1980, whites were no longer a majority in Southwest Philadelphia. As those with requisite economic resources and human capital abandoned the area, some of the white residents who were left behind resorted to violence and intimidation to preclude integration. They attacked African Americans directly and intensified peer pressure against white "traitors" who might consider selling their homes to them.[6]

Whites who feared a repeat of Kingsessing's racial transition committed a series of racist atrocities that swelled between the late 1970s and mid-1980s. In 1979, two white men crawled onto the roof of a factory "looking for a 'nigger' to shoot." They gunned down thirteen-year-old Tracey Chambers, who had the misfortune of being the first African American they saw. In 1980, white youths from Southwest Philly stabbed a Black youth on a trolley. In response, a group of Black youths stabbed a white youth to death. A 1985 incident best exemplified the white homeowners' attempt to keep their neighborhood racially pure. Soon after a Black family moved into an all-white block, a bottle was thrown through their window. Three weeks later, four hundred whites demonstrated on the front lawn of the family's home, demanding that they get out. One month later, arsonists broke into the house and burned it to the ground.[7]

By 1990, much of the white population of the district lived just above the poverty level. But the segregated white areas continued to condense in size, leaving embattled white residents feeling more trapped. In the areas adjacent to McCreesh Playground, only 6.9 percent of all whites aged twenty-five and above had a bachelor's degree, while 41.5 percent had not finished high school. As postindustrial decay negated the economic advantages of white privilege, many opted to maximize what historian David Roediger has labeled the psychological "wages of whiteness." They defended their sense of place and community, which was increasingly rooted in the one factor that stood out in comparison to other impoverished neighborhoods: a high rate of homeownership.[8]

During the 1980s, however, some white homeowners discovered a new escape hatch: They could sell their houses to Asians clandestinely to evade or reduce the social stigma attached to transactions with African Americans. Vietnamese, Cambodian, and Laotian refugees had initially resettled in even more impoverished, majority Black sections of the city. As scholar-activist Ellen Somekawa documented, slumlords contracted with resettlement agencies to fill their "vacant and deteriorating" complexes with refugees given little or no choice in the matter. A marriage of convenience developed between landlords seeking "to milk their properties" for profit and the agencies that were required "to place large numbers of refugees in a short period of time." A glance at the 1980 U.S. Census statistics for a section of West Philadelphia with a concentration of refugees reveals the severe poverty in which they lived. The average household income for Asians was just $7,828 per year, with 36 percent earning below $5,000. Over 85 percent of Asian households had less than $15,000 in annual income. Redlining, troubled public schools, and trickle-down economics led to Black and Asian residents being pitted against each other in a fight for scarce resources and neighborhood turf. Many of these working-class Asians saw moving to the southwest side as a relative step up from their squalid rentals. It was the best among limited options. Furthermore, the unwritten rule prohibiting sales to Black buyers accelerated the fall of housing prices. Dozens of white families, circumventing fair-housing policies, began selling unlisted homes to Southeast Asian refugees for just $15,000–$20,000. From 1980 to 1990, the Asian American population of Southwest Philadelphia skyrocketed 459.2 percent, rising from 174 to 973. Vietnamese comprised the majority, followed by Cambodian and ethnic Chinese refugees.[9]

Shocked by the rapid turnover, some whites began harassing and intimidating their new neighbors. When the true sources of economic and political power seemed distant and untouchable, Asians comprised the most convenient scapegoats. Some white men and boys in the area proudly declared that they were skinheads, neo-Nazis, and/or members of white power gangs. For Asian youths, this made most local hangouts off limits. When he first moved to the neighborhood, one Asian teenager reported, he went to a video rental store, only to be harassed by a group of whites. They chased him home, then threw rocks through a window of his house. Consequently, McCreesh Playground became one of the few public spaces available to Asian youths. Situated in the most concentrated area of white residency, however, there were street rules governing its use. Asian youths might hang closer to the park's eastern end, nearest to where some two hundred Asians lived. They would use part of the field for soccer while whites commanded the baseball diamond. With multiple basketball courts, white, Black, and Asian residents could each have their own. Still, at any time, a group of whites could decide to push Asian youths out of a space it wanted to control.[10]

As I interviewed young Vietnamese American women in Philadelphia during the early 1990s, they shared how the rules governing home and street life were gendered. Most of the public conflicts involved boys and young men because parents expected girls and young women to take on traditional domestic roles. Hue Tran, then a recent college graduate, said her father worked as a janitor in a large hospital, while her mother took care of the children and brought home piecework to supplement the family income. For girls, Tran noted, parental concern for safety conspired with a patriarchal assignment of household chores and caring for younger siblings to keep them indoors. Girls were told, "No, you can't go out." Therefore, one would more frequently see "the guys out on the street." Trang, a high school student, explained that girls like her were also taught to avoid confrontation. "My parents," she said, "they would just say, 'Ignore them 'cause they have no manners.'"[11]

A TWO-SIDED TRAGEDY

Such was the context of the events leading up to David Reilly's untimely death. Robert Sciarrillo, one of his friends, testified for the prosecution at trial. Sciarrillo was drunk, he stated, when he went over with another friend, Brian Parker, to confront some Asians he saw across the park. "I guess we were going to lump 'em up—hit 'em," he admitted. While Sciarrillo claimed he never called them "chinks," he acknowledged having used anti-Asian slurs in the past. He had also been convicted of ethnic intimidation in 1988, when he attacked the car of a Black driver. In fact, the prosecutor admitted that Sciarrillo and Parker called the Asian youths "gooks" and "chinks." One of the pair threatened that his pit bull would bite them; the other warned he was carrying a loaded gun. Some of the Asians responded by leaving the park to retrieve kitchen knives.[12]

On the basis of statements by Reilly's friends, news outlets reported that he was caught in the fighting while attempting to act as a peacemaker. An autopsy concluded he had died from multiple stab wounds. Before a murder weapon was identified, however, reporters repeatedly and without evidence wrote sensationally that he had been "hacked to death with a meat cleaver." Although Reilly was justifiably the focus of the immediate tragedy, it soon became apparent that he and others were casualties of much broader social problems.[13]

Local reporters readily documented extreme racial tension in the days surrounding his death, starting with an aggressive grouping of white men and boys who did not hesitate to share their beliefs that Asians were an alien menace.

"This is our neighborhood," said a white teenager. "We were here first. We're Americans."

Vietnam being synonymous with *war* in the minds of the average American, one of his peers viewed this turf war as global in scope. "They go to war with us," he argued, "and then they try to move into America."

"They should be in gook town," added another.

Linked with physical threats or attacks, such sentiments put terror in the hearts of Asians in the neighborhood. "They've called me chink, gook," said a fourteen-year-old Vietnamese American, who felt trapped in his house. "My mom's scared. She wants to move."[14]

"Some older guys even chased my little sister, and she's only 4," another Asian youth stated. "We were afraid this kind of thing would happen sooner or later, but we thought it would probably be one of us killed."[15]

By contrast, some whites attending a community meeting a few days after Reilly's death insisted that *they* were the true victims. The cops were only "here to protect the nonwhite people," one said. The neighborhood had been taken over by Asian "thugs."[16]

When community organizers from AAU investigated, Southeast Asian residents explained that they had been under siege during months of relentless racist harassment and assaults. Some believed that the Asian youths accused of killing Reilly had acted in self-defense. The police acknowledged there had been a pattern of "ethnic clashes," noting that two Asians had been shot several months prior to Reilly's death. But the response of law enforcement to this death exhibited a pattern of racist profiling and disparate treatment.[17]

As the conflict leading to Reilly's death was transpiring at the playground, restaurant worker Ty Truong, a twenty-four-year-old man from Vietnam, was driving home from a suburban movie theater. Seeing the commotion, he peeked curiously out of his car window. Whites angered at Reilly's death falsely named Truong as the killer. One of Reilly's friends—named in court as the prime instigator of the altercation that led to his death—pointed at him and said, "That's one of the motherfucking gooks." As the police arrested

Truong, the crowd chanted, "Gook, get the gook." A white acquaintance of Reilly swore under oath that he witnessed a group of ten to fifteen knife-wielding Asians led by Truong, who charged at Reilly and stabbed him in the back. Based on nothing more than such spurious witness testimony, Truong was jailed for two months. "I'm 100 percent innocent," he told the press.[18]

After releasing Truong, authorities switched gears. Their new theory was that a "gang" of Asians was responsible for Reilly's death. The district attorney charged Minh La, Tho Tran, Dieu Nguyen, Khoa Ho, Manh Hoang, Tuan Huynh, and Khanh Lam with first-degree murder and held them on bail ranging from $150,000 to $1.1 million. These rates were inflated out of a dubious fear that they might go back to Vietnam, the place they had fled. Deborah Wei, a founder of AAU, had taught five of the defendants in her classes for English language learners. They were "good kids" in her eyes. But there was no place for a "model minority" image of young Asian men put on trial for an alleged gang slaying. The stereotype of faceless Viet Cong aggressors mercilessly killing Americans lurked just beneath the surface. In fact, some of the convicted were mixed-race Amerasians whose American fathers had abandoned them, leaving them to come to the United States in hopes of overcoming a life of hardship.[19]

In the first of two trials, all the defendants except Khanh Lam were tried together. Assistant district attorney Joseph Casey's own words make it easier to understand why the prosecution felt it needed to exploit the racialization of the trial. Casey admitted to the jurors that it was "unlikely that I would be able to prove to you who actually killed David Reilly." Yet, he argued, "regardless of who actually plunged the knives into David Reilly's body, all, all are guilty as accomplices and conspirators." Because the McCreesh Playground altercation was a quick, frantic episode in the middle of the night, the prosecution lacked eyewitnesses who could state with certainty what had happened. Most or all of Reilly's friends had been severely inebriated. On top of the wrongful arrest of Ty Truong, attempts by whites to pick the defendants out of a police lineup proved to be a farce. Neeta Patel, an AAU staff member at the time, attended the lineups. "The people who were identifying them had no idea," she recalled. "They identified a priest!"[20]

The prosecution focused on conspiracy to make up for its lack of hard evidence. Casey pinned mug shots of the defendants on a board to resemble a gang, even though it was some of the white youths and not the Asians who had belonged to a gang. Furthermore, the authorities collected a large assortment of kitchen knives from the houses of the defendants. Although the prosecution could never pinpoint the exact weapon that was used, Casey continually waved this array of knives in front of the jury's watchful eyes for dramatic purposes. Drawing on Orientalism to cast defendant Minh La as an *other*, the prosecutor derisively referred to him as the "whirling dervish" with knives. While speaking of David Reilly being hacked to death, Casey had the gall to brandish a meat cleaver repeatedly, despite published coroner's reports that ruled out the possibility that Reilly's wounds were caused by a meat cleaver.[21]

Asian Americans who attended the trial of the six defendants found Casey's closing argument especially shameful. The prosecutor reinforced an us-versus-them theme by reminding the jury that "we, Americans," hold ourselves to different standards than the defendants. Out of personal concern for their former students, eight of the defendants' teachers came to court voluntarily as character witnesses. Casey dismissed their testimonies out of hand. "There's a difference between reputation and character," declared the prosecutor. "Reputation is what people think of you. Character is what you really are. The true character of all those defendants was spread out before the world at McCreesh Playground on August third of 1991." Further insinuating that the defendants were outside of the *American* circle of humanity, Casey asked jurors to consider the "mindset" of someone who would "plunge" a knife into the back of another human being. His demagoguery reached a crescendo in his closing remarks, when he held up a picture of David Reilly, stood behind each of the defendants, and stated in a "loud" and "angry" tone, "You are guilty!" Although this brought repeated defense motions for a mistrial, all were denied.[22]

In the end, it turned out that the seasoned prosecutor had read the jury correctly. Three of the defendants were found guilty of third-degree murder and six of criminal conspiracy—even though the court never identified who had stabbed David Reilly. In the biggest travesty, Khoa Ho was convicted of criminal conspiracy and sentenced to one to ten years in prison, despite court findings that he never picked up a knife. Minh La, who testified that he retrieved knives, was convicted of third-degree murder, aggravated assault, criminal conspiracy, and possession of an instrument of crime. Among all the defendants, he received the longest sentence: twelve to thirty years. The judge denied the six defendants' appeal for a new trial. The importance of Casey's framing of group culpability was subsequently confirmed when Khanh Lam—the only defendant to be tried and judged as an individual—was found not guilty. The prosecution's reliance on the language of conspiracy could not overcome its lack of specific evidence that Lam was guilty of anything more than being near the crime scene.[23]

MODELS OF COMMUNITY RESISTANCE

Following the height of the Asian American movement from the late 1960s through the 1970s, the development of community organizations bifurcated. Some groups, particularly those that professed themselves radical or left, splintered, faltered, or were dismantled. Simultaneously, many organizations, particularly those in areas with large concentrations of Asian Americans, established themselves as large service providers with relatively stable staff and funding. Many of these organizations proved less likely to espouse consciously oppositional politics, instead getting caught up in what ethnic studies scholar Yen Le Espiritu called the "funding game." Community organizations spent more and more of their resources—and even altered their missions and functions—to reproduce nonprofit and governmental funding.[24]

AAU rather uniquely bucked both trends. Started by a handful of people who met over a kitchen table and engaged in activism during their spare time, AAU grew into a long-standing 501(c) (3) organization with a permanent location and full-time staff. Yet the growth of AAU did not mean abandoning the progressive values in its founding mission. Instead, AAU used its increased resources to project its politics over a wider area and range of issues. Furthermore, AAU stabilized its organizational structure without losing its original grassroots activist approach. Since its inception, AAU has filled its board positions with activists (including youths) and vowed not to pander to elected officials. In fact, AAU has been instrumental in fostering a new generation of activists. What also stands out is the primary role women have played in the organization's development and leadership. Its ethics of care, emphasis on democratic participation, and omnipresent concern with building community are consistent with feminist values in activism.[25]

Through its response to the McCreesh Playground Incident, AAU solidified its grassroots approach to Asian American advocacy. What distinguished AAU from other Asian American nonprofit organizations was its development from the margins of society. In the 1980s, Asian Americans in Philadelphia were marginalized in relation both to other racial groups in the city and to larger Asian American communities, such as those in San Francisco and Los Angeles. At the same time, the disenfranchisement of

Asian Americans and relative lack of established Asian American institutions made Philadelphia a rather hospitable spot for the development of activism carrying on the legacy of the Asian American movement.

Some of the founding members of AAU got started in Asian American community activism in Philadelphia through the pan-Asian collective Yellow Seeds. Founded in 1971, Yellow Seeds sprouted at a time when urban centers were experiencing a proliferation of Third World revolutionary organizations, such as the Black Panther Party, Young Lords, and I Wor Kuen. These young radicals deliberately embraced countries typically cast as enemies of the United States. Inspired by the Chinese Revolution as an example of Asian people overcoming oppression, Yellow Seeds developed "Serve the People" programs in Philadelphia's Chinatown. These included services for the elderly, tutoring, legal aid, recreational programs, and cultural events. Beyond protesting the Vietnam War, the organization proclaimed an internationalist stance: "Yellow Seeds aligns itself with the liberation struggles of people all over the world against all forms of imperialism and colonialism."[26]

Yellow Seeds' militant politics led the group to confront both white elites and the traditional ethnic community leadership over the issue of redevelopment. Mary Yee, a former Yellow Seeds member and founder of AAU, characterized the group as "a major force within Chinatown." It pushed the established Chinese American associations "to take more aggressive stands against urban renewal, which was really threatening to wipe out Chinatown altogether." Yellow Seeds served as a precursor of AAU's grassroots, pan-Asian organizing in Philadelphia. Around 1976, however, it began to break apart as members' political orientation led them away from community-based activism and into the factories to organize workers from the inside. This decline set the stage for AAU's birth.[27]

By the early 1980s, Philadelphia's Asian American community was relatively disconnected from the national Asian American movement and, thus, largely beyond the realm of its influence. But the Asian American population was expanding in size and diversity. Some of the new immigrants were educated professionals falling under the preference categories of immigration law. Owing to the bipolar nature of new migration patterns, however, thousands of poor immigrants and Southeast Asian refugees settled in Philadelphia. A plethora of social ills plagued these fledgling communities: eye-catching acts of racist violence tied to poor housing conditions and problems in public schools. When AAU was in its planning stages, founding member Debbie Wei recounted, "The major area of concern for us was the rising tide of anti-Asian violence nationally and in Philadelphia in particular."[28]

Unlike in major West Coast cities, Philadelphia's Asian American community did not develop a large circle of social service agencies, elected officials, or university institutions. As a result, local activists began to feel a void, a sense that there was no recourse for the problems of working-class Asian communities. Because the largest population growth and the most significant problems with adjustment occurred in the refugee communities, AAU's founders decided to start working with these communities. Only a small assemblage of United Way–sponsored service agencies had been set up to aid Southeast Asian refugees with the resettlement process. Mary Yee, in discussions with activist peers, acknowledged the contributions of those agencies but considered their response to the situation insufficient. A new organization was necessary to confront racism in the schools, city government, and criminal justice system. "We were there to fill a vacuum," Yee stated, "and to give another voice to the Asian community."[29]

The founding of AAU in the summer of 1985 provides another example of how major movements often start with a small group of dedicated and impassioned activists. Initially, it lacked incorporation as a nonprofit organization. Although the members planned for long-term development, it began with no permanent location or paid staff. At its genesis, AAU had no more than twelve members, seven or eight of whom attended meetings consistently. They ranged in age from mid-twenties to mid-thirties. Broken down by occupation, the group included a public school teacher, a librarian, an attorney, two graduate students, a labor organizer, a college professor, and a paralegal. The board comprised mainly college-educated Japanese and Chinese Americans, who recognized a need to support Philadelphia's Southeast Asian communities.[30]

Harkening to the radicalism of the Asian American movement, the concept of "Serve the People" carried decisively political tones within AAU. While the activists did not view the group as the bearer of social revolution, they saw themselves as organizers rather than social service providers. They were not content to ameliorate suffering. They sought to transform the relations of power in Philadelphia, the conditions of the city's Asian communities, and the consciousness of Asian Americans in the city.

Working on the margins meant that there were fewer physical resources to develop community programs. But there was also more political space to foster oppositional culture. The relatively small size of Philadelphia's Asian

American population created a practical necessity for the organization to be pan-Asian, paving the way also for strong identification with other communities of color. Whereas practically no official in power was addressing the issues of Asian Americans, AAU felt both a sense of urgency with its work and a need to start at the grassroots level. Given the lack of an established Asian American community infrastructure in Philadelphia, AAU emerged as an outspoken, progressive representative of the city's Asian American community. Two significant early victories increased its prominence. First, AAU put its principles into action by working with low-income, Southeast Asian tenants to organize a successful rent strike at the Admiral Court apartment complex in West Philadelphia. Second, AAU was party to a victorious lawsuit against the Philadelphia Public School District to enhance services for English language learners of Asian ancestry.[31]

Another breakthrough for the organization came when it launched its youth leadership program in the summer of 1987. The thinking behind this program, which is still active, reflected AAU's emphasis on working with community members in a collective and empowering way. Seeking to build crucial relationships with working-class Southeast Asian refugees, AAU's board determined they could start by connecting with youths. Funded by modest grants from small foundations, the summer program featured high school–age teens hired to tutor elementary school–age children. The tutors, however, did not only teach basic school subjects. Instead, AAU adult members engaged the tutors in consciousness-raising sessions as a requisite part of their training. Because of its novel and unique agenda, AAU's work attracted Southeast Asian youths troubled by questions of racial identity but unable to find solutions from school or society. Hue Tran, one of the first high school students to work for the youth leadership program, recalled writing in her high school journal, "It's really strange. I don't feel like I belong here." When her English teacher failed to relate, she turned to AAU. Debbie Wei, she remembered, "put into words what I felt." Tran felt a new sense of power and purpose: "I felt like I had a lot to invest in an organization and in people like Debbie."[32]

Following its 1985 founding, AAU experienced significant growth. By the early 1990s, the organization reached a milestone, with a full-time staff and highly visible storefront office in Philadelphia's Chinatown. Its base of support expanded from its original members, mostly East Asian Americans, to a wide range of diverse supporters. Moreover, while the founders were primarily American-born professionals, AAU's growing membership became largely working-class immigrants, refugees, and youths.[33]

Prior to the McCreesh Playground campaign, AAU had already developed a focus on anti-Asian violence. Its initial reaction was shaped by the stark contrast between the public's perception of David Reilly's death, which attracted major and extended news coverage, and previous cases in which Asians were victimized. On October 7, 1988, Seung-Ki Cyril Leung, a University of Pennsylvania graduate student from Hong Kong, was beaten over the head by three juveniles and hospitalized in a coma after playing in a touch football game off campus at Clark Park. One of the assailants was on probation at the time for a prior assault on a fourteen-year-old Asian youth. A group of six Asian university student groups and the United Minorities Council issued a statement listing this attack as part of a "chain" of racist events.[34]

No later than October 12, however, the detective in charge of the investigation, Tom Baker, labeled the attack as a "robbery" that "was not racially motivated." Leung, who never woke from the coma, succumbed to his injuries later that month. After two sixteen-year-old youths pled guilty, Maurice Murray was convicted of second-degree murder, robbery, and conspiracy and sentenced to life. He was only seventeen when Leung died but was tried as an adult. Although the three youths provided conflicting accounts, they agreed that Murray was not the one who struck Leung's head with a "heavy" tree branch.[35]

In the summer of 1990, Varin Hok appeared without notice at AAU's Chinatown office bringing news of another horrific tragedy. The story he shared of his brother-in-law, Heng Lim, raised alarm among the staff who met him that day. A thirty-seven-year-old survivor of the Cambodian genocide, Lim had recently moved to Philadelphia from Jacksonville, Florida, to be closer to family. He came with his wife, Mala, who had survived four years of coerced labor under the Khmer Rouge and crossed a minefield to reach a Thai refugee camp. She came to America with nothing but "the clothes on her back." Six-year-old Lisa was their only child. They were traveling through South Philadelphia in a minivan driven by a relative when a minor traffic quarrel turned deadly on June 16. Timothy Meitzler, a twenty-one-year-old South Philly resident, claimed that their vehicle nearly struck his girlfriend at the intersection of Ninth and Tasker Streets. Meitzler cursed at the Asian Americans in the minivan and threw a trash can at them. Seeking to put this behind them, the Lims drove on through the busy, narrow streets of the old neighborhood.[36]

Following on foot, Meitzler caught up with them at the next block. Now wielding a six-foot-long tree stake, he smashed the windshield of a car with Lim's relatives inside. Then he went after the minivan again, beating Lim's father-in-law and breaking his arm. When Lim went to care for the elder, Meitzler beat him over the head—so hard that Lim's head was flattened by the heavy lumber. He fell unconscious before hitting the ground. Three hours later, Lim died in a hospital.[37]

Witnesses gave conflicting accounts of what had happened. At trial, according to the defense, a group of Asians chased and beat Meitzler, who claimed he acted in self-defense. But Lorraine Infante, a neutral bystander who lived near the incident site, said Meitzler called Lim a "fucking Chinese." Jurors considered her the most influential witness. Lim, she testified, was walking away from the confrontation and "didn't do anything" prior to the assault. Meitzler "came up behind him and hit him with the long stick," Infante stated. "The defendant was holding the stick like a bat. He hit him so hard."[38]

The events leading up to the trial further disturbed Lim's family, AAU, and Asian American community advocates. In the immediate aftermath of the murder, the *Philadelphia Daily News* listed Heng Lim as "No. 10" of eleven violent deaths in the city that weekend. This was followed by two generic sentences with no mention of suspect or motive. Even that exceeded the reporting by *The Philadelphia Inquirer*. I could not find any record of the region's leading newspaper mentioning Lim's name until after Meitzler was finally arrested more than five weeks after the incident.[39]

That arrest and the belated media coverage it generated occurred mainly because of a grassroots campaign to draw attention to irregularities and erasures. Lim's family worked with attorney Tsiwen Law, a longtime community advocate and AAU cofounder. On July 20, 1990, the *Philadelphia Daily News* published the first meaningful article in the mainstream media about Heng Lim, noting that his family considered his killing to be "a racial incident." Reporter Dave Davies led the piece by citing the "growing pattern of violence against Asians that has been largely ignored by city agencies and unnoticed by the media." A recent report from the Philadelphia Commission on Human Relations, AAU argued, was "biased and unfair." It failed to recognize that Asians, despite comprising only 2–5 percent of the city's population, were targeted in 25 percent of documented cases of "inter-group tension." Davies highlighted the Lim case as a sign of ongoing injustice, prompting the formation of the Committee for Justice for Heng Lim with a push from AAU. "Family members said police know the identity of the man who struck Lim," Davies wrote, "and community leaders are angry that a month has passed without an arrest." Instead, police kept Lim's family at the precinct for over three hours as he was drawing his last breaths. The article closed by noting that the Committee for Justice planned to meet with police leaders that day, and next with the district attorney.[40]

Within three days of that article's publication, the authorities arrested Meitzler for murder and voluntary manslaughter. In fact, a Philadelphia homicide captain told Davies that the police obtained the arrest warrant the same day the article criticizing police inaction was released. Meitzler "walked away from the incident, and people from the neighborhood surrounded the family as if they were the criminals," said AAU's Debbie Wei. "Without community pressure, we don't know if there ever would have been an arrest." Whether authorities would credit AAU or not, the handling of the case changed noticeably. The DA's office filed "ethnic intimidation" charges against Meitlzer, though these were dismissed by the court. Still, the case proceeded to trial. After ten days in front of the judge and two days of deliberation, a jury of his peers found Meitzler guilty of third-degree murder. Before sentencing, Meitzler, facing up to fifty years in prison, stated that he was "real sorry for what happened." His lawyer argued that he had acted out of fear for his life. Noting the jury's disagreement with that claim, Judge William J. Mazzola sentenced Meitzler to ten to twenty years. Lim's family and AAU were generally satisfied with the outcome. "We wished it could be first-degree murder," said Varin Hok on behalf of the family, "but at least he was convicted."[41]

LESSONS FROM ORGANIZERS

Compared with the murder of Heng Lim, the racial discourse pervading the McCreesh Playground trial was decisively stacked against the Asian American defendants. Nevertheless, AAU dove into this new struggle to expand on the theme that "Asian lives do not come cheap." It pointed out specific incidents of bias within the judicial process and identified strategic places to intervene. In addition, it built a bond of trust with the defendants, their families, and their communities. These relationships not only increased the effectiveness of AAU's advocacy on behalf of the defendants; they also gave AAU the legitimacy to press community concerns in public. Such work demonstrated that the Asian community's passivity could not be assumed: Asian Americans in Philadelphia would organize, fight, and resist when threatened or attacked.

As more Asian Americans learned about the McCreesh Playground Incident, AAU enhanced its reputation as a base for activists and a vehicle for grassroots organizing, particularly breaking through the "model minority" image to connect college students and professionals with the most precarious members of the Asian American population. Other organizations also stepped up their activities, in a different manner. The Asian American Youth Association played an important role in mediating between whites and Southeast Asians in Southwest Philadelphia. Because the organization was based in the neighborhood, it negotiated the tense environment by adopting a more conciliatory tone. In contrast to the firebrands in AAU, Asian American Youth Association president Hoang Tran was characterized by the media as "building bridges."[42]

Initially, AAU members knew of the incident only through the sensational stories that bombarded the electronic and print media. It had some insight into conditions in Southwest Philadelphia from work it had done two years earlier in response to a boycott of a Korean American–owned store. Neeta Patel felt the challenge to cut through the "hysteria and anger and blame." She heard "through the grapevine" that the community was "under lockdown," distraught by news that one man had already been falsely arrested. Concerned for the safety of local residents, Debbie Wei heard from a former student, who reported being "scared to death." Many feared walking to and from school. Wei subsequently recognized that five of the suspects were also former students of hers whom she had grown to trust. Yet none of their life stories appeared in the media, which memorialized Reilly while alluding to the defendants as gang members.[43]

Staff and volunteers at AAU came together to form a new justice campaign under the Committee Against Anti-Asian Violence (distinct from the New York organization of the same name) in early 1992. One was my former college roommate, Lawrence Lee, a Chinese American from the South. He was swayed by a dinner meeting with Khoa Ho, the only defendant able to post bail. After hearing Ho's version of the story, Lee recalled, "it just sounded obvious that the white guys started it." At first, they sat around the table with only five or six people. But all were incensed by how the authorities and media were treating not only the suspects but also their shared Asian American community. As each participant reached out personally to contacts, momentum built. Committee members wrote op-ed pieces for the city's newspapers, produced topical shows on a local public television station, and initiated their own multilingual newspaper, *Asian American Justice Watch*. They exposed disparate treatment by the office of District Attorney Lynne Abraham, contrasting its delay in arresting Heng Lim's killer with the rush to arrest the innocent Ty Truong. Moreover, they drew parallels between the injustices experienced by Asian Americans and other communities of color. The committee developed solidarity work between AAU and a Puerto Rican organization fighting a case similar to the McCreesh Playground case. It also challenged the racial profiling of Black, Puerto Rican, and Asian youths. Some were wrongfully arrested or detained after being identified in a racially coded police "mug book." Community advocates estimated that 50–90 percent of Asian young men and teens they knew had been photographed by police. Philadelphia's organized-crime unit acknowledged that its "Oriental Photo Book" contained 386 photos that were shared routinely with other agencies. Other major cities, like Boston and San Jose, generated similar mug books.[44]

As the court proceedings began, AAU organizers influenced the judicial process in ways that might have been overlooked, curbing the bias against immigrant and refugee communities. They exposed, for example, the court's shoddy handling of translation. In one instance, a Laotian woman who spoke broken Vietnamese was asked to handle major translation duties. They also served as mediators of information when court-appointed defense attorneys had trouble communicating with clients whose first language was not English. By attending the trial regularly, they stood with the defendants' families and helped explain what was transpiring in the court. Some of the abuses they detected, however, proved beyond the reach of their efforts. Patel heard accounts of the police coercing the defendants' girlfriends to cooperate with prosecutors. At least two were told they could be arrested and held in contempt of court unless they responded to the assistant DA whenever he contacted them. While garnering scorn from the prosecution, they attracted media coverage with a public rally at city hall shortly before the trial began.[45]

While the committee's furious level of activity helped consolidate an organizing core, it also provided an avenue of involvement for newcomers to community activism. May Yee (no relation to Mary) first volunteered as a Bryn Mawr College student, then later joined the AAU staff. She developed a sense of self and community that she had lacked in her upbringing. As Yee recalled being bullied in elementary school on the Lower East Side, the campaign connected her concerns about identity to practical activity designed to confront structures of inequality. Approaching the committee's work with caution at first, she attended a meeting and picked "what seemed to be the easiest" task—writing a letter to the defendants in prison. She was soon coordinating a group of ten women from Bryn Mawr for a tutoring program serving seventeen Asian Americans in Holmsburg prison. It was designed to help the defendants and other prisoners study for their GED, since they could not attend public school and would soon be too old to attend.[46]

Despite the unfavorable verdict in the McCreesh Playground trial, community activists at AAU saw the fight against anti-Asian violence as something that transcended any one case. They broadened the scope of their organizing by hosting the East Coast Coalition Against Anti-Asian Violence Conference in November 1992. Over 250 participants attended, building ties among activists across the eastern seaboard. On a personal level, involvement in the campaign deepened their understanding of societal oppression and changed their sense of life priorities. In this regard, community organizing cannot be judged by a simple notion of wins and losses. By striving to uplift voices and concerns that have long been silenced, the first thing movement activism changes is our sense of what is possible.[47]

With broad-based support for its work confronting anti-Asian violence, AAU invested its material resources and cultural capital in community-building efforts. In 1996, it joined with local artists and small-business owners to launch the Mid-Autumn Festival, which became one of the city's signature events, drawing thousands of attendees. Next, it opened the K–8 Chinatown Folk Arts–Cultural Treasures Charter School (FACTS) in 2005. While the school serves students from all racial and ethnic backgrounds, it innovated a place-based, multicultural curriculum that fulfilled a long-identified Chinatown community need. The goodwill these projects generate has been critical to maintaining support for Chinatown in the face of constant threats from redevelopment and demolition. From the postwar era to the early twenty-first century, the district became hemmed in to the east by Independence Mall, cut off to the west by the Pennsylvania Convention Center, and torn in half by the Vine Street Expressway. Through mass demonstrations, AAU has worked with a coalition to stave off a baseball stadium and casino proposed by developers coveting Chinatown's valuable real estate, as well as a prison. Most recently, neighborhood activists faced one of their biggest threats ever with a new plan for the Philadelphia 76ers basketball arena plotted on Chinatown's southern border. Squaring off in a David-versus-Goliath battle against billionaires, AAU and its multiracial allies forced the developers to cancel their plans despite approvals from the mayor and city council. Their continuous efforts highlight the social justice struggles at the core of the city and the nation.[48]

INTO THE TWENTY-FIRST CENTURY

Amid battles spanning four decades, AAU has been made and remade by its connections to the struggles of young people. Yet another such struggle erupted on December 3, 2009. It was an unusually warm Thursday morning, but the day would be remembered for the disturbing events that took place at South Philadelphia High School, less than a mile from the site where Heng Lim was killed. Starting at 8:45 a.m., when an Asian American student was physically attacked in a classroom, beatings continued over the course of the day. An Asian girl was dragged down a staircase. During lunchtime, Chinese American youths were assaulted in the cafeteria by a group of up to seventy students. But the most extensive violence occurred after school. A group of ten Vietnamese American students, mostly girls, told school officials they were afraid to walk outside. Assuring them they would be safe, the principal directed them to walk with her. They quickly became separated, however, as a much larger group of students chased after them. Duyngoc Truong, a petite sixteen-year-old, scrambled and fled until she literally ran into a wall. Trapped by as many as one hundred others, she reported being assaulted. In that moment, she thought, "Oh, my God, maybe I'm going to die." In all, over two dozen Asian American students were attacked that day. Thirteen went to the hospital, and at least seven needed treatment. The sense of fear among Asians at South Philly High may have been eclipsed only by their sense of betrayal by the administrators charged with maintaining a safe learning environment. Drawing news coverage and community support, they waged a mass boycott of the school that lasted eight consecutive days.[49]

Though outraged by the attacks, organizers from AAU were sadly not surprised. They had met with students for more than a year preceding the outburst on December 3, 2009. In the eyes of AAU and the student activists, the principal during the fall 2008 and spring 2009 terms, a white woman, had discounted reports of bullying and harassment. By the start of the fall 2009 term, she had been replaced by a Black woman. In AAU's assessment, both leaders had failed their students: No simple analysis of *white racism* would suffice. While Asian Americans comprised 18 percent of the student body, the majority, 70 percent, was Black. And though a handful of whites and one Cambodian student were reported to be among the assailants, nearly all were Black. The school, the neighborhood, and the city were steeped in histories of racism and violence that held down African Americans until their civil rights activism and political organizing punctured the barriers. Now, as they chastised school and district officials, Asian students and their community allies found themselves in the position of protesting Black leaders who had decision-making authority. With guidance from experienced organizers, the students took the lead. First, while they deemed the violence totally unacceptable, they did not focus on punishing their peers. Instead, the student activists emphasized the structural patterns of racism and inequity. Second, they held the adults responsible for their failure to keep students safe and demanded systemic reforms to increase accountability. Finally, rather than asserting an individual right to safety or issuing only ethnicity-based demands, they proposed measures to improve education for all students and formed multiracial alliances with activists who shared that goal. In sum, they resisted the erasure of anti-Asian racism, as well as a "model minority" framing that would reinforce anti-Black stereotypes.[50]

Considering their marginal starting point, South Philadelphia's Asian American students achieved some breakthrough accomplishments. At first, they felt that administrators were subjecting them to the age-old gaslighting treatment—discounting the notion that Asians were targeted and insinuating that some of the Asian victims had instigated the conflict. In response, they pointed out that the attacks of December 2009 were part of a longer-term pattern that they had meticulously chronicled while embattled school officials found a dearth of solutions. Frustrated by inaction from institutional leaders, the students worked with AAU and two other community-based organizations, Boat People SOS and Victim/Witness Services of South Philadelphia. The organizations then coordinated with a New York–based advocacy group, the Asian American Legal Defense and Education Foundation, to file civil rights complaints at the state and federal levels. This prompted a federal investigation that validated the students' concerns, cocluding that "the District deprived Asian students at SPHS [South Philadelphia High School] the equal protection of the laws by remaining deliberately indifferent to known instances of severe and pervasive student-on-student harassment of Asian students based on their race, color, and/or national origin at SPHS." The coordinated pressure swayed the school district to consent to a package of reforms it had once resisted. These included measures to prevent and remediate harassment, special provisions for English language learners, and commitment to ongoing compliance and monitoring. The state complaint resulted in similar concessions.[51]

As Grace Lee Boggs—a student of Hegel's dialectical philosophy—often said, you cannot expect revolutionary change to happen like a shot out of a pistol. Overcoming oppressive systems requires struggling through "the suffering, the patience, and the labour of the negative" to discover a better pathway forward. While the attacks at South Philadelphia High School caused terrible pain, they exposed contradictions that had been papered over far too long, opening up space for a fresh brand of leadership. The School District of Philadelphia hired a new principal, Otis Hackney, who effectuated substantive reforms. Like his predecessor, Hackney was hired as a Black leader to govern the majority Black high school. But he brought a qualitatively different approach that earned wide praise from the school's and the city's diverse constituencies. In a severely resource-deprived environment in which multiple parties hold legitimate grievances, it is easy for people on all sides to lapse into a crabs-in-a-barrel mentality. As reported by *Chalkbeat*, Hackney "introduced a 'growth mindset' to counteract the zero-sum attitude that permeated the school." He stressed "that doing something for one group did not mean less for another group." Promoting a belief that "adult behavior dictates student behavior," he implemented new training and accountability measures for staff. Finally, he championed multicultural competency to improve communication and understanding between racial/ethnic groups, and he approved a new course in Asian American history. Lauded for such achievements, Hackney was promoted to chief education officer of the district, then tapped to lead the national "I Have a Dream" Foundation.[52]

Through their work to redress anti-Asian violence at South Philly High, Asian American community activists continued to push themselves to the fore of the movement to transform public education. A longtime organizer and former elementary school teacher, Helen Gym served as one of AAU's primary coordinators supporting the students' campaign. As a founder of Parents United for Public Education—a citywide formation—Gym proved especially adroit in explaining how supporting the student boycotters advanced broader social justice interests. These skills proved integral to her election to the Philadelphia City Council in 2015. As a legislator, Gym became a leader of the council's progressive wing. Drawing on her experience with AAU, she sponsored policies to support the rights of tenants, workers, and immigrants, while building a multiracial coalition to increase resources for public education. In response to the 2021 surge in anti-Asian violence, Gym produced a leaflet declaring that "increased policing is not the answer." She equated safety instead with gun control, healthy schools, and protection of immigrant rights. By the time she ran for mayor in 2023, no one could mistake Gym for a demure or conservative Asian American in the "model minority" mold. She attracted endorsements from champions of the left, including Bernie Sanders and Alexandria Ocasio-Cortez. But she also aroused strident opposition from the center and right. Libertarian billionaire Jeff Yass contributed most of the $1 million in funds that a super PAC devoted to negative ads against Gym. Although polls showed a competitive race, Gym had to settle for a respectable third-place finish.[53]

Despite their disappointment with the 2023 election, Philadelphia's dedicated Asian American activists have learned to respond to defeat with reflection and resolve. First, they have become active political players in a long game, particularly through the formation of the Asian Pacific Islander Political Alliance. Permitted to engage in political campaigns as a nonprofit 501(c)(4) organization, the group claims to have doubled their communities' share of the statewide vote between 2016 and 2020. Second, they disrupted conventional ideas about race and politics. Cherelle Parker, a Black Democrat, was elected mayor with a "tough-on-crime" and pro-developer posture that flagged her as a moderate or even a conservative, whereas Gym drew her heaviest support from a coalition of Asian Americans and progressive voters. Finally, there was the voice of the students. In a mock ballot at five high schools, Gym walloped the competition with 60 percent of the vote. In the end, the voice of the community activists and the high school students provided signs of a progressive future—one that is anything but guaranteed but feels far more possible than it once did.[54]

Perhaps the most enduring source of inspiration has come from watching organizers of the student boycott blossom into adult leaders who play critical roles in the city's social movements. In 2006, when Wei Chen came to the United States from Fuzhou, China, he could barely speak English. His most poignant memories of entering South Philly High involved being bullied and beaten up. By the time of the violent incidents in 2009, however, Chen had founded the Chinese American Student Association and connected with AAU. He mobilized students to walk out and attend strategy sessions in Chinatown with veteran activists. They identified common educational and social justice concerns that linked them to Black and Latino student activists.

After graduation, Chen continued his commitment to community organizing by joining the AAU staff, where he remains today.[55]

The parents of Dương Nghệ Lý waited two decades to migrate from Vietnam, arriving in the United States and enrolling their two sons in South Philly High in 2008. Well before the December 2009 incidents, Lý became aware of the school's deep problems, when his brother was assailed twice. Paralleling Gym's work with parents, he connected the boycott to a citywide student organizing drive. After graduating from the University of Pennsylvania, Lý became a youth organizer, then codirector of VietLead. He organizes Vietnamese Americans for social justice and builds solidarity with others around fighting deportation, gentrification, and police brutality. Working from a "heal, resist, and grow" model, VietLead has marched with Black Lives Matter and coalesced around efforts to shift funding from policing to essential human needs.[56]

Reflecting on the lessons he learned, Lý focused on the need to place the attacks into structural context. "If you look straight at the situation," he said, "you would think this is just racial tension between blacks and Asians, but you can also think about it in a more institutional way. The school allowed all these stereotypes and misunderstandings to happen, to continue to escalate, without addressing them, without bringing groups together to understand each other."[57]

The young organizer delivered a vital message for all who are truly committed to stopping anti-Asian violence.

Epilogue

At a community center in a Los Angeles district with one of the highest concentrations of Asian Americans in the region, neighbors and community leaders gathered for two hours for an urgent meeting with the police. Many expressed alarm over what they perceived to be a sharp rise in crime and attacks. One after another, the victims stepped forward to give testimony about house break-ins and assaults on the street. Asian elders especially felt vulnerable in the face of attacks by African Americans and demanded greater protection from the police. The stories aroused such public concern that two TV news channels covered the tense community meeting.

A group of younger Asian American activists showed up in force to present a different perspective. They shared the goal of ending the attacks on elders. But they did not see intensified policing as a solution. It would only harm Black youths—many of whom were already unfairly targeted and profiled by police—and inflame interethnic tensions when community solidarity was most needed. Uniting with Black allies, these Asian American progressives saw the problem and the solution in structural terms.

The account of the meeting was captured in an article by David Monkawa—a Japanese American community organizer from a working-class upbringing. His piece grappled with the difficult issues raised by the attacks. Polarized by race and class, the city lacked jobs and recreation outlets for urban Black youths, leading some to take their frustrations out on nearby scapegoats. Rather than alleviate inequity, schools had turned into "semi-prisons," responding to youth alienation through a framework of criminalization that only served to "escalate violence."[1]

This scene should be recognizable to anyone who has followed the debates arising among Asian Americans since the outbreak of the COVID-19 pandemic—except that it took place nearly half a century earlier, in 1973. It thus draws attention to the long history—largely unknown or forgotten within mainstream media and education—of Asian American activists grappling with cross-racial tensions and solidarities. They have long sought to combat systemic forms of racism and injustice in ways that linked their fates to those of their Black neighbors. Of course, these efforts have yet to bring about the transformative change that is needed. But to deny their existence would exacerbate the erasure of Asian American history, occluding the lessons of past struggles and reducing debate to competing rhetorical postures.

The story of David Monkawa and his generational peers, while not reflective of the entire community, provides insights into the paradigm-shifting developments that changed the course of Asian American political history. In 1973, he was a twenty-two-year-old artist and writer for the radical newspaper *Gidra*. Begun by students at the dawn of the Asian American movement in 1969, *Gidra* broke with a form of ethnic politics and identity the 1960s generation found too steeped in assimilationism and moderation. Its hub was the Crenshaw district, where the Los Angeles community meeting referred to above also took place. During the 1950s and 1960s, Crenshaw was a primary destination for Japanese Americans uprooted by the wartime incarceration and looking to integrate new areas dispersed from the Little Tokyo ethnic enclave. While some Asian American boomers grew up middle class in the suburbs and rebelled against the "model minority" stereotype in college, Monkawa's biography provides us with an appreciation for how political consciousness developed from a transnational upbringing and a working-class neighborhood where Black and Asian Americans lived side by side.

Although he came to the United States for the first time in 1958 at the age of seven, Monkawa was not an immigrant. He was born an American citizen, the son of a Nisei soldier who married a Japanese woman while stationed overseas. David's father had been demoted by the army for sharing blankets and supplies with poor Japanese civilians. He retired as a private, then struggled with health issues as a factory worker and gardener in Los Angeles. His mom worked as a babysitter during the day and as a cocktail waitress at night. The family of four lived in a one-bedroom apartment before the economic and social strain eventually caused the dissolution of his parents' marriage. Monkawa recalled his elementary school as being "90 percent Black and 10 percent Japanese." In this part of Crenshaw, you either learned how to fight or would "get destroyed if you didn't." Most of his fights were with other

Japanese Americans. His childhood best friend was Tony Richmond, a mixed-race Black-Japanese youth, also from a military family, who was being raised by his Black grandmother.[2]

As a teenager during the 1960s, Monkawa underwent a political awakening as he watched the police repress Black Power groups and brutalize African Americans he knew in the neighborhood. The Black Panther Party had an office nearby in West Adams, and three of their members "got slaughtered" by the police in front of a gas station in 1968. "That's only like a block and a half from where I lived," he recalled. Those killed were only one to five years older than Monkawa, who was in high school at the time. While he "didn't see the massacre," he witnessed the scene while the blood was still fresh. The image of the Panthers "slumped inside" their car remains etched in his brain.

Just as crucially, Monkawa began to rebel against the anti-Black prejudice he saw among the older generation of Japanese Americans, which tended to differ from the overt hatred many whites expressed during the civil rights and Black Power eras. It was not usually spoken publicly or part of organized political pressure. Persecuted for looking like the enemy during the war, many Japanese Americans sought to distance themselves during the postwar era from the animosity whites aimed at African Americans. Such prejudice often surfaced through the use of derogatory anti-Black terms from the Japanese language. Some also harbored a fear of Black criminality based on racial stereotypes. Monkawa's parents, for example, used the address of a relative to move him and his sister to Audubon Junior High, which more whites and relatively privileged Japanese Americans attended. When Monkawa progressed to Dorsey High School, however, it fully reflected the changing makeup of the Crenshaw district, which had been an equal mix of Black, Asian, and white but was experiencing white flight. By the mid- to late 1960s, Monkawa clearly sensed that the school and surrounding area was transitioning to majority Black.

To understand how Black-Asian solidarity developed in Crenshaw, one must appreciate that there was not a universal presumption of shared interests. Monkawa stressed that it often emerged from those willing to go against the grain. Malcolm X, the Black Panthers, and many Black Power militants promoted an internationalist vision that highlighted solidarity with Asian revolutionaries. While some Japanese Americans coming of age in this era fit the "model minority" profile of high-achieving students bound for universities, many Sansei youth did not. In response to Japanese and Asian American drug abuse, school dropouts, and gang violence, the Yellow Brotherhood formed in Crenshaw in 1969. Much like the Black Panthers, it aimed to provide youths with self-pride, social consciousness, and positive outlets for fitness and recreation.

In high school, Monkawa defied the "model minority" stereotype by using his artistic talents to make activist and antiwar statements on campus. For this, he was effectively expelled and relegated to low-wage jobs. On a visit to the *Gidra* office, where his best friend volunteered, he was struck by a poster linking corporate production of the "Napalm that blasts Vietnamese civilians" and the "barbiturates that were killing African American and Japanese young people." Monkawa saw the connection between the racist war overseas and his friends of color dying of drug overdoses at home. He joined the *Gidra* collective, becoming an integral contributor for two years before it closed down in 1974. It was one of many radical initiatives of that era to sunset after years of intensive, generally unpaid labor by young activists now reexamining their lives and work. Once driven by the belief that revolution was just around the corner, they adjusted to new political realities, family lives, and careers. Monkawa moved on to the East Wind collective, which merged into the League for Revolutionary Struggle. Continuing a lifelong commitment to social justice, he joined Black, Latino, white, and other Asian American radicals in working with labor unions, civil rights organizations, student activists, and electoral politics.

FIVE LESSONS FROM HISTORY TO STOP
ANTI-ASIAN VIOLENCE

While far from typical, David Monkawa's dedication to overcoming anti-Asian racism provides a fitting conclusion to this book, which seeks to create a dialogue with those who remake and reshape history. In the age of social media, it is easy to be misled into believing that activists sprout up overnight. We can learn much more about organizing as an evolutionary process, however, by listening to those who have been at it for many decades. Monkawa was part of a generation of Japanese Americans who devoted their lives to building the Asian American movement, then continued to advance panethnic and multiracial solidarity to stop anti-Asian violence and all racist attacks. His life story reinforces key points that I have sought to bring forward throughout the preceding pages. While I do not claim to provide a blueprint or prescriptions for implementation, I want to leave readers with five lessons from history that are crucial to breaking the silence and putting a stop to anti-Asian violence.

1. Connect domestic racism with overseas imperialism.

At the outset of Chinese migration to the United States in the mid-nineteenth century, exclusionist acts were precipitated by the colonial Opium Wars, the unequal relations they imposed, and the Orientalist stereotypes they reinforced. Broadly speaking, the sources, purposes, and effects of anti-Asian racism and violence cannot be understood without this type of transnational perspective. As author Viet Thanh Nguyen stated in October 2023, we must not forget that "the greatest acts of anti-Asian violence are carried out in America's wars in Asia." There is, Nguyen added, "total continuity between what the United States has done in the Philippines, in Korea, in Japan, in Laos, in Cambodia, in Vietnam, and now with Palestine." Tragically, the war hatreds have not been isolated but cumulative.[3]

We have seen how the dehumanization of Asian peoples shuttles back and forth across the Pacific. The U.S. government sent troops to massacre independence fighters and civilians in the Philippines, then subjected Filipino immigrants to discrimination and violence when they sought out the beacon of freedom centered in their colonial education. During World War II, an intertwined model of anti-Asian racism underlay the contorted logic behind the mass incarceration of Japanese Americans and the bombing of civilians in Tokyo, Hiroshima, and Nagasaki. Then, amid the trade war of the 1980s, it rebounded in the form of Japan-bashing that took the life of Vincent Chin. And yet, even as that wanton killing brought the concept of anti-Asian violence into mass consciousness, the virulent hatred and resentment of "gooks" overshadowed anti-Japanese discourse to become the most prominent source of such hostilities first in the Vietnam War, and then through the high period of Southeast Asian refugee resettlement from the 1970s to 1990s. With the turn of the twenty-first century, the global war on terror put a target on the backs of West, Central, and South Asians at home and abroad, followed by the xenophobic "China virus" hysteria of the pandemic.

2. Confront the history of erasure.

When the Trump administration's Department of Education issued a "Dear Colleague" guidance letter on February 14, 2025, one of its key stated purposes was ending discrimination against Asian Americans. Yet it did not invoke any of the pillars of anti-Asian racism spanning the past 175 years. Quite to the contrary, the "discriminatory practices" it purported are harming Asian Americans emanated from the specious claim that the nation's "educational institutions have toxically indoctrinated students with the false premise that the United States is built upon 'systemic and structural racism.'" The letter breathtakingly revealed layer upon layer of erasure. The violent history of anti-Asian racism is erased from the official record, which facilitates the equation of Asian American interests with white claims of "reverse" discrimination, thereby erasing the history of oppression against Indigenous, Black, and Brown peoples.[4]

We have seen how narratives of anti-Asian violence have been repeatedly censored: the testimonies of immigrants victimized in the era of *People v. Hall*; the massacre at No Gun Ri; the sexual violence in camptowns; the genocide by proxy in Bangladesh; and the countless attacks dismissed as "not racially motivated." But we have also seen how Asian Americans have broken through the silence to expose the systemic operation of anti-Asian racism within the capitalist system. While the Justice for Vincent Chin movement is the best-documented example, it is far from the only one. After the Rock Springs massacre, 559 Chinese workers issued a joint statement of protest. Yoshi Hattori's family challenged the profiteering and destruction wrought by the rampant sale of guns. Chanel Miller disclosed her name and identity as a sexual assault survivor to expose the favoritism the justice system confers on privileged white men. When we recover that which has been silenced, we demonstrate the power of truth telling and consciousness raising to challenge structures of hierarchy and exclusion.

3. Don't look for the "perfect" victim.

While it is fine to recognize those who study and work hard, the "model minority" stereotype intentionally distorts and misrepresents the experiences of Asian Americans. This pervasive stereotype is a manipulative tool deployed by conservatives to beat down the civil rights claims of other communities of color. It turns achievement into a zero-sum game that reinforces white supremacist ideology while upholding the widening levels of inequality taking place under neoliberalism. When addressing anti-Asian violence, we must take care to avoid championing a form of "model minority" victimhood. In other words, when we justly draw attention to how Asian Americans have been wronged, we should take care not to reinforce other pernicious stereotypes. Given the callous disregard the justice system showed the family and friends of Vincent Chin, we can appreciate why they demanded their right to be heard in court. Nevertheless, we need to be wary of the degree to which an overemphasis on prosecuting offenders serves to exacerbate social problems, while heightening interethnic tensions.

Because victims from minoritized backgrounds are frequently put on trial in court and in the media, it is tempting to look for the "perfect" victim who is above reproach. Doing so, however, not only leads us on a futile search; it can also reinforce the marginalization of survivors and victims. That Vincent Chin was neither an engineer nor a college graduate should be immaterial to his case. Moreover, he did not deserve to die even if he threw the first punch or, especially, if he punched Ebens in response to racist taunting. At the same time, not enough attention has been paid to the roles that anti-Black racism and toxic masculinity played as underlying factors in Chin's killing. We need to understand why there are dozens of victims of similar attacks whose stories are not properly known, which obliges us to detect bias not only within the dominant culture but also among Asian Americans. We are forced to ask whether Thanh Nguyen's story failed to gain traction because he was a gay man shot in a cruising spot with his white lover. Chonburi Xiong's death is less known than Chin's because he was killed by police who portrayed him as a gang member. Asian American sex workers in Red Canary Song have called for us to remedy the precarious conditions under which they and those in the shadows of sex-related industries routinely work.

4. Transcend the hate crimes framework to prioritize meeting human needs.

In the aftermath of the Atlanta spa shootings, Red Canary Song further advised that more criminalization and policing will not make them safer. Their statement was part of an ongoing reassessment of the hate crimes framework. After Ronald Ebens and Michael Nitz escaped with a slap on the wrist for killing Vincent Chin, there was a visceral cry from Asian Americans and their allies to "Jail the Racist Killers." It was an outcry against the bias inherent in law enforcement, which repeatedly fails to arrest, charge, or convict perpetrators of anti-Asian violence. Giving them more authority within a retributive justice framework, however, will not necessarily accomplish what survivors and community advocates seek. Furthermore, the prosecution of hate crimes requires an emphasis on individual motivation and culpability that can inhibit a deeper understanding of the underlying problem.

When President Biden signed the COVID-19 Hate Crimes Act in May 2021, it marked one of the most prominent moments of recognition of anti-Asian violence in U.S. history. But it also came as Asian American activists were highlighting alternatives to policing that address the root causes of violence and vulnerability. With Asian Americans among the numerous victims who have been shot by police while undergoing mental health crises, many are calling for more investments in counseling, health care, and de-escalation training. Drawing inspiration from social movements of the 1960s that predate the professionalization of activism within the nonprofit industry, they are also emphasizing communal self-help and collective care. These moves have aligned with restorative justice measures being carried out by organizers pushing for an end to mass incarceration.

5. Build multiracial alliances.

If we revisit the most devastating moments in the history of anti-Asian racism—such as Chinese exclusion, the Philippine-American War, Japanese American incarceration, and the murder of Vincent Chin—we can find Americans from diverse backgrounds standing with Asians on the right side of history. Moreover, the foundational grounds for Asian American community building, including birthright citizenship and the end of discriminatory immigration restrictions, have been tied to the historic quest for civil rights and Black freedom. When he condemned the U.S. government as "the greatest purveyor of violence in the world" for its bombing and invasion of Vietnam, Dr. Martin Luther King Jr. provided the substance, the means, and the moral clarity to overcome official silence and erasure. In so doing, he established the grounds for international solidarity in the revolutionary movement against the "giant triplets" of racism, militarism, and materialism.

Through the construction of multiracial alliances and coalitions, we can embed the struggle against anti-Asian violence within a transformative movement for systemic change and social justice. We can ensure that true working-class solidarity prevails, so that we expose the underlying sources of violence and conflict under capitalism rather than fall to divide-and-conquer tactics that lead subgroups of workers to seek a marginally better deal from ruling elites. We can further ensure that our work to stop racist violence does not ignore its interconnection to forms of oppression rooted in class, gender, sexuality, disability, religion, and nationality. Finally, we can work to build the most democratic movement possible—the kind that leads to enduring change because it fosters participation and dedication among the multitude of people who represent a just and sustainable future for humanity.

THE STRUGGLE HAS NO ENDING

In December 2021, as both the pandemic and anti-Asian attacks raged on, I felt compelled to catch up with David Monkawa. I learned he had returned to an apartment in Crenshaw and was still engaged in activism, now through the Progressive Asian Network for Action. Though he is critical of leftist dogma, many of his convictions have remained remarkably consistent. Amid ongoing challenges and crises, Monkawa continues to believe escalated policing and criminalization are not the antidote for racist violence. True solutions can only come from grassroots action for systemic change based on multiracial solidarity and self-determination.

During the COVID-19 pandemic, reports from Los Angeles's Koreatown rekindled concerns about Asian American elders and other community members being assailed by non-Asians. In response, Monkawa joined with fellow activists to form Neighborhood Safety Companions. One incident that made headlines clearly fit the profile of a bias incident. Denny Kim was standing on Kenmore Avenue in the heart of Koreatown when he was approached by two men on the night of February 16, 2021. "You have the Chinese Virus, go back to China," he recounted one of the men yelling at him. Kim, a thirty-year-old veteran of the Air Force, had no idea who they were. They hurled racist slurs, he said, while assaulting him. They ran away only when his friend arrived in a rideshare. By then, Kim's eye was swollen, and his nose was broken. Kim's assailants were described as "Hispanic males in their thirties." The attacks reminded some of the interethnic tensions that struck during the 1992 rebellion. Some elders told reporters they were too scared to leave the house. Kim shared their fear, saying his attackers threatened to kill him. He was reluctant to report the attack—only doing so after he attended a rally against anti-Asian violence. There he met a woman activist who convinced him it was necessary to "spread awareness and possibly prevent this from happening to somebody else."[5]

Viewing multiracial solidarity as pivotal to ending all forms of racist violence, Monkawa and Neighborhood Safety Companions created models of mutual aid and community-based care. Formed in 2021, the volunteer group provided escorts to elders so that they could feel safe walking the streets and running errands in the community. (Similar initiatives formed in Oakland and New York City.) They eschewed armed patrols and heightened police presence, knowing that such an ominous presence can harm residents and make others, including system-impacted and houseless persons, feel less safe. They also advocated that policymakers prioritize self-reliance and self-protection. When Congress passed the COVID-19 Hate Crimes Act, much of the funding was allocated to law enforcement. Neighborhood Safety Companions called for those funds to be devoted to "medical expenses and psychological trauma support." They cooperated with Koreatown Immigrant Workers Alliance and other organizations stressing change from the bottom up, including API-RISE, which is led by formerly incarcerated persons and supports Asian Americans and Pacific Islanders in creating healthy lives after prison. Believing that none of us are safe until all of us are safe, they have consistently supported people from diverse racial and ethnic backgrounds who are struggling against violence and repression.[6]

Seeing videos of Asian Americans in their twenties and thirties leading the self-protection patrols made me wonder where Monkawa stood. After all, the youth activist of the 1960s was now an elder in his seventies.

"Are you out on the streets with them?" I asked.

"Yes," he affirmed, "plan to do it till the day I die."

ACKNOWLEDGMENTS

I have been working on this book in one way or another for over thirty-five years. These acknowledgments will at best recognize a fraction of the people from whom I have drawn inspiration and assistance. I apologize in advance for their incompleteness.

Elise Capron and the Sandra Dijkstra Literary Agency helped me refashion the book to reach the widest possible audience. I am grateful for her expert guidance in finding a publisher, lending an ear on a plethora of topics, and being the greatest delight to work with as a collaborator. I am thrilled the book found an ideal home with the University of California Press, and I was most fortunate to have the shrewd editorial insights of Niels Hooper for a third time. Niels particularly saw how the book's radical spirit and scholarly integrity could best come together.

The book was wonderfully served by a close reading by my developmental editor, Melissa Hung, whose comments and suggestions repeatedly provided needed focus and clarity. It also benefited from Diane Fujino's constructive feedback, reports from three anonymous readers, indexing by Do Mi Stauber, and editing by Richard Earles and Emily Park. I also thank everyone who has worked behind the scenes to bring this book into the world.

I first conceived of this project becoming a book while I lived in Detroit and engaged in community organizing with the Detroit Asian Youth Project, American Citizens for Justice, and the Japanese American Citizens League. Thank you to Stephanie Chang, Roland Hwang, Mary Kamidoi, Marcia Lee, Fe Rowland, Toshi Shimoura, Soh Suzuki, Caroline Vang Polly, and Mai Xiong, along with numerous other members and youth participants.

Support from the staff and volunteers at Asian Americans United has been indispensable to this book. Interviewees listed in the endnotes provided firsthand information and directed me to additional sources. The following is a partial list of AAU members and friends who provided additional ideas that shaped my understanding or material support during my trips to Philadelphia: Vivian Chang, Wei Chen, Helen Gym, Eric Joselyn, Debora Kodish, Neeta Patel, Ellen Somekawa,

Hue Tran, Alix Webb, and Debbie Wei. Kaylee Yam provided research assistance to access AAU's organizational records with funding from the School of Interdisciplinary Arts and Sciences at the University of Washington, Bothell.

The many people from whom I requested various forms of help for this project and/or in regard to broader scholar-activist matters include Hōkūlani Aikau, Anida Yoeu Ali, adrienne maree brown, Bruce Burgett, Karam Dana, dream hampton, Evelyn Brooks Higginbotham, Max Krochmal, Curtis Marez, David Monkawa, Glenn Omatsu, David Palumbo-Liu, Kyeyoung Park, Bao Phi, Ai-Jen Poo, Chandan Reddy, Dylan Rodriguez, Cathy Schlund-Vials, Mike Sonksen, Stew Stewart, Masahiro Sugano, Renee Tajima-Peña, Alex Tom, Judy Wu, Jeff Yang, and Paula Yoo. Alexander Jin and Sonya G. Chen generously allowed me to read their unpublished manuscript, "The Uses and Abuses of Asian American History in Responses to Anti-Asian Violence." Special mention to the late Tou Ger Xiong and to scholarly mentors who have joined the ancestors: Yuji Ichioka, Eric Monkkonen, and Don Nakanishi.

I am grateful for the invitations I received to present early versions of talks and papers on topics in the book from Robert Chang and Greg Robinson for a symposium at Seattle University; from Julian Zelizer and Kevin Kruse for a seminar at Princeton; and from Priscilla Liu for a talk at Southern Methodist University.

I am thankful to copyright holders for granting permission to include prior publications. Parts of chapters 6 and 7 draw from Scott Kurashige, "Rereading Vincent Chin: Asian Americans and Multiracial Political Analysis," in *Minority Relations: Intergroup Conflict and Cooperation*, ed. Robert Chang and Greg Robinson, 126–58 (University of Mississippi Press, 2017). Parts of chapter 10 draw from two articles: Scott Kurashige, "Beyond Random Acts of Hatred: Analyzing Urban Patterns of Anti-Asian Violence," *Amerasia Journal* 26, no. 1 (2000): 209–31 (reused courtesy of UCLA Asian American Studies Center), and Scott Kurashige, "Pan-ethnicity and Community Organizing: Asian Americans United's Campaign Against Anti-Asian Violence," *Journal of Asian American Studies* 3, no. 2 (June 2000): 163–90 (reused courtesy of Johns Hopkins University Press and the *Journal of Asian American Studies*). Parts of the epilogue draw from Scott Kurashige, "The Legacy of Multiracial Solidarity in L.A.'s Crenshaw Neighborhood," *PBS SoCal*, April 13, 2022, https://www.pbssocal.org/shows/lost-la/the-legacy-of-multiracial-solidarity-in-l-a-s-crenshaw-neighborhood.

The titanic influence over every word I have thought, written, or spoken since 1998 is Grace Lee Boggs. While I feel Grace's loss with every passing day, I am blessed to continue our relationship through the work of the James and Grace Lee Boggs Foundation with Rob "Biko" Baker, Donald Boggs, Aurora Harris, Gloria House, Alice Jennings, Michelle Lin, and Drew Philp.

None of this work would matter without the love and care of my family. Eternal gratitude to Emily, Kori, and Tula.

NOTES

INTRODUCTION

1. "The Victims," *Atlanta-Journal Constitution*, March 17, 2022, ProQuest US Newsstream.

2. Morning Consult, "National Tracking Poll #210639," June 7–22, 2021, https://www.politico.com/f/?id = 0000017c-27d8-dddc-a77e-27db16040000.

3. Transcript of Atlanta Press Conference, CNN, March 17, 2021, https://transcripts.cnn.com/show/cnr/date/2021–03–17/segment/04; Jina Moore, "How the Atlanta Shooting Shows the Dangers of American Evangelicalism's Trademark 'Purity Culture,'" *Business Insider*, March 20, 2021, https://www.businessinsider.com/the-atlanta-shooting-and-the-dangers-of-evangelical-purity-culture-2021–3; Andrew L. Whitehead and Samuel L. Perry, *Taking America Back for God: Christian Nationalism in the United States* (Oxford University Press, 2020), 10.

4. Jordan Daley, Natalie M. Gallagher, and Galen V. Bodenhausen, "The Pandemic and the 'Perpetual Foreigner': How Threats Posed by the COVID-19 Pandemic Relate to Stereotyping of Asian Americans," *Frontiers in Psychology* 13 (February 16, 2022), https://doi.org/10.3389/fpsyg.2022.821891. The researchers concluded that whites who blamed China for the pandemic, rather than expressing a generally elevated concern about the health risks of COVID-19, espoused "increased foreignness perceptions of Asians."

5. Meryl Kornfield and Hannah Knowles, "Captain Who Said Spa Shootings Suspect Had 'Bad Day' No Longer a Spokesman on Case, Official Says," *Washington Post*, March 18, 2021, https://www.washingtonpost.com/nation/2021/03/17/jay-baker-bad-day/; Li Zhou, "The Stop Asian Hate Movement Is at a Crossroads," *Vox*, March 15, 2022, https://www.vox.com/22820364/stop-asian-hate-movement-atlanta-shootings; Catie Edmondson and Jim Tankersley, "Biden Signs Bill Addressing Hate Crimes Against Asian-Americans," *New York Times*, May 20, 2021, https://www.nytimes.com/2021/05/20/us/politics/biden-asian-hate-crimes-bill.html.

6. Frank Shyong, "Hate Crime or Not, Atlanta Shooter Was Motivated by Racism," *Los Angeles Times*, July 30, 2021, https://www.latimes.com/california/story

/2021–07–30/shyong-atlanta-shootings. Disclosure: I was interviewed by Shyong for this column.

7. "Most AAPI Adults Think K–12 Students Should Learn About Slavery, Racism, Segregation, and the History of AAPI Communities," Associated Press–NORC Center for Public Affairs Research, May 2024, 1–4, https://apnorc.org/wp-content/uploads/2024/05/AAPI-Data-AP-NORC-April-2024-Report.pdf; Briana Mendez-Padilla, "As AAPI Studies Expand Nationwide, Ethnic Studies Can Provide Inroads," *K–12 Dive*, November 6, 2024, https://www.k12dive.com/news/aapi-studies-expand-nationwide-ethnic-studies-provide-inroads/732162/; Neil G. Ruiz, Luis Noe-Bustamante, and Sono Shah, "Diverse Cultures and Shared Experiences Shape Asian American Identities," Pew Research Center, May 8, 2023, 45–47, https://www.pewresearch.org/wp-content/uploads/sites/20/2023/05/RE_2023.05.08_Asian-American-Identity_Report.pdf.

8. Frederick Douglass, "Composite Nation," in *Racism, Dissent, and Asian Americans from 1850 to the Present: A Documentary History*, ed. Philip S. Foner and Daniel Rosenberg (Bloomsbury, 1993), 215–31.

9. Moon-Ho Jung, *Menace to Empire: Anticolonial Solidarities and the Transpacific Origins of the US Security State* (University of California Press, 2022), 8–9.

10. Grace Lee Boggs with Scott Kurashige, *The Next American Revolution: Sustainable Activism for the Twenty-First Century* (University of California Press, 2011), 79; Yuji Ichioka et al., *A Buried Past: An Annotated Bibliography of the Japanese American Research Project Collection* (University of California Press, 1974).

11. Yen Le Espiritu, *Asian American Panethnicity: Bridging Institutions and Identities* (Temple University Press, 1992), 134–60.

12. My use of the terms *invisibility* and *hypervisibility* is indebted to dialogues with scholars in Arab American studies, e.g., Amira Jarmakani, "Arab American Feminisms: Mobilizing the Politics of Invisibility," in *Arab and Arab American Feminisms: Gender, Violence, and Belonging*, ed. Rabab Abdulhadi, Evelyn Alsultany, and Nadine Naber (Rutgers University Press, 2011), 227–41.

13. Movement Advancement Project, *Policy Spotlight: Hate Crime Laws*, July 2021, ii, https://www.lgbtmap.org/file/2021-report-hate-crime-laws.pdf.

14. AAPI Data, *State of Asian Americans, Native Hawaiians, and Pacific Islanders in the United States*, June 2022, 15, 102, https://aapidata.com/wp-content/uploads/2024/02/State-AANHPIs-National-June2022.pdf; U.S. Census Bureau, *1990 Census of Population: General Population Characteristics, Georgia*, 15; Sabrina Tavernise, "A New Political Force Emerges in Georgia: Asian-American Voters," *New York Times*, November 25, 2020, https://www.nytimes.com/2020/11/25/us/georgia-asian-american-voters.html; Kimmy Yam, "Asian American Voter Rates in Georgia Hit Record High," *NBC News*, March 31, 2021, https://www.nbcnews.com/news/asian-america/asian-american-voter-rates-georgia-hit-record-high-how-voting-n1262682.

15. Robert G. Lee, *Orientals: Asian Americans in Popular Culture* (Temple University Press, 1999), 180–203.

16. Lauren Aratani, "'We're Not Taught to Speak Out': Asian Americans Find Their Voice amid Rise in Hate," *Guardian*, April 12, 2021, https://www.theguardian.com/us-news/2021/apr/12/asian-americans-find-their-voice-amid-rise-in-hate; Andrea Woo, "Perseverance and Pride: AAPI Healthcare Workers Get Personal About Racism," *New York Presbyterian Health Matters*, May 13, 2021, https://healthmatters.nyp.org/perseverance-and-pride-aapi-healthcare-workers-get-personal-about-racism/; Morning Consult, "National Tracking Poll #210639."

1. THE VIOLENCE OF EXCLUSION

1. "Memorial of Chinese Laborers Resident at Rock Springs, Wyoming Territory, to the Chinese Consul at New York (1885)," in *"Chink!": A Documentary History of Anti-Chinese Prejudice in America*, ed. Cheng-Tsu Wu (World Publishing, 1972), 151–66.

2. Sucheng Chan, *Asian Americans: An Interpretive History* (Twayne, 1991), 30–32; Manu Karuka, *Empire's Tracks: Indigenous Nations, Chinese Workers, and the Transcontinental Railroad* (University of California Press, 2019), 82–83.

3. Karuka, *Empire's Tracks*, 101; "Memorial of Chinese Laborers Resident at Rock Springs," 152–53; Alexander Saxton, *The Indispensable Enemy: Labor and the Anti-Chinese Movement in California* (University of California Press, 1971), 202–4; Clayton D. Laurie and Ronald H. Cole, *The Role of Federal Military Forces in Domestic Disorders, 1877–1945* (Center of Military History, U.S. Army, 1997), 87–90.

4. Frederick Douglass, "Composite Nation," in *Racism, Dissent, and Asian Americans from 1850 to the Present: A Documentary History*, ed. Philip S. Foner and Daniel Rosenberg (Bloomsbury, 1993), 215–31; Saxton, *The Indispensable Enemy*. On the idea of the West as a "safety valve," see Frederick J. Turner, "The Significance of the Frontier in American History," in *Annual Report of the American Historical Association for the Year 1893* (Government Printing Office, 1894); "Memorial of Chinese Laborers Resident at Rock Springs," 153–54; Michael Luo, "When an American Town Massacred Its Chinese Immigrants," *The New Yorker*, March 3, 2025, https://www.newyorker.com/magazine/2025/03/10/when-an-american-town-massacred-its-chinese-immigrants; "A Deadly Conflict Between White Miners and the Chinese at Rock Springs, Wyoming Territory," *Indiana Sentinel*, September 9, 1885, accessed among a selection of newspaper articles on the Rock Springs massacre held by the Library of Congress, https://guides.loc.gov/chronicling-america-rock-springs-massacre.

5. "Memorial of Chinese Laborers Resident at Rock Springs," 152–64; Luo, "When an American Town Massacred Its Chinese Immigrants."

6. "Memorial of Chinese Laborers Resident at Rock Springs," 156–59; Saxton, *The Indispensable Enemy*, 202; Laurie and Cole, *Role of Federal Military Forces*, 90–99; Luo, "When an American Town Massacred Its Chinese Immigrants"; W. W. Stone, "The Knights of Labor on the Chinese Labor Situation," *Overland Monthly*,

March 1886, 225–30, https://name.umdl.umich.edu/ahj1472.2–07.039; "The Union Pacific, Arrival of the Government Directors in Butte," *The Semi-Weekly Miner* (Butte, MT), September 23, 1885.

7. R. Gregory Nokes, *Massacred for Gold: The Chinese in Hells Canyon* (Oregon State University Press, 2009), 8–31. Nokes lists the eleven known victims as Chea Po, Chea Sun, Chea Yow, Chea Shun, Chea Cheong, Chea Ling, Chea Chow, Chea Lin-chung, Kong Munn-kow, Kong Nhan, and Ah Yow.

8. "Memorial of Chinese Laborers Resident at Rock Springs," 159.

9. John Kuo Wei Tchen, *New York Before Chinatown: Orientalism and the Shaping of American Culture, 1776–1882* (Johns Hopkins University Press, 1999), 3–24; James C. Thomson Jr., Peter W. Stanley, and John Curtis Perry, *Sentimental Imperialists: The American Experience in East Asia* (Harper and Row, 1981), 4–19.

10. Robert G. Lee, *Orientals: Asian Americans in Popular Culture* (Temple University Press, 1999), 2–3, 15–82.

11. Jean Pfaelzer, *Driven Out, The Forgotten War Against Chinese Americans* (University of California Press, 2007), xxvii–xxviii; Beth Lew-Williams, *The Chinese Must Go: Violence, Exclusion, and the Making of the Alien in America* (Harvard University Press, 2018), 1–3.

12. Julia Lovell, *The Opium War: Drugs, Dreams, and the Making of Modern China* (Overlook Press, 2014), 8–12 and elsewhere; "Treaty Between Her Majesty and the Emperor of China, Signed, in the English and Chinese Languages, at Nanking, August 29, 1942," *Gazette* (London), https://www.thegazette.co.uk/London/issue/20276/page/3597/data.pdf.

13. Chan, *Asian Americans*, 7–9; Łukasz Kamieński, "Opium Wars," *The SAGE Encyclopedia of War: Social Science Perspectives*, https://doi.org/10.4135/9781483359878.n486 (accessed May 1, 2025); Teemu Ruskola, "Canton Is Not Boston: The Invention of American Imperial Sovereignty," *American Quarterly* 57, no. 3 (2005): 859–84; Matthew Frye Jacobson, *Barbarian Virtues: The United States Encounters Foreign Peoples at Home and Abroad, 1876–1917* (Hill and Wang, 2000), 33.

14. Chin Keong Ng, *Boundaries and Beyond: China's Maritime Southeast in Late Imperial Times* (National University of Singapore Press, 2017), 316–41; Jason Chang, Benjamin Barson, and Alexis Dudden, *The Cargo Rebellion: Those Who Chose Freedom* (PM Press, 2023), 32–38.

15. Pär Kristoffer Cassel, *Grounds of Judgment: Extraterritoriality and Imperial Power in Nineteenth-Century China and Japan* (Oxford University Press, 2012), 4–13.

16. Edna Bonacich and Lucie Cheng, "Introduction: A Theoretical Orientation to International Labor Migration," in *Labor Immigration Under Capitalism: Asian Workers in the United States Before World War II*, ed. Lucie Cheng and Edna Bonacich (University of California Press, 1984), 1–29.

17. Peter Linebaugh, *Stop, Thief! The Commons, Enclosures, and Resistance* (PM Press, 2014), 65–74; Ian Angus, "The Meaning of 'So-Called Primitive Accumulation,'" *Monthly Review*, April 1, 2023, https://monthlyreview.org/2023/04/01/the-meaning-of-so-called-primitive-accumulation/; Karuka, *Empire's Tracks*, 43.

18. Saxton, *The Indispensable Enemy*, 53–65; Gordon H. Chang, *Ghosts of Gold Mountain: The Epic Story of the Chinese Who Built the Transcontinental Railroad* (Houghton Mifflin Harcourt, 2019), 138–61, 225–30.

19. Saxton, *The Indispensable Enemy*, 40, 211; Jennifer Keohane, "'Honest Toil': Labor, the Body, and Citizenship in the Knights of Labor, 1880–1890," *Rhetoric Society Quarterly* 46, no. 1 (2016): 66–88.

20. Linebaugh, *Stop, Thief!*, 74.

21. "Sentence of Death Passed upon G. W. Hall," *Nevada Journal*, November 25, 1853; "Trial and Conviction for Murder," *Sacramento Daily Union*, October 13, 1853 (both of these sources are located in the UC Riverside Center for Bibliographical Studies and Research, California Digital Newspaper Collection; the latter names the victim as "Sing Sing"); Sucheng Chan, *This Bittersweet Soil: The Chinese in California Agriculture, 1860–1910* (University of California Press, 1986), 48; Saxton, *The Indispensable Enemy*, 53; Pfaelzer, *Driven Out*, 39.

22. Mae Ngai, *The Chinese Question: The Gold Rushes and Global Politics* (W. W. Norton, 2021), 95–98; Sucheng Chan, "A People of Exceptional Character: Ethnic Diversity, Nativism, and Racism in the California Gold Rush," *California History* 79, no. 2 (Summer 2000): 57–67; Chan, *This Bittersweet Soil*, 37–58.

23. "Sentence of Death Passed upon G. W. Hall"; "Trial and Conviction for Murder."

24. "Sentence of Death Passed upon G. W. Hall."

25. "Sentence of Death Passed upon G. W. Hall"; William M. Stewart, *Reminiscences of Senator William M. Stewart of Nevada* (Neale Publishing, 1908), 76–81; Charles J. McClain, *In Search of Equality: The Chinese Struggle Against Discrimination in Nineteenth-Century America* (University of California Press, 1996), 19–20.

26. *People v. Hall*, 4 Cal. 399 (Cal. 1854); Michael Traynor, "The Infamous Case of *People v. Hall* (1854): An Odious Symbol of Its Time," *California Supreme Court Historical Society Newsletter* (Spring–Summer 2017): 1–8.

27. Traynor, "The Infamous Case," 3–6; Stewart, *Reminiscences*, 79.

28. *People v. Hall*.

29. Benjamin Madley, *An American Genocide: The United States and the California Indian Catastrophe, 1846–1873* (Yale University Press, 2016), 2–12, 158–60, 286–87.

30. Chan, "A People of Exceptional Character," 57–76; Chan, *This Bittersweet Soil*, 35–58; Pfaelzer, *Driven Out*, 8–9, 13–16, 36; Kenneth Gonzales-Day, *Lynching in the West: 1850–1935* (Duke University Press, 2006), 205–28; Karuka, *Empire's Tracks*, 87.

31. McClain, *In Search of Equality*, 31–42.

32. Scott Zesch, *The Chinatown War: Chinese Los Angeles and the Massacre of 1871* (Oxford University Press, 2012), 54–84, 117–50, 180–210.

33. Richard Schneirov, "Thoughts on Periodizing the Gilded Age: Capital Accumulation, Society, and Politics, 1873–1898," *The Journal of the Gilded Age and Progressive Era* 5, no. 3 (2006): 189–224; Nicolas Barreyre, "The Politics of Economic Crises: The Panic of 1873, the End of Reconstruction, and the Realignment of

American Politics," *The Journal of the Gilded Age and Progressive Era* 10, no. 4 (2011): 403–23; Christoph Nitschke, "Theory and History of Financial Crises," *The Journal of the Gilded Age and Progressive Era* 17, no. 2 (2018): 221–40.

34. Wong Sam and Assistants, "An English-Chinese Phrase Book," in *The Big Aiiieeeee! An Anthology of Chinese American and Japanese American Literature*, ed. Jeffery Paul Chan et al. (Meridian, 1991), 93–110; Wong quoted in "Program One: Gold Mountain Dreams," *Becoming American: The Chinese Experience* (PBS, 2003), transcript of video at https://www-tc.pbs.org/becomingamerican/program1_transcript.pdf.

35. Saxton, *The Indispensable Enemy*, 60–105.

36. "Governor Haight's Inaugural Address (1867)," in Wu, *Chink!*, 110–11; Lew-Williams, *The Chinese Must Go*, 44–45; Pfaelzer, *Driven Out*, 256.

37. Lucy E. Salyer, *Chinese Immigrants and the Shaping of Modern Immigration Law* (University of North Carolina Press, 1995), 9–12; Ngai, *The Chinese Question*, 39, 101–3; Pfaelzer, *Driven Out*, 61–83, 264; Lew-Williams, *The Chinese Must Go*, 40–44; "Chinese Exclusion Act (1882)," National Archives, https://www.archives .gov/milestone-documents/chinese-exclusion-act (accessed December 7, 2024).

38. Lew-Williams, *The Chinese Must Go*, 5–8; Stone, "Knights of Labor," 229–30.

39. Keohane, "'Honest Toil,'" 67–83; Stone, "Knights of Labor," 225–27.

40. Lew-Williams, *The Chinese Must Go*, 48–51; Madley, *An American Genocide*, 282–84; Saxton, *The Indispensable Enemy*, 212; Pfaelzer, *Driven Out*, 121–43 (emphasis in original).

41. Juliana Hu Pegues, *Space-Time Colonialism: Alaska's Indigenous and Asian Entanglements* (University of North Carolina Press, 2021), 66–75.

42. Lew-Williams, *The Chinese Must Go*, 82–96.

43. Carlos A. Scwhantes, "Protest in a Promised Land: Unemployment, Disinheritance, and the Origin of Labor Militancy in the Pacific Northwest, 1885–1886," *Western Historical Quarterly* 13, no. 4 (1982): 373–83; Lew-Williams, *The Chinese Must Go*, 91–102; City of Tacoma, "Chinese Reconciliation Park," https://www .cityoftacoma.org/government/city_departments/planning_and_development_ services/planning_services/recent_and_completed_projects/chinese_reconciliation_ park (accessed December 7, 2024).

44. Schwantes, "Protest in a Promised Land," 383–85; Lew-Williams, *The Chinese Must Go*, 105–11.

45. Lew-Williams, *The Chinese Must Go*, 137–45, 178–93; McClain, *In Search of Equality*, 201–3.

46. Delber L. McKee, "'The Chinese Must Go!' Commissioner General Powderly and Chinese Immigration, 1897–1902," *Pennsylvania History: A Journal of Mid-Atlantic Studies* 44, no. 1 (1977): 37–51.

2. THE VIOLENCE OF EMPIRE

1. Albert Beveridge, "Policy Regarding the Philippines," January 9, 1900, 33 Cong. Rec., pt. 1, 705.

2. Claude G. Bowers, *Beveridge and the Progressive Era* (The Literary Guild, 1932), 123.

3. Beveridge, "Policy Regarding the Philippines," 705–6; John Braeman, *Albert J. Beveridge: American Nationalist* (University of Chicago Press, 1971), 22.

4. Beveridge, "Policy Regarding the Philippines," 705, 708; Bowers, *Beveridge and the Progressive Era*, 68–70.

5. Beveridge, "Policy Regarding the Philippines," 705–11.

6. Beveridge, "Policy Regarding the Philippines," 711.

7. Luzviminda Francisco, "The Philippine-American War," in *The Philippines Reader: A History of Colonialism, Neocolonialism, Dictatorship, and Resistance*, ed. Daniel B. Schirmer and Stephen Rosskamm Shalom (South End Press, 1987), 19.

8. Beveridge, "Policy Regarding the Philippines," 707, 712.

9. Bowers, *Beveridge and the Progressive Era*, 123.

10. Richard Welch, *Response to Imperialism: The United States and the Philippine-American War, 1899–1902* (University of North Carolina Press, 1979), 159.

11. William McKinley, Executive Order, December 21, 1898, The American Presidency Project, https://www.presidency.ucsb.edu/documents/executive-order-132.

12. Welch, *Response to Imperialism*, 17–20, 58–67; Baltazar Pinguel, "Reframing the Spanish-American War in the History Curriculum," in *Resistance in Paradise: Rethinking 100 Years of U.S. Involvement in the Caribbean and the Pacific*, ed. Deborah Wei and Rachael Kamel (American Friends Service Committee, 1998), 1–12.

13. Gordon H. Chang, "Whose 'Barbarism'? Whose 'Treachery'? Race and Civilization in the Unknown United States–Korea War of 1871," *The Journal of American History* 89, no. 4 (2003): 1331–55.

14. Chang, "Whose 'Barbarism'?," 1355–64.

15. Pinguel, "Reframing the Spanish-American War," 1–12.

16. "A Petition to the President of the United States, October 10, 1901," in "The United States and Its Territories, 1870–1925: The Age of Imperialism," University of Michigan Library Digital Collections, https://name.umdl.umich.edu/ask1009.0001.001 (accessed October 11, 2024); *New York Herald*, October 15, 1900, excerpted at Library of Congress, https://guides.loc.gov/world-of-1898/mark-twain; Welch, *Response to Imperialism*, 75–88.

17. Matthew Frye Jacobson, *Barbarian Virtues: The United States Encounters Foreign Peoples at Home and Abroad, 1876–1917* (Hill and Wang, 2000), 139–72.

18. Gail Bederman, *Manliness and Civilization: A Cultural History of Gender and Race in the United States, 1880–1917* (University of Chicago Press, 1995), 1–44; Kristin L. Hoganson, *Fighting for American Manhood: How Gender Politics Provoked the Spanish-American and Philippine American Wars* (Yale University Press, 1998), 13, 133–79.

19. Hoganson, *Fighting for American Manhood*, 156–179; Beveridge, "Policy Regarding the Philippines," 707–9.

20. Jacobson, *Barbarian Virtues*, 227.

21. Braeman, *Albert J. Beveridge*, 1–26, 64–65, 315.

22. Michele Mitchell, *Righteous Propagation: African Americans and the Politics of Racial Destiny After Reconstruction* (University of North Carolina Press, 2004), 51–75; George P. Marks, *The Black Press Views American Imperialism, 1898–1900* (Arno Press, 1971), 100–71; Michael Morey, *Fagen: An African American Renegade in the Philippine-American War* (University of Wisconsin Press, 2019), 5.

23. Marks, *Black Press*, 160–162.

24. Beveridge, "Policy Regarding the Philippines," 708–10.

25. Francisco, "The Philippine-American War," 10; Stuart Creighton Miller, *Benevolent Assimilation: The American Conquest of the Philippines, 1899–1903* (Yale University Press, 1982), 58; David Roediger, *Towards the Abolition of Whiteness: Essays on Race, Politics, and Working Class History* (Verso, 1994), 117–20; Jacobson, *Barbarian Virtues*, 244.

26. Francisco, "The Philippine-American War," 10–15.

27. Reynaldo C. Ileto, "The Philippine-American War: Friendship and Forgetting," in *Vestiges of War: The Philippine-American War and the Aftermath of an Imperial Dream, 1899–1999*, ed. Angel Velasco Shaw and Luis H. Francia (New York University Press, 2002), 3–21; Francisco, "The Philippine-American War," 22.

28. Glenn A. May, "Resistance and Collaboration in the Philippine-American War: The Case of Batangas," *Journal of Southeast Asian Studies* 15, no. 1 (1984): 69–90; Francisco, "The Philippine-American War," 15.

29. Beveridge, "Policy Regarding the Philippines," 708.

30. Francisco, "The Philippine-American War," 13; Miller, *Benevolent Assimilation*, 225–51; Welch, *Response to Imperialism*, 30–41.

31. Francisco, "The Philippine-American War," 16–17; Miller, *Benevolent Assimilation*, 219–41.

32. Welch, *Response to Imperialism*, 133–46; Miller, *Benevolent Assimilation*, 233–51.

33. Kim A. Wagner, *Massacre in the Clouds: An American Atrocity and the Erasure of History* (PublicAffairs, 2024), 5–6, 25–32, 171–76.

34. Howard A. De Witt, "The Watsonville Anti-Filipino Riot of 1930: A Case Study of the Great Depression and Ethnic Conflict in California," *Southern California Quarterly* 61, no. 3 (1979): 291–302; Dawn Bohulano Mabalon, *Little Manila Is in the Heart: The Making of the Filipina/o American Community in Stockton, California* (Duke University Press, 2013), 25–100.

35. Paul A. Kramer, *The Blood of Government: Race, Empire, the United States, and the Philippines* (University of North Carolina Press, 2006), 229–84.

36. Michael P. Showalter, "The Watsonville Anti-Filipino Riot of 1930: A Reconsideration of Fermin Tobera's Murder," *Southern California Quarterly* 71, no. 4 (1989): 341–48; Fred Cordova, *Filipinos: Forgotten Asian Americans* (Kendall/Hunt, 1983), 115–21; Howard A. De Witt, *Anti-Filipino Movements in California: A History, Bibliography and Study Guide* (R and R Associates, 1976), 31–35; Mabalon, *Little Manila*, 83–99.

37. De Witt, "Watsonville Anti-Filipino Riot," 292–96; Mabalon, *Little Manila*, 132–38.

38. De Witt, "Watsonville Anti-Filipino Riot," 296–99; Showalter, "Watsonville Anti-Filipino Riot," 343–47; De Witt, *Anti-Filipino Movements*, 27–63.

39. Showalter, "Watsonville Anti-Filipino Riot," 343–47.

40. De Witt, "Watsonville Anti-Filipino Riot," 300.

41. *Roldan v. Los Angeles County*, 129 Cal.App. 267 (Cal. Ct. App. 1933); Cordova, *Filipinos*, 115–22; Philippine Commonwealth and Independence (Tydings-McDuffie) Act, Pub. L. 73-127, 48 Stat. 456; Mabalon, *Little Manila*, 143–46.

42. Miller, *Benevolent Assimilation*, 235.

43. Angel Velasco Shaw, "Exquisite Betrayal," in Shaw and Francia, *Vestiges of War*, ix–x; Luis H. Francia, "Excised from the Rind of Things," in *Vestiges of War*, xxiii.

44. Raphael Lorenzo A. Pangalangan, Gemmo Bautista Fernandez, and Ruby Rosselle L. Tugade, "Marcosian Atrocities: Historical Revisionism and the Legal Constraints on Forgetting," *Asia-Pacific Journal on Human Rights and the Law* 19 (2018): 140–90; Cindy Domingo, "Long Road to Justice," in *A Time to Rise: Collective Memoirs of the Union of Democratic Filipinos (KDP)*, ed. Rene Ciria Cruz, Cindy Domingo, and Bruce Occena (University of Washington Press, 2017), 231–39; Jim Douglas, "Defeating the Marcoses in a Court of Law," in *A Time to Rise*, 240–52.

45. Charles J. Hanley, Sang-Hun Choe, and Martha Mendoza, *The Bridge at No Gun Ri: A Hidden Nightmare from the Korean War* (Henry Holt, 2001), 226.

46. Hanley, Choe, and Mendoza, *Bridge at No Gun Ri*, 29, 71–90, 127, 178.

47. Hanley, Choe, and Mendoza, *Bridge at No Gun Ri*, 121–23, 292–94.

48. Hanley, Choe, and Mendoza, *Bridge at No Gun Ri*, 113–45.

49. Hanley, Choe, and Mendoza, *Bridge at No Gun Ri*, xv, 209–10, 257.

50. Hanley, Choe, and Mendoza, *Bridge at No Gun Ri*, x, 143–45, 209; Jeremy Williams, "Kill 'em All': The American Military in Korea," BBC, February 17, 2011, https://www.bbc.co.uk/history/worldwars/coldwar/korea_usa_01.shtml.

3. FROM MASS INCARCERATION TO MASS MURDER

1. "Executive Order 9066: Resulting in Japanese-American Incarceration (1942)," National Archives, https://www.archives.gov/milestone-documents/executive-order-9066 (accessed March 27, 2025).

2. *Problems of Evacuation of Enemy Aliens and Others from Prohibited Military Zones: San Francisco Hearings, February 21 and 23, 1942, Before the Select Comm. Investigating National Defense Migration, House of Representatives,* 77th Cong. 2d Session, Pt. 29, 11010 (1942), Testimony of Hon. Earl Warren, Attorney General of the State of California, San Francisco.

3. *Problems of Evacuation of Enemy Aliens*, 10974, 10981. In addition to live testimony, the Congressional Record of Warren's testimony includes a statement he submitted to the committee, which is quoted here.

4. *Problems of Evacuation of Enemy Aliens*, 11015.

5. *Problems of Evacuation of Enemy Aliens*, 11015–16.

6. *Problems of Evacuation of Enemy Aliens*, 11014.

7. *Problems of Evacuation of Enemy Aliens*, 11011–12 (emphasis added).

8. John Dower, *The Violent American Century: War and Terror Since World War II* (Haymarket Books, 2017), 42.

9. *Nishimura Ekiu v. United States*, 142 U.S. 651 (1892), opinion and arguments at https://casetext.com/case/nishimura-ekiu-v-united-states; Lucy E. Salyer, *Chinese Immigrants and the Shaping of Modern Immigration Law* (University of North Carolina Press, 1995), 26–30; Sarah Song, "Why Does the State Have the Right to Control Immigration?," *Nomos* 57 (2017): 3–50.

10. James C. Thomson Jr., Peter W. Stanley, and John Curtis Perry, *Sentimental Imperialists: The American Experience in East Asia* (Harper and Row, 1981), 145–46; "Willard Straight Hall," Cornell University, https://veteransmemorials.cornell.edu/willard-straight/ (accessed October 2, 2024).

11. Roger Daniels, *The Politics of Prejudice* (University of California Press, 1962), 31–45, 79–105; Yuji Ichioka, *The Issei: The World of the First Generation Japanese Immigrants, 1885–1924* (The Free Press, 1988), 69–72, 210–50.

12. *Ozawa v. United States*, 260 U.S. 178 (1922); *United States v. Bhagat Singh Thind*, 261 U.S. 204 (1923).

13. Gaylord C. Kubota, "The Lynching of Katsu Goto," in *Hawai‘i Chronicles: Island History from the Pages of Honolulu Magazine*, ed. Bob Dye (University of Hawai‘i Press, 1996), 197–214, reprinted at https://www.hawaii.edu/uhwo/clear/home/KatsuGoto.html.

14. Kubota, "The Lynching of Katsu Goto."

15. Ronald Takaki, *Pau Hana: Plantation Life and Labor in Hawaii* (University of Hawai‘i Press, 1983), 127–29.

16. Takaki, *Pau Hana*, 128; Richard S. Kim, *The Quest for Statehood: Korean Immigrant Nationalism and U.S. Sovereignty, 1905–45* (Oxford University Press, 2011), 19–21; Christoper A. Balesteros, "Hanapēpē Massacre," in *The SAGE Encyclopedia of Filipina/x/o American Studies*, ed. Kevin Leo Yabut Nadal, Allyson Tingtiangco-Cubales, and E. J. R. David (Sage, 2022), 447–48.

17. Ichioka, *The Issei*, 114–28.

18. Ichioka, *The Issei*, 251; Ted W. Cox, *The Toledo Incident of 1925: Three Days That Made History in Toledo, Oregon* (Old World Publications, 2005), 34–48, 90–125.

19. Scott Kurashige, *The Shifting Grounds of Race: Black and Japanese Americans in the Making of Multiethnic Los Angeles* (Princeton University Press, 2008), 52–53.

20. Kurashige, *Shifting Grounds*, 53–56.

21. Kim, *The Quest for Statehood*, 3–31.

22. Kim, *The Quest for Statehood*, 32–41; Gary Kamiya, "'I Decided to Kill Him and Kill Myself': When Imperialist Politics Lead to a Murder in SF," *San Francisco Examiner*, April 1, 2024, https://www.sfexaminer.com/our_sections/forum/assassination-of-durham-white-stevens-by-korean-activists/article_921a0a36-b2e9-11ed-8d8e-f30832844f9e.html.

23. Girindra Mukerji, "The Hindu in America," *Overland Monthly*, April 1908, 303–8, South Asian American Digital Archive [hereafter SAADA], https://www.saada.org/item/20111101-443.

24. Joan Jensen, *Passage from India: Asian Indian Immigrants in North America* (Yale University Press, 1988), 43–45; Johanna Ogden, *Punjabi Rebels of the Columbia River: The Global Fight for Indian Independence and Citizenship* (Oregon State University Press, 2024), 1–18; "Mob Drives Out Hindus," *New York Times*, September 6, 1907.

25. Jensen, *Passage from India*, 46–52; Werter D. Dodd, "The Hindu in the Northwest," *World Today* 13 (1907): 1157–60, SAADA, https://www.saada.org/item/20110714-238; "Mob Drives Out Hindus"; Seema Sohi, *Echoes of Mutiny: Race, Surveillance, and Indian Anticolonialism in North America* (Oxford University Press, 2014), 25–27.

26. Dodd, "The Hindu in the Northwest," 1159–60; Jensen, *Passage from India*, 49–53.

27. Jensen, *Passage from India*, 53–54; Vivek Bald, *Bengali Harlem and the Lost Histories of South Asian America* (Harvard University Press, 2013), 63–64, 137–59; Ogden, *Punjabi Rebels*, 32–34.

28. Ogden, *Punjabi Rebels*, 1–42, 59–72, 77.

29. Ogden, *Punjabi Rebels*, 84–135 (quote on p. 89 translated from Urdu).

30. Sohi, *Echoes of Mutiny*, 1–8, 54–67, 152–204; Ram Chandra, "Exclusion of Hindus from America Due to British Influence," 1916, 12, SAADA, https://www.saada.org/item/20100916-121.

31. Ogden, *Punjabi Rebels*, 143–86; Jensen, *Passage from India*, 246–69; "Biography of L. Vaishno Das Bagai," Vaishno Das and Kala Bagai Family Materials, SAADA, https://www.saada.org/item/20130305-1310; "Here's Letter to the World from Suicide," *San Francisco Examiner*, March 17, 1928, SAADA, https://www.saada.org/item/20130513-2748.

32. Kurashige, *Shifting Grounds*, 100–157.

33. Gerhard L. Weinberg, *A World at Arms: A Global History of World War II* (Cambridge University Press, 2005), 894.

34. John W. Dower, *War Without Mercy: Race and Power in the Pacific War* (Pantheon, 1986), 3–14, 36, 80–82; Gary J. Bass, *Judgment at Tokyo: World War II on Trial and the Making of Modern Asia* (Knopf, 2023), 23; "How to Tell Japs from the Chinese," *Life*, December 22, 1941, 81–82.

35. Dr. Seuss, "Waiting for the Signal from Home . . . ," *PM Magazine*, February 13, 1942, UC San Diego Library Digital Collections, https://library.ucsd.edu/dc/object/bb5222708w; David Middlecamp, "Photos from the Vault: He was told he couldn't avoid Japanese internment. He opted for suicide instead," *San Luis Obispo Tribune*, November 2, 2016, https://www.sanluisobispo.com/news/local/news-columns-blogs/photos-from-the-vault/article111249922.html.

36. *Personal Justice Denied: Report of the Commission on Wartime Relocation and Internment of Civilians* (U.S. Government Printing Office, 1982), 66.

37. *Personal Justice Denied*, 51–60, 73–74.

38. *Korematsu v. United States*, 323 U.S. 214 (1944).

39. *Korematsu v. United States*.

40. *Korematsu v. United States*.

41. Michi Weglyn, *Years of Infamy: The Untold Story of America's Concentration Camps* (William Morrow, 1976), 121–25; Kurashige, *Shifting Grounds*, 164–69, 191–93; Greg Robinson, *After Camp: Portraits in Midcentury Japanese American Life and Politics* (University of California Press, 2012), 57–58.

42. War Agency Liquidation Unit, *People in Motion: The Postwar Adjustment of the Evacuated Japanese Americans* (U.S. Government Printing Office, 1947), 18–19; Scott McGaugh, *Honor Before Glory: The Epic World War II Story of the Japanese American GIs Who Rescued the Lost Battalion* (Da Capo Press, 2016), 113–87, 208.

43. Dower, *War Without Mercy*, 33–93.

44. Dower, *War Without Mercy*, 64, 185.

45. Dower, *War Without Mercy*, 38–41; Tim Weiner, "Robert S. McNamara, Architect of a Futile War, Dies at 93," *New York Times*, July 6, 2009, https://www .nytimes.com/2009/07/07/us/07mcnamara.html; Alex Wellerstein, "The Kyoto Misconception: What Truman Knew, and Didn't Know, About Hiroshima," in *The Age of Hiroshima*, ed. Michael D. Gordin and G. John Ikenberry (Princeton University Press, 2020), 40.

46. Bass, *Judgment at Tokyo*, 23–29, 542–564; United Nations, "Convention on the Prevention and Punishment of the Crime of Genocide," https://www.un.org /en/genocide-prevention/1948-convention (accessed November 30, 2024).

47. Bass, *Judgment at Tokyo*, 29, 544–45.

48. James N. Yamazaki, *Children of the Atomic Bomb: An American Physician's Memoir of Nagasaki, Hiroshima, and the Marshall Islands* (Duke University Press, 1995), 60–73; Dower, *War Without Mercy*, 46–47.

49. Ronald Takaki, *Hiroshima: Why America Dropped the Atomic Bomb* (Little, Brown, 1995), 137.

50. Takaki, *Hiroshima*, 22–140; Bass, *Judgment at Tokyo*, 73–82.

51. Takaki, *Hiroshima*, 93–100, 144–51; Wellerstein, "The Kyoto Misconception," 34–55.

52. Takaki, *Hiroshima*, 69–120.

53. Takaki, *Hiroshima*, 47, 71, 149–50; Bass, *Judgment at Tokyo*, 73–80; Dower, *War Without Mercy*, 53–54; Yamazaki, *Children of the Atomic Bomb*, 133–41. See also Wellerstein, "The Kyoto Misconception," 45–48. Truman's earlier draft statement referred to Hiroshima as a "purely military" target. Truman may have wrongly allowed himself to believe that the bomb dropped on Hiroshima would avoid civilian populations, even though Manhattan Project personnel and military leaders knew otherwise.

54. Wellerstein, "The Kyoto Misconception," 49; Yamazaki, *Children of the Atomic Bomb*, 71–88, 141.

55. William Laurence, "Atomic Bombing of Nagasaki Told by Flight Member," *New York Times*, September 9, 1945, https://www.pulitzer.org/winners/william-leonard-laurence.

56. Yamazaki, *Children of the Atomic Bomb*, 65; "Protocol for the Prohibition of the Use in War of Asphyxiating, Poisonous or Other Gases, and of Bacteriological Methods of Warfare (Geneva Protocol)," June 17, 1925, U.S. Department of State, https://2009–2017.state.gov/t/isn/4784.htm; William Laurence, "U.S. Atom Bomb Site Belies Tokyo Tales," *New York Times*, September 12, 1945, https://www.pulitzer .org/winners/william-leonard-laurence.

57. Sean Malloy, "'A Very Pleasant Way to Die': Radiation Effects and the Decision to Use the Atomic Bomb Against Japan," *Diplomatic History* 36, no. 3 (2012): 515–45; Yamazaki, *Children of the Atomic Bomb*, 73–116, 141–43.

58. Charles H. Loeb, "Loeb Reflects on Atomic Bombed Area," *Atlanta Daily World*, October 5, 1945, 1; William J. Broad, "The Black Reporter Who Exposed a Lie About the Atom Bomb," *New York Times*, August 9, 2021, https://www.nytimes .com/2021/08/09/science/charles-loeb-atomic-bomb.html; Malloy, "A Very Pleasant Way to Die," 518.

4. HOW ASIAN WOMEN BECOME TARGETS OF VIOLENCE

1. Mark Berman et al., "The Atlanta Spa Shooting Suspect's Life Before Attacks," *Washington Post*, March 19, 2021, https://www.washingtonpost.com/national /atlanta-shooting-suspect-robert-aaron-long/2021/03/19/9397cdca-87fe-11eb-8a8b- 5cf82c3dffe4_story.html.

2. Berman et al., "Atlanta Spa Shooting."

3. Jonathan Krohn and Sarah Pulliam Bailey, "Atlanta Shooting Suspect Was a Patient at Evangelical Treatment Center Close to First Targeted Spa," *Washington Post*, March 19, 2021, https://www.washingtonpost.com/religion/2021/03/19/robert- aaron-long-evangelical-treatment-facility-sex-addiction/.

4. Tim Craig et al., "A Nationwide Horror: Witnesses, Police Paint a Picture of a Murderous Rampage That Took 8 Lives," *Washington Post*, March 18, 2021, https:// www.washingtonpost.com/national/what-happened-atlanta-shooting/2021/03/18 /163e4de8–8733–11eb-8a8b-5cf82c3dffe4_story.html; Lindsay Whitehurst, "Gun Waiting Periods Rare in US States but More May Be Coming," Associated Press, March 21, 2021, https://apnews.com/article/shootings-atlanta-ahmaud-arbery-violence- georgia-d444884e06c90b625b471b98e48bee24.

5. "Atlanta Spa Shootings: Timeline of Events," *11 Alive*, March 16, 2022, https:// www.11alive.com/article/news/crime/atlanta-spa-shootings-timeline-robert- aaron-long/85–76331761-ae49–40e4-bbb0–2f64d417c377.

6. *The Combahee River Collective Statement*, United States, 2015, Web Archive, https://www.loc.gov/item/lcwaN0028151/; Richard Fausset, "Suspect in Atlanta Spa Killings Pleads Not Guilty to 4 Counts of Murder," *New York Times*, October 18, 2021, https://www.nytimes.com/2021/09/28/us/atlanta-spa-killings-robert-long.html.

7. Jaweed Kaleem and Jenny Jarvie, "Asian American Christians Confront Racism and Evangelical 'Purity Culture' After Atlanta Spa Shootings," *Los Angeles*

Times, April 6, 2021, https://www.latimes.com/world-nation/story/2021–04–06/atlanta-shooting-evangelicals-asian-american.

8. Chauncey DeVega, "Racism, Misogyny, Guns and Religion: Experts Call Atlanta 'an Unmistakable American Stew,'" *Salon*, March 23, 2021, https://www.salon.com/2021/03/23/racism-misogyny-guns-and-religion-experts-call-atlanta-an-unmistakable-american-stew/; Bradley Onishi, *Preparing for War: The Extremist History of White Christian Nationalism—and What Comes Next* (Fortress Press, 2023), 112.

9. Onishi, *Preparing for War*, 10–21, 42, 97–115.

10. Kimberlé Crenshaw and the African American Policy Forum, "AAPF Mourns the Loss of Life in Georgia," March 19, 2021, https://www.aapf.org/post/aapf-statement-on-anti-asian-attacks.

11. Robert G. Lee, *Orientals: Asian Americans in Popular Culture* (Temple University Press, 1999), 85–88; Beth Lew-Williams, *The Chinese Must Go: Violence, Exclusion, and the Making of the Alien in America* (Harvard University Press, 2018), 121–33.

12. Lucie Cheng, "Free, Indentured, Enslaved: Chinese Prostitutes in Nineteenth-Century America," in *Labor Immigration Under Capitalism: Asian Workers in the United States Before World War II*, ed. Lucie Cheng and Edna Bonacich (University of California Press, 1984), 402–34.

13. Peggy Pascoe, *Relations of Rescue: The Search for Female Moral Authority in the American West, 1874–1939* (Oxford University Press, 1990), 14–17; Sucheng Chan, "The Exclusion of Chinese Women, 1870–1943," in *Entry Denied: Exclusion and the Chinese Community in America, 1882–1943*, ed. Sucheng Chan (Temple University Press, 1991), 94–146; Lucy E. Salyer, *Chinese Immigrants and the Shaping of Modern Immigration Law* (University of North Carolina Press, 1995), 11–12.

14. Tamsin Kimoto, "Violence Against Asian Women: The Enduring Legacy of 1875 Page Act," *Blog of the APA*, November 17, 2022, https://blog.apaonline.org/2022/11/17/violence-against-asian-women-the-enduring-legacy-of-1875-page-act/.

15. Cathy Park Hong, *Minor Feelings: An Asian American Reckoning* (One-World, 2020), 176.

16. Hong, *Minor Feelings*, 156.

17. Gwyn Kirk and Carolyn Bowen Francis, "Redefining Security: Women Challenge US. Military Policy and Practice in East Asia," *Berkeley Women's Law Journal* 15 (2000): 229–71; Akemi Johnson, *Night in the American Village: Women in the Shadow of the U.S. Military Bases in Okinawa* (New Press, 2019), 134–38.

18. Katherine H. S. Moon, *Sex Among Allies: Military Prostitution in U.S.-Korea Relations* (Columbia University Press, 1997), 1–22; Ji-Yeon Yuh, *Beyond the Shadow of Camptown: Korean Military Brides in America* (New York University Press, 2002), 9–41; Johnson, *Night in the American* Village, 146–47.

19. Moon, *Sex Among Allies*, 3–7, 21–23, 33–36; Kirk and Francis, "Redefining Security," 257–58; "US Soldier Guilty of Sex Killing," *BBC News*, June 16, 2000, http://news.bbc.co.uk/2/hi/asia-pacific/793426.stm.

20. Moon, *Sex Among Allies*, 3–7, 21–35; Yuh, *Beyond the Shadow of Camptown*, 2–3, 164–72; Marie Myung Ok Lee, "The U.S. Military's Long History of Anti-Asian Dehumanization," *Korean Quarterly*, Spring 2021, https://www.koreanquarterly .org/stop-asian-hate/embedded-stereotypes/.

21. Francis L. Hawks, *Narrative of the Expedition of an American Squadron to the China Seas and Japan Performed in the Years 1852, 1853, and 1854* (D. Appleton, 1856), 566–70.

22. Andrew Yeo, *Activists, Alliances, and Anti-U.S. Base Protests* (Cambridge University Press, 2011), 64–66; Johnson, *Night in the American Village*, 22–29, 112–30.

23. Richard A. Serrano, *Summoned at Midnight: A Story of Race and the Last Military Executions at Fort Leavenworth* (Beacon Press, 2019), 75–102; Yuki Takauchi, "Rape and the Sexual Politics of Homosociality: The U.S. Military Occupation of Okinawa," *Notches*, November 17, 2015, https://notchesblog .com/2015/11/17/rape-and-the-sexual-politics-of-homosociality-the-us-military-occupation-of-okinawa-1955–56/.

24. Yeo, *Activists, Alliances*, 65–67; Johnson, *Night in the American Village*, 110–37; Brandon Marc Higa, "Unpacking Okinawa's 'Suitcase Murder': Revisiting Extra-territoriality Protections for Military Contractors Under the U.S.-Japan SOFA Supplementary Agreement," *Asian-Pacific Law and Policy Journal* 21, no. 2 (2020): 1–50.

25. Johnson, *Night in the American Village*, 1–16, 261–80; Higa, "'Suitcase Murder,'" 40–45.

26. Johnson, *Night in the American Village*, 17–18, 34–46, 119–22, 155–74.

27. Wesley Iwao Ueunten, "Rising Up from a Sea of Discontent: The 1970 Koza Uprising in U.S.-Occupied Okinawa," in *Militarized Currents: Toward a Decolonized Future in Asia and the Pacific*, ed. Setsu Shigematsu and Keith L. Camacho (University of Minnesota Press, 2010), 94–115.

28. Alex Tizon, "Death of a Dreamer—Susana Remerata Blackwell 1969 to 1995," *Seattle Times*, April 21, 1996, https://archive.seattletimes.com/archive/?date = 19960421&slug = 2325181.

29. Tizon, "Death of a Dreamer"; API Chaya, "History," https://www.apichaya .org/history, and "Mission, Vision, Values," https://www.apichaya.org/mission (accessed October 14, 2024).

30. Chetanya Robinson, "API Chaya's 29th Annual Vigil Honors Victims, Empowers Survivors of Violence," *International Examiner*, April 4, 2024, https:// iexaminer.org/api-chayas-29th-annual-vigil-honors-victims-empowers-survivors-of-violence/.

31. Robinson, "API Chaya's Annual Vigil."

32. Chanel Miller, *Know My Name* (Viking, 2019), 335; Sam Levin, "Stanford Sexual Assault: Read the Full Text of the Judge's Controversial Decision," *Guardian*, June 14, 2016, https://www.theguardian.com/us-news/2016/jun/14/stanford -sexual-assault-read-sentence-judge-aaron-persky; Katie J.M. Baker, "Here's the Powerful Letter the Stanford Victim Read to Her Attacker," *BuzzFeed*, June 3, 2016, https://www.buzzfeednews.com/article/katiejmbaker/heres-the-powerful-letter-the-stanford-victim-read-to-her-ra.

33. Miller, *Know My Name*, 333–57; Levin, "Stanford Sexual Assault."

34. Miller, *Know My Name*, 217–21, 288.

35. Miller, *Know My Name*, 355.

36. Miller, *Know My Name*, 87–90; Nicky Woolf, "Chilling Report Details How Elliot Rodger Executed Murderous Rampage," *Guardian*, February 20, 2015, https://www.theguardian.com/us-news/2015/feb/20/mass-shooter-elliot-rodger-isla-vista-killings-report; Mattie Kahn, "Cathy Park Hong and Chanel Miller on Making Art Out of Grief: A Conversation," *Glamour*, March 24, 2021, https://www.glamour.com/story/cathy-park-hong-chanel-miller-in-conversation.

37. Kelly Yang, "Harvard Law School Came After Me for Speaking Up About My Sexual Assault," *Medium*, May 14, 2020, https://medium.com/@kellyyangauthor/harvard-law-school-came-after-me-for-speaking-up-about-my-sexual-assault-779a27fd0195; Meimei Xu, "The Justice of Writing: Kelly Yang's Story of Survival," *Crimson*, April 1, 2021, https://www.thecrimson.com/article/2021/4/1/kelly-yang-parachutes/.

38. Emily Bazelon, "Have We Learned Anything from the Columbia Rape Case?," *New York Times*, May 29, 2015, https://www.nytimes.com/2015/05/29/magazine/have-we-learned-anything-from-the-columbia-rape-case.html; Sylvie McNamara, "Did Emma Sulkowicz Get Redpilled?," *The Cut*, October 28, 2019, https://www.thecut.com/2019/10/did-emma-sulkowicz-mattress-performance-get-redpilled.html; Emma Sulkowicz; "My Rapist Is Still on Campus," *Time*, May 15, 2014, https://time.com/99780/campus-sexual-assault-emma-sulkowicz/.

39. Jessica Roy, "Accused Columbia Rapist Argues in Lawsuit That 'Rapist' Is a Gendered Slur," *The Cut*, April 25, 2016, https://www.thecut.com/2016/04/accused-columbia-rapist-nungesser-refiles-suit.html; Bazelon, "Have We Learned Anything from the Columbia Rape Case?"

40. McNamara, "Did Emma Sulkowicz Get Redpilled?"

41. Sulkowicz, "My Rapist Is Still on Campus."

42. "Red Canary Song Response to Shootings at Gold Massage Spa, Young's Asian Massage, & Aroma Therapy Spa," https://docs.google.com/document/d/1_QomFJnivTZL5fcCS7eUZn9EhOJ1XHtFBGOGqVaUY_8/edit?tab=t.o (accessed March 12, 2025).

43. "Red Canary Song Response to Shootings"; Elena Shih, "How to Protect Massage Workers," *New York Times*, March 26, 2021, https://www.nytimes.com/2021/03/26/opinion/politics/atlanta-shooting-massage-workers-protection.html.

44. Emma Whitford and Melissa Gira Grant, "Family, Former Attorney of Queens Woman Who Fell to Her Death in Vice Sting Say She Was Sexually Assaulted, Pressured to Become an Informant," *The Appeal*, December 15, 2017, https://theappeal.org/family-former-attorney-of-queens-woman-who-fell-to-her-death-in-vice-sting-say-she-was-sexually-d67461a12f1/.

45. Red Canary Song et al., "Un-licensed: Asian Migrant Massage Licensure and the Racialized Policing of Poverty," February 2022, https://static1.squarespace.com/static/5e4835857fcd934d19bd9673/t/6218d9316e93a74b051c9f00/1645795656006/2022_Un-Licensed.pdf.

46. Angelina Chapin, "Every Day, Massage-Parlor Workers Face Violence," *The Cut*, March 19, 2021, https://www.thecut.com/2021/03/every-day-massage-parlor-workers-face-violence.html; Elene Lam, "Survey on Toronto Holistic Practitioners' Experiences with Bylaw Enforcement and Police," May 2018, doi: 10.13140/RG.2.2.27787.72484.

47. "Red Canary Song Response to Shootings."

5. THE VIOLENCE BEYOND VIETNAM

1. Martin Luther King Jr., *Why We Can't Wait* (Signet Books, 1964), 38–112; Frank Sikora, *Until Justice Rolls Down: The Birmingham Church Bombing Case* (University of Alabama Press, 2005), 3–25; Doug Jones, *Bending Toward Justice: The Birmingham Church Bombing That Changed the Course of Civil Rights* (St. Martin's Press, 2019), 19–24.

2. "Read Martin Luther King Jr.'s 'I Have a Dream' Speech in Its Entirety," NPR, January 16, 2023, https://www.npr.org/2010/01/18/122701268/i-have-a-dream-speech-in-its-entirety.

3. Martin Luther King Jr., "Eulogy for the Martyred Children," in *A Testament of Hope: The Essential Writings and Speeches of Martin Luther King, Jr.*, ed. James M. Washington (HarperCollins, 1991), 221 (emphasis in original).

4. Martin Luther King Jr., "Beyond Vietnam," April 4, 1967, YouTube, https://www.youtube.com/watch?v=AJhgXKGldUk (accessed September 29, 2024).

5. King, *Why We Can't Wait*, 15–26, 87, 152; David Garrow, *Bearing the Cross: Martin Luther King, Jr., and the Southern Christian Leadership Conference* (William Morrow, 1986), 571–601 and elsewhere.

6. King, *Where Do We Go from Here*, 186; King, "Beyond Vietnam."

7. James H. Cone, *Martin & Malcolm & America: A Dream or a Nightmare* (Orbis Books, 1991), 240; King, "Beyond Vietnam"; Vincent Bevins, *The Jakarta Method: Washington's Anticommunist Crusade and the Mass Murder Program That Shaped Our World* (PublicAffairs, 2021), 2–3, 41–59, 126–58.

8. Marilyn Young, *The Vietnam Wars 1945–1990* (HarperCollins, 1991), 10–11, 116–23, 331–37 and elsewhere.

9. Nick Turse, *Kill Anything That Moves: The Real American War in Vietnam* (Picador, 2013), 6.

10. Turse, *Kill Anything That Moves*, 6–13; "Vietnam Veterans Memorial," U.S. National Park Service, https://www.nps.gov/places/000/vietnam-veterans-memorial.htm (accessed May 11, 2025).

11. Derrick Z. Jackson, "The Westmoreland Mind-set," *New York Times*, July 22, 2005, https://www.nytimes.com/2005/07/22/opinion/derrick-z-jackson-the-westmoreland-mindset.html.

12. Jackson, "The Westmoreland Mind-set."

13. See Roxane Dunbar-Ortiz, *An Indigenous Peoples' History of the United States* (Beacon Press, 2014); Stephen J. Rockel and Rick Halpern, eds., *Inventing Collateral Damage: Civilian Casualties, War, and Empire* (Between the Lines, 2009).

14. Turse, *Kill Anything That Moves*, 28–50.

15. Bob Dreyfuss, "John McCain's Vietnam," *The Nation*, December 15, 1999, https://www.thenation.com/article/archive/mccains-vietnam/; C. W. Nevius, Marc Sandalow, and John Wildermuth, "McCain Criticized for Slur," *San Francisco Chronicle*, August 26, 2018, https://www.sfgate.com/politics/article/McCain-Criticized-for-Slur-He-says-he-ll-keep-3304741.php; "Bush and McCain Scurry Toward Showdown," *New York Times*, February 18, 2000. The *Times* did a follow-up two weeks later that included comments on its own limited reporting; see Anthony Ramirez, "McCain's Ethnic Slur: Gone, but Not Quite Forgotten," *New York Times*, March 5, 2000, https://www.nytimes.com/2000/03/05/weekinreview/word-for-word-asian-americans-mccain-s-ethnic-slur-gone-but-not-quite-forgotten.html.

16. Turse, *Kill Anything That Moves*, 41–50.

17. Turse, *Kill Anything That Moves*, 45–71, 192–97.

18. Turse, *Kill Anything That Moves*, 78–96; Young, *The Vietnam Wars*, 130.

19. Turse, *Kill Anything That Moves*, 212.

20. Turse, *Kill Anything That Moves*, 158–91; Young, *The Vietnam Wars*, 213.

21. Turse, *Kill Anything That Moves*, 158–91, 237–39.

22. Turse, *Kill Anything That Moves*, 214–58; James S. Olson and Randy Roberts, *My Lai: A Brief History with Documents* (Bedford/St. Martin's, 1998), 20–23.

23. Turse, *Kill Anything That Moves*, 121–22, 193–94, 261.

24. Norman N. Nakamura, "The Nature of G.I. Racism," *Gidra*, June–July 1970, 5, 17; "Quotes from the Asian War," *Gidra*, June–July 1970, 9.

25. Toshio Welchel, *From Pearl Harbor to Saigon: Japanese American Soldiers and the Vietnam War* (Verso, 1999), 16–19 and elsewhere. Names are pseudonyms given by the author.

26. Welchel, *From Pearl Harbor to Saigon*, 67, 83, 104, 107, 165–70.

27. Scott Kurashige, "Growing Up Japanese American in Crenshaw and Leimert Park," *PBS SoCal*, January 30, 2014, https://www.pbssocal.org/shows/departures/growing-up-japanese-american-in-crenshaw-and-leimert-park; Michael Liu, Kim Geron, and Tracy Lai, *The Snake Dance of Asian American Activism: Community, Vision, and Power* (Lexington Books, 2008), 66–67.

28. Gary J. Bass, *The Blood Telegram: Nixon, Kissinger, and a Forgotten Genocide* (Knopf, 2013), xii–xiv, 67–75.

29. Bass, *The Blood Telegram*, 342.

30. Bass, *The Blood Telegram*, 77–87.

31. Bass, *The Blood Telegram*, xvi, 340–42.

32. Seth Jacobs, *The Universe Unraveling: American Foreign Policy in Cold War Laos* (Cornell University Press, 2012), 3–20, 218, 271–74; Keith Quincy, *Hmong: History of a People*, 2nd edition (Eastern Washington University Press, 1995), 171–224; Sucheng Chan, *Hmong Means Free: Life in Laos and America* (Temple University Press, 1994), 1–60.

33. Ben Kiernan, *The Pol Pot Regime: Race, Power, and Genocide Under the Khmer Rouge, 1975–79*, 2nd edition (Yale University Press, 2002), 16–24; Kenton Clymer, *The United States and Cambodia, 1969–2000: A Troubled Relationship* (Taylor and Francis, 2013), 2–34.

34. Clymer, *The United States and Cambodia*, 113–39; Kiernan, *The Pol Pot Regime*, 458; David Chandler, *A History of Cambodia*, 3rd edition (Westview Press, 2000), 4–5, 200–18; Department of State Memorandum of Conversation, Subject: Secretary's Meeting with Foreign Minister Chatchai of Thailand, November 26, 1975, https://nsarchive2.gwu.edu/NSAEBB/NSAEBB193/HAK-11-26-75.pdf, linked from MacMillan Center for International and Area Studies at Yale, "U.S. Involvement in the Cambodian War and Genocide," https://leitner.yale.edu/gsp /us-involvement-cambodian-war-and-genocide-0 (accessed September 28, 2024).

35. My account of the Cleveland Elementary School shooting draws on composite sources: Nelson Kempsky, "A Report to Attorney General John K. Van de Kamp on Patrick Edward Purdy and the Cleveland School Killings," California Department of Justice, October 1989, https://schoolshooters.info/sites/default/files /Purdy%20-%20official%20report.pdf; "Troubled Drifter Left Trail of Crime," *Sacramento Bee*, January 18, 1989; "Day of Anguish, Few Answers: 'Military Hang-Up' Gripped Angry Killer," *Sacramento Bee*, January 19, 1989; "A Short Life Full of Hate," *Sacramento Bee*, January 19, 1989; Robert Reinhold, "After Shooting, Horror but Few Answers," *New York Times*, January 19, 1989; Robert Reinhold, "Killer Depicted as Loner Full of Hate," *New York Times*, January 20, 1989.

36. "TV News Crews Find the Facts, Not the Answers," *Sacramento Bee*, January 18, 1989.

37. "Day of Anguish, Few Answers"; Reinhold, "Killer Depicted as Loner Full of Hate"; Kempsky, "A Report to Attorney General John K. Van de Kamp," 11.

38. Kempsky, "A Report to Attorney General John K. Van de Kamp," 10–12; "Day of Anguish, Few Answers."

39. Kempsky, "A Report to Attorney General John K. Van de Kamp," 17.

40. Reinhold, "After Shooting, Horror but Few Answers."

41. Reinhold, "After Shooting, Horror but Few Answers"; Peter Applebome, "Robert Reinhold, Ex-reporter for the Times, Is Dead at 54," *New York Times*, August 30, 1996, https://www.nytimes.com/1996/08/30/us/robert-reinhold-ex-reporter-for-the-times-is-dead-at-54.html.

42. "Day of Anguish"; "From One Horror to Another Asian Refugees Feel New Fear in Stockton," *Sacramento Bee*, January 19, 1989.

43. "Day of Anguish"; "A Short Life Full of Hate."

44. "Troubled Drifter Left Trail of Crime."

45. Reinhold, "Killer Depicted as Loner Full of Hate."

46. "From One Horror to Another Asian Refugees Feel New Fear in Stockton."

47. Kempsky, "A Report to Attorney General John K. Van de Kamp," 2.

48. Kempsky, "A Report to Attorney General John K. Van de Kamp," 10–11.

49. Kempsky, "A Report to Attorney General John K. Van de Kamp," 5–12.

50. Kempsky, "A Report to Attorney General John K. Van de Kamp," 6.

51. Kempsky, "A Report to Attorney General John K. Van de Kamp," 3–5.

52. Kempsky, "A Report to Attorney General John K. Van de Kamp," 11–17.

53. Kempsky, "A Report to Attorney General John K. Van de Kamp," 26–27.

6. MARTYR IN THE MOTOR CITY

1. Paul Weingarten, "Deadly Encounter: Did Vincent Chin's Assailants Get Away with Murder?," *Chicago Tribune*, July 31, 1983, in "Vincent Chin," Part 1, *FBI Records: The Vault* (hereafter VCFBI), 167–74, https://vault.fbi.gov/vincent-chin/vincent-chin-part-01/view.

2. Don Ball, "Defendant Fuzzy on How Chin Was Slain," *Detroit News*, June 20, 1984, VCFBI, 307–8.

3. Paula Yoo, *From a Whisper to a Rallying Cry: The Killing of Vincent Chin and the Trial That Galvanized the Asian American Movement* (Norton Young Readers, 2021), 204.

4. Transcript of FBI interview with name redacted, DE 44A-2408, September 30, 1983, VCFBI, 161.

5. Robert Lindsey, "Resentment of Japanese Is Growing, Poll Shows," *New York Times*, April 6, 1982; Steven V. Roberts, "In Ohio, the Enemy Is Japan," *New York Times*, April 25, 1982; Robert G. Lee, *Orientals: Asian Americans in Popular Culture* (Temple University Press, 1999), 180–203.

6. John W. Dower, *War Without Mercy: Race and Power in the Pacific War* (Pantheon, 1986), 311–17; Dana Frank, *Buy American: The Untold Story of Economic Nationalism* (Beacon Press, 1999), 160–86.

7. Helen Zia, *The Vincent Chin Legacy Guide: Asian Americans and Civil Rights*, 2nd edition (Vincent Chin Institute, 2022), 6–7.

8. Colin Covert, "Japanese-Americans in Detroit," *Detroit Free Press*, July 10, 1983.

9. Lindsey, "Resentment of Japanese Is Growing"; Francis X. Clines and Warren Weaver Jr., "Briefing," *New York Times*, March 16, 1982.

10. John H. Crider, "Roosevelt Back in Capital, Sees Hull on Far East," *New York Times*, August 18, 1941.

11. Tim Bryant, "Laotian Dies from Beating," United Press International, March 9, 1984, https://www.upi.com/Archives/1984/03/09/Laotian-dies-from-beating/4990447656400/.

12. Weingarten, "Deadly Encounter," 174.

13. Zia, *The Vincent Chin Legacy Guide*, 17.

14. Zia, *The Vincent Chin Legacy Guide*, 30.

15. See Thomas J. Sugrue, *The Origins of the Urban Crisis: Race and Inequality in Postwar Detroit* (Princeton University Press, 1996); Grace Lee Boggs with Scott Kurashige, *The Next American Revolution: Sustainable Activism for the Twenty-First Century* (University of California Press, 2011).

16. FBI interview with name redacted [Jimmy Perry], DE 44A-2408, May 20, 1983, VCFBI, 122–23. In the film *Who Killed Vincent Chin?*, Perry says he was asked to help catch "Chinese guys."

17. Sugrue, *The Origins of the Urban Crisis*, 17–32, 209–358.

18. Scott Kurashige, *The Fifty-Year Rebellion: How the U.S. Political Crisis Began in Detroit* (University of California Press, 2017), 14–29.

19. Kurashige, *The Fifty-Year Rebellion*, 30–50.

20. Covert, "Japanese-Americans in Detroit."

21. Scott Kurashige, ed., "Editor's Introduction," in *Exiled to Motown: A Community History of Japanese Americans in Detroit* (University of Washington Press, 2024), 8–14; Kurashige, *The Fifty-Year Rebellion*, 100–101.

22. Joe T. Darden et al., *Detroit: Race and Uneven Development* (Temple University Press, 1987), 109–50.

23. Scott Kurashige, "Rereading Vincent Chin: Asian Americans and Multiracial Political Analysis," in *Minority Relations: Intergroup Conflict and Cooperation*, ed. Robert Chang and Greg Robinson (University of Mississippi Press, 2017), 134.

24. Kurashige, "Rereading Vincent Chen," 134–35.

25. FBI interview with name redacted, DE 44A-2408, May 20, 1983, VCFBI, 113–14; Kurashige, *The Fifty-Year Rebellion*, 40.

26. Kurashige, "Rereading Vincent Chin," 132–33.

27. Weingarten, "Deadly Encounter," 170–71; Yoo, *From a Whisper to a Rallying Cry*, 184.

28. Tim Kiska, "A Brawl, a Death—and Racism? It's Up to Jury," *Detroit Free Press*, June 26, 1984; Brian Bragg, "Brewers Nail Tigers, 10-3," *Detroit Free Press*, June 20, 1982.

29. Yoo, *From a Whisper to a Rallying Cry*, 29–31.

30. Weingarten, "Deadly Encounter," 168, 172; Yoo, *From a Whisper to a Rallying Cry*, 106–7.

31. Cynthia Lee, "Flak Stuns Judge in Chin Case," *Detroit News*, May 11, 1983, VCFBI, 37–38.

32. Weingarten, "Deadly Encounter," 174.

33. Weingarten, "Deadly Encounter," 174.

34. Cynthia Lee, "Beating Death Stirs Rally," *Detroit News*, May 10, 1983, VCFBI, 35; Zia, *The Vincent Chin Legacy Guide*, 20–22; John Castine, "Judge Agrees to Re-examine His Sentence," *Detroit Free Press*, April 30, 1983, VCFBI, 29.

35. U.S. Commission on Civil Rights, *In the Name of Hate: Examining the Federal Government's Role in Responding to Hate Crimes* (2019), 12; John Castine, "'Dual Prosecution' of Chin's Killers a Rarity," *Detroit Free Press*, November 29, 1983.

36. Cynthia Lee, "Detroit Asians Laud Chin Case Indictments," *Detroit News*, November 4, 1983, VCFBI, 194; Emil Guillermo, "Lessons from Vincent Chin

Murder 35 Years After," June 18, 2017, https://www.aaldef.org/blog/emil-guillermo-lessons-from-vincent-chin-murder-35-years-ago-podcast-helen-zia/; Zia, *The Vincent Chin Legacy Guide*, 27–28.

37. *United States v. Ebens*, 800 F.2d 1422 (1986).

38. "Resolution of Human Rights Commission, City of Detroit," May 18, 1983, VCFBI, 85–86; *United States v. Ebens*, 654 F. Supp. 144 (1987).

39. Yoo, *From a Whisper to a Rallying Cry*, 138; *United States of America v.* redacted [Ebens and Nitz], VCFBI, 184.

40. *United States v. Ebens* (1986); Don Ball, "Prosecutor: Chin Slaying a 'Lynching,'" *Detroit News*, June 27, 1984, VCFBI, 316.

41. Ball, "Defendant Fuzzy on How Chin Was Slain."

42. Transcript of FBI interview with name redacted, DE 44A-2408, June 11, 1984, VCFBI, 277–78; Kurashige, "Rereading Vincent Chin," 151–52.

43. *United States v. Ebens* (1986); Zia, *The Vincent Chin Legacy Guide*, 27.

44. Don Ball, "Chin Jury Could Be Seated by Wednesday," *Detroit News*, June 10, 1984, VCFBI, 284–85.

45. Stanley B. Greenberg, *Middle Class Dreams: The Politics and Power of the New American Majority* (Yale University Press, 1996), 39.

46. Transcript of FBI interview with name redacted, DE 44A-2408, August 18, 1983, VCFBI, 175–76.

47. U.S. Census Bureau, *1990 Census of Population: General Population Characteristics, Metropolitan Areas*, Section 1, 115, 137.

48. Michael Moore, "The Wages of Death," *Detroit Free Press*, August 30, 1987.

49. Jacquelynn Boyle, "Tapes Were Difference in Chin Case," *Detroit Free Press*, May 3, 1987, VCFBI, 381; Yoo, *From a Whisper to a Rallying Cry*, 242.

50. Roberts, "In Ohio, the Enemy Is Japan."

51. Kurashige, *The Fifty-Year Rebellion*, 23.

52. Ball, "Prosecutor: Chin Slaying a 'Lynching.'"

53. Moore, "Wages of Death."

54. Susan Faludi, *Stiffed: The Betrayal of the American Man* (William Morrow, 1999), 3–47. Faludi's book has received overall mixed reviews from academics regarding the so-called crisis of masculinity but presents this argument well.

55. Faludi, *Stiffed*, 35–40; Jay Shambaugh et al., "Thirteen Facts About Wage Growth," The Hamilton Project, September 24, 2017, https://www.hamiltonproject.org/publication/economic-fact/thirteen-facts-about-wage-growth/.

56. See Judith Butler, *Gender Trouble: Feminism and the Subversion of Identity* (Routledge, 1990).

57. Chin was five foot ten and 149 pounds. See FBI report from May 10, 1981, VCFBI, 81.

58. Moore, "Wages of Death."

59. FBI Las Vegas to Detroit office, May 29, 1984, VCFBI, 260–61; Transcript of FBI interview with name redacted, DE 44A-2408, June 16, 1984, VCFBI, 312–13; Weingarten, "Deadly Encounter," 174.

1. Michael Moore, "The Wages of Death," *Detroit Free Press*, August 30, 1987.

2. Michael Moore, "My Afternoon with the Killer of Vincent Chin + #Stop AsianHate with Annie Tan," *Rumble with Michael Moore Podcast*, March 23, 2021.

3. Moore, "Wages of Death."

4. See, e.g., Matthew D. Lassiter, *The Silent Majority: Suburban Politics in the Sunbelt South* (Princeton University Press, 2006).

5. "Philosopher Grace Lee Boggs and Sociologist, Monthly Review Editor John Bellamy Foster on the Financial Meltdown, Social Change and Redefining Democracy," *DemocracyNow!*, September 17, 2009, https://www.democracynow .org/2009/9/17/philosopher_grace_lee_boggs_and_sociologist.

6. Grace Lee Boggs, "In Detroit, We Have Just Begun to Fight," *Common Dreams*, August 18, 2013, https://www.commondreams.org/views/2013/08/18 /detroit-we-have-just-begun-fight.

7. Jay Shambaugh et al., "Thirteen Facts About Wage Growth," The Hamilton Project, September 24, 2017, https://www.hamiltonproject.org/publication/eco nomic-fact/thirteen-facts-about-wage-growth/; Lawrence Mishel et al., "Wage Stagnation in Nine Charts," Economic Policy Institute, January 6, 2015, https:// www.epi.org/publication/charting-wage-stagnation/; Drew Desilver, "For Most U.S. Workers, Real Wages Have Barely Budged in Decades," Pew Research Center, August 7, 2018, https://www.pewresearch.org/short-reads/2018/08/07/for-most-us -workers-real-wages-have-barely-budged-for-decades/.

8. Joe T. Darden et al., *Detroit: Race and Uneven Development* (Temple University Press, 1987), 31; David Riddle, "HUD and the Open Housing Controversy of 1970 in Warren, Michigan," *Michigan Historical Review* (Fall 1998): 1–36. These matters are discussed in greater detail in my book *The Fifty-Year Rebellion*.

9. Darden et al., *Detroit*, 31; Stanley B. Greenberg, *Middle Class Dreams: The Politics and Power of the New American Majority* (Yale University Press, 1996), 39.

10. Ze'ev Chafets, *Devil's Night and Other True Tales of Detroit* (Random House, 1990), 136–37.

11. Moore, "Wages of Death"; Eduardo Bonilla-Silva, *Racism Without Racists: Color-Blind Racism and the Persistence of Racial Inequality in the United States*, 5th edition (Rowman and Littlefield, 2018).

12. Jack Lessenberry, "Storm Center," *Detroit News*, March 17, 1985, clipping from Paula Yoo via Neda Salem and staff (Ethnic Studies Library at the University of California, Berkeley); *Lau v. Nichols*, 414 U.S. 563 (1974); Sucheng Chan, *Asian Americans: An Interpretive History* (Twayne, 1991), 173–74.

13. Helen Zia, *The Vincent Chin Legacy Guide: Asian Americans and Civil Rights*, 2nd edition (Vincent Chin Institute, 2022), 2; Helen Zia, *Asian American Dreams: The Emergence of an American People* (Farrar, Straus and Giroux, 2000), 68; R. W. Apple Jr., "Jackson Triumph Changes Outlook of Top Democrats," *New York Times*, March 28, 1988. Part of a family of migrants from Georgia, Sheffield had begun working at Ford in 1934. He epitomized a form of civil rights unionism,

becoming a leading figure within the left-leaning UAW Local 600 and helping found the Trade Union Leadership Council. See "Horace Sheffield Jr. Papers Now Open," Walter P. Reuther Library, Wayne State University, https://reuther.wayne .edu/node/15318m (accessed December 4, 2024).

14. "Vietnamese Student Killed in Racially-Sparked Fight," *Pacific Citizen*, May 20, 1983; Stephanie Lin, "Anti-Asian Violence: Revisiting the 1983 Murder of Davis High Student Thong Hy Huynh," KCRA, May 20, 2021, https://www.kcra.com /article/1983-murder-thong-hy-huynh-davis-high/36483722.

15. David Freed and Jerry Belcher, "Mass Killer's Angry Odyssey," *Los Angeles Times*, July 19, 1984; Michael Granberry, "A 77-Minute Moment in History That Will Never Be Forgotten," *Los Angeles Times*, July 16, 1989.

16. Kathleen Belew, *Bring the War Home: The White Power Movement and Paramilitary America* (Harvard University Press, 2018), 1–54.

17. Belew, *Bring the War Home*, 35–54; Kirk Wallace Johnson, *The Fisherman and the Dragon: Fear, Greed, and a Fight for Justice on the Gulf Coast* (Viking, 2022), 9–38; see also the film *Seadrift*, directed by Tim Tsai (2019).

18. Johnson, *The Fisherman and the Dragon*, 32–65.

19. Johnson, *The Fisherman and the Dragon*, 71–135, 218–19; Belew, *Bring the War Home*, 40–54.

20. United States Commission on Civil Rights, *Civil Rights Issues Facing Asian Americans in the 1990s* (1992), 26–28; Seth Effron, "Man Guilty in Asian-American's Death," *Greensboro News and Record*, March 19, 1990, https://greensboro.com/man-guilty-in-asian-americans-death/article_bbcba793-faaf-543e-80d3–5b21d45a940f .html.

21. Greg Hernandez, "O.C. Supremacist Gets Death Penalty for Racial Murder," *Los Angeles Times*, December 13, 1997, https://www.latimes.com/archives/la-xpm -1997-dec-13-mn-63735-story.html.

22. Attorney General's Asian and Pacific Islander Advisory Committee [California], "Final Report," December 1988, 30–31, http://doi.org/10.25549/fal-c107 –1698.

23. Chan, *Asian Americans*, 152–65; U.S. Census Bureau, "We the Americans: Asians," September 1993, https://www2.census.gov/library/publications /decennial/1990/we-the-americans/we-03.pdf.

24. Ellen Somekawa, "On the Edge: Southeast Asians in Philadelphia and the Struggle for Space," in *Reviewing Asian America: Locating Diversity*, ed. Wendy L. Ng et al. (Washington State University Press, 1995), 33–47.

25. "Guilty Verdict in Slaying Linked to Racial Hatred," *New York Times*, September 16, 1994 (quote translated from Khmer in original).

26. "Guilty Verdict in Slaying Linked to Racial Hatred."

27. Vijay Prashad, *The Karma of Brown Folk* (University of Minnesota Press, 2000), 75.

28. Tunku Varadarajan, "J. D. Vance and the Indian-American Dream," *Wall Street Journal*, July 16, 2024, https://www.wsj.com/articles/j-d-vance-and-the-zindian -american-dream-2024-election-usha-81ddeddo.

29. William Petersen, "Success Story, Japanese-American Style," *New York Times*, January 9, 1966.

30. Petersen, "Success Story, Japanese-American Style"; Varadarajan, "J. D. Vance and the Indian-American Dream."

31. Varadarajan, "J. D. Vance and the Indian-American Dream."

32. Varadarajan, "J. D. Vance and the Indian-American Dream."

33. Deepa Iyer, *We Too Sing America: South Asian, Arab, Muslim, and Sikh Immigrants Shape Our Multiracial Future* (New Press, 2016), 1–33; Michael J. Mooney, "Could You Forgive the Man Who Shot You in The Face?," *D Magazine*, September 21, 2011, https://www.dmagazine.com/publications/d-magazine/2011/october/how-rais-bhuiyan-forgave-the-man-who-shot-him-in-the-face/; Tony Rizzo, "'Get Out of My Country,' He Said Before Shooting," *Kansas City Star*, May 22, 2018, https://www.kansascity.com/news/local/crime/article211576754.html; John Eligon, Alan Blinder, and Nida Najar, "Hate Crime Is Feared as 2 Indian Engineers Are Shot in Kansas," *New York Times*, February 24, 2017, https://www.nytimes.com/2017/02/24/world/asia/kansas-attack-possible-hate-crime-srinivas-kuchibhotla.html.

34. Amrith Kaur Aakre to Randal Taylor and Paul Keenan, personal correspondence, April 20, 2021, https://www.sikhcoalition.org/wp-content/uploads/2021/04/2021–04–20-FedEx-Facility-Shooting-law-enforcement-final.pdf; Sakshi Venkatraman, "FBI Says FedEx Shooting Not a Hate Crime; Indianapolis Sikhs Still Want Answers," *NBC News*, July 29, 2021, https://www.nbcnews.com/news/asian-america/fbi-says-fedex-shooting-not-hate-crime-indianapolis-sikhs-still-n1275430.

35. "Civilians Killed and Wounded," Watson Institute for International and Public Affairs, Brown University, https://watson.brown.edu/costsofwar/costs/human/civilians (accessed April 12, 2025); *Left in the Dark: Failures of Accountability for Civilian Casualties Caused by International Military Operations In Afghanistan* (Amnesty International, 2014), 7–11, https://www.amnesty.org/en/documents/asa11/006/2014/en/; Patrice Taddonio, "U.S. 'Virtually Never Held Anyone Accountable' for Civilian Deaths in Afghanistan War, Former White House Official Says," *PBS Frontline*, April 11, 2023, https://www.pbs.org/wgbh/frontline/article/afghanistan-civilian-deaths-war-us-night-raids-military-operations/.

36. Mahmood Mamdani, *Good Muslim, Bad Muslim: America, The Cold War, and the Roots of Terror* (Doubleday, 2005), 15.

37. "Coast Police Chief Accused of Racism," *New York Times*, May 13, 1982.

38. See Brenda Stevenson, *The Contested Murder of Latasha Harlins: Justice, Gender, and the Origins of the LA Riots* (Oxford University Press, 2013).

39. Shawn Steel, "The Second Looting of Koreatown," *Korea Times English Edition*, http://www.steelzone.org/newspaper_archives/19920000_TheSecondLooting OfKoreatown.pdf (accessed December 8, 2024).

40. "Deaths During the L.A. Riots," *Los Angeles Times*, April 25, 2012, https://spreadsheets.latimes.com/la-riots-deaths/; "'Let It Fall': Jung Hui Lee," *ABC News*, April 28, 2017, https://abcnews.go.com/Entertainment/fall-jung-hui-lee-son-killed-la-uprising/story?id = 46715436.

41. Claire Wang, "The Landmark Sweatshop Case That Shaped Biden's Labor Secretary Pick," *Guardian*, April 25, 2023, https://www.theguardian.com/us -news/2023/apr/25/julie-su-biden-labor-secretary-pick.

42. The account of this incident presented here is based on *Hattori v. Peairs*, 662 So. 2d 509 (1995); and on Andrew C. McKevitt, *Gun Country: Gun Capitalism, Culture, and Control in Cold War America* (University of North Carolina Press, 2023), 1–7, 206–20.

43. McKevitt, *Gun Country*, 3–7; Toby Luckhurst, "Yoshihiro Hattori: The Door Knock That Killed a Japanese Teenager in US," *BBC News*, October 19, 2019, https://www.bbc.com/news/world-us-canada-50063364.

44. McKevitt, *Gun Country*, 3–13, 210–12. Although gun ownership has historically been low among Asian Americans, some data indicate a significant increase during the pandemic. One academic study particularly found that Asian Americans who experienced discrimination were more likely to buy a gun for protection. See Tsu-Yin Wu et al., "Examining Racism and Firearm-Related Risks Among Asian Americans in the United States During the COVID-19 Pandemic," *Preventive Medicine Reports* 27 (2022), https://doi.org/10.1016/j.pmedr.2022.101800.

45. "U.S. Civil Rights Inquiry Is Sought in Louisiana Slaying," *New York Times*, May 28, 1993; *Hattori v. Peairs*; Luckhurst, "Yoshihiro Hattori."

46. McKevitt, *Gun Country*, 9–13, 205–29.

47. Jonathan Vankin, "California Gun Control Laws: Mass Shootings Have Sparked New Legislation for Three Decades," *California Local*, October 26, 2023, https://californialocal.com/localnews/statewide/ca/article/show/4411-california -gun-control-laws-mass-shootings/; Luckhurst, "Yoshihiro Hattori."

48. McKevitt, *Gun Country*, 228–29.

8. NAMING AND CONFRONTING HATE CRIMES

1. Isha Banerjee, "The Dotbusters Were Not 'a Joke,'" *Juggernaut*, May 23, 2024, https://www.thejuggernaut.com/dotbusters-attacks-anti-indian-hate-crimes-history.

2. Mitch Mitchell, "North Texas Leaders Denounce Hateful Letter Threatening to Shoot Immigrant IT Workers," *Fort Worth Star-Telegram*, September 1, 2020, https://www.star-telegram.com/news/local/crime/article245409905.html.

3. Sneha Dey, "Allen Mall Shooting Alarms Asian Texans as Authorities Search for Gunman's Motive," *Texas Tribune*, May 9, 2023, https://www.texastribune .org/2023/05/09/allen-mall-shooter-neo-nazi-investigation/.

4. Ricardo Kaulessar, "How Indians in Jersey City Fought Back Against the Terror of the 'Dotbusters' in the 1980s," *NorthJersey.com*, January 26, 2022, https:// www.northjersey.com/story/news/new-jersey/2022/01/26/indians-jersey-city-nj-attacks- 1980-s/6397092001/.

5. *The CAAAV Voice*, Fall 1988; Banerjee, "The Dotbusters Were Not 'a Joke'"; United States Census Bureau, *1990 Census of Population, General Population Characteristics, New Jersey*, Section 1, 21–25.

6. Kaulessar, "How Indians in Jersey City Fought Back."

7. Ricardo Kaulessar, "'DotBusters' Victim Looks Back," *Hudson Reporter*, May 3, 2009, archived at https://web.archive.org/web/20160115052814/http://hudsonreporter.com/printer_friendly/2488227; Rekha Borsellino, "Tougher Law Asked in Attacks on Indians," *New York Times*, July 10, 1988, https://www.nytimes.com/1988/07/10/nyregion/tougher-law-asked-in-attacks-on-indians.html.

8. *U.S. v. Evangelista*, 813 F. Supp. 294 (D.N.J. 1993); Robert Hanley, "3 Indicted in Beating of Indian Doctor," *New York Times*, September 12, 1992.

9. Hanley, "3 Indicted in Beating."

10. George James, "Youth in Jersey Denies Account of Man's Death," *New York Times*, March 22, 1989; Kaulessar, "'DotBusters' Victim Looks Back."

11. "Man Acquitted in 1987 Beating of Indian Doctor," *New York Times*, May 29, 1993.

12. George James, "Taunting Led to Killing of Executive, Trial Is Told," *New York Times*, March 15, 1989; George James, "Youths Convicted of Assault in Death of an Indian Man," *New York Times*, April 1, 1989.

13. Michel Marriott, "In Jersey City, Indians Protest Violence," *New York Times*, October 12, 1987.

14. "Protesters Want Four Tried as Adults in Killing of Indian," *New York Times*, December 16, 1987.

15. James, "Youths Convicted of Assault."

16. Borsellino, "Tougher Law Asked in Attacks on Indians"; "'Dotbuster' Trial Ends in Conviction," *Hinduism Today*, July 1, 1989, https://www.hinduismtoday.com/magazine/july-1989/1989-07-dotbuster-trial-ends-in-conviction/.

17. James, "Youths Convicted of Assault."

18. Borsellino, "Tougher Law Asked in Attacks on Indians."

19. Sam Roberts, "A Racial Attack That, Years Later, Is Still Being Felt," *New York Times*, December 18, 2011, https://archive.nytimes.com/cityroom.blogs.nytimes.com/2011/12/18/a-racial-attack-that-years-later-is-still-being-felt/.

20. *Mody v. City of Hoboken*, 959 F.2d 461 (3d Cir. 1992).

21. *Mody v. City of Hoboken*.

22. *Mody v. City of Hoboken*.

23. *Mody v. City of Hoboken*.

24. Marlow Stern, "Mark Wahlberg's Pardon Plea: A Look Back at His Troubling, Violent, and Racist Rap Sheet," *Daily Beast*, April 14, 2017, https://www.thedailybeast.com/mark-wahlbergs-pardon-plea-a-look-back-at-his-troubling-violent-and-racist-rap-sheet.

25. Stern, "Mark Wahlberg's Pardon Plea"; *The CAAAV Voice* 5, no. 1 (Spring 1993); *The CAAAV Voice* 5, no. 2 (Fall 1993).

26. See *The CAAAV Voice*, Vols. 1–3 (Fall 1988–Fall 1991).

27. "The $3,000 License to Kill," *Washington Post*, in "Vincent Chin," Part 1, *FBI Records: The Vault*, 33, https://vault.fbi.gov/vincent-chin/vincent-chin-part-01/view; Helen Zia, *The Vincent Chin Legacy Guide: Asian Americans and Civil Rights*, 2nd edition (Vincent Chin Institute, 2022), 31.

28. "The $3,000 License to Kill"; Sheila Robertson Deming, "Michigan's Sentencing Guidelines," *Michigan Bar Journal* 79, no. 6 (2000), https://www.michbar .org/journal/article?articleID=92&volumeID=8&viewType=archive; Russ McNamara, "How the Killing of Vincent Chin Exposed the Weaknesses of Michigan's Criminal Justice System," WDET, June 16, 2022, https://wdet.org/2022/06/16 /how-the-killing-of-vincent-chin-exposed-the-weaknesses-of-michigans-criminal -justice-system/.

29. Jan Ransom, "Trump Will Not Apologize for Calling for Death Penalty over Central Park Five," *New York Times*, June 18, 2019, https://www.nytimes .com/2019/06/18/nyregion/central-park-five-trump.html.

30. Jon Greenberg and John Kruzel, "Fact-Check: Joe Biden's Defense of His 1994 Crime Bill and Mass Incarceration," *Politifact*, May 30, 2019, https://www .politifact.com/factchecks/2019/may/30/joe-biden/joe-biden-1994-crime-bill-mass- incarceration/; German Lopez, "The Controversial 1994 Crime Law That Joe Biden Helped Write, Explained," *Vox*, September 29, 2020, https://www.vox.com/policy -and-politics/2019/6/20/18677998/joe-biden-1994-crime-bill-law-mass-incarcera- tion; Chelsea Cox, "Fact Check: Hillary Clinton, Not Joe Biden, Used the Phrase 'Super Predators,'" *USA Today*, October 24, 2020, https://www.usatoday.com /story/news/factcheck/2020/10/24/fact-check-hillary-clinton-called-some- criminals-super-predators/6021383002/; "Mrs. Clinton Campaign Speech - Super- Predators," C-SPAN, January 25, 1996, https://www.c-span.org/clip/public-affairs -event/user-clip-mrs-clinton-campaign-speech---super-predators/4558907.

31. U.S. Commission on Civil Rights, *Civil Rights Issues Facing Asian Americans in the 1990s* (1992), 29–30; *Hilla v. State*, 832 S.W.2d 773 (Tex. App. 1992).

32. *Civil Rights Issues Facing Asian Americans in the 1990s*, 29–30; Christopher Haight, "From Hate Crimes to Activism: Race, Sexuality, and Gender in the Texas Anti-Violence Movement" (PhD diss., University of Houston, 2016), 122–24.

33. "Bias Beating and a Death Shock a City," *New York Times*, August 23, 1992; "7 Charged in Death of Student Who Objected to Racial Slur," *New York Times*, September 11, 1992.

34. "50-Year Term in Killing of Vietnamese Immigrant," *New York Times*, December 10, 1992.

35. "Defendant Gets 22 Years for Fatal Beating," *Tampa Bay Times*, June 29, 1994, https://www.tampabay.com/archive/1994/06/29/defendant-gets-22-years-for- fatal-beating/; "Jury Finds One Guilty, One Not in Student Death," *Tampa Bay Times*, April 22, 1995, https://www.tampabay.com/archive/1995/04/22/jury-finds -one-guilty-one-not-in-student-death/; "Guilty Plea to Student's Murder," *Orlando Sun-Sentinel*, August 10, 1994.

36. Buzz Bissinger, "The Killing Trail," *Vanity Fair*, February 1995, https://www .vanityfair.com/news/1995/02/texas-murder-199502.

37. Bissinger, "The Killing Trail."

38. Bissinger, "The Killing Trail"; Daniel A. Kusner, "17 Years After Deadly Shooting in Reverchon Park, Victim All but Forgotten," *Dallas Voice*, January 30,

2008, https://dallasvoice.com/17-years-after-deadly-shooting-in-reverchon-park
-victim-all-but-forgotten/.

39. *State v. Fisher*, 321 N.C. 19 (N.C. 1987); "Executed Man Had Unlikely
Friend," *StarNews*, November 13, 2005, https://www.starnewsonline.com/story
/news/2005/11/14/executed-man-had-unlikely-friend/30248331007/.

40. Jaimie Ding, "Attacker in Asian American Bias Crime Sentenced to Restorative Justice, Not More Jail Time," *Oregon Live*, April 2, 2021, https://www
.oregonlive.com/portland/2021/04/attacker-in-asian-american-bias-crime
-sentenced-to-restorative-justice-not-more-jail-time.html.

41. Carrie Gorringe, "Going Through the Hellfire: An Interview with Arthur
Dong," *Nitrate Online*, September 26, 1997, https://nitrateonline.com/flicensed.html.

42. "In Light of the Matthew Shepard Murder, a Filmmaker Re-examines Anti-
Gay Violence," *Fresh Air*, October 26, 1998, https://freshairarchive.org/segments
/light-matthew-shepard-murder-filmmaker-re-examines-anti-gay-violence.

43. Pew Center on the States, *One in 31: The Long Reach of American Corrections*
(Pew Charitable Trusts, 2009), 9; Christina Hanhardt, *Safe Space: Gay Neighborhood History and the Politics of Violence* (Duke University Press, 2013), 14, 23–24.

44. Grace Wong, "Ileto Family Remembers Joseph Ileto, Slain 15 Years Ago," *Daily
Bulletin* (Rancho Cucamonga, CA), August 9, 2014, https://www.dailybulletin
.com/2014/08/09/ileto-family-remembers-joseph-ileto-slain-15-years-ago/; Jocelyn Y.
Stewart, "Lest Hate Victim Be Forgotten," *Los Angeles Times*, January 25, 2001, https://
www.latimes.com/archives/la-xpm-2001-jan-25-mn-16938-story.html.

45. David Rosenzweig, "Furrow Spared by His Mental History," *Los Angeles Times*,
January 25, 2001, https://www.latimes.com/archives/la-xpm-2001-jan-25-me-16825-
story.html; James Sterngold, "Man with a Past of Racial Hate Surrenders in Day Camp
Attack," *New York Times*, August 12, 1999; Stewart, "Lest Hate Victim Be Forgotten."

46. Stewart Kwoh, "A Family Educates to Prevent Hate Crimes: The Case of
Joseph Ileto," in *Untold Civil Rights Stories: Asian Americans Speak Out for Justice*,
ed. Stewart Kwoh and Russell C. Leong (Asian Pacific American Legal Center,
2009), 42–51; Christian Berthelsen, "Hundreds Remember Slain Letter Carrier,"
New York Times, August 15, 1999.

47. Kwoh, "A Family Educates," 47–48.

48. Wong, "Ileto Family Remembers Joseph Ileto."

49. Bob Rector, "The Legacy of Hate Crime Is Passion with Which to Fight It,"
Los Angeles Times, February 4, 2001, https://www.latimes.com/archives/la-xpm
-2001-feb-04-me-21063-story.html; Joe Mozingo, "Slain Man's Family Marches for
Hate Crimes Law," *Los Angeles Times*, August 19, 1999, https://www.latimes.com
/archives/la-xpm-1999-aug-19-me-1728-story.html; Sunny Kaplan, "Hate Crime
Victims' Kin Meet Clinton," *Los Angeles Times*, April 29, 2000, https://www
.latimes.com/archives/la-xpm-2000-apr-29-me-24766-story.html.

50. AAPI Data, *Making Sense of Anti-AANHPI Hate: A Synthesis of Evidence
from 2020–2024*, January 17, 2025, https://aapidata.com/wp-content/uploads/2025/01
/Hate-Synthesis-Report-Final.pdf.

51. Hate Crimes Statistics Act, H.R. 2455, 99th Cong. (1985); U.S. Commission on Civil Rights, *In the Name of Hate*, 12–13.

52. "A Closer Look at Victims," *CBS News*, July 6, 1999, https://www.cbsnews.com/news/a-closer-look-at-victims/; Francis X. Clines, "Shootings Leave Pittsburgh Suburbs Stunned," *New York Times*, April 30, 2000.

53. U.S. Commission on Civil Rights, *In the Name of Hate*, 13–15.

54. Mark Motivans, "Federal Hate Crime Prosecutions, 2005–19," U.S. Department of Justice, July 2021, https://bjs.ojp.gov/sites/g/files/xyckuh236/files/media/document/fhcp0519.pdf.

55. Sandra Gardner, "New Moves Planned on Bias Crimes," *New York Times*, July 12, 1992, https://www.nytimes.com/1992/07/12/nyregion/new-moves-planned-on-bias-crimes.html; Joseph F. Sullivan, "New Jersey Bias-Crimes Statutes Are Overturned," *New York Times*, May 27, 1994.

56. *State v. Mortimer*, 135 N.J. 517 (N.J. 1994); Joseph Vitale, "The Evolution of New Jersey's Bias Crime Law," *Seton Hall Legislative Journal* 26, no. 2 (2002): 363–88.

57. Haight, "From Hate Crimes to Activism," 120–31.

58. *The CAAAV Voice* 4, no. 2 (Fall 1992), 4; Scott Kurashige, "Pan-ethnicity and Community Organizing: Asian Americans United's Campaign Against Anti-Asian Violence," *Journal of Asian American Studies* 3, no. 2 (2000): 164.

59. Kwoh, "A Family Educates," 45.

60. "Texas Man Sentenced on Hate Crime Charges for Attacking Asian Family," U.S. Department of Justice, August 4, 2022, https://www.justice.gov/archives/opa/pr/texas-man-sentenced-hate-crime-charges-attacking-asian-family; Reagan Hignojos and Brandi Addison, "Sam's Stabbing Victim Offers Lesson in Grace," *Midland Reporter-Telegram*, last updated April 20, 2020, https://www.mrt.com/opinion/article/OPINION-Sam-s-stabbing-victim-offers-lesson-in-15195816.php.

61. Catie Edmondson and Jim Tankersley, "Biden Signs Bill Addressing Hate Crimes Against Asian-Americans," *New York Times*, May 20, 2021, https://www.nytimes.com/2021/05/20/us/politics/biden-asian-hate-crimes-bill.html; COVID-19 Hate Crimes Act, Pub. L. No. 117–13, 135 Stat. 265 (2021).

62. Edmondson and Tankersley, "Biden Signs Bill Addressing Hate Crimes Against Asian-Americans"; Catie Edmondson, "Senate Resoundingly Passes Bill to Target Anti-Asian Hate Crimes," *New York Times*, April 22, 2021, https://www.nytimes.com/2021/04/22/us/politics/senate-anti-asian-hate-crimes.html; "Of Course Josh Hawley Was the Only No on Anti-Asian Hate Crime Bill," *Kansas City Star*, April 23, 2021, https://www.kansascity.com/opinion/editorials/article250875344.html.

63. "100+ Asian and LGBTQ Organizations' Statement in Opposition to Law Enforcement-Based Hate Crime Legislation," *Reappropriate*, May 12, 2021, https://reappropriate.co/2021/05/75-asian-and-lgbtq-organizations-statement-in-opposition-to-law-enforcement-based-hate-crime-legislation/; Joan E. Greve, "What Is the George Floyd Justice in Policing Act and Is It Likely to Pass?," *Guardian*, February 6,

2023, https://www.theguardian.com/us-news/2023/feb/06/george-floyd-justice
-in-policing-act-explainer-tyre-nichols.

64. Jay Caspian Kang, "We Need to Put a Name to This Violence," *New York Times*, March 6, 2021, https://www.nytimes.com/2021/03/06/opinion/asian-american-violence-race.html; Jaeah Lee, "Why Was Vicha Ratanapakdee Killed?," *New York Times*, last updated June 15, 2023, https://www.nytimes.com/2021/08/17/magazine/vicha-ratanapakdee.html.

65. Hurubie Meko, "22-Year Sentence for Man Guilty in Hate-Crime Killing of Asian Immigrant," *New York Times*, March 31, 2023, https://www.nytimes.com/2023/03/31/nyregion/asian-hate-crime-killing-man-sentenced.html; "D. A. Bragg Announces Hate Crime Murder Charges in Anti-Asian Attack of Yao Pan Ma in East Harlem," District Attorney, New York County, February 10, 2022, https://manhattanda.org/d-a-bragg-announces-hate-crime-murder-charges-in-anti-asian-attack-of-yao-pan-ma-in-east-harlem/; Ashley Southall, "Nurse Dies After She Is Knocked to Ground in Times Square," *New York Times*, October 10, 2021, https://www.nytimes.com/2021/10/10/nyregion/nurse-dies-times-square.html; Tracey Tully and Ashley Southall, "Woman Pushed onto Subway Tracks 'Never Saw' Her Attacker," *New York Times*, last updated January 19, 2022, https://www.nytimes.com/2022/01/16/nyregion/michelle-go-man-pushes-woman-subway.html; Danny Petilla, "Pinoy Turns into Symbol of Resistance to Asian Hate in NYC," *Inquirer*, February 27, 2022, https://globalnation.inquirer.net/202619/the-hatred-in-their-eyes; Kimmy Yam, "Man Who Stomped on Asian Woman in Times Square Attack Sentenced to 15 Years in State Prison," *NBC News*, February 21, 2024, https://www.nbcnews.com/news/asian-america/vilma-kari-times-square-attack-rcna139260; Mihir Zaveri, "As Protesters Rally Against Anti-Asian Hate, N.Y.C. Records 5 Attacks," *New York Times*, last updated March 31, 2021, https://www.nytimes.com/2021/03/22/nyregion/nyc-asian-hate-crimes.html; Graham Rayman, "Woman Headed to NYC Protests Against Anti-Asian Violence Punched and Bloodied by Bigot Who Stomps Her Sign Calling for Peace," *New York Daily News*, March 23, 2021, https://www.nydailynews.com/2021/03/22/i-wanted-to-fight-back-woman-headed-to-nyc-protests-against-anti-asian-violence-punched-and-bloodied-by-bigot-who-stomps-her-sign-calling-for-peace/.

66. Troy Closson, "Asian Immigrant Attacked in Hate Crime Last Year Dies," *New York Times*, January 8, 2022, https://www.nytimes.com/2022/01/08/nyregion/anti-asian-hate-crime-death-harlem.html; Yam, "Man Who Stomped on Asian Woman"; Michael Gold and Jonah E. Bromwich, "Man Arrested in Anti-Asian Attack Was on Parole for Killing His Mother," *New York Times*, last updated April 6, 2021, https://www.nytimes.com/2021/03/31/nyregion/brandon-elliot-asian-attack-nyc.html.

67. Andy Newman, Nate Schweber, and Chelsia Rose Marcius, "Decades Adrift in a Broken System, Then Charged in a Death on the Tracks," *New York Times*, last updated June 22, 2023, https://www.nytimes.com/2022/02/05/nyregion/martial-simon-michelle-go.html; Tully and Southall, "Woman Pushed Onto Subway Tracks."

68. Office of Policy Planning and Research, *The Negro Family: The Case for National Action*, U.S. Department of Labor, March 1965; Janelle Wong, "Beyond the Headlines: Review of National Anti-Asian Hate Incident Reporting/Data Collection Published over 2019–2021," June 7, 2021, https://docs.google.com/document /d/19llMUCDHX-hLKru-cnDCqoBirlpNgFo7W3f-qoJoko4/edit?tab = t.o.

69. "'Go Back to China': Racist Rant Suspect ID'd as Daughter of Late NY Senator," *Eyewitness News ABC-7*, March 16, 2021, https://abc7ny.com/asian-american -hate-crime-maura-moynihan-daniel-patrick-moyniohan-racist/10427635/; Sam Roberts, "Elizabeth Moynihan, Engine of the Senator's Success, Dies at 94," *New York Times*, last updated November 20, 2023, https://www.nytimes.com/2023/11/08 /nyregion/elizabeth-moynihan-dead.html; Shannan Ferry, "Daughter of Late Senator Accused of Racist Rant Against Asian-American Couple," *Spectrum News NY1*, March 18, 2021, https://ny1.com/nyc/all-boroughs/news/2021/03/19/daughter-of -late-senator-accused-of-racist-rant-against-asian-american-couple.

70. Council on Criminal Justice, "Trends in Homicide: What You Need to Know," December 2023, https://counciloncj.org/homicide-trends-report/; Neil MacFarquhar, "Murders Spiked in 2020 in Cities Across the United States," *New York Times*, last updated November 15, 2021, https://www.nytimes.com/2021/09/27 /us/fbi-murders-2020-cities.html; Kalley White et al., "Whose Lives Matter? Race, Space, and the Devaluation of Homicide Victims in Minority Communities," *Sociology of Race and Ethnicity* 7, no. 3 (2020), https://doi.org/10.1177/2332649220948184.

71. "100+ Asian and LGBTQ Organizations' Statement."

9. WHEN THE POLICE CAUSE MORE HARM

1. *Estate of Sinthasomphone v. City of Milwaukee*, 838 F. Supp. 1320 (E.D. Wis. 1993).

2. Peter Kwan, "Jeffrey Dahmer and the Cosynthesis of Categories," *Hastings Law Journal* 48 (1997): 1257–92.

3. *Sinthasomphone v. Milwaukee* (1993); "Police Probe Boy's Return to Accused Killer," *Washington Post*, July 26, 1991.

4. Crocker Stephenson, "2 Women Say Officers Failed to Aid 14-Year-Old Boy," *Milwaukee Sentinel*, July 26, 1991, ProQuest US Newsstream; "Police Probe Boy's Return to Accused Killer."

5. *Sinthasomphone v. Milwaukee* (1993).

6. Rogers Worthington, "New Dahmer Revelation: Cops Were in Apartment," *Chicago Tribune*, August 2, 1991, ProQuest US Newsstream.

7. *Sinthasomphone v. Milwaukee* (1993).

8. Worthington, "New Dahmer Revelation."

9. Worthington, "New Dahmer Revelation."

10. Pew Research Center, "American Trends Panel, Final Topline," June 2020, https://www.pewresearch.org/wp-content/uploads/sites/20/2020/06/PSDT_06

.12.20_protest.report-TOPLINE.pdf; May Fu et al., "#Asians4BlackLives: Notes from the Ground," *Amerasia Journal* (2019): 1–18.

11. Gabriel L. Schwartz and Jaquelyn L. Jahn, "Disaggregating Asian American and Pacific Islander Risk of Fatal Police Violence," *Plos One*, October 10, 2022, https://doi.org/10.1371/journal.pone.0274745.

12. "Subject: Jeffrey Dahmer," *FBI Records: The Vault*, File Number: 7-MW-26057-Section 2, August 3, 1992, 8, https://vault.fbi.gov/jeffrey-lionel-dahmer /jeffrey-lionel-dahmer-part-03-of-19.

13. "Police Probe Boy's Return to Accused Killer."

14. Stephenson, "2 Women Say Officers Failed to Aid 14-Year-Old."

15. Worthington, "New Dahmer Revelation."

16. "Woman Who Tried to End Dahmer's Crimes Dead at 56," *Superior Telegram,* January 6, 2011, https://www.superiortelegram.com/news/woman-who-tried-to-end-dahmers-crimes-dead-at-56.

17. Flint Taylor, "In Milwaukee, a History of Racist Violence Fuels Mistrust of the Police Department," *In These Times,* September 7, 2016, https://inthesetimes .com/article/in-milwaukee-a-history-of-racist-violence-fuels-mistrust-of-the-police-depa.

18. *Sinthasomphone v. Milwaukee* (1993).

19. *Sinthasomphone v. Milwaukee* (1993).

20. *Sinthasomphone v. Milwaukee* (1993).

21. "Subject: Jeffrey Dahmer."

22. *Estate of Sinthasomphone v. City of Milwaukee*, 878 F. Supp. 147 (E.D. Wis. 1995); "Milwaukee Council Settles with Dahmer Victim Family," *Orlando Sentinel,* April 26, 1995, https://www.orlandosentinel.com/news/os-xpm-1995–04–26–9504250660-story.html.

23. Kwan, "Jeffrey Dahmer and the Cosynthesis of Categories," 1265–72.

24. *Balcerzak v. City of Milwaukee*, 980 F. Supp. 983 (E.D. Wis. 1997); *Balcerzak v. Chief of Milwaukee Police Department*, 993 F. Supp. 1213 (E.D. Wis. 1998); *John A. Balcerzak and Joseph T. Gabrish v. City of Milwaukee, Wisconsin, Police Department, City of Milwaukee, Philip Arreola, Chief, et al.*, 163 F.3d 993 (7th Cir. 1998).

25. JR Radcliffe, "What's Real and What's Fiction in Netflix's Jeffrey Dahmer Series, 'Monster,'" *Milwaukee Journal Sentinel,* September 23, 2022, https://www .jsonline.com/story/news/2022/09/23/whats-real-fiction-monster-jeffrey-dahmer -story-netflix/8083469001/; "About Us," Trenton Police Department, https://www .usacops.com/wi/p53095/aboutus.html (accessed May 10, 2025); "Gabrish Named Interim Chief," *Ozaukee Press*, August 28, 2019, https://ozaukeepress.com/content /gabrish-named-interim-chief; Marina Watts, "Milwaukee PD Criticized for Old Tweet Congratulating Cop Who Left Dahmer Victim," *Newsweek,* June 19, 2020, https://www.newsweek.com/milwaukee-pd-congratulate-retired-cop-who-laughed-off-teen-victim-dahmer-1512130.

26. Maureen Dowd, "Ryan Murphy Is Having a Very Happy Halloween," *New York Times,* October 29, 2022, https://www.nytimes.com/2022/10/29/style/ryan -murphy-netflix-horror.html.

27. Natalie Oganesyan, "'Dahmer' Becomes Third Netflix Show to Surpass 1 Billion Viewing Hours," *The Wrap*, December 5, 2022, https://www.thewrap.com /dahmer-netflix-billion-hours-viewed-ratings/.

28. Mariana González, "Interview with Kieran Tamondong of Netflix's 'Monster: The Jeffrey Dahmer Story,'" *Rival Magazine*, December 2, 2022, https://www .rivalmagazinela.com/rival-online/interview-with-kieran-tamondong-of-netflixs -monster-the-jeffrey-dahmer-story.

29. "Prosecutor: Warren Police Not at Fault in Fatal Shooting," *Macomb Daily*, last updated June 17, 2021, https://www.macombdaily.com/2006/10/15/prosecutor-warren-police-not-at-fault-in-fatal-shooting/.

30. "Statement of Pang Blia Xiong," n.d. [December 2006], in author's possession.

31. "Statement of Pang Blia Xiong"; Keith Quincy, *Hmong: History of a People*, 2nd edition (Eastern Washington University Press, 1995), 171–224.

32. Eric Tang, *Unsettled: Cambodian Refugees in the New York City Hyperghetto* (Temple University Press, 2015), 8.

33. "Statement of Pang Blia Xiong"; U.S. Census Bureau, "Population by Race and Hispanic or Latino Origin, for the 15 Largest Counties and Incorporated Places in Michigan: 2000," https://www2.census.gov/census_2000/census2000/pdf /mi_tab_5.PDF; U.S. Census Bureau, "QuickFacts: Warren city, Michigan; East-pointe city, Michigan," https://www.census.gov/quickfacts/fact/table/warrencitym ichigan,eastpointecitymichigan/POP010210.

34. Pang Blia Xiong and Tom Vang, interview with author, December 13, 2006.

35. Pang Blia Xiong and Tom Vang interview.

36. Sandra Svoboda, "Shooting Pains," *Metro Times* (Detroit), February 7, 2007, https://www.metrotimes.com/news/shooting-pains-2186589.

37. Svoboda, "Shooting Pains."

38. Svoboda, "Shooting Pains"; *Mitchell v. City of Warren*, 803 F.3d 223 (2015).

39. Aimee J. Baldillo and Vincent A. Eng, "Save a Hunter, Shoot a Hmong," *The Modern American*, Spring 2005, 3–7; Susan Saulny, "Hmong, Shaken, Wonder If a Killing Was Retaliation," *New York Times*, January 14, 2007, https://www.nytimes .com/2007/01/14/us/14hmong.html.

40. Stephen Kinzer and Monica Davie, "A Hunt Turns Tragic, and Two Cultures Collide," *New York Times*, November 28, 2004, https://www.nytimes .com/2004/11/28/us/a-hunt-turns-tragic-and-two-cultures-collide.html; Stephen Kinzer, "Hmong Hunter Charged with 6 Murders Is Said to Be a Shaman," *New York Times*, December 1, 2004, https://www.nytimes.com/2004/12/01/us/hmong -hunter-charged-with-6-murders-is-said-to-be-a-shaman.html; Saulny, "Hmong, Shaken."

41. "Statement of Pang Blia Xiong."

42. According to an archived Wikipedia page from February 3, 2017, Chang represented the sixth district of Michigan's House of Representatives when it was 57.1 percent Black, 21.7 percent Hispanic, 18.4 percent white, 0.9 percent Asian, and 0.5 percent other. See https://en.wikipedia.org/w/index.php?title=Michigan

%27s_6th_House_of_Representatives_district&diff=prev&oldid=763510726 (accessed December 8, 2024). See also Emily Singer, "Democrats Win Back Control of Michigan State House," *Michigan Independent*, April 17, 2024, https:// michiganindependent.com/politics/democrats-win-back-control-of-michigan -state-house/; "State House District 13, MI," Census Reporter, https:// censusreporter.org/profiles/62000US26013-state-house-district-13-mi/ (accessed December 8, 2024).

43. Chinese for Affirmative Action, "Asian Organizations Across the Bay Area Join Forces to Demand Action Against Violence," February 9, 2021, https://caasf .org/press-release/asian-organizations-across-the-bay-area-join-forces-to-demand -action-against-violence/.

44. "Why Was Angelo Quinto's Death Ruled an Accident?," KQED, September 3, 2021, transcript with Sandhya Dirks at https://drive.google.com/file/d /1OfiMksYZLZtInRoxTKPAGx4x12JtFzt-/view; Claire Wang, "The Filipino American Family Behind Calif.'s New Police Reform Laws Speaks Out," *NBC News*, October 15, 2021, https://www.nbcnews.com/news/asian-america/filipino -american-family-califs-new-police-reform-laws-speaks-rcna3030; American Medical Association, "New AMA Policy Opposes 'Excited Delirium' Diagnosis," June 14, 2021, https://www.ama-assn.org/press-center/press-releases/new-ama-policy -opposes-excited-delirium-diagnosis.

45. Kimmy Yam, "A Year After Police Killed Christian Hall, His Parents Continue Calls for Accountability," *NBC News*, December 24, 2021, https://www .nbcnews.com/news/asian-america/christian-hall-police-shooting-anniversary -rcna7254; Danielle Ohl, "Three Years Ago, a Police Officer Killed Christian Hall," *Spotlight PA*, December 28, 2023, https://www.spotlightpa.org/news/2023/12 /mental-health-call-study-christian-hall/; "Justice for Christian Hall," https:// www.apipennsylvania.org/christian-hall (accessed October 14, 2024).

46. Sasha Zhou, Rachel Banawa, and Hans Oh, "The Mental Health Impact of COVID-19 Racial and Ethnic Discrimination Against Asian American and Pacific Islanders," *Frontiers in Psychiatry*, November 16, 2021, https://doi.org/10.3389 /fpsyt.2021.708426; AAPI Data, *Making Sense of Anti-AANHPI Hate*.

47. Erin Nolan and Shayla Colon, "Rare Police Killing of Asian American Woman Has Rattled Her Community," *New York Times*, September 24, 2024, https://www.nytimes.com/2024/09/24/nyregion/victoria-lee-shooting-new-jersey. html; Libor Jany, "LAPD Tactics Faulted in Shooting of Mentally Ill K-Town Man," *Los Angeles Times*, April 10, 2025, https://www.latimes.com/california/story/2025– 04–10/lapd-police-commission-koreatown-shooting. A Korean American mental health clinician responded first to Yang but deferred to police action.

48. Ohl, "Three Years Ago, a Police Officer Killed Christian Hall"; Wang, "Filipino American Family"; Daniel Pardo and Jackson Ellison, "Antioch Family Led the Effort to Ban Excited Delirium Diagnosis in California," *Spectrum News*, December 15, 2023, https://spectrumnews1.com/ca/southern-california/inside-the- issues/2023/12/15/antioch-family-led-the-effort-to-ban-excited-delirium-diagnosis -in-california.

49. Leslie Maitland, "2,500 Chinese Protest Alleged Police Beating Here," *New York Times*, May 13, 1975; Ryan Lee Wong, "Closed to Protest Police Brutality," *Hyphen*, January 8, 2017, https://hyphenmagazine.com/blog/2017/01/closed-protest-police-brutality.

50. Selwyn Raab, "New Militancy Emerges in Chinatown," *New York Times*, June 8, 1975; Wong, "Closed to Protest Police Brutality."

51. Wong, "Closed to Protest Police Brutality"; Deirdre Carmody, "Thousands in Chinatown March in Police Protest," *New York Times*, May 20, 1975; "20,000 Protest Police Brutality," *Yellow Seeds*, August 1975, 1.

52. Dennis Hevesi, "No Indictment for Officer Who Shot Brooklyn Youth," *New York Times*, May 17, 1995; Chris Fuchs, "Decades After a Cop Shot Her Brother, Qinglan Huang Speaks Up for Akai Gurley," *NBC News*, April 11, 2016, https://www.nbcnews.com/news/asian-america/two-decades-after-cop-shot-her-brother-qing-lan-huang-n554146.

53. Vivian Truong, "From State-Sanctioned Removal to the Right to the City: The Policing of Asian Immigrants in Southern Brooklyn, 1987–1995," *Journal of Asian American Studies* (February 2020): 61–92. My analysis also draws on personal interactions with CAAAV staff and volunteers during the 1990s.

54. Fuchs, "Qinglan Huang Speaks Up for Akai Gurley"; Fu et al., "#Asians4BlackLives," 12.

55. Chris Fuchs, "Hmong Family Whose Son Was Shot by White Officer Speaking Out in Solidarity," *NBC News*, June 2, 2020, https://www.nbcnews.com/news/asian-america/hmong-family-whose-son-was-shot-white-officer-speaking-out-n1222281; Jessica Lussenhop, "George Floyd Death: 'The Same Happened to My Son,'" *BBC News*, June 14, 2020, https://www.bbc.com/news/world-us-canada-53023703; Hannah Yang, "'We Need to Help Them': Asian Americans Demand Justice for George Floyd," *MPR News*, June 11, 2020, https://www.mprnews.org/story/2020/06/09/we-need-to-help-them-asian-americans-demand-justice-for-george-floyd.

56. Carolyn Bick, "Le Family Settles, Says KCSO, Deputy Molina Culpable," *South Seattle Emerald*, March 24, 2024, https://southseattleemerald.org/news/2021/03/24/le-family-settles-says-kcso-deputy-molina-culpable-sheriff-email-claims-otherwise.

57. Ashley Nerbovig, "Seattle Police Officer Hurls Racist Slur at Chinese-American Neighbor," *The Stranger*, September 22, 2023, https://www.thestranger.com/news/2023/09/22/79177194/seattle-police-officer-hurls-racist-slur-at-chinese-american-neighbor; Carolyn Bick, "SPD Officer Fired over Racial Slurs, Threats," *Northwest Asian Weekly*, June 18, 2024, https://nwasianweekly.com/2024/06/spd-officer-fired-over-racial-slurs-threats/; Seattle Office of Police Accountability, Closed Case Summary, Case Number: 2023OPA-0413, March 9, 2024, https://www.seattle.gov/Documents/Departments/OPA/ClosedCaseSummaries/2023OPA-0413ccs3-9-24.pdf; Chinese Information and Service Center, "Report an Incident of Hate or Bias," https://cisc-seattle.org/report-an-incident-of-hate-or-bias/ (accessed October 14, 2024).

58. Andrew Engelson, "Seattle Police Knew Officer Who Struck and Killed Pedestrian Had 'Checkered History,' but Hired Him Anyway," *Publicola*, April 13, 2024, https://publicola.com/2024/04/13/seattle-police-knew-officer-who-struck-and-killed-pedestrian-had-checkered-history-but-hired-him-anyway/; "Dispatch Call Reveals More Details of Woman Hit," Fox 13 Seattle, January 26, 2023, https://www.fox13seattle.com/news/dispatch-call-reveals-more-details-of-woman-hit-killed-by-seattle-patrol-car; Amy Radil, "Cleared of Felony, Seattle Cop Who Killed Indian Student Kandula Could End Up in Municipal Court," KUOW, February 23, 2024, https://www.kuow.org/stories/seattle-cop-killed-indian-student-kandula-municipal-court.

59. Laurel Wamsley, "Seattle Officer Recorded Joking About Woman's Death," NPR, September 14, 2023, https://www.npr.org/2023/09/13/1199352063/seattle-officer-recorded-joking-about-womans-death-saying-she-had-limited-value; Karina Vargas, "Group Rallies for Jaahnavi Kandula After Traffic Infraction Filed Against Seattle Officer," *KOMO News*, March 3, 2024, https://komonews.com/news/local/group-rallys-for-jaahnavi-kandula-after-traffic-infraction-filed-against-seattle-officer-kevin-dave-police-fatal-spd-comments-discipline-limited-value-collision-king-county-prosecutors-hire-independent-agency-opa-accountability.

60. Nina Bernstein, "Once Facing Deportation, a Woman Gets Asylum," *New York Times*, September 8, 2007, https://www.nytimes.com/2007/09/08/nyregion/08deport.html.

61. Asian American Legal Defense and Education Fund, "Support the Justice for Jiang Zhenxing Campaign!," March 13, 2006, https://www.aaldef.org/news/support-the-justice-for-jiang-zhenxing-campaign/.

10. BUILDING COMMUNITY IN THE FACE OF VIOLENCE

1. Paul Keegan, "SouthwestSide Story," *Philadelphia Magazine*, October 1992, 77.

2. Jeffrey Fleishman and Martha Woodall, "Tension High After Teen Slain in City," *Philadelphia Inquirer* [hereafter *PHI*], August 4, 1991; Peter Landry, "Neighborhood Strives to Quell Tensions After Slaying," *PHI*, August 5, 1991; Robin Palley, "Uneasy Truce in White-Asian Feud," *Philadelphia Daily News* [hereafter *PDN*], August 5, 1991; Kathy Brennan, "Gang-Slay Trial Racially Charged," *PDN*, June 6, 1992.

3. Maida Cassandra Odom, "Ten Years After MOVE," *Emerge*, vol. 6, no. 8, June 1995, ProQuest Research Library.

4. Noel Ignatiev, *How the Irish Became White* (Routledge, 1995), 130; Carolyn Adams et al., *Philadelphia: Neighborhoods, Division, and Conflict in a Postindustrial City* (Temple University Press, 1991), 11.

5. Adams et al., *Philadelphia*, 81; Allen Scott, *Metropolis: From the Division of Labor to Urban Form* (University of California Press, 1988), 9–25.

6. Keegan, "SouthwestSide Story," 78.

7. Keegan, "SouthwestSide Story"; Adams et al., *Philadelphia*, 22.

8. U.S. Census Bureau, *1990 Census of Population and Housing: Population and Housing Characteristics for Census Tracts and Block Numbering Areas*, Philadelphia-Wilmington-Trenton CMSA (1993); David Roediger, *The Wages of Whiteness: Race and the Making of the American Working Class* (Verso, 1991).

9. Ellen Somekawa, "On the Edge: Southeast Asians in Philadelphia and the Struggle for Space," in *Reviewing Asian America: Locating Diversity*, ed. Wendy L. Ng et al. (Washington State University Press, 1995), 33; Deborah Wei, interview with author, September 15, 1992; U.S. Census Bureau, *1980 Census of Population and Housing: Census Tracts*, Philadelphia, PA-NJ SMSA (1983); U.S. Census Bureau, *1990 Census of Population and Housing . . .* Philadelphia-Wilmington-Trenton CMSA. Data cited for census tract number 87.

10. Fleishman and Woodall, "Tension High After Teen Slain in City"; Neeta Patel, Ellen Somekawa, and Dao X. Tran, "Racial Violence in Southwest Philadelphia: Asian Lives Do Not Come Cheap," *Forward Motion* 11, no. 3 (1992), 24, 30; Trang (pseudonym), interview with author, September 15, 1992.

11. Hue Tran, interview with author, September 15, 1992; Trang interview.

12. Craig R. McCoy, "Witness Tells Court of Night a Friend Died," *PHI*, June 20, 1992; Linda Loyd and Laurie Hollman, "Three Guilty of 3d-Degree Murder," *PHI*, June 30, 1992.

13. Fleishman and Woodall, "Tension High After Teen Slain in City"; Ellen Somekawa, first interview with author, May 30, 1996.

14. Amy S. Rosenberg, "Haunted by Bigotry and Fear, Children Survive a Death," *PHI*, August 10, 1991.

15. "Southwest-Side Story: A Deadly Clash Between White and Asian Youths Leaves a Community Searching for Answers," *PHI*, August 7, 1991.

16. "Southwest-Side Story."

17. Fleishman and Woodall, "Tension High After Teen Slain in City."

18. *Commonwealth v. Minh La et al.*, Court Transcript, First Judicial District of Philadelphia, Court of Common Pleas, 1992, 50; Palley, "Uneasy Truce in White-Asian Feud"; Amy S. Rosenberg and Raoul V. Mowatt, "Witness Tells of Death at Playground," *PHI*, August 21, 1991; Linda Loyd and Thomas Gibbons Jr., "Suspect in Reilly Killing Gets Bail," *PHI*, October 19, 1991.

19. Lloyd and Gibbons, "Suspect in Reilly Killing Gets Bail"; Raoul V. Mowatt, "Trial for 6 in Reilly Slaying," *PHI*, November 26, 1991; Wei interview.

20. *Commonwealth v. Minh La et al.*, 2161; Neeta Patel, interview with author, July 16, 1993.

21. Patel interview. I witnessed Casey at the trial of Khanh Lam and heard the testimony of the coroner on February 11, 1993.

22. *Commonwealth v. Minh La et al.*, 2161, 2195, 2218–19.

23. Susan Caba, "Six Defendants in Reilly Slaying Sentenced to Jail," *PHI*, November 20, 1992; Linda Loyd, "7th Reilly Case Defendant Freed," *PHI*, February 20, 1993.

24. Yen Le Espiritu, *Asian American Panethnicity: Bridging Institutions and Identities* (Temple University Press, 1992), 82–94.

25. Wei interview; Mary Yee, interview with author, February 15, 1993.

26. "This Is Yellow Seeds," *Yellow Seeds*, May 1974, 2.

27. Yee interview.

28. Quote from inactive webpage, previously at http://www.aaunited.org /ourhistory.html.

29. Yee interview.

30. Yee interview.

31. Yee interview; Patel interview.

32. Wei interview; Tran interview; Somekawa first interview.

33. Somekawa first interview.

34. Geoff Taubman, "Police Arrest Three in Grad Student Attack," *Daily Pennsylvanian*, October 12, 1988; Linda Loyd, "Man Says He Witnessed Fatal Attack," *PHI*, December 2, 1988.

35. Geoff Taubman, "U. Student Dies After 3 Weeks at HUP," *Daily Pennsylvanian*, October 31, 1988; "Community Statement on Racial Incidents," *Daily Pennsylvanian*, November 10, 1988; Steven Ochs, "Teen Convicted in Student Murder, Sentenced to Life," *Daily Pennsylvanian*, November 29, 1989. From the articles in the campus paper that I have reviewed between the time of the beating and the end of the trial over a year later, *The Daily Pennsylvanian* never listed the racial identity of the assailants, who presented in broadcast media as Black, and neither apparently did the *Philadelphia Inquirer*. As a University of Pennsylvania student at the time, I recall that the predominantly white campus was surrounded primarily by low-income Black neighborhoods in West Philadelphia. Clark Park sits south of Baltimore Avenue, which then comprised the border between where Penn students and Black Philadelphians resided. The *Philadelphia Daily News* named the suspects in the lead sentence of one article as "thugs." Another article discussed the death of Leung without mention of race, alongside a report of a "racially motivated murder" of a white victim who "was called 'honky' by a group of Hispanics." See Tyree Johnson, "Shortage of Policemen Cited in Park Beating," *PDN*, October 13, 1988; Dave Racher, "Teen Admits Slaying: Had Role in Graduate Student's Death," *PDN*, May 9, 1989.

36. Jeff Gammage, "Anti-Asian Hate Has Long History," *PHI*, May 16, 2021; Murray Dubin, "Suspect Held for Trial in Slaying," *PHI*, August 2, 1990.

37. Ellen Somekawa, second interview with author, October 8, 2024; Linda Loyd, "Words, A Clash, and Maybe a Murder," *PHI*, May 25, 1991.

38. Loyd, "Maybe a Murder"; Dave Racher, "Trial Ordered in Slaying of Cambodian Immigrant," *PDN*, August 2, 1990; Dave Davies, "Man Held in Slaying of Visitor: Victim's Family Cites Time Lapse," *PDN*, July 24, 1990; Linda Loyd, "S. Phila. Man Gets 10 to 20 Years in Fatal Attack on Cambodian Man," *PHI*, December 13, 1991.

39. Debbie Stone and Kurt Heine, "9 Shot, 1 Stabbed, 1 Beaten," *PDN*, June 18, 1990; Murray Dubin, "Residents Press Police over Slaying," *PHI*, July 25, 1990.

40. Dave Davies, "Anti-Asian Crime Ignored? Group Says HRC Should Study Its Own Statistics," *PDN*, July 20, 1990.

41. Davies, "Man Held in Slaying of Visitor"; Racher, "Trial Ordered in Slaying of Cambodian Immigrant"; Kathy Brennan, "Murder Verdict: Conviction Hailed by Asian Group," *PDN*, May 30, 1991; Linda Loyd, "Verdict in Beating Is 3d-Degree Murder," *PHI*, May 30, 1991; Loyd, "S. Phila. Man Gets 10 to 20 Years."

42. Sandy Bauers, "Putting Himself on the Line," *PHI*, September 8, 1992.

43. Patel interview; Wei interview; Trang interview.

44. Lawrence Lee, interview with author, September 14, 1992; Thoai Nguyen, interview with author, September 14, 1992; Jennifer Lin, "Police Photo Sweeps Anger Asians," *PHI*, October 25, 1992.

45. John Fong, interview with author, September 14, 1992; Nguyen interview; Patel interview; Craig R. McCoy, "Prosecution of Asians Denounced in Protest," *PHI*, June 5, 1992.

46. Yee interview.

47. Somekawa first interview; Lee interview.

48. See Kathryn E. Wilson, *Ethnic Renewal in Philadelphia's Chinatown: Space, Place, and Struggle* (Temple University Press, 2015).

49. South Philadelphia High School Asian Student Advocates, "South Philadelphia High School Update," leaflet, April 3, 2010, in author's possession; Kristin A. Graham, "Too Fearful to Go to Class," *PHI*, December 5, 2009; Jeff Gammage and Kristin A. Graham, "Violence at South Philadelphia High," *PHI*, March 14, 2010; Dale Mezzacappa, "Anti-Asian Attacks at a Philadelphia School Led to Landmark Ruling over a Decade Ago," *Chalkbeat*, April 6, 2021, https://www.chalkbeat.org /philadelphia/2021/4/6/22367983/anti-asian-attacks-in-philadelphia-led-to -landmark-ruling-over-a-decade-ago-did-anything-change/.

50. Somekawa second interview; Graham, "Too Fearful to Go to Class."

51. *United States v. The School District of Philadelphia and the School Reform Commission*, Order Approving and Entering Settlement Agreement, December 15, 2010, in author's possession; *Asian Americans United et al. v. The School District of Philadelphia*, Conciliation Agreement, Pennsylvania Human Relations Commission, n.d., in author's possession.

52. Grace Lee Boggs with Scott Kurashige, *The Next American Revolution: Sustainable Activism for the Twenty-First Century* (University of California Press, 2011), 61; Mezzacappa, "Anti-Asian Attacks at a Philadelphia School."

53. Grace Fan, Mohan Seshadri, Ellen Somekawa, and Wolfe Tsuboi, group interview with author, April 29, 2023; Office of Councilmember Helen Gym, "Resources on Anti-Asian Violence," n.d., in author's possession; Anna Orso, "Donor Behind the Anti-Gym Ads," *PHI*, May 7, 2023, ProQuest US Newsstream.

54. Jennifer Stefano, "The Key to Cherelle Parker's Success? Rejecting the Dems' Progressive Wing," *PHI*, May 22, 2023; Committee of Seventy, "High School Students Choose Helen Gym, New Slate of City Council Members in PA Youth Vote Mock Election," https://seventy.org/press-testimony/high-school-students-choose

-gym-new-slate-of-city-council-members-in-pa-youth-vote-mock-election (accessed October 7, 2024).

55. Mezzacappa, "Anti-Asian Attacks at a Philadelphia School"; Anjana Sundaram, "Fighting School Violence, Asian Immigrants Find Their Voice," *Northwest Asian Weekly*, July 30, 2011, https://nwasianweekly.com/2011/07/fighting-school-violence-asian-immigrants-find-their-voice/.

56. Changhee Han, "Penn Freshman Battles Back Against Bullying," *Daily Pennsylvanian*, April 4, 2012, https://www.thedp.com/article/2012/04/college_freshman_takes_antibullying_initiative_to_penn; Tammy Kim, "Immigrant Youth Remake South Philly After Anti-Asian Violence," *Hyphen*, July 22, 2011, https://hyphenmagazine.com/blog/2011/7/22/immigrant-youth-remake-south-philly-after-anti-asian-violence; Lily Suh, "'Heal, Resist, and Grow': VietLead Plants the Seeds for a Better Future," *34th Street*, March 17, 2021, https://www.34st.com/article/2021/03/vietlead-refugee-immigrants-asians-vietnamese-philadelphian-community.

57. Kim, "Immigrant Youth Remake South Philly."

EPILOGUE

1. David Monkawa, "The Westside Community: 'Getting It Together' Against Crime," *Gidra*, December 1973, Densho Digital Repository, https://downloads.densho.org/ddr-densho-297/ddr-densho-297–56-mezzanine-3110b49c67.pdf.

2. David Monkawa, interview with author, December 4, 2021. The remaining quotes and facts related to Monkawa are drawn from this source unless noted.

3. "'A Man of Two Faces': Author Viet Thanh Nguyen on New Memoir, U.S. Imperialism, Vietnam and More," *Democracy Now!*, October 25, 2023, https://www.democracynow.org/2023/10/25/palestine_vietnam.

4. Craig Trainor, "Dear Colleague," United States Department of Education Office for Civil Rights, February 14, 2025, https://www.ed.gov/media/document/dear-colleague-letter-sffa-v-harvard-109506.pdf.

5. Sarah Moon and Claire Colbert, "Attack on Asian American Man in LA's Koreatown Being Investigated as a Hate Crime," CNN, February 26, 2021, https://www.cnn.com/2021/02/26/us/asian-american-man-attack-koreatown-los-angeles-trnd/index.html; Josie Huang, "A Year After a Brutal Beating in Koreatown, Neighbors Push for Action to End Anti-Asian Hate," *LAist*, February 17, 2022, https://laist.com/news/beating-koreatown-anti-asian-attacks-neighborhood-regroups; Jae C. Hong, "Older Korean-Americans in LA Fearful Amid Anti-Asian Attacks," Associated Press, April 19, 2021, https://apnews.com/article/government-and-politics-asia-general-news-health-asia-pacific-04854c78be478fb0f767a5776bba82d3.

6. Huang, "A Year After a Brutal Beating in Koreatown"; Monkawa interview; COVID-19 Hate Crimes Act.

<h1 style="text-align: center">SELECTED BIBLIOGRAPHY</h1>

Research sources include archival documents, interviews, and published works. Below is a selection of books that most shaped my thinking. Please see the notes for full citations of primary sources, government documents, scholarly articles, periodicals, and web-based sources.

Bald, Vivek. *Bengali Harlem and the Lost Histories of South Asian America*. Harvard University Press, 2013.

Bass, Gary J. *The Blood Telegram: Nixon, Kissinger, and a Forgotten Genocide*. Knopf, 2013.

Bass, Gary J. *Judgment at Tokyo: World War II on Trial and the Making of Modern Asia*. Knopf, 2023.

Belew, Kathleen. *Bring the War Home: The White Power Movement and Paramilitary America*. Harvard University Press, 2018.

Bevins, Vincent. *The Jakarta Method: Washington's Anticommunist Crusade and the Mass Murder Program That Shaped Our World*. PublicAffairs, 2021.

Boggs, Grace Lee, with Scott Kurashige. *The Next American Revolution: Sustainable Activism for the Twenty-First Century*. University of California Press, 2011.

Chan, Sucheng. *Hmong Means Free: Life in Laos and America*. Temple University Press, 1994.

Chang, Jason, Benjamin Barson, and Alexis Dudden. *The Cargo Rebellion: Those Who Chose Freedom*. PM Press, 2023.

Clymer, Kenton. *The United States and Cambodia, 1969–2000: A Troubled Relationship*. Taylor and Francis, 2013.

Cox, Ted W. *The Toledo Incident of 1925: Three Days That Made History in Toledo, Oregon*. Old World Publications, 2005.

Cruz, Rene Ciria, Cindy Domingo, and Bruce Occena, eds. *A Time to Rise: Collective Memoirs of the Union of Democratic Filipinos (KDP)*. University of Washington Press, 2017.

Dower, John W. *War Without Mercy: Race and Power in the Pacific War*. Pantheon, 1986.

Espiritu, Yen Le. *Asian American Panethnicity: Bridging Institutions and Identities.* Temple University Press, 1992.

Hanley, Charles J., Sang-Hun Choe, and Martha Mendoza. *The Bridge at No Gun Ri: A Hidden Nightmare from the Korean War.* Henry Holt, 2001.

Hoganson, Kristin L. *Fighting for American Manhood: How Gender Politics Provoked the Spanish-American and Philippine American Wars.* Yale University Press, 1998.

Hong, Cathy Park. *Minor Feelings: An Asian American Reckoning.* OneWorld, 2020.

Ichioka, Yuji. *The Issei: The World of the First Generation Japanese Immigrants, 1885–1924.* The Free Press, 1988.

Ignatiev, Noel. *How the Irish Became White.* Routledge, 1995.

Iyer, Deepa. *We Too Sing America: South Asian, Arab, Muslim, and Sikh Immigrants Shape Our Multiracial Future.* New Press, 2016.

Jacobs, Seth. *The Universe Unraveling: America Foreign Policy in Cold War Laos.* Cornell University Press, 2012.

Jensen, Joan. *Passage from India: Asian Indian Immigrants in North America.* Yale University Press, 1988.

Johnson, Akemi. *Night in the American Village: Women in the Shadow of the U.S. Military Bases in Okinawa.* New Press, 2019.

Jung, Moon-Ho. *Menace to Empire: Anticolonial Solidarities and the Transpacific Origins of the US Security State.* University of California Press, 2022.

Kiernan, Ben. *The Pol Pot Regime: Race, Power, and Genocide under the Khmer Rouge, 1975–79.* 2nd edition. Yale University Press, 2002.

Kim, Richard S. *The Quest for Statehood: Korean Immigrant Nationalism and U.S. Sovereignty, 1905–45.* Oxford University Press, 2011.

Kramer, Paul A. *The Blood of Government: Race, Empire, the United States, and the Philippines.* University of North Carolina Press, 2006.

Kurashige, Scott. *The Shifting Grounds of Race: Black and Japanese Americans in the Making of Multiethnic Los Angeles.* Princeton University Press, 2008.

Lee, Robert G. *Orientals: Asian Americans in Popular Culture.* Temple University Press, 1999.

Lew-Williams, Beth. *The Chinese Must Go: Violence, Exclusion, and the Making of the Alien in America.* Harvard University Press, 2018.

Liu, Michael, Kim Geron, and Tracy Lai. *The Snake Dance of Asian American Activism: Community, Vision, and Power.* Lexington Books, 2008.

Mabalon, Dawn Bohulano. *Little Manila Is in the Heart: The Making of the Filipina/o American Community in Stockton, California.* Duke University Press, 2013.

McClain, Charles J. *In Search of Equality: The Chinese Struggle Against Discrimination in Nineteenth-Century America.* University of California Press, 1996.

McKevitt, Andrew C. *Gun Country: Gun Capitalism, Culture, and Control in Cold War America.* University of North Carolina Press, 2023.

Miller, Chanel. *Know My Name.* Viking, 2019.

Miller, Stuart Creighton. *Benevolent Assimilation: The American Conquest of the Philippines, 1899–1903*. Yale University Press, 1982.

Moon, Katherine H. S. *Sex Among Allies: Military Prostitution in U.S.-Korea Relations*. Columbia University Press, 1997.

Morey, Michael. *Fagen: An African American Renegade in the Philippine-American War*. University of Wisconsin Press, 2019.

Ogden, Johanna. *Punjabi Rebels of the Columbia River: The Global Fight for Indian Independence and Citizenship*. Oregon State University Press, 2024.

Pegues, Juliana Hu. *Space-Time Colonialism: Alaska's Indigenous and Asian Entanglements*. University of North Carolina Press, 2021.

Pfaelzer, Jean. *Driven Out, The Forgotten War Against Chinese Americans*. University of California Press, 2007.

Quincy, Keith. *Hmong: History of a People*. 2nd edition. Eastern Washington University Press, 1995.

Robinson, Greg. *After Camp: Portraits in Midcentury Japanese American Life and Politics*. University of California Press, 2012.

Salyer, Lucy E. *Chinese Immigrants and the Shaping of Modern Immigration Law*. University of North Carolina Press, 1995.

Saxton, Alexander. *The Indispensable Enemy: Labor and the Anti-Chinese Movement in California*. University of California Press, 1971.

Shaw, Angel Velasco, and Luis H. Francia, eds. *Vestiges of War: The Philippine-American War and the Aftermath of an Imperial Dream, 1899–1999*. New York University Press, 2002.

Sohi, Seema. *Echoes of Mutiny: Race, Surveillance, and Indian Anticolonialism in North America*. Oxford University Press, 2014.

Takaki, Ronald. *Hiroshima: Why America Dropped the Atomic Bomb*. Little, Brown, 1995.

Takaki, Ronald. *Pau Hana: Plantation Life and Labor in Hawaii*. University of Hawai'i Press, 1983.

Turse, Nick. *Kill Anything That Moves: The Real American War in Vietnam*. Picador, 2013.

Wagner, Kim A. *Massacre in the Clouds: An American Atrocity and the Erasure of History*. PublicAffairs, 2024.

Wei, Deborah, and Rachael Kamel, eds. *Resistance in Paradise: Rethinking 100 Years of U.S. Involvement in the Caribbean and the Pacific*. American Friends Service Committee, 1998.

Welch, Richard. *Response to Imperialism: The United States and the Philippine-American War, 1899–1902*. University of North Carolina Press, 1979.

Welchel, Toshio. *From Pearl Harbor to Saigon: Japanese American Soldiers and the Vietnam War*. Verso, 1999.

Wilson, Kathryn E. *Ethnic Renewal in Philadelphia's Chinatown: Space, Place, and Struggle*. Temple University Press, 2015.

Yamazaki, James N. *Children of the Atomic Bomb: An American Physician's Memoir of Nagasaki, Hiroshima, and the Marshall Islands*. Duke University Press, 1995.

Young, Marilyn. *The Vietnam Wars 1945–1990.* HarperCollins, 1991.

Yuh, Ji-Yeon. *Beyond the Shadow of Camptown: Korean Military Brides in America.* New York University Press, 2002.

Zesch, Scott. *The Chinatown War: Chinese Los Angeles and the Massacre of 1871.* Oxford University Press, 2012.

Zia, Helen. *Asian American Dreams: The Emergence of an American People.* Farrar, Straus and Giroux, 2000.

Zia, Helen. *The Vincent Chin Legacy Guide: Asian Americans and Civil Rights.* 2nd edition. Vincent Chin Institute, 2022.

INDEX

Einstein, Albert, 84

Eisenhower, Dwight D., 84, 98

electoral politics, 227–28, 261

Elliot, Brandon, 210

Eminem, 224

English-Chinese Phrase Book, An, 34

erasure: Atlanta spa shootings and, 1–2, 90; Bengali genocide, 123; Chinese exclusion era, 20; Vincent Chin murder and, 268; confronting, 57, 267–68; Hiroshima/Nagasaki bombings and, 87–88; Korean War and, 58–61, 96–97; Philippine-American War and, 42, 57–58; resistance to, 57–58, 88; school shootings and, 127–29; sexualized labor and, 96–97; US imperialism and, 3–4; Vietnam War and, 115, 116; violence against Asian women and, 94, 102–3. *See also* lack of accountability for anti-Asian violence

ethnic cleansing, 22, 37, 38, 70–71, 72–74, 170

Ethnic Intimidation Act (New Jersey) (1990), 205

ethnic studies education, 131

Ethnic Terrorism Act (New Jersey) (1981), 205

eugenics, 46–47

evangelical purity culture, 2, 91–92

Evangelista, Mark, 189

Evans, Bruce "Blue," 20

Evans, Terence, 217–18, 219

exclusionary laws, 6, 17

exploitation, 25–26

expropriation, 26–27, 28

extraterritoriality, 25, 95

Fagen, David, 48–49

Faludi, Susan, 155, 156

Fara, Abdul, 74

Feng, Daoyou, 1

Fewel, Jean Kar-Har, 200

Fewel, Tom, 200

Filipino Americans, 53–57; colonial period, 53; Great Depression and, 55–57; hate crimes framework and, 202–3; Hawai'i, 69; immigration exclusion laws and, 53, 56–57; Marcos dictatorship and, 58; Philippine-American War and, 53–54; resistance and, 54–55, 56, 69; scapegoating of, 54; taxi dance halls and, 54; US imperialism and, 24

Filipino Repatriation Act (1935), 57

Floyd, George, murder of (2020), 208, 229, 233

Ford, Gerald, 98

Foreign Miners' Tax Laws (1850 and 1852), 28–29

Founding Fathers, 21

Fourteenth Amendment, 32, 34, 149

France, 113–14

Francia, Luis H., 57

Francis, Carolyn Bowen, 95

Francisco, Luzviminda, 50

From Pearl Harbor to Saigon (Welchel), 120–21

Fung Wai, 38

Funston, Fred, 52

Furrow, Buford, 202

Gabrish, Joseph, 213, 219–20

Gadson, Kenneth, 99

Gardenhire, Michael, 141

Garian, Kalem, 147

gaslighting, 75, 94, 104, 259

Gates, Daryl, 179

Gaza war, 123

Geary Act (1892), 39

Geisel, Theodor (Dr. Seuss), 78

Geneva Protocol (1925), 87

genocide: Bangladesh, 122–23, 268; dehumanization and, 65; Indigenous peoples and, 5, 115; UN Convention on, 83; World War II anti-Japanese rhetoric and, 82

Gentlemen's Agreement (1908), 66–67

George Floyd Justice in Policing Act, 208

Geron, Kim, 122

Ghadar Party, 75–76

Gidra, 264, 266

Gilded Age, 34

Gill, Marcus, 99

Gillooly, John J., 225

Giuliani, Rudy, 232

Ramaswamy, Vivek, 175
rape. *See* violence against Asian women
Ratanapakdee, Vicha, 209
reactive solidarity, 9
Reagan, Ronald, and administration, 8, 125, 131, 151, 163, 165, 172, 195. *See also* neoliberal economic restructuring
Red Canary Song, 107, 108, 269
Reilly, David, 238–39, 244–48, 252, 255
Reinhold, Robert, 127
Remerata, Susana, 101–2
Republican Party: exclusion era, 33, 34, 35; Panic of 1873 and, 33; Philippine-American War and, 44; right-wing resurgence and, 163; US imperialism and, 41–42, 48. *See also specific presidents*
resistance: anti-Asian violence term and, 8, 138, 187; Asian American movement (1960s–70s) and, 7, 81, 122, 143; Atlanta spa shootings and, 2–3; Chinese exclusion era, 6, 27, 32; community empowerment and, 13, 211, 228–29, 238–41, 270, 271–72; consciousness raising, 228; courthouse shootings (1995) and, 102; COVID-19 pandemic and, 2–3; criminal justice system and, 187; culture jamming, 194; electoral politics and, 227–28, 261; erasure and, 57–58, 88; Filipino Americans and, 54–55, 56, 69; funding game and, 248; gun control and, 184; hate crimes framework and, 9–10, 188, 200, 201–4; Hiroshima/Nagasaki bombings and, 84; Indian Americans and, 188, 190, 191; interethnic conflict and, 181; Japanese American incarceration and, 78–79; Japanese Americans and, 68, 70, 73; Justice for Vincent Chin campaign influence on, 8–9, 139, 194, 195; Korean Americans and, 69, 71–72; late 19th–early 20th century exclusion and, 68, 69, 75–76; lessons for, 266–71; mentally ill victims and, 229; MeToo movement and, 103–5; model minority stereotype and, 166, 266, 268–69; police misconduct and, 214, 225, 226, 227–29, 230–33, 234–37, 262; refram-ing of, 10–11, 13, 206–7, 211, 240, 263, 269–70; restorative justice and, 13, 199–200, 270; retributive justice and, 9, 195–96; transcontinental railroad and, 27; urban rebellions, 112; US overseas military bases and, 100–101; Vietnam War and, 7, 121–22; violence against Asian women and, 95, 97, 98, 102, 103–7, 269; white allies, 30; Chonburi Xiong and, 225, 226, 227–28. *See also* Asian Americans United; Black freedom struggle; Justice for Vincent Chin campaign; multiracial solidarity
restorative justice, 13, 199–200, 270
retributive justice, 195–98; anti-Black racism and, 196, 201; Vincent Chin murder and, 195–96, 269; Rudy Giuliani and, 232; hate crimes framework and, 201, 205; limitations of, 9, 269–70; mass incarceration crisis and, 10; police misconduct and, 9–10, 232; resistance and, 9, 195–96; right-wing resurgence and, 163, 232; super predators and, 196, 199; Trump administration and, 196. *See also* hate crimes framework
"reverse racism," 159–60, 161
Reyes, Michelle Ami, 91
Richmond, Tony, 265
right-wing resurgence, 161–85; anti-Asian violence term and, 8; anti-Black racism and, 139, 143–44; as backlash against Black freedom struggle, 139, 163, 165, 168, 169; "Black-Korean conflict" (1992) and, 178–82; color-blind racism and, 163, 165–66, 211; as counterrevolution, 163–64; culture wars and, 162, 164, 175; declining empire mentality and, 169; gun ownership and, 183–84; inner cities and, 243; model minority stereotype and, 92, 162, 178; neoliberal economic restructuring and, 10–11, 131, 144, 146, 162, 164; 9/11 and, 176–77; Obama election and, 163–64; racism denial and, 165–66; retributive justice and, 163, 232; Sikh Americans and, 176–77; Southeast Asian refugees and, 162, 167–74; structural responses and,

Founded in 1893,

UNIVERSITY OF CALIFORNIA PRESS
publishes bold, progressive books and journals
on topics in the arts, humanities, social sciences,
and natural sciences—with a focus on social
justice issues—that inspire thought and action
among readers worldwide.

The UC PRESS FOUNDATION
raises funds to uphold the press's vital role
as an independent, nonprofit publisher, and
receives philanthropic support from a wide
range of individuals and institutions—and from
committed readers like you. To learn more, visit
ucpress.edu/supportus.